Ethical Studies

SECOND EDITION

ROBERT BOWIE

This edition first published in 2004 by:
Nelson Thornes Ltd
Delta Place
27 Bath Road
CHELTENHAM
GL53 7TH
United Kingdom

09 / 10 9

A catalogue record for this book is available from the British Library

First edition ISBN 978 0 7487 5798 5
Second edition ISBN 978 0 7487 8079 2

Page make-up by Northern Phototypesetting Co. Ltd
Illustrations by Angela Lumley and Clinton Banbury

Printed by Multivista Global Ltd

This book could not have been written without the help of many people. I would like to offer my thanks to my RE colleagues and students from my time at St Simon Stock School in Maidstone and St John Fisher School in Chatham, as well as my own teachers from St Ignatius College, Enfield - in particular, those of the RE, Classics and English departments – and St George's Primary School in Enfield. I would also like to thank Nelson Thornes for their enthusiasm, guidance and tolerance.

To Becky and Harry

Acknowledgements

With thanks to the following for permission to reproduce photographs and other copyright material in this book:

Associated Press (p. 193); Blackwell (pp. 60–61, 297, 301); Corel (pp. 13, 54, 112, 219, 309); Duckworth (p. 118); HarperCollins (pp. 236–237); Oxford University Press (pp. 83–84); Pan Macmillan (p. 302); SCM (pp. 60–61, 107–108); Victor Gollancz (pp. 84–85); Westminster Press (p. 108)

Every effort has been made to contact copyright holders. The publishers apologise to anyone whose rights have been inadvertently overlooked, and will be happy to rectify any errors or omissions.

Contents

How to use this book

This book is divided into three parts. The first deals with different approaches or systems for exploring ethical dilemmas, the second examines the links and issues related to ethics and religion, and the third considers a number of today's important ethical issues.

Which chapters to read

The book has been designed to provide the reader with an introduction to the important ethical theories and some current ethical dilemmas. If you're following a structured course that leads to a public exam, such as a GCE AS or A2 level, then you should check the exam board syllabus/specification to see which chapters are relevant for your exam or coursework. It isn't necessary to read the topics in a particular order, although Chapters 1 and 2 are important for putting the rest in context. If you're using this book as your main source for the course, then following the order of chapters will be helpful. If you receive lecture notes or other handouts, then simply read the relevant chapter when your teacher gets to that topic.

The structure of the chapters

The *Key questions* at the beginning of most chapters are meant for discussion, so if you're working as part of a class then talk them through. If you're studying alone, then you should jot down your thoughts before reading on. The tasks are designed to get you thinking about the important aspects of the theory or issue in question. The extracts at the end of most chapters give you a chance to get to grips with some original sources, and are often more difficult than the main body of the text. At the end of each chapter there's a *Chapter summary*, to help you with revision of the topic.

Extras

On the Nelson Thornes website (www.nelsonthornes.com/secondary/re/ethics) you will find information on study skills, which is worth reading before you begin your course. There are also tips on revision, writing essays and sitting exams. The Internet is another valuable source of information, and ICT can be used very effectively to help your study, so Appendix D is devoted to these topics.

At the end of the book you will find a detailed *Bibliography* and a *Glossary* of ethical terms and names. You can also find more information that supports the study of ethics on the website for this book: www.nelsonthornes.com/secondary/re/ethics and also at www.ethicalstudies.co.uk

Part I
Ethical Theories

This first part contains an introduction to **ethics** and nine chapters that cover the major ethical theories. Usually, one or two important philosophers are closely related to the theory, as are a few important philosophical works. Some chapters are divided between two opposing theories, as with **absolutism** and **relativism**. At the beginning of each chapter there are lists of the *Key philosophers and texts* and the *Key terms* associated with the theories under scrutiny. There are also *Key questions* to illustrate the kind of problems that the theories address and to initiate the topic. At the ends of most chapters there are important *Extracts from key texts* that are closely associated with the theory.

Chapter 1

An introduction to ethics

One of the things that distinguishes humans from other animals is our ability to make moral decisions. We deliberate before making choices. We may feel guilt when we do things that we feel are wrong. We're motivated to take great risks because of what we believe is right. We disagree passionately with each other over how we should live. Humans have a moral dimension.

This book explores how human beings decide what is right and wrong, good and bad. It examines the ways in which different thinkers have tried to define what it means to be a good person. It also investigates some of the most prominent ethical issues of our time.

The big questions in ethics

There are a number of big ethical questions that commonly interest philosophers. You will learn how different philosophers try to answer them, but consider them here for yourself:

- If I do a good thing for a bad reason, does it matter?
- Do ends justify means?
- Do the needs of the many outweigh the needs of the few or the one?
- Is what's wrong for you necessarily wrong for me?
- Is an action right or wrong depending on the situation?
- Are we free to make moral choices?
- Is being moral about following rules?

- Should we use our heads or our hearts when deciding what's moral?
- Can we have morals without religion?
- Should I help my father before I help a stranger?
- Are human beings selfish or selfless?
- Should we follow our **consciences**?
- Is ethics a special kind of knowledge or are moral views just personal feelings?
- Is killing an unborn human as immoral as killing a born human being?
- Should people who want to die be helped to die?
- Do animals have rights?
- Is it ever right to fight?
- Is it wrong to use embryos for experimentation?
- Should business think only about profits?

If you're going to study ethics seriously, you must be prepared to examine your views critically and be open to a range of ideas that may be quite different from your own. What you read may challenge your convictions. At the very least, it will require you to re-examine them.

Task

Consider the following scenarios:

1 You witness a car crash. The wreckage is burning, but you may be able to save one of the two passengers. To your horror, you realise that one is your father and the other is a famous cancer specialist on the brink of a breakthrough. Who do you save?

2 Your mother comes home with an appalling hat and asks you what you think. She's clearly delighted with her purchase. Do you tell the truth?

3 You're close to a breakthrough with a new medical treatment, but to complete your work you must carry out some particularly slow and painful experiments on animals. What do you do?

4 Your ship goes down and you're lost in the sea with two others, in a life raft. You have no food. Without a supply of food, there's no hope of rescue before you starve to death. Two would survive by eating the third: otherwise, all three will die. What do you do?

5 The parents of a car crash victim allow their son's body to be used for transplants, but only if the parts go to white patients. Do you accept their condition?

Ethical theories

6 One night in a concentration camp, a boy is raped and some of his uniform is taken away by the rapist. Prisoners who are incorrectly dressed are shot at dawn by the guards. Should he accept his fate or steal from someone else?

7 Siamese twins are born, attached at the abdomen and sharing several major organs. If nothing is done, both will die. If the twins are separated, one will die and one will live. What should be done?

8 A railway drawbridge operator is closing the bridge for the express train that's about to arrive when he sees his son trapped in the machinery. To close the bridge will kill his son but save the train. To open the bridge will save his son, but the train will not be able to stop in time. What should he do?

9 An unattractive man offers to give a million pounds to the charity of your choice if you spend one night with him. What do you do?

What is ethics?

The term **ethics** comes from the Greek word *ethikos*, meaning 'character'. It may be translated as 'custom' or 'usage'. It refers to the customary way to behave in society.

The term **morality** comes from the Latin word *moralis*, and is concerned with which actions are right and which are wrong, rather than the character of the person. Today, the two terms are often used interchangeably.

Ethics is a branch of philosophy concerned with morality. It explores actions and consequences, motives, moral decision-making and human nature. Ethics can be broadly divided in two:

1 **Ethical theory**, which covers philosophical systems or methods for making moral decisions or analysing moral statements.

2 **Practical, or applied, ethics**, which focuses on debates about specific dilemmas, such as abortion or euthanasia.

Three ways of 'doing' ethics

There are three main ways of 'doing' ethics:

- the **normative** approach
- the **descriptive** approach
- **meta-ethics**

Normative ethics was prevalent until the end of the nineteenth century. It begins by asking what things are good and what things are bad, and what kind of behaviour is right and wrong. It decides how people ought to act, how moral choices should be made and how the rules apply. These decisions may come from an established group or culture, such as the Christian tradition, or they may be based on some philosophical or ideological way of thinking. This is the traditional way of doing ethics. A normative ethical question would be 'Is sex before marriage right?' Many of the theories in this book are normative theories.

Descriptive ethics describes and compares the different ways in which people and societies have answered moral questions. It can be described as moral sociology or moral anthropology. A descriptive ethical question would be 'What do the Christian and Muslim traditions believe about sex before marriage?'

Meta-ethics, sometimes called philosophical ethics, attracts a great deal of interest today. Meta-ethics explores the meaning and function of moral language. What, if anything, do we mean when we use words such as 'good' or 'bad', 'right' or 'wrong'? A meta-ethical question is 'What do we mean when we say that sex before marriage is good?' Theories important to the meta-ethical debate include ethical **naturalism** (definism), **ethical non-naturalism** (**intuitionism**) and ethical non-cognitivism (emotivism).

Task

Identify the kind of ethical approach that these phrases fit best:

1 Adultery is wrong because God's law forbids it.

2 When you say euthanasia is wrong, you're only saying you don't like euthanasia.

3 In some Muslim communities men may take a number of wives, while in most Christian communities only one wife is permitted.

Now think of a new statement of your own for each ethical approach.

Normative ethics: teleological and deontological

There are two main ethical systems within normative ethics.

Teleological ethics is concerned with the ends or consequences of actions. The word *telos* is Greek for 'end'. Teleological theories, sometimes known as **consequentialist**, hold up the link between the act and the consequence as extremely important in moral decision-making. A teleological theory maintains that the rightness or wrongness of an action is decided by the consequences that it produces. If my action causes pain and suffering, then it is bad. If my action causes happiness and **love**, then it is good. The action isn't good in itself (not **intrinsically good**), but good by virtue of the result. Two teleological theories are **utilitarianism**, which values actions that produce the greatest amount of happiness and well-being for the most people, and **situation ethics**, which values actions that produce the most love-filled result.

There are some weaknesses with teleological approaches: How can you be sure what the result will be? Do ends justify all **means**? Aren't there some things, such as rape and the murder of children, that can never by justified by a noble result and simply shouldn't be done?

Deontological ethics is concerned with the nature of the **acts** themselves. Deontologists maintain that acts are right or wrong in themselves (they are intrinsically right or wrong) because of some **absolute** law perhaps laid down by God, or because they go against some **duty** or obligation. A deontologist might say that murder is wrong because the very act of murder is intrinsically evil. Pacifists claim that all physical violence is wrong, and many religious groups maintain that certain acts are inherently sinful. Deontologists have the advantage of being able to take strong moral positions on certain actions, as illustrated by anti-abortion campaigners. They can prevent certain moral boundaries from being crossed. On the other hand, they aren't flexible enough to take into account special circumstances, or culture groups with different religious perspectives on life. Examples of deontological theories investigated in this book are **absolutism**, **natural moral law** and **Kantian ethics**.

Task

Which statement shows teleological thinking and which shows deontological thinking:

1 We should permit the abortion because she's too young and too poor to look after the child.
2 You should help your mother because it's your duty.
3 Do what your father says.
4 It's okay to steal if you're starving.
5 If you tell her the truth she'll be really upset.
6 Whatever you say, just tell the truth.

Now add two statements of your own to each of the two categories.

What do we mean when we say something is good?

The philosopher G. E. Moore thought that there is a difference between good things and goodness itself. The aspects or qualities that make something good are different from goodness itself. An action may be good because it is a generous action, but good isn't identical to generosity.

When we add 'good' to a sentence it has an effect that's different from that of the adjectives. If we call a hat 'a red hat' then it adds a quality, or aspect, to the description. If we call a person 'a good person', the word good certainly adds something to the person, but 'good' is just another word like 'red' or 'old' or 'tall'. A good knife is better than a bad knife, but here when we use the word 'good' we're probably talking about sharpness or shininess. A good knife isn't *morally* better than a bad knife. In fact, I may use a good knife to stab someone – a morally bad thing to do. I may drink good coffee that has been produced by farmers who aren't fairly paid for their work, in which case I may think that it is morally bad.

There are good footballers who aren't morally good at all. When we call someone a 'good' person we're saying something very different from calling them 'tall' or 'short', or 'old' or 'young'. We may be referring to the nature of their character, the kind of things that they do or the way in which they weigh up a situation. The moral sense of **good** refers to actions, consequences, situations, people, characters, choices and lifestyles.

Tasks

1 We use the word 'good' in many different ways. Try to describe in different words what 'good' means in each of these sentences:

   a He was a good dog.

   b It was a good film.

   c We gave it a good shot.

   d They made us a good breakfast.

   e It was good that we double-checked the time of the flight.

   f She had a good soul.

   g This car's as good as any other.

2 Different philosophers explain the word 'good' in many different ways, according to their preferred ethical theory. Consider these examples and decide which you most and least agree with. Good means:

   a In accordance with the will of God.

   b The thing that produces the greatest good for the greatest result.

Ethical theories

   c Following the moral rules.

   d The thing that produces the most loving result.

   e Doing your duty.

   f Becoming a virtuous person.

   g Things you like.

3 Describe, in no more than 20 words, a good person – someone, who helps others, follows the Commandments, has good intentions ...?

4 Write definitions for each of these words: right, wrong, good, bad, moral, immoral, amoral.

5 Is there any difference between good things and goodness?

6 Are pleasurable things always good?

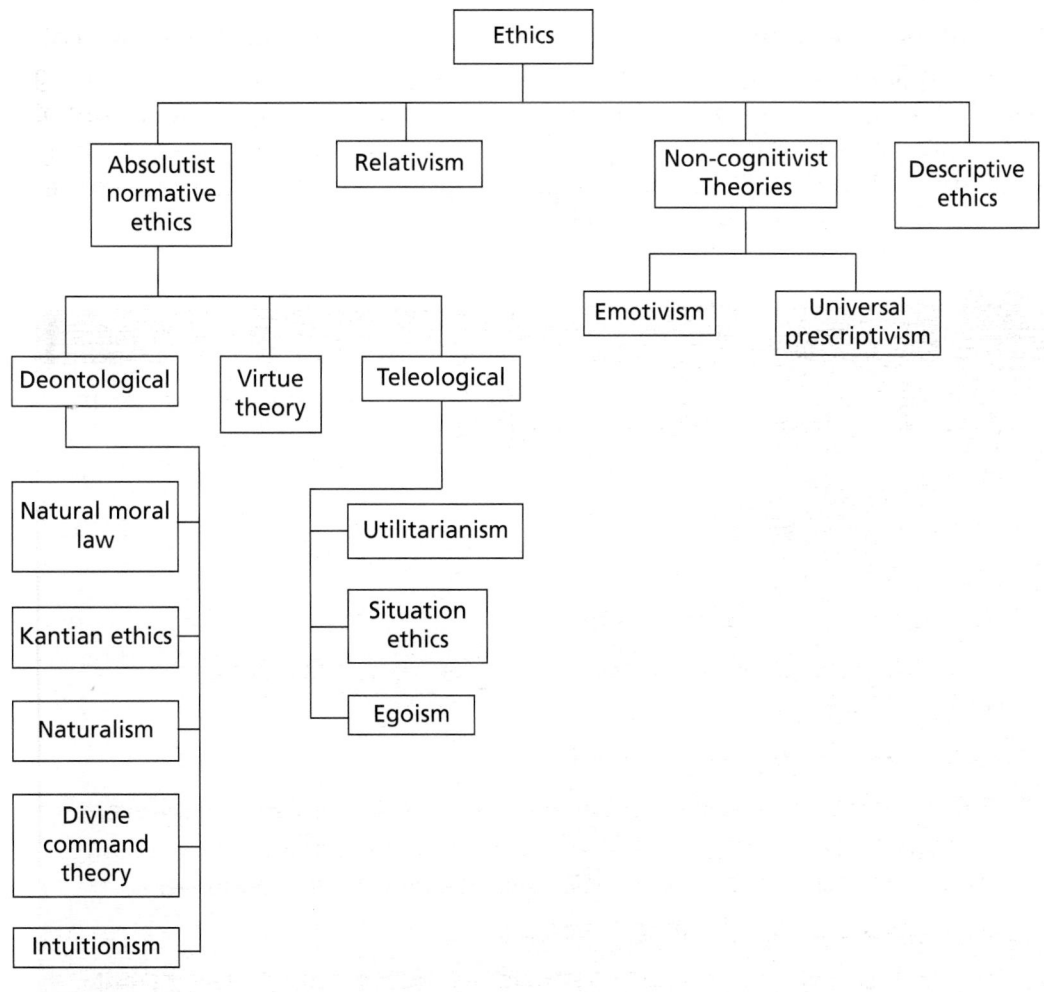

Ethical theories

CHAPTER SUMMARY

- The term 'ethics' comes from *ethikos* – a Greek word meaning 'character'.
- The term 'morality' comes from *moralis* – a Latin word concerned with which actions are right and which are wrong.
- Ethics is a branch of philosophy concerned with morality.
- Ethical theory explores philosophical systems or methods for making moral decisions or analysing moral statements.
- Practical, or applied, ethics focuses on debates about specific dilemmas, such as abortion or euthanasia.
- Ethics is studied in three ways:
  - normative – a traditional approach that asks what is right and what is wrong, and how we know
  - descriptive ethics – a form of anthropology that compares differing ethical **beliefs** without making **value judgements**
  - meta-ethics – a twentieth-century approach that explores the meaning of ethical language such as 'good', 'bad', 'right' and 'wrong'
- Normative ethical theories are divided into two broad kinds:
  - deontological theories, according to which acts are intrinsically right or wrong (such as absolutism or natural moral law)
  - teleological theories, according to which the consequences (or ends) determine the **goodness** of actions (actions are extrinsically right or wrong)
- There is a difference between good things and goodness.

Chapter 2

Absolutism and relativism

Introduction

Key philosophers and texts

Aristotle (384–322 BCE): *Nicomachean Ethics*

Plato (428–347 BCE): *The Republic*

Protagoras (490–420 BCE): only fragments surviving

J. L. Mackie (1917–1981): *Ethics, Inventing Right and Wrong*, 1977

William Graham Sumner (1840–1910): *Folkways*, 1906

Key terms

Absolutism, cultural relativism, forms, moral absolutes, objective truth/knowledge/value, relativism, subjective

What you will learn by the end of this chapter

- The theory of ethical absolutism and the contribution of Plato.
- The theory of relativism, and the contributions of Protagoras, Sumner and Mackie.
- The respective strengths and weaknesses of those theories.
- Examples that illustrate the ethical dilemma.

Key questions

1 Do moral rules really exist?
2 Should moral rules ever be broken?

3 Are there times when an action might be right and other times when the same action is wrong? What are they?

4 Are there any actions which are always wrong? What are they?

5 Is one culture's view of morality as good as another?

6 Are things that are true for you necessarily true for me?

7 Are all moral opinions equally valid, or are some moral opinions better than others?

Absolutism

Consider the following:

- A man has an affair with his secretary.
- A gang leader murders a member of a rival gang.
- A youth mugs an old lady and takes her purse.

Many people would say that each of these examples shows someone doing wrong. It is wrong to have affairs, wrong to murder and wrong to mug old ladies. To help an old lady across the road is right, just as it is to remain faithful to your partner. People make moral judgements about right and wrong all the time. Some organisations are quite vocal about what is right and wrong. Christian Churches preach the Commandments as a guide to knowing what one should not do: 'Do not murder', 'Do not steal', 'Do not bear false witness' and so on. Islamic law gives clear guidelines on morally good and bad behaviour. Politicians often make statements about right and wrong. In ethical terms, to maintain that some things are right and other things are wrong, and that these things are fixed for all time and all people, is called **absolutism**.

An ethical **absolute** is a moral command or prohibition that's true for all time, in all places and in all situations. Absolutists hold that some things are wrong from an **objective** point of view, not just wrong from your or my perspective. In the Middle Ages, the principle 'Follow the good and avoid the evil' expressed an absolutist perspective. It implies that the moral way of living is to do things that are objectively good and avoid things that are objectively bad. In ethical absolutism, things that are right or wrong can't change. They aren't affected by mitigating circumstances. They don't depend on the situation. For example, absolutists might say that torturing children, rape and murder are always wrong. They don't change according to the culture in which you live. What is right and wrong for you is the same for me and for every other person in the world. **Immoral** acts are **intrinsically wrong**, which means wrong in themselves. The thing isn't made wrong by the situation or the result it causes. It is wrong because the act in itself breaks a moral rule.

Plato and the forms

Plato was an ethical absolutist. He thought that moral absolutes such as good-ness and **justice** really existed in some way, beyond our normal perceptions of the world. This other-world was inhabited by the **forms** or **ideas**, which were the true reality. What we perceived around us was a shadow of this truth.

Plato

We might find a piece of music beautiful. We might use the word 'beautiful' to describe a statue or painting, or the way a mother holds her baby, or the sound of a bird. Plato believed that a beautiful painting had 'form beauty' participat-ing in it. Without the form beauty there would be no beautiful things. He held that there were many forms. The form 'green' participated in the grass, the form 'red' participated in wine, and so on. The highest of all the forms was goodness itself. While Protagoras thought that you could only ask the question 'What's good for you?', Plato thought that you could ask the question 'What is goodness itself?' Goodness itself was the highest form of reality – an objective or absolute thing that existed eternally, beyond our limited world. Plato was an absolutist.

Plato described his view of reality using similes. In the simile of the Sun (see Table 2.1), he illustrated the importance of the form 'good' for truth, by draw-ing an analogy with the importance of the Sun.

He felt that we must escape from the mistake of believing that our percep-tions of reality were the truth. Our mind was distorted by pleasure and pain, and so the search for truth was a struggle to get beyond our physical percep-tions and sensations. He described this journey in *The Republic*, in the simile of the cave. An extract from that book is given at the end of this chapter.

Table 2.1 Plato's simile of the Sun

Visible world	Intelligible world of the forms
The Sun Source of growth and light, which gives visibility to the objects of sense and the power of seeing to the eye. The faculty of sight.	The Good Source of reality and truth, which gives intelligibility to objects of thought and the power of knowing to the mind. The faculty of knowledge.

Tasks

1 Individually, list five things that you would say might be wrong in certain situations.

2 In groups, compare your lists and come up with a common list with which you all agree. Order the items, from 'most likely to be always wrong' to 'least likely to be always wrong'.

3 For each of the five things, give a plausible exception where you might be justified in breaking the rule.

Relativism

People don't always agree about what's right and what's wrong. Some people feel that it is acceptable for a man to marry more than one wife, while others feel that such a practice is a crime. Different cultures express different moral codes of conduct. An ancient observer of this cultural diversity was King Darius. In a story recorded by Herodotus in the *Histories* (Book 3, p. 38), Darius observed that while certain Greeks burnt the bodies of their fathers, a different people called Callations ate the bodies of their fathers. He brought the two groups together and asked each how much he would have to pay them to adopt the practice of the other. In both cases, the groups were outraged at the suggestion and refused to follow the practice of the other for any amount of money. What was right for one tribe was wrong for the other.

An ancient Greek philosopher called Protagoras held that there's no truth in anything beyond the way it seems. There's no objective knowledge, because all knowledge depends on the perceptions of the person. There's no objective truth. Truth is only true for you, or true for me. Man is the measure of all things. Things are good or bad relative to our perspective. A sick person eating food may find that it tastes horrible, while a healthy person eating the same food will find it delicious. Each view is true relative to each person's perspective. If I say I don't like spaghetti and you say you do like spaghetti, both of us are right. Protagoras thought that moral statements were like this: so when I say 'Abortion is wrong' and you say 'Abortion is right', we're both saying things that are true, because what we're saying is true for you, and true for me.

A debate between an absolutist and a relativist might go something like this:

> Sam: Abortion is wrong. It's killing and killing is wrong. It's something that should not be done. People should not ask for abortions and they should not carry out abortions. Killing is wrong. It's one of those rules that can't be broken.

> Ben: Who says it's wrong? May be it's wrong for you, perhaps because of your religion, but just because you feel it's wrong doesn't actually mean it is wrong, except in your eyes. It's just your view. I have a view that's different – and who is to say that your view is better or more accurate than my view? How do you know for sure that abortion is wrong? You can't tell me what to think. There isn't just one set of morals that everyone agrees with or follows.

Another ancient Greek philosopher to be more relativistic was Plato's pupil, Aristotle, whose ethics were collected into a book called *Nicomachean Ethics* in the fourth century BCE. Aristotle did not believe in universal forms which are absolute and beyond our world. He felt that the forms were in the world, and therefore not absolute. He believed in a rule-of-thumb approach to moral characteristics whereby we should seek a midway approach of behaviour between two extremes. Virtue is the mean between two extremes. For example, we should not be rash in our behaviour or cowardly but should chose a 'midway' courageous approach. Human circumstances are infinite and it is not possible to have a general rule which will cover every situation. Moral rules hold for the most part, but there are times when they won't. This makes Aristotle more relativistic than Plato. We shall learn more about Aristotle's ethics in Chapter 10.

Cultural relativism

Modern anthropologists have observed cultural differences and some have concluded that the existence of diverse moral codes implies that morality is not absolute. Morality simply means 'socially approved habits'. The anthropologist William Graham Sumner expressed this view in 1906:

> The 'right' way is the way which the ancestors used and which has been handed down. The tradition is its own warrant ... The notion of right is in the folkways. It is not outside of them, of inde-

pendent origin, and brought to test them. In the folkways, whatever is, is right. This is because they are traditional, and therefore
contain in themselves the authority of the ancestral ghosts. When
we come to the folkways we are at the end of our analysis.

Sumner (1906)

This approach to ethics is **cultural relativism**. Moral rules are expressions of
the culture and nothing more. There's no set of moral rules that applies to
all. There's nothing absolute or universal about morality; When in Rome, do
as the Romans do. This theory directly challenges ethical absolutism.
Cultural relativism celebrates the variety of **beliefs** and **values** held by different peoples. There's no way of deciding between one set of morals and
another, because there's no objective measure. What is right and wrong
depends upon the perspective of the group.

If you're in a strict Islamic country, the women are right to cover themselves. In
a Western country, the women are right to expose more skin. This ethical theory
suits the multicultural nature of the world, as it gives equal measure to the different ethnic and religious groupings. It doesn't raise one particular cultural
expression to supremacy over others, as happened during the period of
European colonial expansion, and more recently in Nazi Germany. Cultural relativism seems a more modern and open ethical system than this early view.

Relativism also explains other differences. What is right and wrong not only
differs from culture to culture, but also from one time to another. In the past,
it was considered acceptable to leave highwaymen in hanging cages to
starve and rot. Today, that form of punishment is considered morally unacceptable. In the past, women didn't have the vote or the same property rights
as men. Today, many countries grant men and women equal status. Moral
points of view vary from time to time, from culture to culture, from religion
to religion and from place to place.

Relativism and J. L. Mackie

A modern relativist, J. L. Mackie, writes that 'There are no objective values'
(Mackie, 1977, p. 15). He maintains that values, the good, rightness and wrongness, aren't part of the fabric of the world. They don't exist. He sees the existence
of diverse ethical values expressed in different times and cultures as evidence
that no moral absolutes exist. An absolutist might argue that there are common
values beneath many of these cultural expressions, but Mackie thinks that a
more convincing **argument** is to assume that people participate in different
ways of living because they actually follow different codes. Mackie agrees with
Plato that if moral rules existed they would have to be entities of a strange sort,
uniquely different from all other things, but he finds this idea unconvincing.

Ethical theories

Tasks

1 What, in your view, does Darius' experiment prove?

2 In Christian cultures it is believed that monogamy is the only acceptable way of arranging marriage. In Islamic law, husbands have the right of **polygamy** and may be validly married at the same time to a maximum of four wives. The nomadic Masai of East Africa practise **polygamy** and wife-lending between men of the same age group. Some Westerners practise open marriages whereby husbands and wives engage other husbands or wives in sexual relations openly. What are the arguments that:

   a these are different but equally valid ways of arranging marriage – OR

   b one way is right (or morally better) and the others are wrong (or morally worse)?

3 Think of any other differences, and in each case consider the arguments for **a** and **b** in each case.

4 Construct an argument against the claim that views about moral issues are similar to views about chocolate – some prefer dark chocolate, others prefer milk, but both are equally valid.

Evaluating relativism and absolutism

Moral relativism has several attractions. It explains the different values that people hold and it encourages diverse cultural expressions. It prohibits a dominant culture from enforcing itself over others simply because 'we're right and they are wrong'. Relativism is a flexible ethical system that can accommodate the wide diversity of lifestyles found in the modern world. However, it does have some weaknesses. Cultural relativism observes that as different **value systems** exist, there can't be one **moral truth**. However, the existence of different views doesn't mean that they are all equal, and the existence of many views doesn't mean that all views are equally true. In a dialogue between Socrates and Crito, Socrates argues that 'one should not regard all the opinions that people hold, but only some and not others ... one should regard the good ones and not the bad ...'. He goes on to illustrate his point by observing a male athlete who doesn't take all the praise or criticism that he receives to be equally important. He only listens to the comments of a qualified person such as his trainer, and he disregards anything said by people who don't have any expertise in athletics (Crito 46B–47C, in Plato, 1969).

For Plato, not all views are of equal worth. This is quite apparent when we consider the Nazi Reich. To argue that the Nazi ethic was 'right for them' seems very dangerous. Most people today consider an ideology that justified the extermination of millions of innocent people to be morally corrupt and utterly wrong. Many people see the Second World War as a battle against evil, but this is an absolutist perspective. Cultural relativists are unable to criticise a different culture. Relativists can't prefer one moral opinion rather than another.

Another problem is that a cultural relativist can't condemn any practices that are accepted by society, because there's no objective measure by which those practices can be judged. Ultimately, cultural relativism reduces the meaning of 'good' to 'that which is socially approved'. If a culture endorses wife-beating, then wife-beating is morally acceptable.

There's also a paradoxical consequence of adopting relativism. If the relative belief that differing moral codes should all be supported was adopted universally, relativism itself would become an absolute moral code. Put another way, to say that the statement 'what is right is what is approved by the culture' is always true is to make an absolute claim about relativism.

Ethical absolutes overcome some of these problems. Absolutism provides a fixed ethical code with which to measure actions. An ethical absolutist can condemn Nazi Germany or the wife-beater. Absolutism gives people clear guidelines of behaviour that reinforce a global view of the human community. One country may judge the actions of another country as wrong and act on that judgement. The United Nations Declaration of Human Rights suggests a set of absolutes that apply to all people, no matter where they live. Absolutism can support the Declaration, while relativism might have difficulty when the Declaration differs from a particular culture's way of doing things.

Absolutism also has its weaknesses. It can't take into account the circumstances of the situation. An absolutist might consider stealing to be wrong. If the thief is a starving child who needs money for food, and the victim is a rich tourist, the absolutist must still condemn the thief, while the relativist could tolerate the action. An absolutist with strong beliefs about the treatment of animals might find the Islamic practice of ritually killing a lamb immoral, while a relativist can recognise the religious significance and the importance of the activity to that community. Absolutism can seem intolerant of cultural diversity in the way in which European nations were in the past.

Despite various limitations, relativism remains a popular ethic, although it is rejected by most religions, which remain staunchly absolutist (see Chapters 3, 5, 6 and 11). However, it has been accommodated by one Christian ethic in **situation ethics**. Other ethical theories – such as **utilitarianism**, which defines goodness relative to the amount of happiness created, and **emotivism**, which takes relativism to an extreme individualistic position – have relativistic aspects.

1 If you believe that a certain thing is wrong, should you try to persuade others not to do it?

2 Explain the view that there are objective moral truths.

3 Explain that view that all moral statements are relative.

4 What are the strengths and weaknesses of relativism and absolutism?

5 What is the most plausible argument for and the most plausible argument against moral absolutism?

Extracts from key texts

Plato, *The Republic*

The simile of the cave, Part seven, Book six

Imagine an underground chamber like a cave ... in this chamber are men who have been prisoners there since they were children, their legs and necks being so fastened that they can only look straight ahead of them and cannot turn their heads. Some way off, behind and higher up, a fire is burning, and between the fire and the prisoners and above them runs a road, in front of which a curtain-like wall has been built, like a screen at puppet shows between the operators and their audience ... Imagine further that men are carrying all sorts of gear along behind the curtain-wall, projecting above it and including figures of men and animals made of wood and stone and all sorts of other materials, and that some of these men, as you would expect, are talking and some are not ... Then if they [the prisoners] were able to talk to each other, would they not assume that the shadows they saw were the real things? ... that whenever one of the passers by on the road spoke, that the voice belonged to the shadow passing before them? ... And so in every way they would believe that the shadows of the objects we mentioned were the whole truth ...

... Suppose one of them were let loose, and suddenly compelled to stand up and turn his head and look and walk towards the fire ... and if he was forcibly dragged up the steep and rugged

Absolutism	Relativism
Moral truth is objective	There is no objective moral truth, or if there is we cannot know it
Moral actions are right or wrong intrinsically (in themselves)	What is morally true for you is not necessarily true for me
Moral truth is universal and unchanging in all circumstances, cultures, times and places	Morals are subject to culture, religion, time and place
Absolutists: Plato, Aquinas, Bradley	Relativists: Protagoras, Aristotle, Sumner, Mackie

Absolutism and Relativism – Essentials

ascent and not let go till he had been dragged out into sunlight ... he would need to grow accustomed to the light before he could see things in the upper world outside the cave. First he would find it easier to look at the shadows, next at the reflections of men and other objects in water, and later on at the objects themselves. After that he would find it easier to observe the heavenly bodies and the sky itself at night, and to look at the light of the moon and stars ... The thing he would be able to do last would be to look at the sun itself ... Later on he would come to the conclusion that it is the sun that produces the changing seasons and years and controls everything in the visible world, and is in a sense responsible for everything that he and his fellow prisoners used to see.

... Now my dear Glaucon, this simile must be connected throughout with what preceded it. The realm revealed by sight corresponds to the prison, and the light of the fire in the prison to the power of the sun. And you won't go wrong if you connect the ascent into the upper world and the sight of the objects there with the upward progress of the mind into the intelligible region. That at any rate is my interpretation, which is what you are anxious to hear; the truth of the matter is, after all, known only to God. But in my opinion, for what it is worth, the final thing to be perceived in the intelligible region, and perceived only with difficulty, is the form of the good; once seen, it is inferred to be responsible for whatever is right and valuable in anything ...

CHAPTER SUMMARY

Absolutists:

- Believe in moral truths that are fixed for all time and all people.
- Believe that moral actions are right or wrong in themselves, irrespective of circumstance, culture or opinion.
- Deontological thinkers are concerned with acts, not ends.
- 'Follow the good and avoid the evil' (a saying from the Middle Ages).

Examples of ethical absolutists:

- Plato, believing that goodness itself really exists beyond this world.
- St Thomas Aquinas (see Chapter 3), believing in a fixed divine law.
- F. H. Bradley (see Chapter 6), believing that morals are fixed, part of a concrete universe.

Relativists:

- Believe that moral truth varies depending on culture, time, place and religion.
- Believe that there's no fixed objective moral reality – or if there is, that it can't be discovered.
- Believe that morals are **subjective** – subject to the culture, religion, time and place.

Examples of ethical relativists:

- Aristotle believed that forms were in the world and therefore not absolute. Differing human circumstances mean we cannot have a general rule for all situations.
- Protagoras: 'Man is the measure of all things' (attributed).
- William Graham Sumner: 'The "right" way is the way which the ancestors used and which has been handed down.' Sumner was an anthropologist who investigated and appreciated cultural diversity.
- J. L. Mackie: 'there are no objective values' – different culture's ethics are evidence against the existence of moral absolutes, and people participate in different ways of living, or codes.

Evaluate:

- Relativism explains the existence of the different values that people hold.

- Relativism supports diverse cultural expressions.
- Relativism prohibits the dominance of a single culture.
- Relativism is a flexible ethical system that can accommodate the wide diversity of lifestyles found in the modern world.

However –

- The existence of different views doesn't mean that they are all equal.
- The Nazi culture was morally wrong, not 'right for them'.
- Cultural relativists are unable to criticize a different culture.
- Cultural relativists can't condemn any cultural practices – if a culture endorses wife-beating, then wife-beating is morally acceptable.
- If the relative belief that differing moral codes should all be supported was adopted universally, relativism itself would become an absolute moral code.

On the other hand:

- Absolutism provides a fixed ethical code to measure actions.
- Absolutism gives clear guidelines of behaviour.
- The UN Declaration of Human Rights suggests a set of absolutes that apply to all people, no matter where they live.

However –

- Absolutism can't take into account the circumstances of the situation.
- Absolutism can seem intolerant of cultural diversity in the way European nations were in the past.

Chapter 3

Natural moral law

Contents of Chapter 3

Introduction

Key philosophers and works

St Thomas Aquinas (1224–1274): *Summa Theologica*, 1273

Aristotle (384–322 BCE): *Nichomachean Ethics*

Cicero (106–43 BCE): *On The Republic*

Key terms

Exterior and interior acts, natural moral law, primary and secondary precepts, real and apparent goods, right reason

What you will learn by the end of this chapter

■ The ancient background of natural law.

■ St Thomas Aquinas' natural moral law theory, including the importance of reason, the purpose of human beings, real and apparent goods, exterior and interior acts, and primary and secondary precepts.

■ The strengths and weaknesses of natural moral law.

■ Examples that illustrate the ethical issues at stake.

Key questions

1 Is there a universal moral code within all people?

2 What makes a thing wrong, the nature of the act or the consequence of the action?

3   Are human beings essentially good or bad?

4   Do all humans have a common purpose and, if so, what is it?

Background

The roots of **natural law** can be found in the ancient Greek and Roman world. In the play *Antigone*, written in the fifth century BCE by Sophocles, Creon, the ruler of Thebes, forbids the burial of Antigone's brother as punishment for his treason against Thebes. Antigone breaks Creon's law and buries her brother. She argues that the state cannot overrule the immortal laws of the Gods, which in this case require the dead to be buried. In *Nicomachean Ethics*, the Greek philosopher Aristotle wrote that natural justice was not always the same as that which was just by law. He observed that while laws may vary from place to place, natural justice is independent and applies to everyone no matter where they live:

> The natural is that which everywhere is equally valid, and depends not upon being or not being received ... that which is natural is unchangeable, and has the same power everywhere, just as fire burns both here and in Persia.
>
> *Nicomachean Ethics*, Book V, Chapter 7, Natural Justice

The Ancient Stoics emphasised the importance of Logos, or rationality that governs the world and sees human nature as part of one natural order. They considered natural law a law of **right reason**. In his letter to the Romans, St Paul wrote (Romans 2:14–15) about a law that is 'written in the hearts' of Gentiles. The Roman lawyer Cicero formulated the classic description of natural law in his work *On the Republic*:

> True law is right reason in agreement with nature; it is of universal application, unchanging and everlasting; it summons to duty by its commands, and averts from wrongdoing by its prohibitions ... We cannot be freed from its obligations by senate or people, and we need not look outside ourselves for an expounder or interpreter of it. And there will not be different laws at Rome and at Athens, or different laws now and in the future, but one eternal and unchangeable law will be valid for all nations and all times, and there will be one master and ruler, that is, God, over us all, for he is the author of this law, its promulgator, and its enforcing judge.
>
> Cicero, *De Republica* (*On the Republic*), III, xxii

1 Give some examples of moral beliefs held by most or all people which might indicate a common law in all people.

2 Can you give examples of differing moral beliefs that counter the suggestion of a common moral law?

St Thomas Aquinas' theory of natural law

St Thomas Aquinas (1224–1274), an important Christian philosopher and theologian developed a fuller account of natural law in the thirteenth century. His ethical theory is absolutist and deontological, which means that it is focused on the ethicacy of actions. In his work, *Summa Theologica*, Aquinas described natural law as a moral code existing within the **purpose** of nature, created by God: 'Law is nothing else than an ordination of reason for the common good promulgated by the one who is in charge of the community' (II.i Q. 90 art. 4).

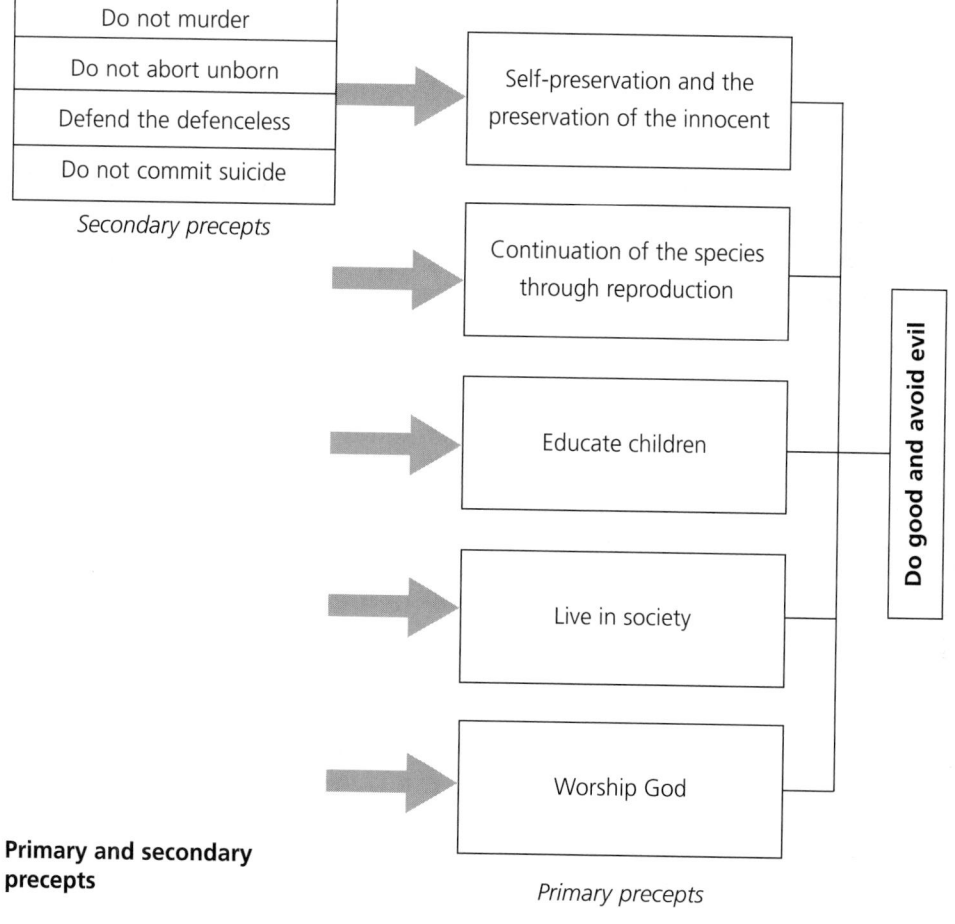

Primary and secondary precepts

This natural law exists to assist humans to direct their actions in such a way that they may reach their eternal destiny with God. This divinely inspired law covers both the outward external view of actions and the internal motivation for doing so. Natural law evaluates both what I do and why I do it. Natural law affects all aspects of human behaviour, because '... man needs to be directed to his supernatural end in a higher way' (II.i Q. 91 art. 4).

Aquinas maintained that there was a basic law, or precept, within which all the other natural laws played a part: 'A certain order is to be found in the things that are apprehended by men ... that good is to be done and pursued, and evil is to be avoided. All the other precepts of the law of nature are based on this...' (II.i Q. 94 art. 2).

Reason and human purpose

The eternal law of divine **reason** is perceived through revelation, in the form of the Word of God (the Bible), and through the use of human reason. A moral life is a life lived according to and in accordance with reason, and an immoral life is a life lived at odds with reason: 'To disparage the dictate of reason is equivalent to condemning the command of God' (II.i Q. 19 art. 4). Aquinas deduced that, fundamentally, humans should do good and avoid evil.

Reason determines that the ultimate **purpose** and destiny of human life is fellowship with God. Humans naturally tended towards this destiny and should live according to their design. They should avoid being enslaved by non-natural, non-rational desires.

For Aquinas, man's first precept (rule) is self-preservation. He established a series of **primary precepts** (rules) that are required to ensure this goal: the continuation of the species through reproduction, the education of children, to live in society and to worship God. These primary precepts don't change: 'Natural law is the same for all men ... there is a single standard of truth and right for everyone ... which is known by everyone' (II.i Q. 94 art. 4).

Real and apparent goods

Aquinas believed that human nature was essentially good, as natural law is within everyone. He maintained that humans were oriented towards the achievement of perfection and that they could never knowingly pursue evil: 'No evil can be desirable, either by natural appetite or by conscious will. It is sought indirectly, namely because it is the consequence of some good' (1a Q. 19 art. 9). Human actions that are not in the pursuit of perfection can be explained as the pursuit of an *apparent* good – something that doesn't fit the perfect human ideal: 'A fornicator seeks a pleasure which involves him in moral guilt' (1a Q. 19 art. 9). Sin consists of falling short of God's intention

---

Ethical theories

for humans. To choose an apparent good is an error, because it isn't really good for us. The adulterer or adulteress commits adultery because he or she believes that it is good. This is an error of reason, because adultery prevents a human from drawing close to what God intended. A parent advises a child to get as much education as possible, but the child wastes time watching TV. The child thinks that watching TV in large amounts is good, although in fact less time should be given to such things, and more to learning. To correctly distinguish between apparent and real goods is to use reason rightly and to choose the right thing to do. It isn't necessarily easy, as we're tempted by what we like doing, which may not be truly good for us.

Reason identifies 'natural' or 'cardinal' virtues: prudence, temperance, fortitude and justice. Scripture reveals theological virtues: faith, hope and charity (1 Corinthians 13:13). To adhere to natural law, an individual should seek to develop these virtues – this development requires practice. The virtues must become habitual. It is also possible for the very opposite to become habitual if people are not careful, and for a habit of sinful unnatural activity to develop. For more on virtue, see Chapter 10.

Exterior and interior acts

For Aquinas, both the **intention** and the **act** are important. To act in a good way for the wrong reason is to perform a good exterior act but a bad interior act. For example, to help an old lady across the road (good exterior act) to impress someone (bad interior act) is wrong. It should be done out of charity and not for the sake of admiration by others. On the other hand, good intentions don't always lead to good actions. If I steal money to give it to a friend, the theft isn't made good by my intention to help my friend. The only end that Aquinas values is God. Physical pleasures can't be the final end, as animals can experience them. Academic pleasures aren't accessible to everyone, so the ultimate aim open to all humans is God. Aquinas believes that acts are intrinsically good or bad (good or bad in themselves) because when human beings act in accordance with their ultimate purpose, God is glorified. The act of helping the old lady across the road is good in and of itself, because it accords with the destiny of how humans should be and that glorifies God.

Primary and secondary precepts

Whether or not acts lead towards God depends upon whether the action fits the purpose that humans were made for. We have seen that the main purpose of human nature is to preserve the self and the innocent, to reproduce, to acquire knowledge, to live in an ordered society and to worship God. These are called **primary precepts**. Acts that accord with the main human purpose are good. Acts not in accordance with human purpose are bad. **Secondary precepts** are rulings about things that we should or shouldn't do because they uphold, or fail to uphold the primary precept.

Aquinas deduces the secondary precepts from the primary ones. Reproduction is a primary precept. The purpose of human genitals is reproduction. Masturbation is wrong because it doesn't lead to new life, doesn't fulfil its purpose and doesn't glorify God. Having hetrosexual intercourse with one's partner is good because it involves using the genitalia for their purpose, to pursue the primary precept of reproduction, and so it leads towards God as an end, and the action itself glorifies God. For more on sexual ethics see chapter 14.

Tasks

1 Suggest three apparent goods that aren't at all good, and explain your choices.

2 Aquinas believes that humans never choose evil, although they sometimes choose apparent goods which are in fact bad. Suggest examples that challenge this view; in other words, examples of evil actions that humans choose purposefully and knowingly. Are they convincing? Is Aquinas' view convincing?

3 Aquinas suggests that reason is the principle tool for making moral decisions. Can you suggest any alternative tools for making moral decisions? Can it ever be morally right to go against reason? Give a possible example.

4 Is it clear that the purpose of humanity is to preserve self and the innocent, to reproduce, to acquire knowledge, to live in an ordered society and to worship God? Are any of these disputable and, if so, on what grounds? Are there any other purposes that could be added to the list?

5 Does it matter if I do a good thing for a wrong reason, such as giving to charity for the admiration and praise that I'll receive? Why might some say that this isn't the best way to act?

6 Aquinas rejects teleological ethics and embraces deontological ethics. Explain what is meant by these terms and how they apply to Aquinas.

7 Suggest an ethical theory that opposes Aquinas' view and identify two aspects of that theory that oppose aspects of natural moral law.

8 Consider the following and decide, with reference to the primary precepts why Aquinas would think them wrong: the use of contraception, murder, homosexual sex, rape and adultery. Are there any which are unclear or raise concerns? Explain your answers.

Ethical theories

Evaluating natural moral law

The strengths of natural moral law are the strengths of an absolutist deontological view of morality. It enables people to establish common rules in order to structure communities. In a relativist era that is suffering from a breakdown in traditional social structures and moral uncertainty, this can be an attractive option.

Aquinas' view of reason as a tool for moral understanding and his idea of a common nature and morality for all people gives natural law a universality that goes beyond any one religion or culture. This is attractive in a world that suffers from intercultural strife and disharmony. Different cultures can all be seen to have the same basic principles of preserving life, continuing the species, education and building a society. A considerable portion of the human population still believes in God, even if in Western European countries such as the UK there is a decline in religious practice.

Natural moral law gives a concrete reason to be moral and a firm basis from which to refuse to step over moral boundaries. It provides justification and support for certain core ideas which are popular in modern times, such as human rights and equality. It judges actions, such as torture or rape, irrespective of consequences. Natural moral law isn't simply a set of rules, but a way of living. It gives guidance on day-to-day questions of how to live and links them to the fundamental principles of life. It provides a complete system of moral living in step with what it is to be human.

Some have challenged Aquinas. They question whether there's a common natural law that is apparent and self-evident, whether there's a single 'one size fits all' human nature and whether day-to-day rules can be deduced from the fundamental laws (primary precepts).

In his article 'An examination of the Thomistic theory of natural moral law' (1959; in Sigmund, 1988, p. 215), Kai Neilson argues against Aquinas' belief in a basic human nature that is present across all societies and cultures: 'from the point of view of science, there is no such thing as an essential human nature which makes a man man. The concept of human nature is a rather vague cultural concept; it is not a scientific one.' The challenge is that an essential human nature isn't as obviously self-evident as Aquinas claims. Neilson notes that anthropologists have investigated practices in other cultures. At one time, the Eskimos killed members of their families who would not make it through the winter, and new-born girls if there were no husbands to support them. Scandinavians killed their elderly family members to allow them into Valhalla. These differing moral standards challenge the idea of a common natural law within all human societies. Natural law obscures these basic moral differences.

Perhaps human beings have different or changeable natures, as indicated by people of different or variable sexual orientations. Homosexual men and women argue for recognition as normal human beings. Their acts are classed as unnatural by Aquinas as they can't lead to new life, but they themselves find love and purpose in life through the expression of their sexuality. Perhaps a common natural law does exist, but in a more complex form than Aquinas thought. Perhaps primary precepts differ in certain circumstances.

In their book *The Puzzle of Ethics* (1994, p. 60), Peter Vardy and Paul Grosch challenge the way in which Aquinas works from general principles to lesser purposes. Aquinas maintains that as human beings must preserve the species, every discharge of semen should be associated with life generation. To use the genitals in other ways is immoral. However, it isn't necessary that every discharge of semen should produce a new life to maintain the human species. Sexual acts could be justified on account of the benefits to the couple's relationship. Aquinas could be wrong about his deductions, as they may be based on an incorrect view of human life. Vardy and Grosch also consider Aquinas' moral view of human nature as unholistic. Perhaps the genitals are for pleasure rather than reproduction, or some other purpose, or for a number of different purposes. Sexual activity isn't only found in the genitalia. Psychologists have drawn much more complex pictures of human nature than Aquinas' simplistic account. Today, the human body is seen as one psycho-physical whole, not the fragmented collection of parts that Aquinas seems to believe in.

Aquinas' natural moral law is a Christian ethic and yet Jesus opposes **legalistic morality** in the New Testament. He debated sharply with the moral legalists of his time, the Pharisees. Natural moral law appears to be similar to Pharisaic law, and some, such as Joseph Fletcher (see Chapter 9), argue that Jesus rejected this approach. Some Christian ethicists argue for a morality that's based more on the person involved than the acts committed. One such writer is Kevin T. Kelly. In his book *New Directions in Moral Theology* (1992), Kelly identifies two traditions found in Christian morality, one that is centred on acts, and another that is centred on the dignity of the human person. He sees both of these strands of morality at work in recent Christian thinking. The Constitution of the Roman Catholic Church, *Gaudium et Spes*, maintains that 'the moral aspect of any procedure is influenced by intentions and motives but also objective standards, based on the nature of the human person and his acts' (p. 29). Kelly argues for a morality based on the human person as author and director of any actions, and moves away from the idea that actions have moral value in themselves. A more extreme form of **personalism** is found in **situation ethics**, where 'a one size fits all' legalistic approach to morality is virtually entirely abandoned. In situation ethics, the situation and the results of actions determine the goodness or badness of an action, not the action in itself.

Ethical theories

Given these criticisms, it is worth noting that natural law may not be as rigid as it first appears. Aquinas observed that although the primary precepts were unchangeable, the secondary precepts may change in some particular aspects, or in a case in which special reasons make it impossible to observe them. The conclusions of the Roman Catholic Church regarding the prohibitions of artificial contraception and homosexual acts may be challengeable in certain special cases. However, in the absence of guidelines to establish what is changeable, this may equally render the whole of natural moral law approach impossibly **subjective**. Vardy and Grosch (1994, pp. 62–63) note that this opens a door to the possibility of the proportionalist form of **situationism**, whereby rules apply to all proportionately extreme cases (see Chapter 9).

Tasks

1 Make a case arguing that all humans share a common nature.
2 What benefits does this view have for society?
3 Consider the evidence against the claim in **1**.
4 Identify sexual issues affected by natural moral law and suggest what Aquinas' view of these issues would be.
5 Explain what it means to base morality on actions (**deontology**).
6 What does it mean to say that morality should be person-centred, and what are the merits of this approach?

Extracts from key texts

St Thomas Aquinas, *Summa Theologica*

Of the Natural Law, II.i 94, Article 2

Now a certain order is to be found in those things that are apprehended universally. ... the first principle of practical reason is one founded on the notion of good, viz. that 'good is that which all things seek after'. Hence this is the first precept of law, that 'good is to be done and pursued, and evil is to be avoided'. All other precepts of the natural law are based upon this: so that whatever the practical reason naturally apprehends as man's good (or evil) belongs to the precepts of the natural law as something to be done or avoided ...

... Wherefore according to the order of natural inclinations, is the order of the precepts of the natural law. Because in man there is first of all an inclination to good in accordance with the nature which he has in common with all substances: inasmuch as every substance seeks the preservation of its own being, according to its nature: and by reason of this inclination, whatever is a means of preserving human life, and of warding off its obstacles, belongs to the natural law. Secondly, there is in man an inclination to things that pertain to him more specially, according to that nature which he has in common with other animals: and in virtue of this inclination, those things are said to belong to the natural law, 'which nature has taught to all animals' [*Pandect. Just. I, tit. i], such as sexual intercourse, education of offspring and so forth. Thirdly, there is in man an inclination to good, according to the nature of his reason, which nature is proper to him: thus man has a natural inclination to know the truth about God, and to live in society: and in this respect, whatever pertains to this inclination belongs to the natural law; for instance, to shun ignorance, to avoid offending those among whom one has to live, and other such things regarding the above inclination.

The Catechism of the Roman Catholic Church

Chapter Three – God's Salvation: Law and Grace
Article 1 – the Moral Law

I. The Natural Moral Law

1954   Man participates in the wisdom and goodness of the Creator who gives him mastery over his acts and the ability to govern himself with a view to the true and the good. The natural law expresses the original moral sense which enables man to discern by reason the good and the evil, the truth and the lie:

> The natural law is written and engraved in the soul of each and every man, because it is human reason ordaining him to do good and forbidding him to sin ... But this command of human reason would not have the force of law if it were not the voice and interpreter of a higher reason to which our spirit and our freedom must be submitted. [Leo XIII, *Libertas praestantissimum*, 597.]

1955   The 'divine and natural' law [*GS* 89 ' 1] shows man the way to follow so as to practice the good and attain his end. The natural law states the first and essential precepts which govern the moral life ...

Ethical theories

> The natural law is nothing other than the light of understanding placed in us by God; through it we know what we must do and what we must avoid. God has given this light or law at the creation. [St Thomas Aquinas, *Dec. praec.* 1.]

1956   The natural law, present in the heart of each man and established by reason, is universal in its precepts and its authority extends to all men. It expresses the dignity of the person and determines the basis for his fundamental rights and duties:

> For there is a true law: right reason. It is in conformity with nature, is diffused among all men, and is immutable and eternal; its orders summon to duty; its prohibitions turn away from offense ... To replace it with a contrary law is a sacrilege; failure to apply even one of its provisions is forbidden; no one can abrogate it entirely. [Cicero, *Rep.* III, 22, 33.]

1957   Application of the natural law varies greatly; it can demand reflection that takes account of various conditions of life according to places, times, and circumstances. Nevertheless, in the diversity of cultures, the natural law remains as a rule that binds men among themselves and imposes on them, beyond the inevitable differences, common principles ...

1959   The natural law, the Creator's very good work, provides the solid foundation on which man can build the structure of moral rules to guide his choices. It also provides the indispensable moral foundation for building the human community. Finally, it provides the necessary basis for the civil law with which it is connected, whether by a reflection that draws conclusions from its principles, or by additions of a positive and juridical nature.

1960   The precepts of natural law are not perceived by everyone clearly and immediately. In the present situation sinful man needs grace and revelation so moral and religious truths may be known 'by everyone with facility, with firm certainty and with no admixture of error'. [Pius XII, *Humani generis*: DS 3876; cf. *Dei Filius* 2: DS 3005.] The natural law provides revealed law and grace with a foundation prepared by God and in accordance with the work of the Spirit.

CHAPTER SUMMARY

Background:

- Aristotle wrote 'The natural is that which everywhere is equally valid.'
- Stoics emphasised Logos, or rationality, which governs the world.
- St Paul wrote about a law that is 'written in the hearts' of Gentiles.
- The Roman lawyer Cicero wrote 'True law is right reason in agreement with nature.'

St Thomas Aquinas' theory of natural moral law (thirteenth century):

- His ethical theory is absolutist and deontological, which means that it is focused on the ethicacy of actions.
- Natural law exists to assist humans: '... man needs to be directed to his supernatural end in a higher way'.
- There was a basic law '... that good is to be done and pursued, and evil is to be avoided'.
- Eternal law was perceived through revelation, in the form of the Word of God (the Bible) and human reason.
- 'To disparage the dictate of reason is equivalent to condemning the command of God.'
- The primary precepts are concerned with self-preservation, the continuation of the species through reproduction, the education of children, living in society and worshipping God.
- The secondary precepts are deduced from the primary ones.
- When humans do bad 'things' or 'acts' they are pursuing apparent goods, falsely believing them to be really good.
- For Aquinas, both the intention and the act are important. To act in a good way for the wrong reason is to perform a good exterior act but a bad interior act.
- Acts are intrinsically good or bad (good or bad in themselves) because when human beings act in accordance with their ultimate purpose, God is glorified.

Evaluating natural moral law:

- Natural moral law enables people to establish common rules to structure communities.
- Different cultures can be seen to have basic principles of preserving life, continuing the species, education and building a society, so natural law seems reasonable.

- Natural moral law gives guidance on day-to-day questions of how to live and links them to the fundamental principles of life.

However –

- Some dispute the presence of a common natural law and whether humans have a single nature.
- Humans may have different or changeable natures, as indicated by the different sexual orientations in society.
- Aquinas could be wrong about his primary precepts, his definition of human purpose.
- Natural moral law is a Christian ethic and yet Jesus' opposition to legalistic morality is apparent in the New Testament. Some, such as Joseph Fletcher, argue that Jesus rejected this approach.
- Natural moral law may not be as rigid as it first appears, as secondary precepts may change in some particular aspects.

Utilitarianism: a theory of usefulness

Introduction

Key philosophers and works

Jeremy Bentham (1748–1832): *Principles of Morals and Legislation*, 1789; *A Fragment on Government*, 1776

John Stuart Mill (1806–1873): *Utilitarianism*, 1863

Henry Sidgwick (1838–1900): *The Methods of Ethics*, 1874

Key terms

Act utilitarianism, consequentialism, hedonic calculus, hedonist, principle of utility, rule utilitarianism, teleological, *telos*, utilitarianism

What you will learn by the end of this chapter

- The difference between teleological and deontological theories of ethics.
- The utilitarian theory, including the utility principle, the hedonic calculus, and act and rule utilitarianism.
- Key utilitarian philosophers, including Jeremy Bentham and John Stuart Mill.
- The strengths and weaknesses of utilitarianism.

Key questions

1 A moral world is one in which as many people as possible are as happy as they can be. Do you agree?
2 Do the ends justify the means? Suggest an example where a desirable end justifies an undesirable action.

Ethical theories

3 What makes an action good or bad – the action in itself, or the consequence of that action?

4 'The good of the many outweighs the good of the few, or the one.' Is this true or false? Can you think of examples that support each view?

Teleological and deontological theories

Ethical theories that concentrate on moral rules that can't be broken are **deontological**. For deontological ethics, the important thing isn't the result or consequence of the action, but the action itself. If the action is wrong, in and of itself, then don't do it. A deontologist might say 'You should never kill, because the act of killing is wrong.' For a deontologist, the end never justifies the means.

Another group of philosophers argue that whether something is right or wrong depends on the result or end of that action. Theories that are interested in ends are called **teleological**, from the Greek word for 'end' – *telos*. For a teleological ethical thinker, the end justifies the means. You decide the rightness of an action by the end it produces. A choice that results in good end is morally better than one that results in a bad end. Stealing or lying is right if it leads to a better situation afterwards – for example, if the theft feeds a starving family, or the lie conceals a secret from a spy. Qualities such as love, honesty and kindness are not good in themselves. They are only good in an instrumental way because they cause good results.

Consider torture. A deontologist may argue that torturing prisoners is always wrong, no matter what the situation. On the other hand, a teleologist will want to look at the consequences of either choosing to torture or not choosing to torture before deciding whether or not it is right. Let us suppose that the prisoner has secrets that, once revealed, will save the lives of many innocent people. The prison guards know he has this information. The teleological thinker will maintain that it is right to go ahead and torture to discover the truth, as it will save the lives of many innocents.

Tasks

1 Would you authorise someone to be tortured to save innocent lives?

2 Make a list of deontological moral statements and teleological moral statements. Read them to your partner to see if he or she can correctly identify which is which.

3 A naval warship is in a battle. It receives a severe hit to the engineering section and a fire breaks out. If the fire continues, the ship's munitions could explode, killing the whole crew. The captain can use

a fast-acting extinguisher that would result in blasts of steam putting out the fire, but this will kill the men trapped in engineering. What should he do? What would a teleological thinker do? How would a deontological thinker respond?

4 Can you think about the sort of criteria that you would have to use to judge the ends of an action? What things would you want to consider when deciding whether or not a result or consequence was morally acceptable?

For teleological theories to work there needs to be some way of measuring how good or bad a consequence is. To answer this question, we need to investigate the most famous teleological theory – utilitarianism.

The theory of utilitarianism

Jeremy Bentham (1748–1832)

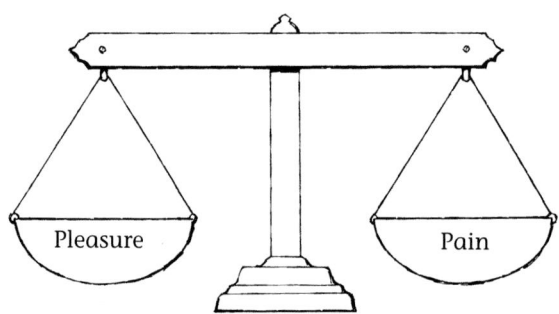

Weighing up pleasure and pain

The theory of **utilitarianism** was devised by Jeremy Bentham. He was born in London and lived at a time of great scientific and social change. With revolutions in France and America, demands were being made for human rights and greater **democracy**. Bentham worked on legal reform and wrote *The Principles of Morals and Legislation* (1789), in which he put forward his ethical theory. We can divide his theory into three parts:

1 His view on what drove human beings, and what goodness and badness was all about.

2 The principle of utility (from the Latin *utilis*, meaning 'useful'), which is his moral rule.

3 The hedonic calculus, which is his system for measuring how good or bad a consequence is.

Ethical theories

The motivation of human beings

Bentham maintained that human beings were motivated by pleasure and pain, and so he can be called a **hedonist** (*hedone* is Greek for 'pleasure'). He said, 'Nature has placed mankind under the governance of two sovereign masters, pain and pleasure. It is for them alone to point out what we ought to do, as well as to determine what we shall do.' (Bentham, 1789, Chapter I, I)

Bentham believed that all human beings pursued pleasure and sought to avoid pain. He saw this as a moral fact, as pleasure and pain identified what we should and shouldn't do. As a hedonist, Bentham believed that pleasure was the sole good and pain the sole evil: hence Bentham's utilitarianism is called hedonic utilitarianism.

The principle of utility

Once Bentham had established that pleasure and pain were the important qualities for determining what was moral, he developed the **utility principle**. The rightness or wrongness of an action is determined by its 'utility' or usefulness. Usefulness refers to the amount pleasure or happiness caused by the action. The theory is known as the greatest happiness principle, or a theory of usefulness:

> By the principle of utility is meant that principle which approves or disapproves of every action whatsoever, according to the tendency which it appears to have to augment or diminish the happiness of the party whose interest is in question: or, what is the same thing in other words, to promote or to oppose that happiness. I say of every action whatsoever; and therefore not, only of every action of a private individual, but of every measure of government.
>
> Bentham (1789), Chapter I, II

This can be shortened to 'An action is right if it produces the greatest good for the greatest number', where the greatest good is the greatest **pleasure** or happiness and the least **pain** or sadness, and the greatest number are the **majority** of people. Good is the maximisation of pleasure and the minimisation of pain. The end that Bentham's theory identify are those with the most pleasure and least pain. His theory is democratic, because the pleasure can't be for one person alone. When faced with a moral dilemma, Bentham argued that one should choose to act in such a way that brings about the maximum possible happiness for the most people. However, the possible consequences of different actions must be measured clearly to establish which option generates the most pleasure and the least pain. To measure the results, Bentham proposed the hedonic calculus.

The hedonic calculus

The **hedonic calculus** weighs up the pain and pleasure generated by the available moral actions to find the best option. It considers seven factors:

1. Its intensity.
2. Its duration.
3. Its certainty or uncertainty.
4. Its propinquity or remoteness ...
5. Its fecundity, or the chance it has of being followed by, sensations of the same kind: that is, pleasures, if it be a pleasure: pains, if it be a pain.
6. Its purity, or the chance it has of not being followed by, sensations of the opposite kind: that is, pains, if it be a pleasure: pleasures, if it be a pain ...

And one other; to wit:

7. Its extent; that is, the number of persons to whom it extends; or (in other words) who are affected by it.

Bentham (1789), Chapter IV, II

The balance of pleasures and pains is compared with those of other options and the best result determined. The action that leads to this best consequence is the morally correct one to pursue.

Tasks

1 Why might the fact that we aren't always able to predict the future be a problem for utilitarianism? Give an example.

2 Suggest examples of pains that are good and pleasures that are bad. How do these cause difficulties for utilitarianism?

3 Are affection or honesty good in themselves, or only because they have good results?

4 Why might a critic of utilitarianism argue that the theory doesn't protect the interests of minority groups?

5 One contemporary utilitarian, Peter Singer, goes as far as to consider animals in the equation, the greatest good for the greatest number. When making moral decisions, should you include the happiness and well-being of non-human beings? Justify your view.

6 Why does Bentham's theory pose a problem for those who believe we have a special obligation for certain people (parents, family and so on)?

Ethical theories

7 Sadistic guards torture a wrongly imprisoned innocent man. What difficulty does this example pose for Bentham's theory.

8 'Jim finds himself in the central square of a small South American town. Tied up against the wall are a row of Indians, mostly terrified, a few defiant, in front of them several armed men in uniform. A heavy man in a sweat-stained khaki shirt turns out to be the captain in charge and, after a good deal of questioning of Jim which establishes that he got there by accident while on a botanical expedition, explains that the Indians are a random group of the inhabitants who, after recent acts of protest against the government, are just about to be killed to remind other possible protestors of the advantages of not protesting. However, since Jim is an honoured visitor from another land, the captain is happy to offer him a guest's privilege of killing one of the Indians himself. If Jim accepts, then as a special mark of the occasion, the other Indians will be let off. Of course, if Jim refuses, then there is no special occasion, and Pedro here will do what he was about to do when Jim arrived, and kill them all. Jim, with some recollection of schoolboy fiction, wonders whether if he got hold of the gun, he could hold the Captain, and the rest of the soldiers to threat, but it is quite clear from the set-up that nothing of that kind is going to work: any attempt at that sort of thing will mean that all the Indians will be killed and himself. The men against the wall, and the other villagers, understand the situation, and are obviously begging him to accept. What should he do?'

Williams (1973), pp. 98–99

a On what grounds would a utilitarian kill the single prisoner?

b Would you agree with a utilitarian that the action of choosing and killing the single prisoner was good? If so, why – and if not, why not?

c Bernard Williams thinks that utilitarians find the decision to kill one too easy to take. What might he mean by this?

John Stuart Mill (1806–1873)

John Stuart Mill was a child prodigy who was able to read several languages at an early age, and the son of a follower of Jeremy Bentham. Perhaps the greatest British philosopher of the nineteenth century, he was an administrator for the East India Company and a Member of Parliament. Amongst his other works, he wrote *On the Subjugation of Women*, one of the inspirations behind modern **feminism**. His works concerning ethics were *On Liberty* (1859) and *Utilitarianism* (1861).

Mill maintained that the well-being of the individual was of greatest importance and that happiness is most effectively gained when individuals are free to pursue their own ends, subject to rules that protect the common good of all. While Mill accepted the utility principle of the greatest good for the greatest number, he was concerned about the difficulty raised in the example of the sadistic guards (see p.41, 7). If the greatest good for the greatest number was purely quantitative, based on the quantities of pleasure and pain caused, what would stop one person's pleasure from being completely extinguished if the majority gained pleasure from that act. To address this difficulty, Mill focused on qualitative pleasures. He developed a system of higher and lower pleasures, preferring the higher pleasures to the lower ones: 'It is better to be a human being dissatisfied than a pig satisfied; better to be Socrates dissatisfied than a fool satisfied.' (Mill, 1863, Chapter 2)

Mill maintained that the pleasures of the mind were higher than those of the body. There's a link between the two, as to be able to enjoy poetry or art, we need to eat and drink in order to survive. Nevertheless, Mill clearly believed that to pursue purely bodily pleasures – food, drink, drugs and sex – was not as high an objective as those that are intellectually demanding. When confronted with a choice between a pleasure of the body or a pleasure of the mind, that of the mind is to be preferred.

Ethical theories

1 Are bodily pleasures lower than intellectual pleasures?

2 a Working on your own, arrange the following pleasures in qualitative order, from higher to lower quality: eating, listening to music, making music, drinking alcohol, watching a good movie, viewing beautiful artwork, spending time with your partner, spending time with your friends, attending family gatherings, eating chocolate, reading or hearing poetry, playing sport, achieving fame.

  b Now compare your list with that of a partner or group, and try to come to an agreement.

  c What issues does this activity raise for Mills' utilitarianism?

Act and rule utilitarianism

Utilitarianism also exists in act form and rule form. **Act utilitarians** maintains that, whenever possible, the principle of utility must be directly applied for each individual situation. When faced with a moral choice, I must decide what action will lead to the greatest good in this particular situation. If I'm in a situation in which lying will create the greatest pleasure, then I should lie. If, in the next situation, lying brings about a lesser result than telling the truth, then I should tell the truth. According to act utilitarians, when determining whether the act is right, it is the value of the consequences of the particular act that count. I may break any law if, in that situation, greater happiness will result.

Act utilitarianism has the benefit of flexibility, being able to take into account individual situations at a given moment, although the actions that it justifies can change. This form of utilitarianism is more closely associated with Jeremy Bentham.

There are a number of criticisms of act utilitarianism. First, it has the potential to justify virtually any act if, in that particular case, the result generates the most happiness. A second problem is that it's impractical to suggest that we should measure each and every moral choice every time, especially as we may not have all the information required by the hedonic calculus. A third difficulty is that act utilitarianism can have some quite extreme results.

For example, an act utilitarian goes out to see a film. On the way to the cinema, she sees someone collecting money for charity. She gives her money to the collector instead of buying the ticket, and then goes home. A week passes and she sets out to the cinema again. She meets the collector again, hands over her money and again returns home. In each case, giving up her money to help the greatest number generates the greatest happiness. However, taken to extreme, all leisure activity would end – which seems a little hard to stomach. The other form of utilitarianism – rule utilitarianism – addresses this difficulty.

Rule utilitarianism focuses on general rules that everyone should follow to bring about the greatest good for that community. Rule utilitarianism establishes the best overall rule by determining the course of action which, when pursued by the whole community, leads to the best result. This form of utilitarianism is more closely associated with John Stuart Mill (1861) and John Austin (*The Province of Jurisprudence*, 1832). In a particular situation, I must obey the rule even if it doesn't lead to the greatest pleasure for me in this particular situation. A rule utilitarian will maintain that I must always drive on the left-hand side of the road in the UK, even in situations in which that doesn't bring about the greatest pleasure for me – such as when I'm in a traffic jam – because that will ensure the greatest good when everyone acts in such a way. I should never lie because, as a general community rule, lying doesn't bring about the greatest good for the community. In each case, the rule takes priority over my immediate situation.

Rule utilitarianism seems to overcome some of the difficulties encountered in act utilitarianism. In the case described above, the woman would be able to see a film, because a rule that allows people leisure time would be acceptable. On the other hand, it creates difficulties of its own. The British philosopher R. M. Hare notes a weakness with rule utilitarianism. Suppose that a maniac is chasing someone who hides in my shop. The maniac runs into the shop and asks me where the person is. Our gut feeling would be to lie. A rule utilitarian would state that I have to be honest, because I'm not allowed to break a rule even though, in this instance, the result isn't the greatest good. (R. M. Hare; in Childress and Macquarrie, 1986, p. 642). In addition, it's possible that a rule utilitarian could still permit certain practices, such as slavery, that appear to be morally unacceptable. There's no guarantee that minority interests will be protected. As long as the slaves are the smaller proportion of the people, the greatest good might be to keep them enslaved, because of the benefits that this would give to the majority.

Tasks

1 Give an example of where breaking a rule is arguably the right thing to do.

2 Give an example of where following a rule is arguably the wrong thing to do.

3 Read the following quotations and comment on them with regard to utilitarianism:

Ethical theories

a 'Rules and models destroy genius and art.' [William Hazlitt (1778–1830), British essayist, 'On taste'.]

b 'The good of the people is the chief law.' [Cicero (106–43 BCE), Roman orator and statesman, *De Legibus*, III.]

c 'Laws grind the poor, and rich men rule the law.' [Oliver Goldsmith (1728–1774), Irish-born British writer, 'The traveller'.]

d 'Laws were made to be broken.' [Christopher North (John Wilson; 1785–1854), Scottish writer, *Noctes Ambrosianae*, 24 May 1830.]

e 'Pleasure after all is a safer guide than either right or duty.' [Samuel Butler (1835–1902), British writer, *The Way of All Flesh*, Chapter 19.]

Evaluating utilitarianism

Jeremy Bentham's theory has a number of clear benefits. It seems reasonable to link morality with the pursuit of happiness and the avoidance of pain and misery, and this connection would receive popular support. It also seems natural to consider the consequences of our actions when deciding what to do. Utilitarianism offers a balanced, democratic morality that promotes the general happiness. Utilitarianism doesn't support individual pursuits that are at the expense of the majority. It is a commonsense system that's practically applicable to real-life situations. It has no need for a special wisdom.

These benefits are considerable, as they signify a working morality that can be brought into operation in organisational rather than simply individual matters. One could envisage the benefits of using utilitarianism in the management of hospitals, where fixed budgets must be best used to alleviate the suffering of the many.

However, there are a number of difficulties with utilitarianism. The first difficulty concerns all theories that rely on the consequences for deciding which actions are good. I need to be sure that what I think will come about as a result of a particular action *will* actually come about. Utilitarianism depends upon accurate predictions of the futures, but human beings don't always display accurate foresight. The consequences of actions may not become apparent until years into the future.

A second difficulty is found in measuring pleasure. The balancing process brought about using the seven criteria of the hedonic calculus appears straightforward. However, can different pleasures and different pains be so easily quantified? Can I compare the pleasure of seeing children grow up into adults with the pleasure of eating a chocolate bar? How do I quantify those two pleasures? What about pain that's good for you? When we hurt ourselves, the pain is a reminder that we have the injury and must take care of it. People who suffer from conditions that prevent their sensation of pain are at risk of serious injury. Some pain is good for us – it's there for a reason. The hedonic calculus formula isn't as straightforward as it at first appears. It's questionable whether an action can be declared good by an empirical test in the way the hedonic calculus suggests.

A third and more profound difficulty concerns the issue of justice. While utilitarianism ensures a maximum-pleasure result, it doesn't set out how that pleasure is distributed. It ensures that the most people receive pleasure, but it guarantees nothing for minorities. There's nothing in utilitarianism that prevents the total sacrifice of one pleasure for the benefit of the whole. Five bullies get pleasure from torturing a single boy. His pleasure is sacrificed for the greater benefit of theirs. In *A Theory of Justice*, John Rawls (1972, pp. 26–27) identifies this issue: 'The striking feature of justice is that does not matter, except indirectly, how this sum of satisfactions is distributed among individuals any more than it matters, except indirectly, how one man distributes his satisfactions over time.' In his book *A Short History of Ethics* (1966), Alasdair MacIntyre notes that utilitarianism could justify horrendous acts as being for the pleasure of the many. The Nazi policy of persecution and, eventually, extermination of Jews could be considered good if the greater population thought it pleasurable (p. 238). He identifies the focus on happiness as the cause of the problem: 'That men are happy with their lot never entails that their lot is what it ought to be. For the question can always be raised of how great the price is that is being paid for the happiness.' (p. 239)

A fourth difficulty is utilitarianism's failure to consider different views on what happiness is. It asserts that there's common agreement about what brings pleasure and what brings pain. This can be challenged on many levels. Not only do people have different tastes with regards to art, music and literature, but there are even extreme exceptions with regard to physical sensations – there are people who find pleasure in experiencing pain. If human beings don't have the same idea of what gives them pain and pleasure, then the premise on which utilitarianism is built severely weakened. The identification of one's interests with those of others becomes artificial.

Despite these weaknesses, utilitarianism has proved popular and useful in the centuries since its original formation. In *The Methods of Ethics* (1874), Henry Sidgwick (1838–1900) produced a more complex account of utilitarianism. He rejected Bentham's view that people pursued their own pleasure and replaced it with ethical **hedonism** – the view that individuals should seek general happiness. A contemporary adherent is the ethicist Peter Singer, who also argues, in *Practical Ethics* (1993), for a modified view of utilitarianism. He suggests that our ethical decisions should benefit the best interests of those affected, rather than simply pleasure, and that no individual's interests can be considered more valuable than another's interests. Modern formulations of utilitarianism don't fully address all its opponents' criticisms. The current concern for justice and minority issues in the light of human rights abuses raises powerful arguments against adopting a utilitarian stance. Nevertheless, utilitarianism will remain a persuasive ethical theory due to its practical dimension, which provides organisations with clear-cut systems for making decisions.

Long questions

1 Explain what is meant by the definition 'Goodness means the greatest happiness of the greatest number.'

2 Explain the distinctive features of utilitarianism.

3 Identify and evaluate three strengths of utilitarianism.

4 Identify and evaluate three weaknesses of utilitarianism.

Extracts from key texts

Jeremy Bentham, *Principles of Morals and Legislation*, 1781

Chapter I: Of The Principle Of Utility

I   Nature has placed mankind under the governance of two sovereign masters, pain and pleasure. It is for them alone to point out what we ought to do, as well as to determine what we shall do. On the one hand the standard of right and wrong, on the other the chain of causes and effects, are fastened to their throne. They govern us in all we do, in all we say, in all we think: every effort we can make to throw off our subjection, will serve but to demonstrate and confirm it. In words a man may pretend to abjure their empire: but in reality he will remain subject to it all the while ...

II   ... By the principle of utility is meant that principle which approves or disapproves of every action whatsoever, according to the tendency which it appears to have to augment or diminish the happiness of the party whose interest is in question: or, what is the same thing in other words, to promote or to oppose that happiness. I say of every action whatsoever; and therefore not, only of every action of a private individual, but of every measure of government.

III By utility is meant that property in any object, whereby it tends to produce benefit, advantage, pleasure, good, or happiness, (all this in the present case comes to the same thing) or (what comes again to the same thing) to prevent the happening of mischief, pain, evil, or unhappiness to the party whose interest is considered: if that party be the community in general, then the happiness of the community: if a particular individual, then the happiness of that individual ...

Chapter IV: Value Of A Lot Of Pleasure Or Pain, How To Be Measured

I Pleasures then, and the avoidance of pains, are the ends which the legislator has in view: it behoves him therefore to understand their value. Pleasures and pains are the instruments he has to work with: it behoves him therefore to understand their force, which is again, in other words, their value.

II To a person considered by himself, the value of a pleasure or pain considered by itself, will be greater or less, according to the ... following circumstances:

1. Its intensity.

2. Its duration.

3. Its certainty or uncertainty.

4. Its propinquity or remoteness ...

5. Its fecundity, or the chance it has of being followed by, sensations of the same kind: that is, pleasures, if it be a pleasure: pains, if it be a pain.

6. Its purity, or the chance it has of not being followed by, sensations of the opposite kind: that is, pains, if it be a pleasure: pleasures, if it be a pain ...

And one other; to wit:

7. Its extent; that is, the number of persons to whom it extends; or (in other words) who are affected by it.

Sum up all the values of all the pleasures on the one side, and those of all the pains on the other. The balance, if it be on the side of pleasure, will give the good tendency of the act upon the whole, with respect to the interests of that individual person; if on the side of pain, the bad tendency of it upon the whole.

John Stuart Mill, *Utilitarianism*, 1863

Chapter 2: What Utilitarianism Is

The creed which accepts as the foundation of morals, Utility, or the Greatest Happiness Principle, holds that actions are right in proportion as they tend to promote happiness, wrong as they tend to produce the reverse of happiness. By happiness is intended pleasure, and the absence of pain; by unhappiness, pain, and the privation of pleasure ...

To suppose that life has (as they express it) no higher end than pleasure – no better and nobler object of desire and pursuit – they designate as utterly mean and grovelling; as a doctrine worthy only of swine, to whom the followers of Epicurus were, at a very early period, contemptuously likened; and modern holders of the doctrine are occasionally made the subject of equally polite comparisons by its German, French, and English assailants ...

It is quite compatible with the principle of utility to recognise the fact, that some kinds of pleasure are more desirable and more valuable than others. It would be absurd that while, in estimating all other things, quality is considered as well as quantity, the estimation of pleasures should be supposed to depend on quantity alone ...

Now it is an unquestionable fact that those who are equally acquainted with, and equally capable of appreciating and enjoying, both, do give a most marked preference to the manner of existence which employs their higher faculties. Few human creatures would consent to be changed into any of the lower animals, for a promise of the fullest allowance of a beast's pleasures; no intelligent human being would consent to be a fool, no instructed person would be an ignoramus, no person of feeling and conscience would be selfish and base, even though they should be persuaded that the fool, the dunce, or the rascal is better satisfied with his lot than they are with theirs. They would not resign what they possess more than he for the most complete satisfaction of all the desires which they have in common with him. If they ever fancy they would, it is only in cases of unhappiness so extreme, that to escape from it they would exchange their lot for almost any other, however undesirable in their own eyes. A being of higher faculties requires more to make him happy, is capable probably of more acute suffering, and certainly accessible to it at more points, than one of an inferior type; but in spite of these liabilities, he can never really wish to sink into what he feels to be a lower grade of existence. We may give what explanation we please of this unwillingness; we may attribute it to pride, a name which is given indiscriminately to some of the most and to some of the least estimable feelings of which mankind are capable: we may refer it to the love of liberty and personal independence, an appeal to which was with the Stoics one of the most effective means for the inculcation of it; to the love of power, or to the love of excitement, both of which do really enter into and contribute to it: but its most appropriate appellation is a sense of dignity, which all human beings possess in one form or other, and in some, though by no means in exact, proportion to their higher faculties, and which is so essential a part of the happiness of those in whom it is strong, that nothing which conflicts with it could be, otherwise than momentarily, an object of desire to them.

Whoever supposes that this preference takes place at a sacrifice of happiness – that the superior being, in anything like equal circumstances, is not happier than the inferior – confounds the two very different ideas, of happiness, and content. It is indisputable that the being whose capacities of enjoyment are low, has the greatest chance of having them fully satisfied; and a highly endowed being will always feel that any happiness which he can look for, as the world is constituted, is imperfect. But he can learn to bear its imperfections, if they are at all bearable; and they will not make him envy the being who is indeed unconscious of the imperfections, but only because he feels not at all the good which those imperfections qualify. It is better to be a human being dissatisfied than a pig satisfied; better to be Socrates dissatisfied than a fool satisfied. And if the fool, or the pig, are of a different opinion, it is because they only know their own side of the question. The other party to the comparison knows both sides.

CHAPTER SUMMARY

- Deontological theories concentrate on actions.
- Teleological thinkers believe that the end justifies the means.

Jeremy Bentham:

- Jeremy Bentham devised the utilitarian theory. Human beings are motivated by pleasure and pain (hedonism) and all humans pursue pleasure, which is good, and seek to avoid pain, which is bad.
- The utility principle: the rightness or wrongness of an action is determined by its 'utility', or usefulness.

Ethical theories

- Usefulness refers to the amount pleasure or happiness caused by the action.
- 'An action is right if it produces the greatest good for the greatest number.'
- The hedonic calculus: this weighs up pain and pleasure based on intensity, duration, certainty or uncertainty, propinquity or remoteness, fecundity, purity and extent.

John Stuart Mill:
- The well-being of the individual is of greatest importance, and that happiness is most effectively gained when individuals are free to pursue their own ends, subject to rules that protect the common good of all.
- Focused on qualitative pleasures – some pleasures are higher (mind) and others lower (body).
- 'It is better to be a human being dissatisfied than a pig satisfied; better to be Socrates dissatisfied than a fool satisfied.'

Act and rule utilitarianism:
- Act utilitarians maintain that the good action is the one that leads to the greatest good in a particular situation.
- Act utilitarianism is flexible, being able to take into account individual situations at a given moment.
- However, it has the potential to justify virtually any act.
- It may be impractical to suggest that we should measure each moral choice every time.
- Rule utilitarians establish the best overall rule by determining the course of action which, when pursued by the whole community, leads to the greatest result.
- Rule utilitarianism overcomes some of the difficulties encountered in act utilitarianism.
- However, it may still permit certain practices, such as slavery, that appear to be morally unacceptable, because minority interests are not protected.

Evaluating utilitarianism:
- It's reasonable to link morality with the pursuit of happiness and the avoidance of pain and misery.
- It's natural to consider the consequences of our actions when deciding what to do.

- Utilitarianism offers democratic morality that promotes general happiness and opposes individual pursuits.
- It's a commonsense system that doesn't require special wisdom.

Difficulties:

- Utilitarianism relies on knowledge of consequences, but predictions may be mistaken or not apparent until years into the future.
- It's difficult to quantify pleasure.
- Some pain is good for us and some pleasure may be bad.
- The problem of justice: utilitarianism doesn't set out how that pleasure is distributed.
- Utilitarianism fails to consider different views on what happiness is.
- Utilitarianism has proved popular and useful in the centuries since its original formation, with updated versions suggested by Henry Sidgwick and Peter Singer.
- Utilitarianism remains persuasive due to its practical dimension, which provides organisations with clear-cut systems for making decisions.

Chapter 5

Kant

Contents of Chapter 5

Introduction
Kant's deontological ethics
The moral law
Good will and duty
The categorical imperative
Freedom
Dilemmas
Evaluating Kant

Introduction

Key philosophers and works

Immanuel Kant (1724–1804): *Groundwork for the Metaphysics of Morals*, 1785; *Critique of Practical Reason*, 1788; *The Metaphysics of Morals*, 1797

Key terms

a posteriori, a priori, analytic, categorical imperative, deontological ethics, duty, hypothetical imperative, kingdom of ends, maxim, moral agents, 'ought' implies 'can', prescriptive, *summum bonum*, synthetic, univeralisability

What you will learn by the end of this chapter

- The theory of deontological ethics.
- Kant's theory of the moral law, good will and duty, the categorical imperative and freedom.
- The strengths and weaknesses of Kantian ethics.
- Examples that illustrate the ethical issues at stake.

Key questions

1 Should moral decisions be made by following reason or feelings?
2 Is it wrong to do good for selfish motives?
3 Are actions more important than consequences when deciding what to do?

4 Are moral statements universally true in every circumstance?

5 Is honesty the best policy?

6 Are there ever times when it's justified to use human life as a means to an end?

Kant's deontological ethics

Deontological theories are concerned with actions, not consequences. Moral value is conferred by virtue of the actions in themselves. If a certain act is wrong, then it is wrong in all circumstances and all conditions, irrespective of the consequences. This view of ethics stands in opposition to teleological views such as utilitarianism, which holds that the consequences of an action determine its moral worth. Kant's theory is deontological because it's based on **duty**. To act morally is to do one's duty, and one's duty is to obey the moral law. Kant argued that we should not be side-tracked by feeling and **inclination**. We should not act out of love or compassion. Kant also stated that it isn't our duty to do things that we're unable to do. For Kant, the fact that we ought to do something implies that it is possible to do it. Moral statements are **prescriptive**; they prescribe an action. 'Ought' implies 'can'. If I say 'I ought to do x', it means 'I can do x'.

Kant maintained that humans seek an ultimate end called the supreme good, the **summum bonum** – a state in which human virtue and happiness are united. However, since it is impossible for human beings to achieve this state in one lifetime, he deduced that we had to have immortal souls to succeed. While Kant rejected theological arguments for the existence of God, his ethical theory assumes immortality and God's existence. Kant believed that the afterlife and God must exist to provide an opportunity for reaching this supreme good. So, for Kant, morality led to God.

The moral law

> Two things fill the mind with ever new and increasing admiration and awe ... the starry heavens above me and the moral law within me.

Kant (1788), pp. 193, 259

Kant believed that there is an objective moral law and that we know this law through reason. Moral rules exist and they are binding. Kant argued that we know the moral law without reference to any consequences.

What kind of statements did Kant think moral ones are?

Statements of knowledge can be *a priori*, knowable without reference (or prior) to experience, or *a posteriori*, knowable through experience. An example of *a priori* knowledge would be '1 + 1 = 2'. You don't need experience to know that when you add two 1's together you get 2. An example of *a posteriori* knowledge is 'the squirrel is behind the tree'. You can only know for certain by looking, and this looking is experience.

Another division can be made. Knowledge may be **analytic**: the predicates (parts of the sentence) may say something that is necessarily true about the subject. For example, consider the sentence 'all spinsters are women' (the word 'spinster' refers to an unmarried woman). The statement needs no further facts from an exterior source – we don't need to go round checking! It is necessarily true – true by its own authority. The '*a priori*' example '1 + 1 = 2' is also 'analytic', as we don't need further information apart from the sum itself. It can be called '*a priori* analytic'.

Alternatively, knowledge may be **synthetic**. It may require empirical tests, such as observations, measurements or experiments. The statement 'Jack is a butler' isn't necessarily true, because we need exterior information to support the claim that he's a butler. There's nothing inextricably linked to the word 'Jack' that means he must be a butler. Not all Jacks are butlers. It may in fact turn out that Jack isn't a butler at all. Synthetic statements may be true or false. The statement 'Jack is a butler' is also *a posteriori*, as it's knowable after experience. Therefore, we can call it '*a posteriori* synthetic'.

Moral statements are '*a priori* synthetic'.

Kant believed that statements of fact are either '*a priori* analytic', such as '1 + 1 = 2' or 'all spinsters are women', or '*a posteriori* synthetic', such as 'Jack is a butler'. Moral statements, however, fall into a different category. We can't prove what people should do by looking, so moral statements must be *a priori*. Moral knowledge is gained by pure reason, not sense experience. However, as moral statements may be right or wrong, they are also synthetic, so moral statements are called '*a priori* synthetic'.

To summarise, non-ethical statements are either:

- *a priori* analytic = necessarily true and knowable without experience (for example, '1 + 1 = 2'), or
- *a posteriori* synthetic = possibly true and to be validated through experience (for example, 'Jack is a butler')

Ethical statements are *a priori* synthetic = knowable through reason, not sensation or experience, and may or may not be true.

This places Kant in direct opposition to utilitarians, who consider the consequences of an action (experience) as fundamental in deciding what is moral.

Good will and duty

> Good will shines forth like a precious jewel.
>
> It is impossible to conceive anything at all in the world, or even out of it, which can be taken as good without qualification, except a good will.
>
> Kant (1785), p. 394

In Kant's book, *Groundwork for the Metaphysics of Morals* (1785), he argues that the highest form of good is **good will**. To have a good will is to do one's duty. To do one's duty is to perform actions that are morally required, and to avoid actions that are morally forbidden. Doing one's duty is doing the right thing, not the wrong thing. Why do we do our duty? – because it's our duty to do it! To perform a moral action out of a desire for the good consequence it brings is to act in self-interest, and is not a morally good action. To tell the truth because it's in our interest to do so isn't a moral action. We don't do our duty because of the consequences of doing it – we do it for duty itself. Duty is good in itself. Kant acknowledged that happiness is also good, and that it comes as a reward for acting through good will, but that duty is the highest good.

Kant's theory directly opposes utilitarian ethics. If a murderer asked us whether our friend, who he was pursuing, was hiding in our house, Kant would insist we were honest. The utilitarian would see greater happiness being caused by a lie, but Kant doesn't consider consequences, only the action, and to lie would be wrong.

Task

Do you agree that 'To tell a falsehood to a murderer who asked us whether our friend, of whom he was in pursuit, had not taken refuge in our house, would be a crime'? How might you argue that it's true?

Kant believed that we should act out of duty and not emotion. A human action isn't morally good because we feel that it's good, or because it's in our own self-interest. A human action is good when it's done for the sake of duty. I may act out of kindness, generosity or compassion, but in these circumstances, the act confers no virtue on me. Even if duty demanded the same action, but it was done for a motive such as compassion, the act would be a good act, but the person wouldn't be moral for choosing it. If I give money to a beggar out of compassion, then my act may be good, but I'm not virtuous for doing it. If I give to the beggar because duty demands it, then I'm virtuous for doing so. For Kant, we're not moral for the sake of love – we're moral for the sake of duty. This makes Kant seem rather austere and uninterested in human emotions. In fact, he argued that duty and reason can help to guide our emotions, so that we aren't ruled by them.

Kant is described as having produced a system of ethics based on reason and not intuition. A moral person must be a rational being. Being good means having a good will. A good will is when I do my duty for the sake of duty alone. I do my duty because it's right, and for no other reason. But what does it mean to act out of duty? Kant explained that to act out of duty is to perform actions that are morally obligatory and not to perform those that are forbidden.

The categorical imperative

The **categorical imperative** helps us to know which actions are obligatory and which are forbidden. It tells us what we ought to do:

> All imperatives command either hypothetically or categorically ...
> If the action would be good simply as a means to something else,
> then the imperative is hypothetical; but if the action is represented
> as good in itself ... then the imperative is categorical.
>
> Kant (1797), p. 414

Kant argued that morality is prescriptive; it prescribes moral behaviour. Once you're aware of a moral requirement, your awareness is a reason for doing something. Moral statements are categorical in that they prescribe actions irrespective of the result.

A categorical imperative differs from an **hypothetical imperative**, which doesn't prescribe or demand any action. Hypothetical imperatives are conditional: 'If I want x, I must do y'. If I want to lose weight, I ought to go on a diet. If you want a sandwich, open the fridge. These imperatives are not moral. For Kant, the only moral imperatives were categorical: I ought to do such and such. For example, I ought to tell the truth. This makes no reference to desires or needs.

There are three principles of the categorical imperative, as follows.

The universal law

> There is ... only one categorical imperative. It is: Act only accord-
> ing to that maxim by which you can at the same time will that it
> should become a universal law.
>
> Kant (1785), pp. 80–87

The categorical imperative is 'Do not act on any principle that cannot be universalised'. In other words, moral laws must be applied in all situations and all rational beings universally, without exception. If an action is right for me, it's right for everyone. If it's wrong for one person, then it's wrong for all people. I can't maintain the proposal 'stealing is wrong for everyone, but because I haven't got enough to pay the rent this month I can steal'.

> For an action to be morally valid, the agent – or person performing
> the act – must not carry out the action unless he or she believes
> that, in the same situation, all people should act in the same way.
>
> Kant (1785), pp. 80–87

The moral law permits certain actions and forbids others. Why adopt such an emphatic absolutist stance? Kant argued that to allow exceptions would harm someone and have an eroding effect on society. He gave an example using the case of lying. In certain circumstances we might think that a lie is better than the truth. It might get us out of trouble! Kant argued that a lie always harms someone – if not the liar then mankind generally, because it violates the source of law. If everyone was to act in this way, society would become intolerable.

Treat humans as ends in themselves

Kant's second principle in the categorical imperative is:

> So act that you treat humanity, both in your own person and in
> the person of every other human being, never merely as a means,
> but always at the same time as an end.
>
> Kant (1797), p. 428

You can never treat people as means to an end. You can never use human beings for another purpose, to exploit or enslave them. Humans are rational and the highest point of creation, and so demand unique treatment. This guarantees that individuals are afforded the same moral protection. There can be no use of an individual for the sake of the many – as is the case with utilitarians, who can sacrifice the few for the greater good of the greater number.

Kant argued that we have a duty to develop our own perfection, developing our moral, intellectual and physical capabilities. We also have a duty to seek the happiness of others, as long as that is within the law and allows the **free-**

dom of others. So we should not promote one person's happiness if that happiness prevents another's happiness.

Act as if you live in a kingdom of ends

The third principle of Kant's categorical imperative is:

> So act as if you were through your maxim a law-making member of a kingdom of ends.

Kant (1797), p. 74

Kant required moral statements to be such that you act as if you, and everyone else, were treating each other as ends. You can't act on a rule that assumes that others don't treat people as ends. You can't create a **maxim** such as 'I may lie as all others lie'. If such rules were pursued, society would become intolerable.

Task

During the Second World War, the Allies pursued a policy of bombing civilian targets (area bombing), in the hope that the Axis powers would be weakened by the loss of morale.

1 Explain the difficulties that Kant would have with this policy.

2 Do you agree with Kant's view?

3 What's the strength of never treating people as a means to an end?

Freedom

> ... [I]n morals, the proper and inestimable worth of an absolutely good will consists precisely in the freedom of the principle of action from all influences ...

Kant (1785), pp. 80–87

Kant believed that humans were free to make rational choices. If people were not free, the possibility of making moral choices would be denied. This ability to freely rationalise, or reason, is what distinguishes humans from animals, who lack this ability.

We have to be free to do our duty. Our duty is to follow the categorical imperative. But if our choices aren't free, and our actions are controlled by factors beyond our control, then we can't truly be **moral agents**. Kant thought that 'ought' implied 'can' – in other words, something that's impossible can't be a moral option, and therefore every moral option must be possible. For example, two people are mugged one night. The gang of ruffians quickly overpowers them, and one is tied up fast. The other is then seriously assaulted, before the gang runs off. The person who has been tied up can't defend his friend. He has no choice and so he hasn't done anything wrong. Human reason means that we're able to choose what to do: we can freely make moral decisions.

Task

1

One day Jack's mother notices that he has a new football. She asks him where he got the money for it and he says he found it. When Jack's father discovers that some money is missing from his wallet, Jack owns up. His parents are very angry and give him a firm talking to about stealing always being wrong and lying always being wrong.

The next day there's a ring at the door. Jack opens it to see an agitated, angry man holding a large baseball bat. The man asks where his father is. Jack knows that his father is asleep in the back garden. What should he do?

Later on, in his adult life, Jack owns a small shop. He can see out into the street and he notices a very poorly looking beggar on the other side of the road. From time to time, Jack notices the beggar stealing fruit from the grocer's shop. Jack remembers his parents' words about stealing. One day, the police call by and ask Jack if he's noticed the beggar stealing, as the grocer has made a complaint. What should Jack do?

2

A friend of yours has, for some time, been going out with a local boy. She's besotted with him and believes that he's the perfect gentleman. One day, you discover that he's been two-timing your friend, but before you have a chance to say anything the boy is killed in a car crash. Your friend is devastated and decides to write a eulogy to him, to be read out at the funeral. She asks you to help. Should you tell her the truth or keep quiet?

3 – the *Casablanca* example

The film Casablanca is set in Morocco at the beginning of the Second World War. An anti-Nazi writer, Victor (played by Paul Henreid), and his wife Ilsa (Ingrid Bergman) arrive in Morocco as refugees. Victor needs to escape to America to continue the struggle, but he does not have the necessary documents. Ilsa meets a club owner, Rick (Humphrey Bogart), with whom she had been in love in the past. Towards the end of the film Rick persuades Ilsa to run away with him leaving Victor behind. In fact, he is making it possible for Victor and Ilsa to leave together to continue their anti-Nazi work. She only realizes this at the last moment, and then he tells her that his feelings for her are an attachment to past and not present passion, which is also false. (And 'I'm not much good

Ethical theories

at being noble, but it isn't hard to see that the troubles of three little people don't amount to a hill of beans in this crazy world.') Rick has lied to Ilsa in order to be part of the struggle against something evil. And the motives are self-sacrificing ones. What stronger justification could be given?

Morton (1996), p. 221

Did Rick do the right thing? What would you have done? What would Kant have done?

Evaluating Kant

The categorical imperative is a powerful set of moral principles that prohibit acts that would be commonly considered wrong such as theft, murder, fraud, violence and sexual abuse. They bind us to set rules that apply to everyone and that command respect for human life.

The contribution that Kant made is apparent in three ways. Firstly, he makes a distinction between duty and inclination. We may be inclined to do what benefits ourselves individually, but morality is more than personal preference. Secondly, he corrects the utilitarian presumption that the punishment of the innocent can be justified if the majority benefit. Kant insists you can't promote happiness if that happiness undermines another's happiness. The moral value of an action comes from its **intrinsic** rightness in itself. This means that justice is impartial, and that justice for individuals is safeguarded by the universal character of the categorical imperative. Finally, Kant's theory gives humans intrinsic worth, as the rational high point of creation. Humans can only ever treated as ends in themselves, never as means. Therefore, humans can't be expended for some apparent greater good. They can't be enslaved or exploited.

However, there are a number of difficulties with Kant's deontological ethics. The refusal to allow exceptions in using people as a means to an end places severe restrictions on our behaviour. A government can't sacrifice the few for the many, and yet sometimes – as in war – such a sacrifice is politically necessary for the good of the majority. Arguably, Kant's theory isn't well-suited to world politics, which occasionally require hard decisions to be made. In some circumstances, duties conflict. If you run a hospital with a fixed budget, you have to makes decisions about how many patients of each category of illness you can treat. There comes a point at which the money runs out, and so difficult decisions must be made as to who gets what treatment. Kant would find making such decisions very difficult

A weakness with **universalisability** is the problem of different but similar moral dilemmas. Are any two moral dilemmas the same? How similar do they have to be to be covered by the same maxim? Are murder, self-defence and the defence of the realm all to be covered by one maxim about taking human life, or can some kinds of killing be justified and excluded because they are different?

Teleological thinkers look to consequences and act out of compassion, but Kant rejects both which is a challenge in moral deliberation. Nevertheless, Kant proposes a "reason-based" case for moral behaviour

Kant's *Groundwork of the metaphysic of morals* trans. H. J Paton

All imperatives command either hypothetically or categorically. Hypothetical imperatives declare a possible action to be practically necessary as a means to the attainment of something else that one wills (or that one may will). A categorical imperative would be one which represented an action as objectively necessary in itself apart from its relation to a further end.

Every practical law represents a possible action as good and therefore as necessary for a subject whose actions are determined by reason. Hence all imperatives are formulae for determining an action which is necessary in accordance with the principles of a will in some sense good. If the action would be good solely as a means to something else, the imperative is hypothetical; if the action is represented as good in itself and therefore as necessary, in virtue of its principle, for a will which of itself accords with reason, then the imperative is categorical.

Questions

1 What are the distinguishing features of deontological ethical theories?

2 'An act is morally good if it's done entirely from motives of duty.' What does Kant mean by duty? Consider the strengths *and* weaknesses of the claim.

3 a Can you explain the principle 'You ought to act in such a way that you would be willing to universalise the act'?

b Why do some philosophers reject this view?

4 Does 'ought' imply 'can'? Explain Kant's view of freedom.

CHAPTER SUMMARY

Kant's deontological ethics:

■ Deontological theories are concerned with actions, not consequences.

■ Kant's theory is deontological because it's based on duty. To act morally is to do one's duty, and one's duty is to obey the moral law.

- 'Ought' implies 'can'. If I say 'I ought to do *x*', it means 'I can do *x*'.
- Humans seek an ultimate end called the supreme good, the *summum bonum*, so, for Kant, morality led to God.
- 'Two things fill the mind with ever new and increasing admiration and awe … the starry heavens above me and the moral law within me.'
- Moral statements are '*a priori* synthetic' (reason, not sense experience).
- 'Good will shines forth like a precious jewel' – the highest form of good is good will. To have a good will is to do one's duty.
- To do one's duty is to perform actions that are morally required.
- We should act out of duty, and not emotion; Kant's ethic is reason-based, not intuitive.
- Moral statements are categorical – they prescribe irrespective of the result.
- Universal law: 'Act only according to that maxim by which you can at the same time will that it should become a universal law.' Treat humans as ends in themselves. Act as if you live in a kingdom of ends.
- Humans are free to make rational choices. If people were not free, the possibility of making moral choices would be denied.

Evaluating Kant:
- The categorical imperative prohibit acts that would commonly be considered immoral.
- Kant distinguishes between duty and inclination.
- Kant's theory gives humans intrinsic worth, which can't be sacrificed for the majority.
- Kant's system can't resolve conflicting duties.
- **Universalisability** generalises different but similar moral dilemmas.

Chapter 6

Naturalism and intuitionism

Contents of Chapter 6

Introduction

Key philosophers and works

F. H. Bradley (1846–1924): *Ethical Studies*, 1876

G. E. Moore (1873–1958): *Principia Ethica*, 1903

H. A. Prichard (1871–1947): 'Does moral philosophy rest on a mistake?' in *Mind* (1912); *Moral Obligation: Essays and Lectures*, 1949

W. D. Ross (1877–1971): *The Right and the Good*, 1930; *The Foundations of Ethics*, 1939

Key terms

Ethical naturalism, good, intuition, intuitionism, meta-ethics, naturalistic fallacy, normative ethics, *prima facie* duties

What you will learn by the end of this chapter

■ The theory of ethical naturalism.

■ The contribution that F. H. Bradley makes to naturalism.

■ The theory of intuition and the different contributions of G. E. Moore, H. A. Prichard and W. D. Ross.

Key questions

1 How do we perceive morals? Do we use the same facilities and evidence as used for mathematical or scientific proofs? Do we use some sort of separate intuition?

2 Do moral truths exist at all, or are they simply an expression of our likes and dislikes?

Background

The ethical theories that we have looked at so far have been concerned with how you demonstrate whether something is right or wrong, whether it be by some set of absolute truths or a special system such as the hedonic calculus or the categorical imperative. By the end of the nineteenth century, this normative approach to ethics produced **naturalism**, which maintained that ethical values could be substantiated in the same way that scientific ones were, using evidence and proofs. This chapter examines naturalism and its contender **intuitionism**, which rejected the scientific approach to moral facts in favour of an intuitive approach. As the different forms of intuitionism have their own strengths and weaknesses, they are considered specifically within each section rather than at the end.

Ethical naturalism

With the rise of modern science in the seventeenth century, and the criticisms that science was making of traditional views of the world, which were based partly on religious traditions, a view of ethics emerged that tried to link morals with this new scientific knowledge. Ethical naturalism is the view that:

1 Ethical terms can be defined or explained using the same 'natural' terms that we would use to define mathematics or science.

2 Morals could be based on the same kind of observation of the world as used in science.

Our sense perceptions – the things we see, hear, touch, smell and taste – and our **logic** faculty are the tools that a moral person uses to conclude ethical truths. Moral truths are facts like numbers or chemical properties. Naturalists believe that moral conclusions can be deduced from non-moral premises. I can conclude that something is wrong from observation and analysis. When I see the murder of an innocent, what I see isn't only the facts of how the person is killed, who the killer is and what actually happens – I also perceive the fact that it's despicable and wrong. The wrongness of murder is as much a fact of the universe as the fact that plunging a knife into the heart can stop it. This means that moral facts aren't views or opinions, likes or dislikes. Nor are they based on some sort of spiritual or intuitive sense. When I observe that something is wrong, it's a moral fact of the universe.

Naturalists fall into different categories. Theological naturalists (such as St Thomas Aquinas) maintain that goodness is linked to the will of God as seen in nature. God's will defines morality: murder is wrong because God commands against murder. Alternatively, hedonic naturalists see goodness as a fact of pleasure or happiness. R. B. Perry suggests that 'good' means 'being an object of favourable interest' and 'right' means 'being conducive to harmonious happiness' (Perry, 1954, pp. 3, 1–7, 109). For Perry, '*x* is good' is the same as '*x* is an object of desire', while '*y* is right' is the same as '*y* is conducive to harmonious happiness'.

Naturalists come to their ethical conclusions using non-ethical evidence. In the case of the hedonists, pleasure is the non-ethical element. In the case of the theological naturalist, God's will is the non-ethical element. Consider the two statments 'Stalin helped defeat Germany' and 'Stalin was an evil man'. The first statement is factual. We can prove it true or false by looking at the evidence. The ethical naturalist holds that the second statement may also be proved true or false in much the same way. We can find out whether Stalin was evil by investigating his actions and behaviour. The evidence that we come up with verifies the moral fact 'Stalin was an evil man'.

For Naturalists, 'good' doesn't really exist on its own. It can be reduced to pleasure, happiness or God's will. Charles R. Pigden (1991, p. 422) writes 'Naturalists, in short, resort to all sorts of supposed facts – sociological, psychological, scientific, even metaphysical or supernatural.'

Naturalism – F. H. Bradley (1846–1924)

The naturalist F. H. Bradley, writing in his book *Ethical Studies* (1876), believed that a moral perspective was determined from self-realisation and from observing one's position in society. He rejected hedonism, as pleasure provides no final self-understanding. He opposed Kant's idea of duty for the sake of duty, on the grounds that it doesn't guide us in morality or give human satisfaction. Bradley concluded that the better approach was to pursue self-realisation within the community: '... we have found the end, we have found self realisation, duty, and happiness in one – yes, we have found ourselves, when we have found our station and its duties, our function as an organ of the social organism' (Bradley, 1927, p. 163).

Our place and role in the historical community provide a satisfying life. We must realise our true self, which we learn in the family and community, and adopt the values of our society – and those of other societies that offer sound criticisms of our society. This places us firmly in the concrete universe and offers the best satisfaction. To be a good person, we must know our station and its duties. The good of society is about hard work and **obedience**. Once your position in life is decided, you have a duty to perform the function of that station.

Tasks

1 According to naturalists, what are moral laws?

2 According to naturalists, how is moral knowledge investigated?

3 What according to Bradley provides human satisfaction?

4 Suggest one benefit of giving moral knowledge a scientific basis.

5 Suggest examples of how linking moral knowledge to society's view of your role in life may be undesirable.

Intuitionism – G. E. Moore (1873–1958) and the naturalistic fallacy

The philosopher G. E. Moore criticised naturalism in his work *Principia Ethica* (1903). In his book, he asserted that moral judgements are based on an infallible intuitive knowledge of good things. When we make a moral decision we simply choose the action that brings about more of these good things. Any disagreements are simply about the actions that might bring about the good things – not the good things themselves, as these are self-evident. In his book, Moore argued that the things that are intrinsically good can't be defined or analysed: 'If I am asked "What is good?" my answer is that good is good, and that is the end of the matter. Or if I am asked "How is good to be defined?" my answer is that it cannot be defined, and that is all I have to say about it.' (Moore, 1903, p. 6)

Good is indefinable, because it's a simple idea. Moore differentiates between complex ideas that can be broken down into smaller ideas, and simple ideas that can't be broken down. 'Yellow' is a simple idea, like 'good'. Moore says that 'yellow' and 'good' are not complex. 'Yellow' can't be described in any other way than to say it is yellow. On the other hand, a 'horse' is a complex idea that can be defined and reduced: 'You can give a definition of a horse because a horse has many different properties and qualities [but] when you have reduced a horse to its simplest terms, then you can no longer define these terms' (p. 7). You can analyse a horse and divide up the various elements – quadruped, mammal, vegetarian and so on – but with 'yellow' and 'good' you can't go any further.

To define an ethical judgement as a factual one is an error. To define goodness as the greatest pleasure or the most happiness is to propagate a fallacy, the **naturalistic fallacy**, because such a definition isn't possible. In trying to do this, naturalists confuse the property of goodness with some other non-moral property that good things happen to possess. They are confusing moral judgements with factual judgements.

Moore maintained that you can't use a non-moral premise to establish a moral conclusion. You can't go from observing pleasure to saying that goodness is pleasure. Likewise, 'good' can't be identified with a metaphysical entity such as God. Moore wrote 'everything is what it is and not another thing'. The good is the good – not pleasure or happiness – and it can't be broken down into pleasure or happiness or some other description. Moore believed that his 'open question' argument disproved naturalism. If a naturalist claims that goodness consists of things that lead to pleasure, we can then identify a thing that leads to pleasure and still ask the open question 'But is it good?' We can also say that a thing leads to pleasure but isn't good. Moore concludes that naturalistic definitions can't be correct.

Moore believed that moral judgements could never be proved empirically. We don't use scientific observation or logical analysis to perceive the good, as the naturalists might. We recognise good things intuitively when we see them, and in this sense Moore is an intuitionist – but not an ordinary intuitionist. He believed that moral judgments were incapable of being proved, not that the origin of moral judgments lay in human intuitions. What's more, moral intuitions can be wrong. However, Moore maintained that all human beings know by intuition that '… the most valuable things which we know or can imagine … are certain states of consciousness, which may roughly be described as the pleasures of human intercourse and the enjoyment of beautiful objects' (p. 188).

What is right or good is that which brings about this end. It's fair to say that while Moore claims this is the case, he doesn't demonstrate it conclusively. This is the greatest weakness in his theory. He asserts many things about good and its indefinability but, he can't prove his own case. Moore also leaves a doubtful explanation to account for moral disagreements. He maintains that either you agree with his list of intrinsic and indefinable goods, or you haven't thought about it properly. The only thing left to argue about is which action produces more of the goods. It seems unreasonable to summarise all moral debate in these terms.

Intuitionism – H. A. Prichard (1871–1947)

In his article 'Does moral philosophy rest on mistake? (1912), the intuitionist H. A. Prichard set out his moral theory. Prichard argued that to justify moral obligation by reducing it to an interest or something else was a mistake. Moral obligation presented itself directly to our intuitions: 'This apprehension is immediate, in precisely the same sense in which a mathematical apprehension is immediate ...'.

Prichard thought that there were two different kinds of thinking – intuition and reasoning. Reason collected together the facts concerned and intuition determined which course to follow. In deciding whether to have an abortion, reason collects all the data on the nature of abortion – the people concerned, and the various possible outcomes – and then intuition determines what we should do. Ethical dilemmas are about making a choice between different actions where there are conflicting moral obligations. In the case of abortion, for example, one would weigh up the obligation to the unborn human with that owed to the mother. Prichard held that intuition would identify which obligation was the greater. He didn't believe in linking moral obligations to the intrinsic goodness of any action. One simply had to consider the different obligations in the situation at hand.

This didn't mean that all people could clearly intuit moral truth. People's morals differed because some had clearer moral intuitions than others. Our intuitions don't all reach the same degree of moral enlightenment. The main weakness in Prichard's theory is that it doesn't adequately explain how we discriminate between the conclusions when our intuitions differ. How we decide which option is more enlightened isn't clear.

Intuitionism – W. D. Ross (1877–1971)

W. D. Ross built on the work of Prichard and Moore in his works *The Right and the Good* (1930) and *The Foundations of Ethics* (1939). He accepted Moore's argument that goodness could not be defined in natural terms and argued that moral principles can't be absolute. Many philosophers see a moral theory as a list of basic moral principles from which daily activities are deduced. Utilitarianism, natural moral law and Kantian ethics all have sets of moral principles that operate in this way. Ross developed *prima facie* duties – *prima facie* means 'at first appearance'. Ross believed that, in a moral dilemma, the various duties or obligations that we have are apparent. A *prima facie* duty is a moral obligation that binds us to follow it unless there's an overriding obligation. We follow a particular duty unless a higher duty exists that compels us to pursue that instead.

Ross set out seven foundational *prima facie* duties that he acknowledged might not be complete but were correct: promise keeping, reparation for harm done, gratitude, justice, beneficence, self-improvement and non-malefi-cence. These principles emphasise a personal character of duty rather than one set on certain absolutes. Ross rejected the idea that you simply do the thing that leads to the greatest good for the greatest number. These duties are important in moral decision-making, but ultimately choosing is a matter of judgement. The duties don't tell us what to do. The duties should not be listed in any order, as they can only be considered in the particular situation: 'it is more important that our theory fit the facts than it be simple' (Ross, 1930, p. 19). In making a moral decision, our intuition identifies our *prima facie* duties, although our actual action isn't self-evident. Our choice of action is down to judgement, which is improved through our experience or knowledge of making moral decisions.

Task

Your father asks you what you think of his new false hair piece. You think it's extremely unflattering. The duties of truthfulness and non-harm need to be considered. What would you do, using Ross's ethical intuitionism?

Ross also thought that things that were right or obligatory were just as indefinable as good. In a given moral situation, you have the facts of what's going on and the way in which it's viewed. When considering an abortion, the person doesn't have absolute certainty about the situation and what is right. They can't truly be in this position of absolute knowledge. All they really know is what they think is right to do in the situation that they think they are in.

Lastly, Ross differentiated between things that are right to do and things that are good to do. To help an old lady across the road is the right action – the right thing to do – but if I'm doing it to gain praise from my minister who is walking along the same road, then it isn't good, because my motivation or intention isn't good.

Ross' theory is a more fully developed form of intuitionism, which goes some way to addressing the difficulty that absolutist theories of ethics face when two absolutes conflict. When a dilemma forces a choice that must lead to the abandonment of one principle or another, Ross provides a way forward. Kant believed that a son should be honest to a murderer about the whereabouts of his father, because one must always be truthful. The preservation of the life of the father can't overrule the requirement to be truthful. Ross offers a way round this problem by being able to set aside the principle for truthfulness for the higher duty of preserving the life of the father. Likewise, utilitarianism would insist that you save a drowning famous scientist in preference to your father, on the basis of the greatest good for the greatest number; Ross allows for the personal nature of duty and the obligation that we have to our parents, which could overrule the need to provide any greater good.

However, there are a number of difficulties with Ross' theory, and these are identified in Michael Palmer's book, *Moral Problems* (1991, p. 110). Ross seems to take no account of rights, even in life-or-death situations. The consideration of different duties when considering extreme cases such as sex abuse or abortion may be unpalatable. Ross made the general comment that his foundational duties were correct but incomplete, but he didn't justify his choice. How do we know what is or is not a *prima facie* duty, and how can we be sure that Ross' choices are correct?

Tasks

1 What is the naturalistic fallacy?
2 Why, according to Moore, is 'good' like 'yellow' and not like a 'horse'?
3 Explain the roles of reason and intuition according to Prichard.
4 How do Moore, Prichard and Ross each explain moral disagreement?
5 According to Ross, how do we make moral decisions?
6 Explain a criticism of each of Moore's, Prichard's and Ross' views of intuitionism.
7 In your own view, are moral facts different from scientific facts? Justify your view.

Evaluating naturalism and intuitionism in general

Naturalism came under criticism because of its simplistic account of moral knowledge, which ultimately didn't stand up to criticism. Bradley's suggestion that morals were a feature of the concrete universe no longer carries much weight outside religious groups. Nor does it stand up in the light of the new science being developed in quantum physics, where traditional mechanistic approaches to the universe are being challenged by more radical accounts such as chaos theory. To anchor ethics to science leaves it vulnerable to the vagaries of scientific discovery.

There are also some general difficulties with intuitionism. Intuitionists don't agree on the moral principles that they maintain are self-evident. Moore was essentially teleological in his contention that the good is whatever maximises human happiness for most. Ross emphasised the importance of duty, rejecting the teleological approach. The moral sense that intuitionists maintain that we have isn't fully explained, and has led philosophers such as G. J. Warnock to suggest that they offer only a confession of bewilderment when trying to explain how intuition works (see Dancy, 1997, p. 415).

1 Examine the theory of naturalism and consider its strengths and weaknesses.

2 Compare the naturalistic approach to moral knowledge with the intuitionist approach.

3 Critically examine the strengths and weaknesses of intuitionism.

Extracts from key texts

F. H. Bradley, *Ethical Studies*, 1876

From the second edition, pages 173–174

What is it then that I am to realize? We have said it in 'my station and its duties'. To know what a man is (as we have seen) you must not take him in isolation. He is one of a people, he was born in a family, he lives in a certain society, in a certain state. What he has to do depends on what his place is, what his function is, and that all comes from his station in the organism. Are there then such organisms in which he lives, and if so, what is there nature? ... there are such facts as the family, then in a middle position, a man's own profession and society, and, over all, the larger community of the state.

G. E. Moore, *Principia Ethica*, 1903

From pages 6–10 and 188

... If I am asked 'What is good?' my answer is that good is good and that is the end of the matter. Or if I am asked 'How is good to be defined?' my answer is that it cannot be defined, and that is all I have to say about it ... You can give a definition of a horse because a horse has many different properties and qualities, all of which you can enumerate. But when you have enumerated them all, when you have reduced a horse to its simplest terms, then you can no longer define these terms ... 'Good', then, if we mean by it that quality which we assert to belong to a thing ... is incapable of definition ... 'good' has no definition because it is simple and has no parts. It is one of those innumerable objects of thought which are themselves incapable of definition, because they are the ultimate terms of reference by which whatever is capable of definition must be defined ... There is no intrinsic difficulty in the contention that 'good' denotes a simple and indefinable quality. There are many other instances of such qualities ... By far the most valuable things, which we know or can imagine, are certain states of consciousness which may be roughly described as the pleasures of human intercourse and the enjoyment of beautiful objects.

W. D. Ross, *The Right and the Good*, 1930

From pages 21–22

There is nothing arbitrary about these *prima facie* duties. Each rests on a definite circumstance which cannot seriously be held to be without moral significance. Of *prima facie* duties I suggest, without claiming completeness or finality for it, the following division.

(1) Some duties rest on previous acts of my own. These duties seem to include two kinds, (a) those resting on a promise or what may fairly be called an implicit promise, such as the implicit undertaking not to tell lies which seems to be implied in the act of entering into conversation (at any rate by civilized men), or of writing books that purport to be history and not fiction. These may be called the duties of fidelity. (b) Those resting on a previous wrongful act. These may be called the duties of reparation. (2) Some rest on previous acts of other men, i.e. services done by them to me. These may be loosely described as the duties of gratitude. (3) Some rest on the fact or possibility of a distribution of pleasure or happiness (or of the means thereto) which is not in accordance with the merit of the persons concerned; in such cases there arises a duty to upset or prevent such a distribution. These are the duties of justice. (4) Some rest on the mere fact that there are other beings in the world whose condition we can make better in respect of virtue, or of intelligence, or of pleasure. These are the duties of beneficence. (5) Some rest on the fact that we can improve our own condition in respect of virtue or of intelligence. These are the duties of self-improvement. (6) I think that we should distinguish from (4) the duties that may be summed up under the title of 'not injuring others'. No doubt to injure others is incidentally to fail to do them good; but it seems to me clear that non-maleficence is apprehended as a duty distinct from that of beneficence, and as a duty of a more stringent character. It will be noticed that this alone among the types of duty has been stated in a negative way.

An attempt might no doubt be made to state this duty, like the others, in a positive way. It might be said that it is really the duty to prevent ourselves from acting either from an inclination to harm others or from an inclination to seek our own pleasure, in doing which we should incidentally harm them. But on reflection it seems clear that the primary duty here is the duty not to harm others, this being a duty whether or not we have an inclination that if followed would lead to our harming them; and that when we have such an inclination the primary duty not to harm others gives rise to a consequential duty to resist the inclination.

CHAPTER SUMMARY

Ethical naturalism:

- Ethical terms can be defined or explained using the same 'natural' terms that we would use to define mathematics or science.
- Morals could be based on the same kind of observation of the world as used in scientific observation.
- Naturalists come to their ethical conclusions using non-ethical evidence. In the case of the hedonists, pleasure is the non-ethical element.
- F. H. Bradley believed that a moral perspective was determined from self-realisation and observing one's position in society.
- The good of society is about hard work and obedience. Know your station and its duty.

Intuitionism:

G. E. Moore –

- Moore asserted that moral judgements are based on an infallible intuitive knowledge of good things.
- Good is indefinable.
- 'Good' is a simple idea – like 'yellow'.
- The naturalistic fallacy is to define an ethical judgement as factual.
- Moore argued that you can't use non-moral premise to establish a moral conclusion.
- Moore asserted many things about good and its indefinability, but he didn't actually prove his own case.

H. A. Prichard –

- Prichard argued that moral obligation presents itself directly to our intuitions.
- Reason collects together the facts concerned and intuition determines which course to follow.
- Not all people can intuit moral truth, because some people have clearer moral intuitions than others.
- Prichard's main weakness is that he doesn't adequately explain how we discriminate between the conclusions when our intuitions differ.

W. D. Ross –

- W. D. Ross accepted Moore's argument that goodness could not be defined in natural terms and argued that moral principles can't be absolute.
- Ross developed *prima facie* duties (at first appearance) – in a moral dilemma, the various duties or obligations that we have are apparent.
- There are seven *prima facie* duties, which may not be complete but are correct: promise keeping, reparation for harm done, gratitude, justice, beneficence, self-improvement and non-maleficence.
- In making a moral decision, our intuition identifies our *prima facie* duties, although our actual action isn't self-evident.
- Ross differentiated between things that are right to do and things that are good to do depending on our motivation or intention.
- Ross offers a solution when duties conflict.
- Ross allows for the personal nature of duty and the obligation that we have to our parents, which could overrule the need to provide any greater good.
- However, Ross seems to take no account of rights, even in life-or-death situations.
- How do we know what is or is not a *prima facie* duty, and how can we be sure Ross' choices are correct?

Evaluating naturalism and intuitionism in general:

- Naturalism came under criticism because of its simplistic account of moral knowledge, which ultimately didn't stand up to criticism.
- Intuitionists don't agree on the moral principles that they maintain are self-evident.

Chapter 7

Emotivism and prescriptivism

Introduction

Key philosophers and works

David Hume (1711–1776): *Enquiry Concerning the Principles of Morals*, 1751

A. J. Ayer (1910–1989): *Language, Truth and Logic*, 1936

C. L. Stevenson (1908–1979): *Ethics and Language*, 1945; 'The emotive meaning of ethical terms', 1937; 'Persuasive definitions', 1938

R. M. Hare (1919–): *The Language of Morals*, 1952; *Freedom and Reason*, 1963

Key terms

Analytic, emotivism, ethical non-naturalism, 'hurrah/boo' theory, logical positivism, meta-ethics, prescriptivism, sentiment, synthetic, universalisability, verification, Vienna Circle

What you will learn by the end of this chapter

- The emotive theory, including the contributions of Ayer and Stevenson.
- The strengths and weaknesses of emotivism.
- The theory of prescriptivism formulated by R. M. Hare.
- The strengths and weaknesses of prescriptivism.

Key questions

1 Can morals be proved like other facts, or are they simply emotional responses?
2 Do moral statements simply express an opinion, or do they also affect behaviour?

Background

How can we 'know' something is wrong? Naturalists claim that we can examine morals in the same way as we examine other features of the universe. They believe that morals are part of the natural world and are discovered using reason. Intuitionists believe that we have a special faculty within us that considers the facts that our senses perceive and then makes a moral judgement. However, there are some philosophers who reject this idea of moral knowledge entirely.

In the 1920s, a group of philosophers known as the **Vienna Circle** developed a theory called **logical positivism**, which sought to give an account of ethical language that was scientific rather than intuitive or naturalistic.

Emotivism (ethical non-naturalism) – A. J. Ayer (1910–1989)

The logical positivists embraced a scientific method for verifying knowledge – a process of **verification** – which excluded the possibility of moral facts. This shows the influence of the Scottish philosopher David Hume (1711–1776), who also rejected naturalism. He believed that **sentiment** was the source of right and wrong. If you decide to help someone in need, you do so because you have feelings, not because you have reason. Hume believed in a common feeling for each other's welfare. We all have a capacity for compassion, but it has nothing to do with reason. You can't go from a factual statement (an 'is') to a moral one (an 'ought'). Logical positivism acknowledged that moral facts were not like scientific ones, but went on to conclude they were not facts at all.

The leading British exponent of this theory was A. J. Ayer. Ayer argued that meaningful statements had to be verified either synthetically or analytically. **Synthetic** facts are those that can be tested by sense perceptions, such as what we can see, hear, smell, touch or taste. Examples of synthetic statements are 'it's snowing' and 'there's a squirrel in that tree'. **Analytic** facts are true by definition. Examples of **analytic statements** include '1 + 1 = 2', 'all widows are women' and 'all bachelors are men'. Only facts that can be verified analytically or synthetically are meaningful. Any other fact, such as a religious belief or a moral opinion, can't be verified analytically or synthetically and so isn't meaningful. Moral beliefs are not true by definition and can't be observed by sense perceptions. They are no kind of fact or knowledge at all.

Ayer explained ethical statements and moral judgements as emotive responses such as expressions of preference, attitude or feeling. Ayer's theory is known as **emotivism** or **ethical non-naturalism** (it's opposed to naturalism). Ethical statements express our feelings about something or somebody. 'Henry is good' simply expresses my positive feelings towards Henry – perhaps in relation to his behaviour. Such statements are like grunts, screams or cheers, to arouse feelings or express pain. Hence, this is sometimes called the 'hurrah/boo' theory. To say that 'lying is wrong' is to say 'boo to lying'. In so doing, we're expressing a feeling against lying. To say that charity work is good is to say 'Hurrah to charity work', and nothing more. We're simply saying that we feel positive about it. In his book *Language, Truth and Logic* (1936), Ayer writes:

> For in saying that a certain type of action is right or wrong, I am not making any factual statement, not even a statement about my own state of mind. I am merely expressing certain moral sentiments. And the man who is ostensibly contradicting me is merely expressing his moral sentiments. So there is plainly no sense in asking which of us is in the right. For neither of us is asserting a genuine proposition.
>
> Ayer (1936), pp. 107–108

Moral arguments serve no real purpose, because they are an expression of feeling. Ayer did not even think that ethical statements asserted views. They only express feelings, a bit like the one you would get when you tread barefoot on a pin. To say that 'the ouch I express when I tread on a pin is true' is meaningless. In the same way, moral statements are meaningless. They are not an argument for someone's belief, although Ayer thought that they were calculated to arouse feelings and stimulate action: 'In fact we may define the meaning of the various ethical words in terms both of the different feelings they are ordinarily taken to express, and also the different responses which they are calculated to provoke' (Ayer, 1936, p. 106).

People may reject Ayer's theory – suggesting a whole variety of causes for their moral beliefs, which they believe justify their view. I might say that murder is wrong because Jesus taught against it in the New Testament and because it disrupts civilised society. Ayer explains this as an attempt to find other things that appeal to my emotions. Ayer's theory rejects traditional normative explanations of ethics, both deontological and teleological. His contribution to the study of ethics is to take seriously the language of ethics. At the very least, philosophers writing after Ayer have had to respond to his radical critique of traditional moral philosophy.

Tasks

1 What did Hume mean when he said 'all is sentiment' with regard to ethics?

2 'You can't go from an "is" to an "ought."' Explain what this means.

Ethical theories

3 Which group of philosophers believe that you can go from an 'is' to an 'ought'?

4 Explain the difference between synthetic and analytic statements.

5 Categorise the following statements as synthetic, analytic or meaningless, in emotivist terms:

   a You're a bad person.

   b The book is under the bed.

   c All cats are feline.

   d Hitler was a German Chancellor.

   e The boiling point of water is 100°C.

   f God exists.

   g Horses exist.

   h It's wrong to murder.

   i He was murdered.

   j All murder victims have a murderer.

6 Ayer's theory is known as the 'hurray/boo' theory. Explain what this means with reference to the statements 'Euthanasia is wrong' and 'A just war is right'.

Emotivism – C. L. Stevenson (1908–1979)

Another important emotivist who developed Ayer's ideas was C. L. Stevenson. While Ayer thought that arguments were people simply expressing their emotions towards each other, Stevenson maintained there was actually a disagreement in attitudes.

In his book *Ethics and Language* (1945), Stevenson argued that moral judgements contain two elements, an expression of an attitude based on a belief, and a persuasive element which seeks to influence others. Instead of describing the properties of people or actions, moral judgements express approval and disapproval. Stevenson thought that to say 'this is good' meant 'I approve of this, do so as well'. Moral statements were not simply expressions of emotion, but were the result of attitudes based on fundamental beliefs. If I say **capital punishment** is wrong, it's because I have an attitude opposed to capital punishment which is formed by my fundamental beliefs against capital punishment – be they religious, moral or political. Ayer thought that moral statements were emotive expressions. Stevenson maintained that a moral disagreement tells us more about the people's beliefs, rather than simply illustrating a 'hurray/boo' emotive shouting match. Stevenson appreciated the strong roots that underlie people's disagreements more fully than Ayer.

Stevenson noted that many moral disagreements were not really moral disagreements at all. Two doctors may disagree about which method to employ to treat a patient, but they aren't disagreeing about the necessity of treating the patient. In such cases, the principle was agreed upon but the best course of action was disputed. Real moral disagreements exist where people actually consider a certain action or process to be right or wrong. If you maintain that it's wrong for a wife to commit adultery and I maintain that it's right, then we disagree over the moral principle. In this situation, where two opposite positions are held, it's due to differing fundamental beliefs.

The other ingredient in a moral statement is the intention to influence the feelings of approval and disapproval of others. If I say that abortion is wrong, my moral statement is seeking, in part, to influence others to hold my attitude against abortion. I'm trying to persuade you to adopt my view, or at least to express the attitude that I express.

Stevenson's development of emotivism gave more meaning to moral disagreements, which in Ayer's view were simply noisy shouting matches. However, moral judgements didn't imply any kind of objective truth or fact. Stevenson ultimately considered moral statements as the result of **subjective** opinions, views or beliefs. Unlike the normative theories – naturalism or intuitionism – there's no universal truth or absolute right or wrong in emotivism.

Tasks

1 According to Stevenson, what are the two ingredients of a moral statement?

2 Using the terms 'expression', 'attitude' and 'belief', explain, first, what Ayer argues is meant by the following moral statements and, secondly, what Stevenson argues is meant by the following moral statements:

   a Murder is wrong.

   b Abortion is good.

   c Euthanasia is bad.

   d Genocide is despicable.

3 How does Stevenson's explanation of moral disagreements differ from Ayer's?

Ethical theories

Evaluating emotivism

James Rachels has criticized the emotive theory of ethics in his book *The Elements of Moral Philosophy* (Rachels, 1993a). He argues that Ayer and Stevenson are wrong to remove reason from moral judgements. He criticises Ayer for drawing a parallel between the 'ouch' reaction to stubbing your toe and the 'that's wrong' reaction to reading about a murder in the newspaper (see Rachels, 1993b). Rachels thinks that Ayer is wrong to make this association, and that there's much more to moral statements than simply an expression of feeling. Moral judgements appeal to reasons, just as any judgement appeals to reasons. The statement 'I like coffee' needs no reason. Moral judgements require reasons or else they are arbitrary.

Emotivism doesn't have much of a following; in part, because it seems to reduce moral discussions to, at best, expressions of opinion and, at worst, a shouting match. In the words of Peter Vardy and Paul Grosch (1994, p. 101), emotivism leaves moral debate as 'just so much hot air and nothing else'.

Ethical views of the perception and existence of moral norms

Bradley

Naturalism

Naturalists and Emotivists agree that empirical tests reveal facts about the universe but disagree about whether those tests reveal Objective Morals

Naturalists and Intuitionists agree that Objective Morals exist but disagree about whether they are perceived empirically or intuitively

Emotivism

Ayer   Stevenson

Emotivists and Intuitionists disagree about whether Objective Morals exist but agree they cannot be perceived empirically

Intuitionism

Moore   Prichard   Ross

Emotivism reduces moral reactions about atrocities such as genocide, murder or rape to subjective personal feelings. Whether I tell lies or the truth, whether I betray my friends or remain loyal, my moral sense is an emotive feeling or personal belief. Ayer and Stevenson have no place for reason in moral investigation. Nevertheless, people do express common reactions to horrific crimes such as mass murder and genocide, which suggests the possibility of a reasonable basis for moral behaviour. Ultimately, emotivism can only be right if every attempt to give morality an objective rational justification has failed – and this seems a rather sweeping dismissal of all normative ethics.

Despite these criticisms, Ayer and Stevenson made an important contribution to the discussion of morality in the twentieth century. They took seriously the importance of language in ethical studies, and they have forced philosophers to consider the meaning of ethical statements. They also raised fundamental questions about normative systems of morality, which must adequately substantiate or justify the principles on which they are based.

Prescriptivism – R. M. Hare (1919–)

Naturalists used reason to justify moral statements, intuitionists used a special moral sense, and emotivists denied the existence of moral facts as being meaningful in any way beyond personal opinion. In his books *The Language of Morals* (1952) and *Freedom and Reason* (1963), the philosopher R. M. Hare produced a meta-ethical theory that sought to make moral statements objective.

While Stevenson had given moral statements a descriptive quality in that they described a belief, and a persuasive quality in that they sought to have others agree with that view, Hare took meta-ethics a step further. In his view, moral judgements were both prescriptive and universal, and the only coherent way to behave morally was to act on judgements that you're prepared to universalise.

Prescriptivism

The British emotivist A. J. Ayer had argued that moral statements don't describe anything factual. The American emotivist C. L. Stevenson had maintained that moral statements expressed attitudes founded on individual beliefs, and that they attempted to persuade people to agree with us. Hare rejected the subjective idea of morality in emotivism. He believed that moral statements did more than describe behavior or express attitudes. Hare argued that moral statements had a prescriptive quality because they commanded behaviour, guiding our actions. Moral statements are to guide choices – our own and other peoples. When I say that abortion is wrong, I'm trying to prescribe an attitude and behavior. I want you to come round to my way of thinking and act in my way of acting.

Universalisability

Unlike the emotivists, Hare believed that reason had a role to play in moral statements. He believed that moral statements had a universal character about them. If I say a thing is red, I'm committed to the view that anything which is like it in colour will likewise be red. The judgement that a thing is red is descriptive (it describes), but it's also universal (it applies to everything similar). Moral judgements have this universal quality too. The essence of this is clear in the New Testament and the writings of Kant. The **Golden Rule** states 'Do unto others as you would have done unto yourself', and Kant writes 'Act only on the maxim through which you can and at the same time will that it should become a universal law.' When we make moral statements there are qualities about those statements which, when found elsewhere, mean in those situations that the same rule applies. Hare argued that moral statements had a universal quality, and it's in our best interests to prescribe the advice to others, as we would want to have such advice given to ourselves. It would be inconsistent to do otherwise.

Evaluating prescriptivism

Hare made a case for moral statements having universal and prescriptive qualities, while accounting for the work done on ethical language by Ayer and Stevenson. It seems beneficial for a moral system to require common rules, and people seem to intend their moral statements to have some influence on others. However, some – such as J. L. Mackie (see Chapter 2) – reject the idea that morals are universal. Your preferences may be different from mine, and so the universalistic rule 'do unto others as you would have done unto yourself' may not be helpful. There may be special situations that require a different approach to moral rules. Nevertheless, R. M. Hare's development of a meta-ethical theory which retains objective moral norms presents a radical alternative to traditional normative ethics and twentieth-century relativism.

Extracts from key texts

R. M. Hare, *The Language of Morals* (1952)

From Sections 8.1 and 8.2

> I have said that the primary function of the word 'good' is to commend. We have, therefore, to enquire what the commending is.

When we commend or condemn anything, it is always in order, at least indirectly, to guide choices, our own or other people's, now or in the future. Suppose that I say 'The South Bank Exhibition is very good'. In what context should I appropriately say this, and what would be my purpose in so doing? It would be natural for me to say it to someone who was wondering whether to go to London to see the Exhibition, or, if he was in London, whether to pay it a visit. ...

It should be pointed out that even judgements about past choices do not refer merely to the past. As we shall see, all value judgements are covertly universal in character, which is the same as to say that they refer to, and express acceptance of, a standard which has an application to other similar instances. If I censure someone for having done something, I envisage the possibility of him, or someone else, or myself, having to make a similar choice again; otherwise there would be no point in censoring. Thus, if I say to a man whom I am teaching to drive 'You did that manoeuvre badly' this is a very typical piece of driving-instruction; and driving-instruction consists in teaching a man to drive not in the past but in the future; to this end we censure or command past pieces of driving, in order to impart to him the standard which is to guide him in his subsequent conduct.

When we commend an object, our judgement is not solely about the particular object, but is inescapably about objects like it. Thus, if I say that a certain motor-car is a good one, I am not merely saying something about that particular motor-car ... It extends to every motor-car that is like that one in the relevant particulars; and the relevant particulars are its virtues – those of its characteristics for which I was commending it, or which I was calling good about it.

A. J. Ayer, *Language, Truth and Logic* (1936)

From page 107

We begin by admitting that the fundamental ethical concepts are unanalysable, inasmuch as there is no criterion by which one can test the validity of the judgements in which they occur. So far we are in agreement with the absolutists. But, unlike the absolutists, we are able to give an explanation of this fact about ethical concepts. We say that the reason why they are unanalysable is that they are mere pseudo-concepts. The presence of an ethical symbol in a proposition adds nothing to its factual content. Thus if I say to someone, 'You acted wrongly in stealing that money,' I am not stating anything more than if I had simply said, 'You stole that money.' In adding that this action is wrong I am not making any further statement about it. I am simply evincing my moral disapproval of it. It is as if I had said, 'You stole the money,' in a peculiar tone of horror, or written it with the addition of exclamation marks. The tone, or the exclamation marks, adds nothing to the literal meaning of the sentence. It merely serves to show that the expression of it is attended by certain feelings in the speaker ... It is clear that there is nothing said here which can be true of false. Another man may disagree with me about the wrongness of stealing ... in saying that a certain type of action is right or wrong, I am not making any factual statement, not even a statement about my own mind. I am merely expressing certain moral sentiments. And the man who is ostensibly contradicting me is merely expressing his moral .

CHAPTER SUMMARY

Emotivism:

- The logical positivists embraced a scientific method for verifying knowledge, which excluded the possibility of moral facts.
- They were influenced by David Hume, who believed that sentiment was the source of right and wrong.
- Logical positivism acknowledged that moral facts were not like scientific ones, but went on to conclude that moral facts were not facts at all.
- A. J. Ayer argued that meaningful statements had to be verified either synthetically or analytically.
- Religious beliefs or moral opinions can't be verified analytically or synthetically and so aren't meaningful.
- Ethical statements and moral judgements are emotive responses, to arouse feelings or express pain – this is sometimes called the 'hurrah/boo' theory.
- Moral arguments serve no purpose, because they only express feelings.
- Ayer's theory rejects traditional normative explanations of ethics, both deontological and teleological.

C. L. Stevenson:

- Stevenson believed that moral disputes reflected a disagreement in attitudes.
- Moral judgements express an attitude based on a belief, and include a persuasive element that seeks to influence others.
- Real moral disagreements exist, where people actually consider a certain action or process to be right or wrong.
- Stevenson's emotivism gave more meaning to moral disagreements, which in Ayer's view were simply noisy shouting matches.
- Stevenson ultimately considered moral statements as being the result of subjective opinions, views or beliefs.

Evaluating emotivism:

- Ayer might be wrong to compare emotive responses to moral statements, as moral judgements appeal to reasons.
- Emotivism reduces moral discussions to a shouting match.
- Emotivism reduces moral reactions about atrocities such as genocide, murder or rape to subjective personal feelings.
- People express common reactions to horrific crimes such as mass murder and genocide, which suggests the possibility of a reasonable basis for moral behaviour.
- Emotivism can only be right if every attempt to give morality an objective rational justification has failed.
- Ayer and Stevenson took seriously the importance of language in ethical studies, and have forced philosophers to consider the meaning of ethical statements.

Prescriptivism – R. M. Hare:

- Hare produced a meta-ethical theory that sought to make moral statements objective.
- Moral judgements are both prescriptive and universal, and the only coherent way to behave morally is to act on judgements that you're prepared to universalise.

Chapter 8

Determinism and free will

Introduction

Key philosophers and works

St Thomas Aquinas (1224–1274): *Summa Theologica*, 1273

St Augustine of Hippo (AD 354–430): *Divine Election*

John Calvin (1506–1564): *Institutes*, 1559

David Hume (1711–1776): 'Liberty', in his *An Enquiry Concerning Human Understanding*, 1748

John Locke (1632–1704): *Essay Concerning Human Understanding*, 1690

Benedict Spinoza (1632–1677): *Ethica Ordine Geometrico Demonstrata* (*Ethics Demonstrated with Geometrical Order*), 1674

Key terms

Autonomous moral agents, blameworthy, compatiblists, determinism, freedom, moral responsibility, genetics, hard determinism, incompatibilitists, libertarians, moral culpability, 'ought' implies 'can', predestination, soft determinism

Key questions

1 What influences how we behave?
2 Are we always free to act?
3 What factors limit our ability to act freely?
4 Can we be morally **blameworthy** for our actions if we aren't free?
5 Should the drunk driver be just as responsible for his actions as the sober driver?

What you will learn by the end of this chapter

■ The link between freedom and moral responsibility.

- The religious doctrine of predestination.
- The ethical theories of hard determinism, libertarianism and soft determinism.
- The strengths and weaknesses of these theories.

Freedom and moral responsibility

What if it's shown that all human actions have a cause beyond their control?

What if the ability to make free moral choices is an illusion?

Would we be morally responsible for our actions if they were influenced by fixed external forces?

There's an important relationship between **freedom** and **moral responsibility**. It's commonly held that we should be morally responsible for actions that we freely perform. I should be ready to accept the **blame** for the things that I freely do wrong. If I'm *forced* to commit an immoral action, then I'm not blameworthy. If I'm forced at gunpoint to drive a getaway car from a bank robbery, then it isn't my fault. Likewise, if I'm forced to commit a moral action, I'm not praiseworthy. If I'm forced at gunpoint to give money to charity, I'm not praiseworthy. We can only attribute moral **blame** or **praise** to actions that are freely undertaken.

If, in **ignorance**, I perform an action that has an unpredictable immoral effect, then I'm not blameworthy. If a general in a war sends his troops into a valley that he believes to be safe, he isn't morally blameworthy if there's a secret ambush that kills all his troops assuming he could not have known what was going to happen. If, on the other hand, he had sent the troops to their deaths knowingly, or without taking appropriate checks, then he would be morally blameworthy. A company producing cosmetics that uses an untested chemical that causes harmful side-effects is morally responsible, because it should have tested that chemical for side-effects. In instances such as these, ignorance is no excuse and negligence is immoral.

If someone isn't in control of his or her actions because of drugs, alcohol or some other disorientating influence – such as an emotional trauma or a psychological condition – then that person isn't entirely morally responsible for his or her actions. The drunk who kills a pedestrian may be morally blameworthy, but he hasn't committed as great a crime as a sober person who deliberately runs down an innocent, because the person's intention is important. If a person chooses to enter into a state of uncontrolled behaviour, such as choosing to get drunk before driving home, then that person may have greater blame than a person who unwillingly enters a disorientated state. If I kill a pedestrian because I'm disorientated after someone has spiked my orange juice, I'm not as responsible for my actions as the person who chooses to drink and then drive. Intention has some bearing on moral culpability. Did they mean to kill or was it an accident? We punish criminals who intend to commit their crimes more heavily than those who commit unplanned crimes.

If we can only blame or praise people for actions they freely and knowingly undertake, then it's vital that human beings have freedom to act. Morality depends on freedom. Immanuel Kant wrote ' "Ought" implies "can" '. Moral actions are freely undertaken actions. We can't blame Smith for not doing what he couldn't do. If people aren't free, the possibility of making moral choices is denied. If human actions are caused by external influences, then people can't be morally responsible for those actions. This is the challenge brought about by the Christian idea of predestination and the determinist ethical viewpoint.

Task

Consider these five situations:

a A policeman, who is a poor shot, shoots dead an innocent civilian by mistake.

b A policeman intentionally shoots dead an innocent civilian.

c A policeman, hallucinating after taking drugs, shoots dead an innocent civilian.

d A policeman, believing it his duty to obey the orders of the state, is commanded to shoot dead an innocent civilian and does so.

e A policeman, threatened with execution if he doesn't obey orders, is commanded to shoot dead an innocent civilian and does so.

1 With regard to the policeman, arrange the examples in order, from the least blameworthy to the most blameworthy.

2 Is the policeman morally responsible for the death of the innocent civilian in each case?

3 Should there be any difference in the way the policeman is dealt with (that is, punished)? Explain your answer.

Historically, there has been a great deal of concern over human freedom and moral responsibility. Before considering the background to the current discussion, we shall explore the Christian view of predestination.

Predestination

The traditional Judeo-Christian view is that human beings are free, **autonomous** agents, responsible for their actions. In Genesis, Adam and Eve

---

exercise **free will** in choosing to eat the forbidden fruit. They are held responsible for their actions by God, who punishes them. St Thomas Aquinas, the Christian theologian and philosopher, wrote ' … man chooses not of necessity but freely' (*Summa Theologica*, 1 PT 1, qu 13 a 6). The main Christian denominations hold to the view that we are free to choose to do good or sin. However, there is an alternative view in Christian writings, which was and is held by some Protestant Churches. This is the view that God has already decided who will be saved and who will not. This idea, which originates in St Paul's letter to the Romans, is called '**predestination**':

> And we know that in all things God works for the good of those who love him, who have been called according to his purpose. For those God foreknew he also predestined to be conformed to the likeness of his Son, that he might be the firstborn among many brothers. And those he predestined, he also called; those he called, he also justified; those he justified, he also glorified.
>
> Romans 8: 28–30 (New International Version)

Augustine's writing on the Divine Election suggests predestination: 'The potter has authority over the clay from the same lump to make one vessel for honour and another for contempt.' (*Sermon* 26 xii,13)

The Protestant reformer John Calvin described predestination as 'the eternal decree of God, by which he determined that he wished to make of every man. For he does not create everyone in the same condition, but ordains eternal life for some and eternal damnation for others' (John Calvin, *Institutes*, 1559; quoted in McGrath, 1994, pp. 396–397).

The idea that God decides who receives salvation and who doesn't at creation suggests that humans don't have free will with regard to their moral or religious behaviour. This idea has significance in the debate about whether human beings save themselves by their actions or whether they are saved by God's grace alone. As regards the ethical ramifications of such a view, the notion that human beings aren't **autonomous moral agents** raises a number of problems. If you aren't free, how can you be morally responsible for your actions? How can you then be punished for those actions?

Three ethical views on freedom

In ethics, there are three philosophical approaches to freedom. There are those who maintain that humans can't be morally blameworthy for their actions because all of their actions are determined – hard determinists. There are those who maintain that we are free to act and morally responsible – libertarians. There are those who maintain that some human actions are determined, but that we still have moral responsibility – soft determinists.

Ethical theories

Hard determinism

We are not free and cannot be held morally responsible for our actions

> And the first Morning of Creation wrote / What the Last Dawn of Reckoning shall read.
>
> Omar Khayyam, Persian poet, Copyright 1994–1999 Encyclopædia Britannica, 'Determinism'

> Pear trees cannot bear bananas. The instincts of a spaniel cannot be the instincts of an ostrich. Everything is planned, connected, limited.
>
> Voltaire, *Dictionaire Philosophique* (1764), article on destiny

Hard determinism has some ethical similarity to predestination. Ted Honderich summarises it as the view that '... all our choices, decisions, intentions, other mental events, and our actions are no more than effects of other equally necessitated events' (Honderich, 1995, p. 194).

The view is also expressed in this limerick:

> There once was a man who said damn!
> It is borne in upon me I am
> An engine that moves
> In predestinate grooves;
> I'm not even a bus, I'm a tram.
>
> Young (1997b)

Hard determinism maintains that all actions have a prior cause. Humans aren't free to act. Our actions are determined by a complex set of prior

Everything we do is determined

causes. It's as if we are trams, running along fixed rails. Determinism sometimes draws on the Newtonian view that all physical objects, living or otherwise, must exist in accordance with natural laws.

Genetics may have a powerful influence on how we respond. Our socio-eco-
nomic backgrounds, religio-cultural backgrounds and experience of life may
affect us in such a way that our behaviour is determined rather than free.
While few scientists would argue that genes cause people to do things, the
combinations of all these elements might. This lends weight to the hard
determinists' cause. If our actions are truly determined, then in what sense
can we be morally responsible for them? Is it fair to punish people for committing actions beyond their control?

Clarence Darrow was an American attorney who defended two boys who
murdered a 14-year-old called Bobby Franks. The two murderers were rich
and very intelligent, and had planned a perfect crime to illustrate their superiority over society. They were brought to trial facing the death penalty, but
Darrow argued successfully for their sentence to be commuted to life imprisonment, because the boys were products of their upbringing. Darrow thought
that criminals should still be sent to prison to protect society, but argued in
court that it should not be assumed that they are responsible for their
actions.

The law considers people who have limited control over their actions because
of extreme psychological or emotional difficulties as having 'diminished
responsibility'. The emotionally distraught and beaten wife who kills her husband isn't acting in total moral freedom. Her emotional state has distorted
her judgement and she's treated differently in court from the cold, calculating killer. But what if we all suffer from diminished responsibility, because all
of our actions are determined by prior causes?

Evaluating hard determinism

Hard determinism has a number of profound consequences. It puts into
doubt our hopes for the future and how we consider the morality of others.
Determinism means that we're mistaken to praise some people for being
good or to blame others for being bad. In addition, if our actions are determined, then we can't deliberate rationally. The idea that we make choices
ourselves and that we decide what to do is illusory. The whole notion of
moral responsibility is called into question. Murderers murder because they
have the wrong genes, poor upbringing, poor parents or poor teachers. This
impacts on notions of punishment. It seems wrong to punish people for
acting immorally if they aren't responsible for their actions.

Libertarians argue that determinists confuse things that are necessarily true
with those that are contingently true (true depending on the circumstances).
While it's necessarily true that all widows are women, it's only contingently

true that a particular man is a footballer. Libertarians argue that a mechanical view of the world is incorrect. Writers on quantum mechanics have challenged the mechanistic approach: 'A fundamental concept in quantum mechanics is that of randomness, or indeterminancy. In general, the theory predicts only the probability of a certain result.' (Copyright 1994–1999 Encyclopædia Britannica, 'The interpretation of quantum mechanics')

Libertarianism

We are free and morally responsible for our actions

Some people reject determinism because it rules out moral responsibility, and also because there is a sense that we have self-determination or freedom to act. They are called incompatibilitists (because they maintain that free will is incompatible with determinism) or libertarians.

David Hume (1711–1776) described liberty in his *An Enquiry Concerning Human Understanding* (1748): 'By liberty, then, we can only mean a power of acting or not acting, according to the determinations of the will; that is, if we choose to remain at rest, we may; if we choose to move, we also may.' (Section 8, Part 1, para. 73) Libertarians believe that we're free to act, and morally responsible for those actions. They believe that we're not compelled to act by forces outside our moral consciousness. Moral actions are not chance or random events, but result from the values and character of the moral agent.

We have an idea that when we act, we're choosing our actions. We perceive ourselves as free agents, capable of making moral choices and responsible for those choices. Humans have a sense of decision-making. Sometimes we're torn between two options, both of which we feel equally uncertain about and deliberate before making a decision. C. A. Campbell (1976) writes:

> Here, and here alone, so far as I can see, in the act of deciding whether to put forth or withhold the moral effort required to resist temptation and rise to duty, is to be found an act which is free in the sense required for moral responsibility; an act of which the self is sole author, and of which it is true to say that 'it could be' (or, after the event, 'could have been') otherwise ...

The pool ball is hit by the cue and moves across the table. While humans are constrained by the laws of physics, they aren't like the ball in moral behaviour. If I stub my toe against a rock, I'll feel pain. In my moral behaviour I am autonomous. If I'm brought up among criminals I may be predisposed to think that stealing is acceptable, but moral perception can present the idea that it's wrong. Some people give in to temptation, while others hold out.

Evaluating libertarianism

An important argument for **libertarianism** is the human sense of decision-making. While we have a sense of freedom, a sense of deliberating over our options, determinists maintain this is an illusion of freedom. Benedict Spinoza (1632–1677) wrote 'men think themselves free on account of this alone, that they are conscious of their actions and ignorant of the causes of them' (*Ethics*, 1674, III ii note). John Locke (1632–1704) illustrates the view with the idea of a sleeping man who is moved into a locked room. He wakes and chooses not to try to leave the room. He believes that he could leave the room by walking through the door, while in fact the door is locked and he could never do it. We may believe that we have free will and we may feel that we can choose any number of options, when in truth our moral choices are determined by factors beyond our control. Perhaps we spend a long time deliberating over the possible choices; perhaps we feel unsure what to do. In the end, we make a decision, believing that we've freely done so. Determinists hold that in actual fact it was inevitable that we would come to this decision, because of the background causes.

Libertarianism doesn't explain human action, yet surely our actions are caused by something? Libertarianism attributes our moral judgement to an objective source, unaffected by environment or upbringing, but this is questionable. Just as it's difficult to show how one thing causes another, it's difficult to show that there are no causes beyond our control. Libertarianism doesn't seem to account for human motive, which is caused by *something*.

Soft determinism

Some aspects of human beings are determined, but we are morally responsible for our actions

Soft determinists argue that determinism doesn't rule out free will. They believe that determinism and free will are **compatible**. For them, freedom to act is acting voluntarily and not out of coercion.

This midway position suggests that some of our actions are conditioned, while others have so complex a collection of causes that they may properly be described as freely decided or willed. We may be constrained by external circumstances to certain forms of behaviour. If I have no food, I can't eat. If I have food but wish to lose weight, I eat less. If I have food but it's a religious fast day, I choose not to eat although I might want to. If I have to keep to a diet set by my doctor, I may only eat some of the food for the good of my health. In each case, the relationship is different. I may feel compelled to observe the religious fast or to follow a special diet for health reasons, but this is different from poverty, where there's simply no food to eat.

Soft determinists are criticised by hard determinists for failing to realise the extent to which human freedom is limited, and by libertarians for failing to realise the true extent of human freedom. **Soft determinism** offers an agreeable account of moral freedom. However, a line still has to be drawn between that which is determined and that which is open to choice. Soft determinists have to agree on precisely what is and what isn't a determining factor. The complexities of physics, genetics and psychology make such a line difficult for them to draw.

Task

1 Look at the following examples and decide whether or not the people concerned are morally blameworthy, and why?

   a The soldier, for saving his life by collaborating with the enemy.
   b The spy, for giving away secrets under torture.
   c The lover, who kills at the behest of his partner.
   d The kleptomaniac, for stealing.
   e The starving boy, for stealing food.
   f The motorist, for speeding in ignorance of the limit.
   g The wife, for murdering her adulterous husband.
   h The mother, for hiding her criminal son from the police.
   i The drunken motorist, for killing a pedestrian.
   j The linguist, for failing the maths exam.
   k The drug addict, for stealing from the chemist.

2 Can we blame German civilians indoctrinated by Nazi propaganda about the Jews, and living in fear of Hitler's tyranny, for exposing Jews in hiding rather than protecting them?

3 In Shakespeare's *Romeo and Juliet*, did Juliet act freely when she took her own life on seeing that her lover was dead?

Questions

1 What is meant by the phrase ' "ought" implies "can" '?
2 What is the relationship between freedom and moral responsibility?
3 Can you outline two Christian views of human freedom?
4 Can you explain the differences between hard determinism, soft determinism and libertarianism? Critically evaluate each view.

Extracts from key texts

Aristotle (384–322 BCE), *Nicomachean Ethics* 1110a

Actions are commonly regarded as involuntary when they are performed (a) under compulsion, (b) as the result of ignorance. An act, it is thought, is done under compulsion when it originates in some external cause of such a nature that the agent or person subject to the compulsion contributes nothing to it. Such a situation is created, for example, when a sea captain is carried out of his course by a contrary wind or by men who have got him in their power. But the case is not always so clear ... An involuntary act being one performed under compulsion or as the result of ignorance, a voluntary act would seem to be one of which the origin or efficient cause lies in the agent, he knowing the particular circumstances in which he is acting.

Benedict Spinoza, *Ethics*, 1674, III ii note

An infant thinks it freely seeks milk, an angry child thinks that it freely desired vengeance, or a timid child thinks it freely chooses flight. Again, a drunken man thinks that he speaks by the free decision of the mind those things which, if he were sober, he would keep to himself. ... So experience teaches as clearly as reason that men think themselves free on account of this alone, that they are conscious of their actions and ignorant of the causes of them.

Pierre Laplace (1749–1827), eighteenth-century French physicist and mathematician

From *Philosophy in Practice* (Morton, 1996), an introduction to the main questions, page 396

An intelligence knowing all the forces acting in the nature at a given instant ... would be able to comprehend in one single formula the motions of the largest bodies as well as the lightest atoms in the world, provided that its intellect were sufficiently powerful to subject all data to analysis; to it nothing would be uncertain, the future as well as the past would be present to its eyes.

A. J. Ayer, *Philosophical Essays*, 1959

From page 275

Either it is an accident that I choose to act as I do or it is not. If it is an accident, then it is merely a matter of chance that I did not choose otherwise; and if it is merely a matter of chance that I did not choose otherwise, it is surely irrational to hold me morally responsible for choosing as I did. But if it is not an accident that I choose to do one thing rather than another, then presumably there is some causal explanation of my choice: and in that case we are led back to determinism.

Frances S. Collins, M.D., Ph.D., Director, National Center for Human Genome Research

From foreword, in Peters (1997)

As genetic predispositions to everything from cancer or diabetes to novelty-seeking behavior or homosexuality are being reported almost daily in the scientific literature (and regrettably often over-stated in the popular press), a new and dangerous brand of genetic determinism is subtly invading our culture. Carried to its extreme, this 'Genes R Us' mentality would deny the value of social interventions to maximize individual potential, destabilize many of our institutions (perhaps especially the criminal justice system), and even deny the existence of free will. Surely a world in which every aspect of human behavior is hard-wired into our genes cannot comfortably exist with the concept of personal responsibility and free will to try (albeit not successfully for very long) to follow the moral law of right and wrong which people of faith believe has been written into our hearts by a loving and holy God.

CHAPTER SUMMARY

- Predestination – a Protestant view that God has already decided who will be saved and who will not.
- Hard determinism – we are not free and cannot be held morally responsible for our actions:
  - '... all our choices, decisions, intentions, other mental events, and our actions are no more than effects of other equally necessitated events' (Honderich)
  - all actions have a prior cause
  - determinism means that we're mistaken to praise some people for being good or for blaming others for being bad, as the idea of moral responsibility is called into question

- Libertarianism – we are free and morally responsible for our actions:
    - human beings believe that they have self-determination or freedom to act
    - 'By liberty, then, we can only mean a power of acting or not acting, according to the determinations of the will; that is, if we choose to remain at rest, we may; if we choose to move, we also may.' (David Hume)
    - moral actions are not chance or random events, but result from the values and character of the moral agent
    - humans have a sense of decision-making or deliberation
    - some people give in to temptation, while others hold out
    - libertarianism doesn't provide any explanation for human action
    - libertarianism doesn't account for a human motive, which has a cause
- Soft determinism – some aspects of human beings are determined, but we are morally responsible for our actions:
    - determinism doesn't rule out free will; the two are compatible
    - some of our actions are conditioned, while others have so complex a collection of causes that they may properly be described as freely decided or willed
    - soft determinists are criticised by hard determinists for failing to realise the extent to which human freedom is limited, and by libertarians for failing to realise the degree of human freedom that exists
    - soft determinism offers an agreeable account of moral freedom
    - soft determinists haven't agreed on precisely what is and what isn't a determining factor in human action

Chapter 9

Situation ethics

Contents of Chapter 9

Introduction
A radical Christian ethical approach
The theory of situation ethics
Evaluating situation ethics
A note on proportionalism
Extracts from key texts

The morality of an action depends on the situation.

Joseph Fletcher (1963)

Introduction

Key philosophers and works

Joseph Fletcher (1905–1991): *Situation Ethics, the New Morality*, 1963

Key terms

Agape love, Antinomian ethics, conscience, four working principles, individualistic, intrinsically good, justice, law of love, legalistic ethics, personalism, positivism, pragmatism, prescriptive, proportionalism, relativism, situation ethics, subjective

What you will learn by the end of this chapter

- ■ The theory of situation ethics.
- ■ The weaknesses and strengths of situation ethics.
- ■ The theory of proportionalism.

Key questions

1 Is moral behaviour about following rules or working things out for ourselves?

2 Are there unbreakable laws to govern moral behavior, or should we make our own moral decisions?

---

3 Is abortion for health reasons just as bad as abortion for convenience?

4 Are there ever situations when you should ignore established moral rules?

5 When deciding what is right, should the situation be taken into account?

A radical Christian ethical approach

> There is only one ultimate and invariable duty, and its formula is 'Thou shalt love thy neighbour as thyself.' How to do this is another question, but this is the whole of moral duty.
>
> William Temple (1923), p. 206

> The law of love is the ultimate law because it is the negation of law; it is absolute because it concerns everything concrete. ... The absolutism of love is its power to go into the concrete situation, to discover what is demanded by the predicament of the concrete to which it turns. Therefore, love can never become fanatical in a fight for the absolute, or cynical under the impact of the relative.
>
> Tillich (1951), Vol. 1, p. 152

Joseph Fletcher starts his book by noting the words of Bishop Robinson, 'there is no one ethical system that can claim to be Christian' and of Rudolf Bultmann, who argued that Jesus had no ethics apart from 'love thy neighbour as thyself', which is the ultimate **duty**. Ethics had traditionally been seen by Catholics as something defined by natural moral law. Protestants tended to deduce morality from the moral laws in the Bible. In *Situation Ethics*, Joseph Fletcher offers ethical principles that he maintains can accommodate Christian beliefs. His work is a radical departure from traditional Christian ethics and has been condemned and castigated by traditional Christian moralists. In his foreword, Joseph Fletcher writes:

> Let an anecdote set the tone. A friend of mine arrived in St. Louis just as a presidential campaign was ending, and the cab driver, not being above the battle, volunteered his testimony. 'I and my father and grandfather before me, and their fathers, have always been straight-ticket Republicans.' 'Ah,' said my friend, who is himself a Republican, 'I take it that means you will vote for Senator So-and-So.' 'No,' said the driver, 'there are times when a man has to push his principles aside and do the right thing.'
>
> Fletcher (1963, p. 13)

For Fletcher, that St Louis cabbie is the hero of **situation ethics**. To understand the theory, we need to look at the detail.

Ethical theories

A rich man asked a lovely young woman if she would sleep the night with him. She said 'No.' He then asked if she would do it for $100 000. She said 'Yes!'

1 Is it wrong to have sex for money:

a To survive?

b For luxury purchases?

c To fund a life-saving operation for a friend or relative?

In each case, explain your answer.

2 Why might your answers for **a**, **b** and **c** differ?

The theory of situation ethics

Three kinds of ethical theories

Fletcher maintains that there are essentially three different ways of making moral decisions. **Legalistic ethics** has a set of prefabricated moral rules and regulations. Judaism and Christianity both have legalistic ethical traditions. Pharisaic Judaism has a law-based approach to life, founded on the Halakah oral tradition. Christianity has been focused either on natural law or biblical commandments. According to Fletcher, this runs into problems when life's complexities require additional laws. For example, once murder has been prohibited, one has to clarify killing in self-defence, killing in war, killing unborn human beings and so on. The legalist must either include all of the complex alternatives in the law or create new laws to cover the result. This can produce a puritanical, choking web of laws, a kind of textbook morality that leaves people simply to check the manual to decide what is right and wrong. This error has been made by Catholics through their adherence to natural law, and by Protestants through puritanical observance of the sayings of the Bible. Fletcher rejects legalistic ethics.

Antinomian ethics is quite the reverse of legalistic ethics. The term 'antinomian' literally means 'against law'. A person using **antinomianism** doesn't really use an ethical system at all. He or she enters decision-making as if each occasion was totally unique. Making a moral decision is a matter of spontaneity: 'it is literally unprincipled, purely *ad hoc* and casual. They follow no forecastable course from one situation to another. They are, exactly, anarchic – i.e. without a rule.' (Fletcher, 1963, p. 23) Fletcher is equally critical of antinomianism as an acceptable approach to ethics, because it's unprincipled.

The third approach to ethics is the situational approach. The situationist enters into the moral dilemma with the ethics, rules and principles of his or her community or tradition. However, the situationist is prepared to set aside those rules in the situation if love seems better served by doing so. **Situation ethics** agrees that reason is the instrument of moral judgements, but disagrees that the good is to be discerned from the nature of things. In Fletcher's words, 'The situationist follows a moral law or violates it according to love's need' (p. 26). For the situationist, all moral decisions are hypothetical. They depend on the what best serves love. The situationist doesn't say that 'giving to charity is a good thing'; they only ever say 'giving to charity is a good thing if …'. Lying is justified if love is better served by it.

An insane murderer who asks you the whereabouts of his next victim should be lied to. In that situation, a legalist must tell the truth. A situationist must best serve love but he or she doesn't deduce rules from that principle. In the words of William Temple (1881–1944), 'What acts are right may depend on the circumstances … but there is an absolute obligation to will whatever may on each occasion be right' (Temple, 1923, p. 27). Situation ethics identifies its roots in the New Testament. St Paul writes 'Christ Jesus … abolished the law with its commandments and legal claims' (Ephesians 2:13–15).

Situation ethics is sensitive to variety and complexity. It uses principles to illuminate the situation, but not to direct the action. Fletcher divides his principles into two categories: The four working principles and the six fundamental principles.

Task

A teenage girl has become pregnant as a result of being raped by a close family member. She's very poor and very young. How would legalists, antinomians and situationists go about considering what the moral thing to do is?

Four working principles

There are some presuppositions that Fletcher makes before setting out situation ethics theory:

1 **Pragmatism** – a practical or success posture. The proposed course of action must work, and must work towards the end, which is love.

2 **Relativism** – situation ethics is relativistic: 'The Situationist avoids words like "never" and "perfect" and "always" and "complete" as he avoids the plague, as he avoids "absolutely".' (Fletcher, 1963, p. 44) There are no fixed rules that must always be obeyed. However, nor is it a free for all! Fletcher maintains that all decisions must be relative to Christian love.

Situation ethics 'relativizes the absolute, it does not absolutize the relative' (Fletcher, 1963, p. 45).

3 **Positivism** – religious knowledge or belief can only be approached by one of two ways. With natural positivism reason deduces faith from human experience or natural phenomena. Nature provides the evidence and reason grasps hold of it. With theological positivism faith statements are made and people act in a way that is reasonable in the light of these statements. Reason isn't the basis for faith, but it works within faith. Situation ethics depends on Christians freely choosing faith that God is love, so giving first place to Christian love.

4 **Personalism** – the legalist puts the law first. The situationist puts people first. He asks what to do to help humans best: 'There are no "values" in the sense of inherent goods – value is what happens to something when it happens to be useful to love working for the sake of persons.' (Fletcher, 1963, p. 50)

Conscience isn't a bag of reliable rules and principles to tell you what to do. It in no way guides human action. For the situationist, conscience describes the weighing up of the possible action before it's taken.

With these presuppositions acknowledged, Fletcher goes on to lay out the main theory.

Six fundamental principles

First proposition

> Only one thing is intrinsically good; namely love: nothing else at all.
>
> Fletcher (1963, p. 56)

Only love is good in and of itself. Actions aren't intrinsically good or evil. They are good or evil depending upon whether they promote the most loving result. They are extrinsically good, depending on their circumstances and consequences.

Second proposition

> The ruling norm of Christian decision is love: nothing else.
>
> Fletcher (1963, p. 69)

Jesus replaced the Torah with the principle of love. Take, for example, his decision to heal (work) on the Sabbath day, rejecting the obligations of Sabbath observance. The Commandments are not absolute. Jesus broke them when love demanded it. Love replaces law. It isn't equaled by any other law.

Third proposition

> Love and Justice are the same, for justice is love distributed, nothing else.
>
> Fletcher (1963, p. 87)

Love and **justice** can't be separated from each other. Fletcher writes, 'Justice is Christian love using its head, calculating its duties, obligations, opportunities, resources ... Justice is love coping with situations where distribution is called for.' (p. 95) Justice is love at work in whole community, for the whole community.

Fourth proposition

> [L]ove wills the neighbour's good, whether we like him or not.
>
> Fletcher (1963, p. 103)

The love that Fletcher is concerned about isn't a matter of feeling, but of attitude. It isn't sentimental or erotic but, rather, a desire for the good of the other person. This is the New Testament **agape love**. Your neighbour is anybody and agape love goes out to everyone; not just those we like but those we don't like as well. Agape love is unconditional; nothing is required in return.

Fifth proposition

> Only the end justifies the means, nothing else.
>
> Fletcher (1963, p. 120)

To consider moral actions without reference to their ends is a haphazard approach. Actions acquire moral status as a means to an end. For Fletcher, the end must be the most loving result. When weighing up a situation, one must consider the desired end, the means available, the motive for acting and the foreseeable consequences.

Sixth proposition

> [L]ove's decisions are made situationally, not prescriptively.
>
> Fletcher (1963, p. 134)

Jesus reacted against the kind of rule-based morality that he saw around him. There were Jewish groups that lived on rule-based moral systems, but Jesus distanced himself from them. Whether something is right or wrong depends on the situation. If an action will bring about an end that serves love most, then it's right. Fletcher believes that if people don't feel that it's wrong to have sexual relations outside marriage, then it isn't, unless they hurt themselves, their partners or others.

It's clear from these six propositions that Fletcher's moral theory radically differs from traditional Christian ethics. It embraces a form of relativism as actions are not intrinsically right or wrong. Actions are right or wrong depending on their result. For Fletcher, the good result is that which serves agape love best. Any action that leads to that end is right: 'Whether any

Ethical theories

form of sex is good or evil depends on whether love is fully served.' (Fletcher, 1963, p. 139)

Evaluating situation ethics

A clear benefit of situation ethics is that it provides an alternative Christian ethic that is consistent with the Gospel representation of Jesus. Orthodox Christianity today often seems to take on the character of the kind of Pharisaic Judaism that Jesus opposed. The approach of situation ethics develops a principle from Jesus' action of breaking the law when the situation demanded it for reasons of love. In this sense, it could be argued that situation ethics is more consistent with the New Testament than natural moral law ethics, providing a corrective to that and other **legalistic** approaches.

Situation ethics is flexible and practical. It takes into account the complexities of human life, and can make tough decisions where, from a legalistic perspective, all actions seem wrong. This gives it a dynamism that can free up deadlocked moral dilemmas. It's able to take the least bad of two bad options, which legalistic approaches cannot. A legalist may always feel bound to tell the truth, but when faced with a murderer seeking his victim the legalist is in an impossible position. The situationist can lay aside the rule of not lying for the better outcome of saving a person's life.

Traditional Christian thinkers rejected situation ethics. In 1952, Pope Pius XII called situation ethics 'an individualistic and subjective appeal to the concrete circumstances of actions to justify decisions in opposition to the natural law or God's revealed will'. The Roman Catholic Church hasn't abandoned St Thomas Aquinas' natural law approach, and views situation ethics as a subjective and individualistic moral approach. Here are three criticisms of situation ethics:

1 Situation ethics is subjective, because decisions must be made from within the situation as it's perceived to be. It isn't easy to be certain that one's perception of the situation is correct. How can individuals safely decide which is the most loving action? We don't have an objective perspective, a bird's eye view of morality and could end up justifying unloving actions on the basis of loving results that never emerge. Situation ethics could prove unworkable because it isn't easy to determine all the consequences of an action.

2 Situation ethics is individualistic, because humans see things from their own perspective. There's a danger that the ideals of unconditional love may be polluted by a selfish human tendency. Agape love is an ideal. How many parents can show equal love to strangers as to their children? Attaining and living out agape love is fundamental to situation ethics.

How do we judge when love is unconditional and when it isn't? How can we be sure when an action comes from agape love, and who is to decide whether the motive is pure?

3 Situation ethics seems to be prepared to accept any action at all if it fits the required criteria. After a century of some of the most horrendous acts of genocide and the rise of a concern for the absolute protection of human rights, there's a common sense that there are some things that are just wrong and can never be right on any grounds. What is believed to be a loving end could justify actions that many people regard as simply wrong.

Tasks

1 Explain what's meant by the term **situation ethics**.

2 Choose a moral dilemma and explain how a legalist, an antinomian and a situationist might approach the dilemma.

3 Try to think of the two most plausible examples whereby killing a human being could serve love. Then evaluate how convincing your arguments are.

4 In what sense is situation ethics relativistic?

5 What does it mean to take a personalist approach when considering a moral dilemma, and how does this differ from a legalistic approach? Use a moral dilemma to illustrate your answer.

6 Is the end the only thing that can justify the means?

7 Can humans act out of unconditional love for each other, or are they selfish?

8 Evaluate the strengths and weaknesses of situation ethics.

A note on proportionalism

Situation ethics opposes natural moral law on several grounds. Natural law states that actions are intrinsically good or bad according to the law of nature, while situationists maintain that actions are extrinsically good or bad according to whether they produce the most loving result. Natural law is deontological and situation ethics is teleological.

There is a midway position in between the two theories, that tries to combine elements of both. Bernard Hoose's **proportionalism** modifies both theories to come up with the maxim 'It is never right to go against a principle unless there is a proportionate reason which would justify it' (Hoose, 1987). Proportionalism isn't an entirely new ethical theory. It can be found in Aquinas' understanding of a 'just war' (see Chapter 17). The **just war theory** makes it possible for a Church that opposed killing to justify a certain amount of killing in particular circumstances. In other words, the basic rule of 'Do not kill' usually applies, but there are certain proportionate circumstances when it can be right to overrule the moral principle.

Proportionalism might be a way forward for Christian morality to resolve the different approaches currently adopted. However, it is not clear when it's acceptable to put moral laws aside or how proportionalism can produce a consistent ethical theory.

Extracts from key texts

John A. T. Robinson, *Honest to God*, 1963

From pages 110–115

The Teaching of Jesus

… 'The clear teaching of our Lord' is taken to mean that Jesus laid down certain precepts which were universally binding. Certain things were always right, other things were always wrong – for all men everywhere.

But this is to treat the Sermon on the Mount as the new Law, and, even if Matthew may have interpreted Jesus that way, there would hardly be a New Testament scholar today who would not say that it was a misinterpretation. The moral precepts of Jesus are not intended to be understood legalistically, as prescribing what all Christians must do, whatever the circumstances, and pronouncing certain courses of action universally right and others universally wrong. They are not legislation laying down what love always demands of every one: they are illustrations of what love may at any particular moment require of anyone …

… Jesus' teaching on marriage, as on everything else, is not a new law prescribing that divorce is always and in every case the greater of two evils (whereas Moses said there were some cases in which it was not). It is saying that love, utterly unconditional love, admits of no accommodation; you cannot define in advance situations in which it can be satisfied with less than complete and unreserved self-giving …

… Jesus never resolves these choices for us: he is content with the knowledge that if we have the heart of the matter in us, if our eye is single, then love will find the way, its own particular way in every individual situation.

… Love alone, because, as it were, it has a built-in moral compass, enabling it to 'home' intuitively upon the deepest need of the other, can allow itself to be directed completely by the situation. It alone can afford to be utterly open to the situation, or rather to the person in the situation, uniquely and for his own sake, without losing its direction or unconditionality. It is able to embrace an ethic of radical responsiveness, meeting every situation on its own merits, with no prescriptive laws.

Joseph Fletcher, *Situation Ethics, the New Morality*, 1963

From pages 138–140

For real decision-making, freedom is required, an open-ended approach to situations. Imagine the plight of an obstetrician who believed he must always respirate every baby he delivered, no matter how monstrously deformed! ...

... No wonder that Jesus, in the language of a French Catholic moralist whose concern is contemporary, 'reacted particularly against code morality and against casuistry,' and that his 'attitude toward code morality [was] purely and simply one of reaction.' Modern Christians ought not to be naive enough to accept any other view of Jesus' ethic than the situational one ...

As we know, for many people, sex is so much a moral problem, largely due to the repressive effects of **legalism**, that in newspapers and popular parlance the term 'morals charge' always means a sex complaint! 'Her morals are not very high' means her sex life is rather looser than the mores allow. Yet we find nothing in the teachings of Jesus about the ethics of sex, except adultery and an absolute condemnation of divorce – a correlative matter. He said nothing about birth control, large or small families, childlessness, homosexuality, masturbation, fornication or pre- marital intercourse, sterilization, artificial insemination, abortion, sex play, petting, and courtship. Whether any form of sex (hetero, homo, or auto) is good or evil depends on whether love is fully served. The Christian ethic is not interested in reluctant virgins and technical chastity. What sex probably needs more than anything is a good airing, demythologizing it and getting rid of its mystique-laden and occult accretions, which come from romanticism on the one hand and puritanism on the other. People are learning that we can have sex without love, and love without sex; that baby-making can be (and often ought to be) separated from love-making. It is, indeed, for recreation as well as for procreation. But if people don't believe it is wrong to have sex relations outside marriage, it isn't, unless they hurt themselves, their partners, or others. This is, of course, a very big 'unless' and gives reason to many to abstain altogether except within the full mutual commitment of marriage.

Situation ethics always suspects prescriptive law of falsifying life and dwarfing moral stature, whether it be the Scripture legalism of Biblicist Protestants and Mohammedans or the nature legalism (natural law) of the Catholics and disciples of Confucius ... To learn love's sensitive tactics, such people are going to have to put away their childish rules.

CHAPTER SUMMARY

- 'The law of love is the ultimate law because it is the negation of law'. (Tillich)
- ' "Love thy neighbour as thyself" is the ultimate duty.' (Bultmann)
- Ethics is either legalistic, antinomian or situational.
- The situationist enters into the moral dilemma with the ethics and rules and principles of his or her community or tradition. However, the situationist is prepared to set aside those rules in the situation if love seems better served by doing so.
- 'The situationist follows a moral law or violates it according to love's need.' (Fletcher)
- Moral decisions are guided by what best serves love.

Four working principles, and conscience:

- Pragmatism, which is a practical or success posture.
- Relativism – situation ethics is relativistic: 'The Situationist avoids words like "never" and "perfect" and "always" and "complete" as he avoids the plague, as he avoids "absolutely".'
- Positivism – situation ethics depends on Christians freely choosing faith that God is love, so giving first place to Christian love.
- Personalism – the legalist puts the law first, but the situationist puts people first.
- 'Conscience' describes the weighing up of the possible action before it's taken.

Six fundamental principles:

- First proposition: 'Only one thing is intrinsically good; namely love: nothing else at all.' (Fletcher)

- Second proposition: 'The ruling norm of Christian decision is love: nothing else.'
- Third proposition: 'Love and Justice are the same, for justice is love distributed, nothing else.' (Fletcher)
- Fourth proposition: 'Love wills the neighbour's good, whether we like him or not.' (Fletcher)
- Fifth proposition: 'Only the end justifies the means, nothing else.' (Fletcher)
- Sixth proposition: 'Love's decisions are made situationally, not prescriptively.' (Fletcher)

Evaluating situation ethics:
- Situations ethics provides an alternative Christian ethic that is consistent with the Gospel representation of Jesus.
- Situation ethics is flexible and practical. It takes into account the complexities of human life and can make tough decisions where, from a legalistic perspective, all actions seem wrong.
- In 1952, Pope Pius XII called situation ethics 'an individualistic and subjective appeal to the concrete circumstances of actions to justify decisions in opposition to the natural law or God's revealed will'.
- Situation ethics is subjective, because decisions must be made from within the situation as it's perceived to be.
- Situation ethics is individualistic, because humans see things from their own perspective. There's a danger of a selfish human tendency polluting agape love.
- What is believed to be a loving end could justify actions that many people regard as simply wrong.

Chapter 10

Virtue theory

Introduction

Key philosophers and texts

Aristotle (384–322 BCE): *Nichomachean Ethics*

Alasdair MacIntyre (1929–): *A Short History of Ethics*, 1966; *After Virtue, a Study in Moral Theory*, 1981

Key terms

Heroic society, vice, virtue, virtue theory

What you will learn by the end of this chapter

- The contributions of Aristotle and MacIntyre to virtue theory.
- The weaknesses and strengths of virtue theory.

Key questions

1 How can you be a better person?
2 What are the qualities of a good person?
3 Can practice make you a better person?

After virtue – Alasdair MacIntyre

Most moral theories seek try to work out what the right or good thing to do is. They tend to suggest a set of principles for working out the best choice. According to utilitarians, the right thing to do is that which results in the greatest good for the greatest number. For situationists, it's the thing that causes the most loving consequence. In natural law, the right thing is that

Aristotle

which is in accordance with the purpose of what it is to be human. Other moral theories suggest that there are no moral laws as such – morality is whatever's right for you, or moral statements are simply emotive expressions (relativism and emotivism, respectively). Some moral theories understand good in terms of duties (Kant & Ross). **Virtue theory** rejects these approaches. Instead of concentrating on what the right thing to do is, virtue theory asks how you can be a better person. Most theories concentrate on defining good acts or good consequences. Virtue theory is interested in defining good people and the qualities that make them good. The roots of virtue theory are in Greek literature, especially Aristotle, but new interest has been generated by a number of modern writers, most notably Alasdair MacIntyre in his book *After Virtue, a Study in Moral Theory* (1981).

Alasdair MacIntyre thinks that morality has suffered a catastrophe. He writes '… we have – very largely, if not entirely – lost our comprehension, both theoretical and practical, of morality' (MacIntyre, 1981, p. 2). It's as if a global catastrophe has thrown us back into the Dark Ages. But instead of losing scientific knowledge, we have lost moral wisdom.

MacIntyre looks back to the writings of the ancient Greeks. The writings that told of great heroes such as Achilles and Odysseus show a vision of morality – you are what you do. The epic stories describe man in terms of his actions. His identity is defined by what he does. To judge a man is to judge his actions. The way in which we behave provides an opportunity for others to judge our **virtues** and **vices**. It's in this society that the word virtue, **arête**, emerges.

In heroic society, courage is a measure of the quality of an individual and is essential to sustain a household and community. A courageous person is someone who can be relied on and so is important in friendship. Fidelity is also crucial for friendship, as it guarantees a person's will to support and help. A person who displays these virtues is a good person.

Aristotle (384–322 BCE)

Aristotle was born in 384 BCE at Stagirus, a Greek colony on the coast of Thrace. At the age of 17 he was sent to the intellectual capital of the Greek world, Athens, joined the Academy and studied under Plato. In later years, he gave his own lectures and set up his own school called the Lyceum. In the end, he had to flee Athens and he died in 322 BCE.

In his work *Nicomachean Ethics*, Aristotle, writing in 350 BCE, argues that whenever we do something, we do it to gain an end, and that the ultimate end of all ends is the chief good, the greatest good. While this is teleological there is another important principle. In order to achieve that end we must practise, like archers who want to hit the target. By practising we improve our skills (**virtue/arête**), and so become happy and live good lives. There are moral virtues that are qualities of character, such as courage, liberality, temperance and modesty, and we cultivate these by habit. There are 12 such moral virtues, but they fall between two vices, that of excess and that of deficiency. Courage is one of the virtues. If I don't have enough, then I'm a coward. If I'm excessively courageous, then I may become rash. Aristotle believed that all virtues lay at the mid-point between two vices, as illustrated in Table 10.1.

Although all of us could develop these virtues, only a few will do so. To cultivate them we must find the mean, controlling our emotions and behaviour towards others in different situations. We must behave in a proportionate way. We should not be excessively self-deprecating in the manner of Dickens' Uriah Heap in *David Copperfield* – we should be sincere. Our humour should not descend into buffoonery or extend to boorishness. If we're to be virtuous rather than simply emotive in our responses to people, self-control is essential. Aristotle believed that virtuous behaviour could become a habit, but at no time should we forget that we're behaving virtuously because it's right. By the same measure, we know how virtuous we are by how we spontaneously respond to situations. By doing virtuous things, we become virtuous.

Table 10.1 Aristotle's view of virtues and vices

Vice of deficiency	Virtuous mean	Vice of excess
Cowardice	Courage	Rashness
Insensibility	Temperance	Intemperance
Illiberality	Liberality	Prodigality
Pettiness	Munificence	Vulgarity
Humble-mindedness	High-mindedness	Vaingloriness
Want of ambition	Right ambition	Over-ambition
Spiritlessness	Good temper	Irascibility
Surliness	Friendliness/civility	Obsequiousness
Ironical deprecation	Sincerity	Boastfulness
Boorishness	Wittiness	Buffoonery
Shamelessness	Modesty	Bashfulness
Callousness	Just resentment	Spitefulness

Aristotle believed that every action is directed towards an aim. I get up in the morning because I want to go to work; I go to work because I want to earn a living and have a good career; I want earnings and career success so that I can live life well. There are superior and subordinate aims. Getting up in the morning is subordinate to earning a living. We do one thing to accomplish a greater thing. Ultimately, everything is subordinate to the supreme good, which is happiness. People have different ideas of happiness. Some seek pleasure, others seek honour (such as those who serve the community), and there are those who love contemplation (philosophers). It's the last of these that Aristotle believes to be the best.

Aristotle acknowledged that the virtues of one city may differ from those of another. He didn't believe in an absolute platonic good beyond our world. He thought that good was found within this world. The **supreme happiness** that he talks about is one for the community, not just an individual.

In 1958, G. E. M. Anscombe in 'Modern moral philosophy' wrote that modern moral philosophy was misguided, and that the mistake has been to associate good with actions rather than people. She believed that we should return to Aristotle. Alasdair MacIntyre agreed and argued that modern ethics has lost sight of its roots. Modern philosophers have thrown the baby out with the bathwater.

James F. Keenan (1998) summarises virtue theory in three questions: Who am I? Who ought I to become? How do I get there? Virtues provide a way of estimating character, and suggest a direction in which you should go in order to become a better person. Virture theory is person-centred and focused on our development. By practising actions that embody the virtue, we can grow in the virtues. Being virtuous requires practice, because we can be **excessive** or **deficient** in our behaviour. Our spontaneous behaviour illustrates the degree to which we're behaving in a virtuous manner. Self-knowledge is central – by knowing and understanding ourselves, we can practise to be better. Keenan likens this to good parenting. Good parenting is knowing how to help children to grow according to their own strengths and weaknesses.

MacIntyre sees a moral society as one in which people recognise commonly agreed virtues and aspire to meet them. Those virtues improve and clarify themselves over time. MacIntyre looks back and identifies the virtues that have been picked up and passed on: from Aristotle, Christianity, democracy and so forth. We're left with two kinds of people in society – those who speak from within that tradition of thinking and those who stand outside it. Modern moral philosophy is the latter and McIntyre the former.

There are differences between the virtues of the ancient Homeric world, which saw human excellence in terms of the warrior; Aristotle's Athenian gentlemen; and the Christian virtues outlined by St Thomas Aquinas, who drew on Plato, Cicero, Ambrose, Gregory and Augustine to list four cardinal virtues – prudence, justice, temperance and fortitude/bravery – together with the theological virtues of faith, hope and charity. Prudence was central to both Aristotle and Aquinas. We must have both feet firmly on the ground so that we think practically and realistically. Our goals must be achievable and we should be moderate in reaching them. For MacIntyre, the virtues improve and clarify themselves over time. For the modern era Keenan suggests prudence, justice, fidelity, self-care and the distinctive Christian virtue of mercy. James Rachels suggests courage, honesty and loyalty to support friendship and stand up to the struggles of life.

Tasks

1 Compile a set of virtues suitable for the twenty-first century. Use Table 10.1 and the paragraph above to help you.

2 Decide the 'vice of deficiency' and 'vice of excess' for each of your virtues.

Evaluating virtue theory

Virtue theory encompasses all aspects of life rather than particular actions. It sees every moment as the possibility for acquiring or developing a virtue.

Aquinas said that every human action is a moral action. What we do is what we are. This approach is more proactive than dilemma-based ethics, which responds to a difficult moral situation. It is involved in every aspect of human life.

Virtue theory provides an alternative route for drawing on the tradition of moral philosophy in a way that's different from the natural law approach. It avoids the pitfalls of ethical systems that espouse moral absolutes and then struggle with the consequences of those absolutes. It's an alternative ethical model that fits Christian ethics and also reaches beyond religious ethics. Rather than simply looking for rules, it looks at the fundamental issue of what it means to be human.

One criticism levelled against virtue theory is that far from replacing the arguments about moral duty and moral absolutes, it ultimately depends on them. In 'Are virtues no more than dispositions to obey moral rules?', Walter Schaller (1990) argues that moral virtues have only 'instrumental or derivative value'. Virtue theory relies on the concept of duty, our responsibility for acting in a certain way, and the idea that there are moral norms or absolutes. By being virtuous we do good things. This point undermines the significance of virtue theory, as MacIntyre was trying to get away from the arguments about duty and moral actions.

Julia Annas (1992) rejects the idea that ancient values are simply outdated. She suggests that there may well be something of value in them, but she also offers a warning: '... there is another attitude, equally harmful, I think, of romantic nostalgia: the feeling that it would be nicer if we could shed the problem-era that we have and go back to a very different set of problems, that ethics would be a kinder, gentler place if we could forget about hard cases and talk about friendship and the good life instead. Like much nostalgia, this is misplaced.' (p. 136) An old idea isn't necessarily a good idea. MacIntyre may be in danger of this misplaced nostalgia. Perhaps modern philosophers may have more to contribute to ethics than MacIntyre suggests because they are critical of past ethical systems.

In 'On some vices of virtue ethics' (1984), Robert Louden identifies a number of difficulties. Virtue theory doesn't provide answers to specific moral dilemmas such as euthanasia, and nor does it provide a list of intolerable acts such as murder which we might want to condemn outright. In addtion, it is difficult to decide who is virtuous, as external acts that appear virtuous on the outside may have doubtful inner motives which canot be perceived, and vice versa.

These difficulties must be resolved if virtue theory is to work in practice, and it may have to borrow principles from another ethical system such as utilitarianism or Kantian ethics to do so. However, virtue ethics raises the importance of the person when many theories simply address acts and consequences.

1 What criticism does MacIntyre make against recent modern philosophy?

2 What does MacIntyre mean by virtue theory?

3 What are the strengths and weaknesses of virtue theory?

Extracts from key texts

Aristotle, *Nichomachean Ethics*

Book II, Chapter 1

Virtue, then, being of two kinds, intellectual and moral, intellectual virtue in the main owes both its birth and its growth to teaching (for which reason it requires experience and time), while moral virtue comes about as a result of habit, whence also its name (ethike) is one that is formed by a slight variation from the word ethos (habit). From this it is also plain that none of the moral virtues arises in us by nature; for nothing that exists by nature can form a habit contrary to its nature. For instance the stone which by nature moves downwards cannot be habituated to move upwards, not even if one tries to train it by throwing it up ten thousand times; nor can fire be habituated to move downwards, nor can anything else that by nature behaves in one way be trained to behave in another. Neither by nature, then, nor contrary to nature do the virtues arise in us; rather we are adapted by nature to receive them, and are made perfect by habit.

Again, of all the things that come to us by nature we first acquire the potentiality and later exhibit the activity ... but the virtues we get by first exercising them, as also happens in the case of the arts as well. For the things we have to learn before we can do them, we learn by doing them, e.g. men become builders by building and lyreplayers by playing the lyre; so too we become just by doing just acts, temperate by doing temperate acts, brave by doing brave acts ...

... Again, it is from the same causes and by the same means that every virtue is both produced and destroyed, and similarly every art; for it is from playing the lyre that both good and bad lyre-players are produced. And the corresponding statement is true of builders and of all the rest; men will be good or bad builders as a result of building well or badly. For if this were not so, there would have been no need of a teacher, but all men would have been born good or bad at their craft.

This, then, is the case with the virtues also; by doing the acts that we do in our transactions with other men we become just or unjust, and by doing the acts that we do in the presence of danger, and being habituated to feel fear or confidence, we become brave or cowardly.

The same is true of appetites and feelings of anger; some men become temperate and good-tempered, others self-indulgent and irascible, by behaving in one way or the other in the appropriate circumstances. Thus, in one word, states of character arise out of like activities. This is why the activities we exhibit must be of a certain kind; it is because the states of character correspond to the differences between these. It makes no small difference, then, whether we form habits of one kind or of another from our very youth; it makes a very great difference, or rather all the difference.

Alasdair MacIntyre, *After Virtue, a Study in Moral Theory*, 1985 (2nd edn)

The Nature of Virtues, page 191

A virtue is an acquired human quality the possession and exercise of which tends to enable us to achieve those goods which are internal to practices and the lack of which effectively prevents us from achieving any such goods. Later this definition will need amplification and amendment. But as a first approximation to an adequate definition it already illuminates the place of the virtues in human life. For it is not difficult to show for a whole range of key virtues that without them the goods internal to practices are barred to us, but not just barred to us generally, barred in a very particular way.

It belongs to the concept of a practice as I have outlined it – and as we are all familiar with it already in our actual lives, whether we are painters or physicists or quarterbacks or indeed just lovers of good painting or first-rate experiments or a well-thrown pass – that its goods can only be achieved by subordinating ourselves within the practice in our relationship to other practitioners. We have to learn to recognize what is due to whom; we have to be prepared to take whatever self-endangering risks are demanded along the way; and we have to listen carefully to what we are told about our own inadequacies and to reply with the same carefulness for the facts. In other words we have to accept as necessary components of any practise with internal goods and standards of excellence the virtues of justice, courage, and honesty.

CHAPTER SUMMARY

- Virtue theory asks how you can be a better person – it defines good people and the qualities that make them good.

- To judge a man is to judge his actions. The way in which we behave provides an opportunity for others to judge our virtues and vices.

- Aristotle argued that whenever we did something, we did it to gain an end, and that the ultimate end of all ends was the chief good, the greatest good.

- To achieve that end we must practise, like archers who want to hit the target. By practising, we improve our skills (virtue/**arête**) and so become happy and live good lives.

- G. E. M. Anscombe wrote that modern moral philosophy was misguided.

- Alasdair MacIntyre argues that modern ethics has lost sight of its roots and has forgotten all that has gone before.

- Virtues provide a way of estimating character, and suggest a direction in which you should go in order to become a better person.

- Virtue theory is person-centred and focused on our development.

- By knowing and understanding ourselves, we can practice to be better.

- MacIntyre sees a moral society as one in which people recognise commonly agreed virtues and aspire to meet them. Those virtues improve and clarify themselves over time.

Evaluating virtue theory:

- Virtue theory encompasses all aspects of life rather than particular actions.

- Rather than simply looking for rules, virtue theory looks at the fundamental issue of what it means to be human.

- Arguably, virtue theory ultimately depends on moral duty and moral absolutes.

- Julia Annas warns that an old idea isn't necessarily a good idea.
- Virtue theory demands that you adequately define the virtues, but how you do this is far from clear.
- Virtue theory offers a reintroduction of an important dimension of ethics that focuses on the person, rather than just acts or consequences.

Part II

Religion and Ethics

In Part II, we consider three ethical areas of debate that are closely associated with religion. Chapters consider the link between **religion** and **ethics**, different religions and non-religious approaches to ethics and debates surrounding the idea of **conscience**. As with Part I, each chapter opens with lists of the *Key philosophers and texts* and the *Key terms* associated with the theories under scrutiny, and in some cases there are important *Extracts from key texts*.

Chapter 11

Religion and morality

Introduction

Key philosophers and works

Plato (428–347 BCE): *Euthyphro*

Bertrand Russell (1872–1970): *Why I Am Not a Christian*, 1927

J. L. Mackie (1917–1981): *Ethics, Inventing Right and Wrong*, 1977

Gottfried Leibniz (1646–1716): *Discourse on Metaphysics*, 1686

Joseph Fletcher (1905–1991): *Situation Ethics, The New Morality*, 1963

Immanuel Kant (1724–1804): *Critique of Practical Reason*, 1788

James Rachels (1941–): *Elements of Moral Philosophy*, 1986

Key terms

Divine command theory, Euthyphro dilemma, moral absolutes, moral autonomy, *summum bonum*

What you will learn by the end of this chapter

- The meaning of the Euthyphro dilemma.
- The links that some philosophers make between religion and morality.
- The arguments that some philosophers make for separating religion from morality.

Key questions

1 Do morals come from God? If not, where do they come from?
2 Suggest evidence for and against the argument that religion is immoral.

---

3 Do religious people stand a better chance of being moral than non-religious people?
4 Could God command a wicked act?

The Euthyphro dilemma

In Plato's *Euthyphro*, Socrates says:

> Consider this question: Is what is pious loved by the gods because it is pious, or is it pious because it is loved?
>
> Plato, *Euthyphro*, 9A–10B

In other words, Plato is asking 'Is *x* good because God loves it or does God love *x* because *x* is good?' Put another way, is murder wrong because God says murder is wrong, or is murder wrong because it's wrong in itself, independent of God? Socrates presents us with two possible visions of the universe. In one there's God, a set of immutable **absolute** moral rules and the human race. In this universe, God commands humans to follow the moral rules because they are absolutely true in themselves, separate from God. God agrees with them and wants humans to follow them. Now let us consider an alternative universe. In this second universe, there only exists God and the human race. God commands humans to do certain things and they are good things because God has commanded them.

The view that moral rules are true by virtue of being commanded by God is called the **divine command theory**. It's concisely put by Emil Brunner (1947): 'The Good consists in always doing what God wills at any particular moment.' If you decide that moral actions are good or bad because they are commanded or forbidden by God, certain things follow. First, if they had not been commanded or forbidden by God then they wouldn't have been good or bad. Secondly, if God has said the opposite to what He did in fact say, then the things that would have been good are now bad and vice versa. If God has said 'Hate your neighbour', then that indeed would be the Christian and Jewish code of behaviour. This makes the moral codes appear somewhat arbitrary. Surely murder is wrong not just because God said it but because it is wrong. For some philosophers, morality can't depend on authority alone. In the words of A. J. Ayer, 'No morality can be founded on authority, even if the authority were divine.' Commanding something doesn't make it morally right.

What is more, if God chose his commands arbitrarily, then why worship Him? The philosopher Gottfried Leibniz writes '... in saying that things are not good by any rule of goodness, but merely the will of God, it seems to me that one destroys, without realising it, all the love of God and all his glory. For why praise him for what he has done if he would be equally praiseworthy in doing exactly the contrary?' (Leibniz, 1686) Perhaps God is so unlike humans that He is beyond comprehension. While it seems impossible to imagine that His com-

Religion and ethics

mands make things good or bad, nevertheless, since he created morality this is within His power.

Plato was an absolutist and may have believed in the first universe with a set of absolute moral rules which are true in themselves, and not by virtue of being commanded. If we do choose this first universe, with God and moral absolutes separate from one another, we have to answer another question. If there's an objective standard of right and wrong separate from God, which He agrees with or follows, what do we then make of God? We're left with no religious reason to be good. God seems diminished, because He defers to a higher set of absolutes. This challenges the traditional view of God as all powerful. God no longer has the same ultimate nature. The absolute moral rules seem to occupy that position in the universe.

There are ways around this difficulty, which we shall consider at the end of this chapter, but first we must also address the other questions related to the link between religion and morality.

Is religion immoral?

An **atheist** would refute the argument that morals come from God. Humanists hold strong ethical beliefs, but deny the existence of a supernatural being. They often argue that religion, on balance, is bad for humanity, citing crusades and inquisitions as evidence for the **immorality** of religion. Lucretius, writing in the first century BCE, stated that 'Tantum religio potuit suadere malorum' – 'Such evil deeds could religion provoke' (*De Rerum Natura*, c. 60 BCE, I, 101). More recently, philosophers have identified religion as preventing the improvement of human civilisation. Bertrand Russell states, 'I say quite deliberately that the Christian religion, as organized in its churches, has been and still is the principal enemy of moral progress in the world .... [religion] ... prevents our children from having a rational education; religion prevents us from removing the fundamental causes of war; religion prevents us from teaching the ethic of scientific co-operation in place of the old fierce doctrines of sin and punishment. It is possible that mankind is on the threshold of a golden age; but if so, it will first be necessary to slay the dragon that guards the door, and this dragon is religion.' (Russell, 1927, pp. 15 and 37)

Galileo was kept under house arrest because his scientific theories didn't accord with those preferred by the religious authorities. Some religions today will not accept medical procedures such as blood transfusions, transplants and IVF – procedures that many people consider life-enhancing. In *A Treatise on Human Nature* (1739–1740), David Hume wrote 'Generally speaking, the errors in religion are dangerous; those in philosophy only ridiculous.' (see Hume, 1962 edn, p. 272) Perhaps religion is in fact a source of immorality, a cause of wars and disunity among the human race. It holds back technological advancement, is unscientific and encourages belief in the supernatural. Furthermore, those who hold particular religious beliefs have often been shown to be **intolerant** of others who hold differing beliefs – as in the case of the Christian crusades against Jews and Muslims.

Some argue that religion is a source of moral absolutes. The saintly behaviour of people such as Mother Teresa was inspired by religious belief. The abolition of slavery in the UK came about partly because of strongly held Christian convictions. Those convictions inspired Martin Luther King is his assertion that all were equal in the eyes of God. All the major world religions teach about the primacy of love or compassion in human relations. Religion enables people to develop in more than simply material ways and justifies a **sceptical** view of the materialistic culture prominent in the West. In countries where religion has been suppressed – such as in Stalin's Russia and Hitler's Nazi Germany – horrendous injustices and crimes still took place. Perhaps immorality has more to do with human nature than a set of beliefs with a supernatural element. In AD 392, St Augustine wrote, 'God is not the parent of evils ... Evils exist by the voluntary sin of the soul to which God gave free choice.' (*Acta seu Disputatio Contra Fortunatum Manichaeum* [*Acts or Disputation Against Fortunatus, the Manichaean*], Chapter 20)

Religion and morality are linked

Immanuel Kant argued that morality supports religion. In his *Critique of Pure Reason* (1781), he dismissed traditional attempts of philosophers to prove the existence of God, but maintained that there's something about morality that makes it reasonable to believe in God. Morality pointed towards God. Human beings have a moral obligation to bring about a perfect state of affairs called the **summum bonum**. Since it's impossible to do so in one lifetime, there must be an afterlife where such a *summum bonum* exists.

In *A Grammar of Assent* (1947), John Henry Newman argued that feelings of responsibility and guilt point to God. In *Absolute Value* (1947), D. I. Trethowan suggested that an awareness of obligation is an awareness of God, and in *The Moral Argument for Christian Theism* (1965), H. P. Owen writes that it's impossible to think of a command without also thinking of a commander. Each of these writers considers the presence of moral values as an indicator of the existence of God.

Religion is a reason to be moral

Without religion, what is the reason for being good? In Dostoyevsky's *The Brothers Karamazov* (1879–1880), the character Ivan says that 'without God, everything is permitted'. Religion provides people with a reason to be moral, because if there were no God everything would be permitted or permissible. It justifies a set of moral absolutes and saves us from moral relativism. If we don't have God or religion, then we don't need to justify acting morally at all. Arguably, it's reasonable to act morally, to do our duty to others, perhaps on the basis of harmony, or the desire to have a civilised society. However, it could be reasonable to act selfishly and look after your own best interests. J. L. Mackie calls this the dualism of practical reason (Mackie, 1977, p. 227); it can seem reasonable to be both self-seeking and selfless.

Joseph Butler thought that, in most cases, the same moral choices would be pursued if you acted out of self-interest as you would make if you acted out of duty to others, but even he noted that this might not be true in every situation if there wasn't an afterlife: 'Duty and interest are perfectly coincident; for the most part in this world, but entirely and in every instance if we take in the future …' (Butler, 1726; quoted in Mackie, 1977, p. 227). If there was no judgement, heaven or hell, then there might be instances in which immorality was in our best interests. The existence of religion and God make doing good right from both selfish and selfless perspectives.

If we do good out of **obedience** to God, then are we being good for the right reasons? Are we simply obeying a tyrant who commands us to obey, rather than making our own moral choices? D. Z. Phillips (1966) wrote that 'To a Christian, to do one's duty is to do the will of God.' There are a number of possible reasons for obeying the will of God. Perhaps God is in a unique position, being all knowing (omniscient) and wanting to act in our best interests because He is all-loving. God has the full picture of what's best for humanity when laying down the moral rules. Since we're not in such a position, we should follow His guidelines. Alternatively, we might decide that we should obey the commands of God out of gratitude for His creating us in the first place. His loving action demands a obedient response. Finally, we might argue that we should obey God because He is our superior and His orders must be obeyed. There are difficulties with each of these suggestions, not least the question of how we can be sure what God's commandments are. There are plenty of religious beliefs on offer, with different holy books. Even within a single religious tradition, there are different denominations or sects who don't agree on the meanings of the holy books.

James Rachels argues that it's unacceptable for religious belief to involve unqualified obedience to God's commands. Rachels maintains that such obedience is inappropriate for a moral agent: 'to be a moral agent is to be an autonomous or self-directed agent … The virtuous man is therefore identified as the man of integrity, i.e. the man who acts according to the precepts which he can, on reflection, conscientiously approve in his own heart.' (Rachels, 1971, p. 334) He concludes that a being such as God can't exist, as no God that requires a human being to abandon his or her moral **autonomy** is worth worshipping – and the only kind of God that can exist is one that's worth worshipping. However, we could argue that God doesn't require us to abandon moral autonomy. Perhaps, in a given situation, God wants us to work out what the right thing to do is – as Joseph Fletcher believes, with his situation ethics theory, (Chapter 9). Even religious authorities such as the Roman Catholic Church identify the importance of conscience in moral living (see Chapter 12). Alasdair MacIntyre (1966, p. 115) is concerned about the motives for moral actions. If the motive for doing good is a fear of going to hell, then it's a selfish and potentially corrupting act.

Ways forward

Theologians and philosophers have recognised important ethical dilemmas posed by certain beliefs about the link between religion and morality. There are some ways forward in getting through these difficulties. Mackie has suggested one solution, which is to maintain that moral truths exist independently but are the product of the creative will of God, who has made humans for which these rules are right. Just as humans were created by God but are now free and separate from God, moral laws were also part of the creation of God. They are now separate from Him. God might require humans to follow the moral rules, but humans might not be able to infer directly what these rules are. Humans may then infer from God's commands that they are worth following.

James Rachels uses an example to illustrate another possibility. Suppose that a leader commands a follower to do something. The follower performs the action, not because he's ordered to do so, but because he thinks that the action is right in itself. In this situation the rightness of the moral action isn't conferred because it's commanded by God. The rightness of the action comes from the fact that it's right in itself (Rachels, 1971, p. 334).

MacIntyre (1966, p. 115) concludes that there must be a secular reason for being moral, which religion sheds light on. Kevin T. Kelly states that '... Christian revelation opens our eyes to the wonder of wise and loving human living' (Kelly, 1992, p. 105). The Roman Catholic Church in *Veritatis Splendor* (1993, verse 22) states that, 'the Ten Commandments are part of God's Revelation. At the same time, they teach us man's true humanity. They shed light on the essential duties, and so indirectly on the fundamental rights, inherent in the nature of the human person.'

Tasks

1 In your own words, explain the **Euthyphro dilemma**.
2 Explain the criticisms that Bertrand Russell makes of Christianity earlier in this chapter and try to think of arguments against each one.

3 On the whole, is religion good or bad for humanity? Justify your view.

4 Should religious people try to work out what's right themselves, or should they simply do what the law of God says in their Holy Scriptures and through their religious authorities?

5 Is it appropriate for a Christian to do good things out of a desire to get to heaven, rather than out of a simple desire to do good things?

6 Do you agree with A. J. Ayer that 'No morality can be founded on authority, even if the authority were divine'? Give reasons for your view.

7 Construct a reason to be good which doesn't require any religious or supernatural source. Can you link this reason to an ethical theory that you have already studied?

Extracts from key texts

Plato, *Euthyphro* 9A–11B

The phrase pious is no longer commonly used. Pious refers to things which are morally right.

Socrates:	Consider this question: Is what is pious loved by the gods because it is pious, or is it pious because it is loved by the gods?
Euthyphro:	I don't understand what you mean, Socrates.
Socrates:	Well, I will try and explain more clearly. Do we seek of things as carried and carrying, led and leading, seen and seeing? And do you understand that in all such pairs of terms each is different from the other?
Euthyphro:	Yes I think I understand.
Socrates:	Is there also something that is loved and someone else that is loving?
Euthyphro:	Of course.
Socrates:	Tell me, then: is a carried thing carried because one carries it, or for some other reason?
Euthyphro:	No; the reason is just that.
Socrates:	And a led thing is led because one leads it and a seen thing because one sees it?
Euthyphro:	Certainly.

...

Socrates:	Then what do we say about piety? Isn't it loved by all the gods, according to your definition?
Euthyphro:	Yes.
Socrates:	Just because it is pious, or for some other reason?
Euthyphro:	No; because it is pious.
Socrates:	So it is loved because it is pious, not pious because it is loved?
Euthyphro:	It seems so.
Socrates:	But it is because a thing is loved by the gods that it is an object of love or god-beloved.
Euthyphro:	Of course.
Socrates:	Then what is god-beloved is not the same as what is pious, Euthyphro, nor is what is pious the same as what is god-beloved, as you assert; they are two different things.
Euthyphro:	How do you make that out Socrates?
Socrates:	Because we agree that what is pious is loved because it is pious, and not pious because it is loved; isn't that so?
Euthyphro:	Yes.
Socrates:	And we agree that what is god-beloved is god-beloved because the gods love it, from the very fact of their loving it; and that they do not love it because it is god-beloved.
Euthyphro:	That is true.
Socrates:	But if what is god-loved were identical with what is pious, my dear Euthyphro, then if what is pious were loved because it is pious, what is god-beloved would be loved because it is god-beloved; and if what is god-beloved were god-beloved because it is loved by the gods, then what is pious would be pious because it is loved by them. As it is, you can see that the relation between them is just the opposite; which shows that they are entirely different from each other. The one is lovable because it is it loved, and the other is loved because it is lovable.

Sørren Kierkegaard (1813–1855), *Fear and Trembling*, 1843

It was early in the morning, and everything in Abraham's house was ready for the journey ... They rode along in harmony, Abraham and Isaac, until they came to mount Moriah. Abraham made everything ready for the sacrifice, calmly and gently, but when he turned away and drew the knife, Isaac saw that Abraham's left hand was clenched in despair, that a shudder went through his whole body – but Abraham drew the knife.

Then they returned home again, and Sarah hurried to meet them, but Abraham had lost faith. Not a word is ever said of this in the world, and Isaac never talked to anyone about what he had seen, and Abraham did not suspect that anyone had seen it.

CHAPTER SUMMARY

- 'Consider this question: is what is pious loved by the gods because it is pious, or is it pious because it is loved?' (Plato)

- 'Is *x* good because God loves it or does God love *x* because *x* is good?'

- Divine command theory: 'The Good consists in always doing what God wills at any particular moment.' (Emil Brunner)

- If morals are separate from God, there's no religious reason to be good, so it diminishes God.

- If morals are good because God commands them, they seem arbitrary, not good in themselves – the opposite would have been good if God had commanded the opposite. 'No morality can be founded on authority, even if the authority were divine.' (A. J. Ayer)

Is religion immoral?

For –

- Atheists and humanists refute the argument that morals come from God

- 'Such evil deeds could religion provoke.' (Lucretius)

- Religion obstructs human civilization: 'the Christian religion ... is the principal enemy of moral progress in the world ... prevents our children from having a rational education; ... prevents us from removing the fundamental causes of war; ... prevents us from teaching the ethic of scientific co-operation in place of the old fierce doctrines of sin and punishment. It is possible that mankind is on the threshold of a golden age; but if so, it will first be necessary to slay the dragon that guards the door, and this dragon is religion.' (Bertrand Russell)

■ Religion can be accused of not tolerating scientific progress, rejecting new medical procedures and sometimes actively opposing scientific discoveries – as in the case of Galileo – and one religion can sometimes be accused of intolerance towards others.

Against –

■ Religion is a source of moral absolutes.

■ Some religious people are moral figures (Martin Luther King, Mother Teresa).

■ Religion does good: charity, campaigns (abolition of slavery).

■ Religion offers an alternative to materialism.

■ Non-religious countries can be immoral (Stalin's Russia and Hitler's Nazi Germany).

■ 'God is not the parent of evils ... Evils exist by the voluntary sin of the soul to which God gave free choice.' (St Augustine)

Religion and morality are linked:

■ Immanuel Kant argued that morality supports religion.

■ Feelings of responsibility and guilt point to God (John Henry Newman).

■ An awareness of obligation is an awareness of God (D. I. Trethowan).

■ It's impossible to think of a command without also thinking of a commander (H. P. Owen).

Religion is a reason to be moral:

For –

■ 'Without God, everything is permitted.' (Dostoyevsky)

■ It can seem reasonable to be both self-seeking and selfless (J. L. Mackie).

■ 'Duty and interest are perfectly coincident; for the most part in this world, but entirely and in every instance if we take in the future ...'. (Butler)

■ 'To a Christian, to do one's duty is to do the will of God.' (D. Z. Phillips)

Against –

■ There are different religious truths.

■ One shouldn't just obey religious truths: 'To be a moral agent is to be an autonomous or self-directed agent.' (James Rachels)

- No God that requires a human being to abandon his or her moral autonomy is worth worshipping.

Ways forward:

- Moral truths exist independently but are the product of the creative will of God (J. L. Mackie).
- A command can give orders that you see as in your best interest to follow (James Rachels).
- There must be a secular reason for being moral, which religion sheds light on (Alasdair MacIntyre).
- '...Christian revelation opens our eyes to the wonder of wise and loving human living.' (Kevin T. Kelly)

Chapter 12

Buddhist, Christian and Muslim ethics

Contents of Chapter 12

Introduction
Buddhist ethics
Christian ethics
Muslim ethics

Introduction

Key terms

Effacement, virtues, deontological, natural law, conscience, Ummah, Qur'an, Sunnah, Shari'a

What you will learn by the end of this chapter

- The basis for Buddhist ethics.
- The basis for liberal and conservative Christian ethics.
- The basis for Muslim ethics.

Key questions

1 How do Buddhists, Christians and Muslims decide what is right?
2 What are the Buddhist, Christian and Muslim sources of moral authority?

Buddhist ethics

There are a number of philosophical presumptions underpinning Buddhist ethics. Padmasiri de Silva (1997) notes that free will, the distinction between good and bad and the idea that our moral behaviour has a causal effect on our next life underpin Buddhist ethics. To determine whether or not an act is bad, the motive must be considered. De Silva writes:

If the action has as its roots greed, hatred and delusion, it is an unwholesome or bad action, and if it was generated by the opposite roots of liberty, compassionate love and wisdom, it is a good action.

De Silva (1997), p. 61

The consequences for ourselves and others also play an important part. By doing a good act we form good habits and are likely to repeat them, and we also build up happiness in our next life:

Buddhism may be described as a consequentialist ethic embodying the ideal of ultimate happiness for the individual, as well as a social ethic with a utilitarian stance concerned with the material and spiritual well-being of mankind.

De Silva (1997), p. 62

As it is concerned with human moral improvement, Buddhist ethics can be described in terms of vices and virtues. In the Sutta in *The Simile of the Cloth*, 16 vices are listed:

And what, monks, are the defilements of the mind? [1] Covetousness and unrighteous greed are a defilement of the mind; [2] ill will is a defilement of the mind; [3] anger is a defilement of the mind; [4] hostility ... [5] denigration ... [6] domineering ... [7] envy ... [8] jealousy ... [9] hypocrisy ... [10] fraud ... [11] obstinacy ... [12] presumption ... [13] conceit ... [14] arrogance ... [15] vanity ... [16] negligence is a defilement of the mind.

Thera (1988), Number 3

These must be avoided and positive practices should be employed. A wide variety of moral virtues are involved in building a moral character. These can be said to fall into three groups:

1. Virtues of conscientiousness:
   Veracity, truthfulness and righteousness.

2. Virtues of benevolence:
   Loving kindness, compassion, sympathetic joy and equanimity.

3. Virtues of self restraint:
   Self control, abstinence, contentment, patience, celibacy, chastity, purity.

Thera (1988)

In *The Discourse on Effacement*, the progress of pursuing the virtues and avoiding the vices is outlined, and in the notes to that discourse Nyanaponika Thera summarises the process: '(Sec. 12) "Effacement" means the radical removal of detrimental qualities of mind.' There are many modes of efface-ment, but Nyanaponika Thera notes that the first is very important:

> 'Others will be harmful, we shall not be harmful here,' and so
> forth through all the other items. This bespeaks of the Buddha's
> realistic outlook as befitting a world that cannot be improved by
> mere wishing nor by 'preaching at it.' There is no use nor hope in
> waiting for our neighbor to change his ways. 'Clean-up cam-
> paigns' should start at our own door, and then the neighbours
> may well be more responsive to our own example than to our
> preaching. Besides, if the aim is the radical effacement of mental
> defilements, we cannot afford to waste time and be deviated from
> our task by side-long glances at the behavior of others. Here lurks,
> in addition, the danger of pride. Hence the Sutta Nipata (v. 918)
> warns that 'though possessing many a virtue one should not com-
> pare oneself with others by deeming oneself better or equal or
> inferior. It is a virtue that squints (Chungtze) that will deprive the
> progress on the path of the element of self-forgetting joyous spon-
> taneity.'
>
> Thera (1988)

The practice of virtues itself is essential both in terms of personal improve-ment and its effect on others. Five ways of maintaining the virtues in the face of vices are explained in *The Practice of Loving-Kindness (Metta), as Taught by the Buddha in the Pali Canon*, from the Anguttara Nikaya, 5:161 (spoken by the Buddha):

> Loving-kindness can be maintained in being towards a person
> with whom you are annoyed: this is how annoyance with him
> can be removed. Compassion can be maintained in being towards
> a person with whom you are annoyed; this too is how annoyance
> with him can be removed. Onlooking equanimity can be main-
> tained in being towards a person with whom you are annoyed;
> this too is how annoyance with him can be removed. The forget-
> ting and ignoring of a person with whom you are annoyed can be
> practiced; this too is how annoyance with him can be removed.
> Ownership of deeds in a person with whom you are annoyed can
> be concentrated upon thus: 'This good person is owner of his
> deeds, heir to his deeds, his deeds are the womb from which he is
> born, his deeds are his kin for whom he is responsible, his deeds
> are his refuge, he is heir to his deeds, be they good or bad.' This
> too is how annoyance with him can be removed.
>
> Thera (1987)

Christian ethics

How does a Christian decide what is right and what is wrong? What needs to be taken into account, and what principles should be applied? What sources of authority should Christians seek advice from or follow in making a decision?

The ethics of Catholic Christianity

There are a number of ethical systems that come into play in Catholic moral theology. **Natural moral law** is a key ethical theory underpinning Roman Catholic Christianity with its emphasis on reason as a tool to perceive natural law, and its deontological emphasis on the application of the primary precepts. Orthodox Catholic teaching about moral decision has remained fundamentally deontological, with an emphasis on certain acts being either right or wrong, and that it is intrinsically evil to commit wrong acts. The Church teaching on natural contraception is an example of this, whereby the act of using artificial contraception is intrinsically evil in itself: 'excluded is any action which either before, at the moment of, or after sexual intercourse, is specifically intended to prevent procreation' (*Humanae Vitae*, 1968, 14). This is also apparent in the Church's view of abortion, which it sees as intrinsically evil in all circumstances.

Catholic Christianity has traditionally maintained that there are absolutes that cannot be changed by the circumstances. However, the Catholic Church also maintains that **conscience** plays an important role in moral decision-making with Aquinas' view that conscience is reason making moral decisions (Cardinal Newman's view that conscience is of primary importance in moral decision-making is considered in Chapter 13). Conscience must be informed by prayer and worship, the teaching of the Church, experience and the inner voice of the Holy Spirit. The Catholic Church also has an important place for the virtues and so **virtue theory** is an additional source for Catholic ethics. Aristotle's idea that our moral actions determine the nature of our character is adopted. Sacred Scripture is an important source of guidance in Catholic Christianity that cannot be changed, and so the place of the Ten Commandments, the Sermon on the Mount and other key texts about Christian discipleship and behaviour form what is known as Divine positive law and no human can change it. It is also the case that the role of the person is important as well as the acts themselves:

> Human activity must be judged insofar as it refers to a human person integrally and adequately considered.
>
> *Acta Synodalia Concilii Vaticani* II, vol. IV, part 7, p. 502, n. 37

In *The Law of Christ* (1954), Bernard Haring stressed the importance of Scripture in making moral choices and argued that moral choices are responses to God's gift of Christ. We need to look on the whole life and calling of a Christian, and not just individual acts. In *Principles of Catholic Morality* (1990), Timothy E. O'Connell argued that moral theology is an attempt to answer the question 'How ought we, who have been gifted by God, to live?' (p. 7). He stressed that a person is more important than an act and that individual freedom is important:

> For one can only be morally responsible when one has knowledge and freedom, when one is fully in control of the events that conspire.
>
> O'Connell (1990), p. 53

Conscience is crucial and it is not a feeling of guilt but a guide for decision-making. Humans must do what they believe is right even if they are mistaken (O'Connell, 1990, p. 113). O'Connell stresses the practice of the virtues and says that certain values may conflict with each other. The moral challenge is to do what is right – to do as much good as possible and as little evil. He maintains that **natural law** is important but our understanding of it is incomplete, so while we can use it, it is not the ultimate decision-making tool:

> If the law guides us to the good, so much the better. But if it does not, then the law must be forsaken, it must be violated, it must be ignored. The good must be sought, always and in all things. For the good after all, is where God is finally to be found.
>
> O'Connell (1990), p. 238

For further details, see Chapters 3, 10 and 13.

Liberal Protestant Christian ethics

A number of writers represent more liberal and evangelical Protestant ethics. In his work *An Interpretation of Christian Ethics* (1935), Reinhold Niebuhr applies the Gospel to social issues through love. Niebuhr writes:

> I still believe, as I believed then, that love may be the motive of social action but that justice must be the instrument of love in the world in which self-interest is bound to defy the canons of love at every level.
>
> Niebuhr (1935), p. 9

and

> The primary issue is to derive a social ethics from the absolute ethic of the gospel. The gospel ethic is absolute because it merely presents the final law of human freedom: the love of God and the neighbour. A social ethics must be concerned with the establishment of tolerable harmonies of life, tolerable forms of justice ...'
>
> Niebuhr (1956 edition), pp. 9–11

In *Basic Christian Ethics* (1950), Paul Ramsey has argued that 'The central ethical notion or "category" in Christian ethics is "obedient love" – the sort of love the gospels describe as "love fulfilling the law" and St. Paul designates as "faith working through love"' (p. xi) and that 'Analyzing ethical problems from the viewpoint of Christian love simply means that Jesus Christ is the center' (p. xvii). Ramsey argues that Christian love is rooted in the righteousness of love (justice), God's nature and His activity. Ramsey argues that Christian ethics are 'An ethic without rules' – as in the case of Jesus, who was a faithful Jew even when he had to ignore the law (e.g. the Sabbath). He goes on to say 'Everything is lawful, everything is permitted which Christian love permits' and 'everything is demanded which Christian love requires' (p. 79). The most powerful expression of this trend is in **situation ethics** (Fletcher, 1963) and this theory is dealt with in full in Chapter 9.

The views of Ramsey and Niebuhr contrast with those of more conservative Protestants, who offer more absolutist Christian ethics. Robertson McQuilkin in *An Introduction to Biblical Ethics* (1995), sees the Bible as 'a revelation by God of his will for human nature' (p. ix) and asserts that universal Bible norms are absolute. The teachings found in the Commandments, beatitudes and elsewhere take on absolute authority. He writes 'Those laws or other teachings that derive from, interpret, or reinforce one of the Ten Commandments should thus be recognised as having enduring authority' (p. 52). The law is the expression of God's love, not law for law's sake, and McQuilkin uses the Bible to address modern issues. Crook identifies Lewis B. Smedes' book *Mere Morality* (1983) as an example of evangelical ethics. Smedes focuses on the Commandments, fulfilled by the coming of Jesus, as embodying an enduring human law. They provide authoritative guidance for people today. Within Protestant ethics, there is a sharp divide between those who take a deontological approach to moral norms espoused in the Bible and those who focus on Jesus' love as a power that overcomes the constraints of all other moral laws. This division is reflected in the varying approaches of Protestant Christians to current issues such as abortion and homosexuality. While evangelicals prohibit abortion and homosexual sex as acts that contravene biblical laws, more liberal Protestants make exceptions through the application of love. For more on these topics, see Chapter 15.

Muslim ethics

Azim Nanji (1997) notes that the two main sources for the principles found within Islam come from the Qur'an and the exemplification of the Qur'an found in the Sunnah, which contains the Prophet's actions, sayings and norms (Nanji, 1997, p. 106). He writes that in one of the chapters of the Qur'an, entitled 'The Criterion' (Furqan: Sura 25), revelation becomes the point of reference for determining right and wrong, and that the biblical prophets of the past are also mediators of God's word (Nanji, 1997, p. 107). This provides Islam with a divine command basis for its ethics.

Nanji goes on to write that there is a human quality that represents

> on the one hand, the moral grounding that underlies human action, while on the other, it signifies the ethical conscience which makes human beings aware of their responsibilities to God and society.
>
> Nanji (1997), p. 108

The community, or Ummah, is the instrument through which the ideals and commands of the Qur'an are applied at the social level, so Muslims are accountable to both God and the community.

The Qur'an and Sunnah were elaborated and applied as God's commands and prohibitions, and are understood as Shari'a law, a system of duties based on Allah's commands, to which people's submission must be total and unqualified. Muslim books of law contain categories for evaluating actions:

1. Obligatory acts, such as the duty to perform ritual prayer, paying of zakat and the practice of fasting.

2. Recommended acts, which are not considered obligatory, such as … acts of charity, kindness, prayer, etc.

3. Permitted actions, regarding which law adopts a neutral stance, that is there is no expectation of reward or punishment for such acts.

4. Acts that are discouraged and regarded as reprehensible, but not strictly forbidden; Muslim jurists differ about what actions to include under this category.

5. Actions that are categorically forbidden, such as murder, adultery, blasphemy, theft, intoxication, etc.

Nanji (1997), p. 113

The divine command basis leads to a deontological approach as illustrated by the categories listed above. These moral norms are applied to contemporary issues as outlined by Frederick M. Denny:

> Although the Qur'an provides no systematic legal corpus, there is much in it pertaining to how humankind should rightly live in the Ummah: marital relations and family life, inheritance, commercial activities and relations, social welfare, slaves, punishment for crimes, and so on, all of which and more are to be understood as implicit as the 'urging what is reputable and restraining from what is disreputable', a key phrase for Qur'anic ethics.
>
> Denny (1985)

Qur'anic ethical teachings cover personal morality and social issues such as economic social justice, especially with regard to poverty. Nanji notes that Muslims are urged to spend their wealth on family relatives, orphans, the poor, the travelling homeless and the needy, and on freeing the enslaved (Nanji, 1997, p. 108).

Questions

1 What comparisons can be made between Buddhist ethics and virtue theory?

2 Identify the different sources of Christian approaches to ethics and the broad ethical theories to which they relate.

3 To what extent are all religious ethics deontological?

4 Critically examine how effectively the three religions might approach an ethical issue of your choice.

CHAPTER SUMMARY

Buddhist ethics:

- Free will, the distinction between good and bad and the idea that our moral behaviour has a causal effect on our next life underpin Buddhist ethics.

- The motive must not be greed, hatred or delusion, but liberty, compassionate love and wisdom.

- By doing a good act we form good habits and are likely to repeat them, and we also build up happiness in our next life, so consequences are important.

- Buddhist ethics can be described as an ethic of vices and virtues.

- Buddhists should avoid covetousness and unrighteous greed, ill will, anger, hostility, denigration, domineering behaviour, envy, jealousy, hypocrisy, fraud, obstinacy, presumption, conceit, arrogance, vanity and negligence.

- Moral virtues are involved in building a moral character and include the following:
  - Virtues of conscientiousness: veracity, truthfulness and righteousness.
  - Virtues of benevolence: loving-kindness, compassion, sympathetic joy and equanimity.

- Virtues of self-restraint: self-control, abstinence, contentment, patience, celibacy, chastity and purity.

■ The practice of virtues itself is essential both in terms of personal improvement and its effect on others.

Christian ethics:

Catholic Christianity –

■ Natural moral law underpins Roman Catholic Christianity with its emphasis on reason and its deontological emphasis on the application of the primary precepts.

■ Certain acts are intrinsically right or wrong: 'excluded is any action which either before, at the moment of, or after sexual intercourse, is specifically intended to prevent procreation'.

■ Conscience is also of primary importance, although it must be informed by prayer and worship, the teaching of the Church, experience and the inner voice of the Holy Spirit.

■ Virtue theory is also a source for Catholic ethics – our moral actions determine the nature of our character.

■ Personalism is also a feature: 'Human activity must be judged insofar as it refers to a human person integrally and adequately considered.'

■ Bernard Haring stressed the importance of Scripture in making moral choices and argued that moral choices are responses to God's gift of Christ.

Protestant Christianity –

■ 'I still believe, as I believed then, that love may be the motive of social action but that justice must be the instrument of love in the world in which self-interest is bound to defy the canons of love at every level'. (Reinhold Niebuhr)

■ 'The central ethical notion or "category" in Christian ethics is "obedient love" – the sort of love the gospels describe as "love fulfilling the law".' (Paul Ramsey)

■ Christian ethics are 'An ethic without rules ... Everything is lawful, everything is permitted which Christian love permits.' (Paul Ramsey)

■ Robertson McQuilkin sees the Bible as 'a revelation by God of his will for human nature' and that universal Bible norms are absolute.

■ Lewis B. Smedes focuses on the Commandments, fulfilled by the coming of Jesus, as embodying an enduring human law.

- This division is reflected in the varying approaches of Protestant Christians to current issues such as abortion and homosexuality.

Muslim ethics:

- There are two main sources – the Qur'an and the Sunnah.
- The Qur'an is the reference point for determining right and wrong, so Islam has a divine command basis for its ethics.
- The community is the instrument through which the ideals and commands of the Qur'an are applied, so Muslims are accountable to both God and the community.
- Muslim books of law contain categories for evaluating actions: obligatory acts, recommended acts, permitted actions, acts that are discouraged and regarded as reprehensible, and actions that are categorically forbidden.
- Muslim ethics are based on divine commands and are deontological.
- Muslim ethics cover personal morality and social issues – Muslims are urged to spend their wealth on family relatives, orphans, the poor, the travelling homeless and the needy, and on freeing the enslaved.

Chapter 13

Conscience

Introduction

Key philosophers and works

St Augustine of Hippo (AD 334–430): *De Trinitate*

St Thomas Aquinas (1224–1274): *Summa Theologica*, 1273

Joseph Butler (1692–1752): *Fifteen Sermons*, 1726

Sigmund Freud (1856–1939): *The Essentials of Psychoanalysis*; *The Outline of Psychoanalysis*, 1938

Key terms

Atheist, benevolence, conscience, immature conscience (super-ego), mature conscience, self-love, synderesis rule, *synderessi*

What you will learn by the end of this chapter

■ Different theories of what conscience is.

■ Arguments for and against relying on conscience for moral decision-making.

■ Arguments for and against the link between God and conscience.

Key questions

1 Is it right to do what we really believe or feel is right, even when that differs from what others believe (always, sometimes, never)?

2 Should we ever go against our conscience?

3 Can conscience be wrong?

4 If we believe that what we're doing is right, can we be held responsible if it's wrong?

Definitions of conscience

The word **conscience** is used in common language. **Conscientious objectors** refuse to fight wars that they disapprove of. People are often advised to follow their conscience. When people feel guilty, they sometimes say that their conscience is telling them that they shouldn't have done it. Many definitions of conscience exist, and there are a number of philosophical theories about conscience and its connection with moral decision-making.

Task

Are the following acting morally or immorally, and should they be punished for their actions?

a A conscript who refuses to fight because he or she believes that war is wrong.

b A regular soldier who refuses to fight because he or she believes that a particular war is wrong.

c A mother who sends her daughter to school in trousers despite school rules insisting on skirts.

d Environmental activists who destroy a field of experimental genetically modified crops.

e Teachers who go on strike demanding better pay.

f A priest who refuses to preach a teaching of his Church on sexual morality, which he believes is wrong.

g Anti-abortionists who burn down an abortion clinic.

h A citizen who refuses to pay tax to the government because he believes that the country's nuclear deterrent is immoral and doesn't want his money to support it.

i A demonstrator who blocks traffic in the street to make his or her protest known.

j An animal rights activist who breaks into a pharmaceuticals laboratory and destroys the research equipment and the results of animal experimentation.

k Local families who drive out a paedophile living near their homes, who has been released after serving a prison sentence.

l A person who breaks into the premises of a British arms dealer and damages war planes due for export.

Three theories of conscience

Although there's no Hebrew word for conscience, there is a Greek word 'synderessi', which appears in the Book of Wisdom 17:11. In the New Testament, St Paul mentions conscience many times. He describes it as an awareness of what is good and bad, and observes that it can be weak and mistaken (1 Corinthians 8:10–12). Christian writers in the first few centuries developed explanations of conscience and its role in moral decision-making. St Jerome (AD 147–240) saw conscience as the power to distinguish good from evil, writing '... the spark of conscience ... with which we discern that we sin'.

St Augustine of Hippo (AD 334–430) considered conscience to be a tool for observing the law of God within human hearts: '... men see the moral rules written in the book of light which is called Truth from which all laws are copied' (De Trinitate, 14, 15, 21). God gives us conscience to determine his law, which is laid down. St Augustine identified conscience as the **voice of God** speaking to us, which we must seek within ourselves. This intuitive activity reveals the most God-like behaviour, so bringing us into close unity with God.

Task

Consider the following definitions of conscience. Choose one which you find most plausible and justify your choice.

- 'Knowledge within oneself', 'The faculty or principle which pronounces upon the moral quality of one's actions or motives, approving the right and condemning the wrong.' (*Oxford English Dictionary*)
- 'Conscience is thus ... the voice of our true selves which summons us ... to live productively, to develop fully and harmoniously. It is the guardian of our integrity.' (Erich Fromm)
- 'It is the reason making moral judgements or choice values.' (St Thomas Aquinas)
- 'The built in monitor of moral action or choice values.' (John Macquarrie)

Conscience is the power of reason – St Thomas Aquinas (1224–1274)

St Thomas Aquinas didn't think that conscience was an inner knowledge of right and wrong but, rather, that it was a device or faculty for distinguishing right from wrong actions. He thought that people basically tended towards the good and away from evil (the 'synderesis rule'). Working out what the good things and evil things were was the main problem. Aquinas thought that the reason people sometimes did evil deeds was because they had made a mistake. They had pursued an apparent good and not a real good – their consciences were mistaken. Aquinas writes:

> If a mistaken reason bids a man to sleep with another man's wife, to do this will be evil based on ignorance of divine law he ought to know; but if the misjudgment is occasioned by thinking the woman really is his own wife and she wants him then his will is free from fault.

Rather than being a voice that commands one thing or another, conscience is 'reason making right decisions' (*Summa Theologica*, I–II, I). In other words, conscience deliberates between good and bad. There are two parts to making moral decisions. **Synderesis** is right reason, the awareness of the moral principle to do good and avoid evil. **Conscientia** distinguishes between right and wrong and makes the moral decision.

Intuitive conscience – Joseph Butler (1692–1752)

Joseph Butler was an Anglican priest and theologian. He saw conscience as the final moral decision-maker: 'There is a principle of reflection in men by which they distinguish between approval and disapproval of their own actions … this principle in man … is conscience' (Butler, 1726, p. 21). Butler believed that humans were influenced by two basic principles, **self-love** and **benevolence** (love of others). Conscience directs us towards focusing on the happiness or interest of others and away from focusing on ourselves.

Like Aquinas, Butler held that conscience could both determine and judge the rightness and wrongness of actions. However, Butler went on to state that conscience comes into play in situations without any introspection and has the ultimate authority in ethical judgements. For Butler, conscience gives us instant intuitive judgements about what we should do. He wrote: 'Had it strength as it has right; had it power as it had manifest authority, it would absolutely govern the world.'

Butler identified conscience as 'our natural guide, the guide assigned us by the Author of our nature'. It's our guide to moral behaviour, put there by God, and it must be obeyed: 'it is our duty to walk in that path, and follow this guide without looking about to see whether we may not possibly forsake them with impunity'. The fact that your conscience instructs to act in a certain way is adequate justification to behave in that way. You should not even consider alternatives. If your conscience commands, you must obey unquestioningly. This is a far more intuitive view of conscience than Aquinas' account:

> But allowing that mankind hath the rule of right within himself, yet it may be asked, 'What obligations are we under to attend to and follow it?' I answer: it has been proved that man by his nature is a law to himself, without the particular distinct consideration of the positive sanctions of that law; the rewards and punishments

which we feel, and those which from the light of reason we have ground to believe, are annexed to it. The question then carries its own answer along with it. Your obligation to obey this law, is its being the law of your nature. That your conscience approves of and attests to such a course of action, is itself alone an obligation. Conscience does not only offer itself to show us the way we should walk in, but it likewise carries its own authority with it, that it is our natural guide, the guide assigned us by the Author of our nature; it therefore belongs to our condition of being, it is our duty to walk in that path, and follow this guide without looking about to see whether we may not possibly forsake them with impunity.

Butler (1726), p. 6

Butler gives intuitive moral judgements of conscience absolute authority and this is questionable. Surely it's at least possible that consciences could be misled or simply misinformed, and so could err. An intuitive conscience, which is obeyed unquestioningly, could be used to justify all sorts of acts. For this reason, Catholic Christianity has tended towards Aquinas' position, which gives weight to conscience but allows for the possibility of error where conscience directs a person to go against the law of God through ignorance.

Conscience as guilt – Sigmund Freud (1856–1939)

Freud believed that at its most fundamental, the human psyche was inspired by powerful instinctive desires that had to be satisfied. However, children quickly learn that the world restricts the degree to which these desires are satisfied. Humans create the **ego**, which takes account of the realities of the world and society. A '**super-ego**' internalises and reflects anger and disapproval of others. A guilty conscience is created, which grows into a life and power of its own irrespective of the rational thought and reflection of the individual. This conscience is pre-rational. Rather, it's the inevitable outcome of conflict and aggression.

Psychologists since Freud have amended Freud's theory. They suggest an explanation in terms of a mature and immature conscience. The mature and healthy conscience can be identified with the ego's reflection about the best way of achieving integrity. It can be characterised as something that's concerned with what is right and wrong, and that acts on things of value. It looks out to the world, developing new insights into situations. The mature conscience is dynamic, responsive and focused on the future.

The immature conscience (super-ego) can be identified with the mass of feelings of guilt that have been put there at an early pre-rational stage by parents, schooling, and so on. It may inspire actions simply to gain approval. It's concerned with feelings and it blindly obeys. It is backward-looking and the amount of guilt has little to do with the importance of the action.

These two consciences may conflict. I may feel guilty about going shopping on a Sunday, because it was instilled in me as a child that this was wrong, although I no longer believe that it's wrong. The super-ego reflects human social nature. We belong to a group and our life depends on our relationship with others. The group imposes controls over our desires, and in this way harmony can be achieved and society can survive. The mature conscience, on the other hand, is the expression of an individual search for self-fulfillment. It claims autonomy over social pressures. The individual is not content to do what everyone else does and be part of the crowd.

This psychological account of conscience is a recent explanation which can undermine both of the previous religious views of conscience, expressed by Aquinas and Butler. It doesn't rule out the possibility that God has some involvement with conscience, but if this is the case the original theories will need reworking.

Issues surrounding conscience

Do we always obey our conscience?

It's difficult to know whether anyone deliberately goes against his or her conscience. There's no objective way of measuring what someone else's conscience is telling them and why. People may be able to manipulate their consciences to justify their actions. It is of course possible to have a sense of knowing what one ought to do, but lack the strength or will to do it. This factor was noted by St Paul in his letter to the Romans: 'I do not understand my own actions. For I do not do what I want, but I do the very thing I hate ... I can will what is right, but I cannot do it. For I do not do the good I want, but the evil I do not want, is what I do.' (Romans 7:15,18)

Is conscience a moral guide?

St Paul believed that conscience was within the centre of the soul: 'They can demonstrate the effects of the law engraved on their hearts, to which their own conscience bears witness.' (Romans 2:15) Acting on your conscience is acting on your innermost convictions and involves an act of integrity. St Jerome thought it the capacity to make judgements and a power of the soul.

The Roman Catholic Church adopted Aquinas' understanding that not following conscience was always wrong. It's a deep sense of right and wrong from God, although He also taught that conscience can never motivate you to do something that goes against what is morally right (as determined by natural law). Aquinas believed that consciences should be informed, as ignorance can lead conscience astray.

The Catholic cardinal John Henry Newman (1801–1890) took a more intuitionist approach to conscience. Newman believed that to follow conscience is to follow a divine law as it is a messenger from God. Newman was a devout Catholic, but the quote 'I toast the Pope, but I toast conscience first' is attributed to him. Ultimately, the Roman Catholic Church's teaching on conscience reflects both Newman and Aquinas, maintaining that conscience is the law that speaks to the heart: '... a law written by God' (Pastoral Constitution, *Gaudium et Spes*). Obedience to conscience sustains human dignity, and human beings are judged by it.

Today, Catholics are encouraged to **inform** their consciences before acting on them. In the Declaration on Religious Freedom, the Vatican II Council said, 'In all his activity a man is bound to follow conscience faithfully, in order that he may come to God for whom he was created. It follows that he is not to be forced to act in a manner contrary to his conscience.'

However, there's disagreement about what you should do when your informed conscience goes against the established teaching of the Church. In principle, this should be impossible, but many Catholics have difficulty in accepting certain aspects of the Church's sexual teachings. The teaching on the use of artificial contraception is widely ignored – Catholics are prepared to ignore it on the basis of conscience. The Church teaches that it's intrinsically wrong to use artificial methods of contraception, but the experience of many Catholic couples brings them into disagreement with this teaching.

Difficulties with linking conscience with God

One consequence of taking conscience to be a voice of God is the difficulty of conflicting consciences. There are a number of religions with competing claims about truth. People sincerely and conscientiously believe different things on a wide variety of ethical and religious issues. If we're to claim that God has some input into the human conscience, then we must address this disparity. Butler gives ultimate authority to conscience as it commands, while Aquinas notes that consciences may be misled or misinformed. This allows for a margin of error, which might explain the different conclusions that people come to and the apparent failure of people to be moral sometimes. Perhaps people don't listen to their consciences correctly, or perhaps they don't inform their consciences correctly.

However, this may simplify the observation that many Christians feel doubt in situations in which they are making moral decisions. People can feel torn and genuinely unsure about what they ought to do. This would seem to question whether it's possible to give conscience the clear-cut 'voice of God', or guide from God, that is suggested in some views.

Athiests may also claim that conscience is important to them, with no need of a supernatural element in their decision-making. They may feel that a psychological explanation of conscience is adequate, while still giving it some authority in their moral choices. The non-religious case for, and use of, conscience is an important challenge to the traditional religious use of conscience.

Task

1 What is meant by **conscience**? Give three different accounts.

2 What factors might influence the formation of conscience?

3 Why could it be argued that we have a duty to follow our consciences, and what could be said against that claim?

4 When, if ever, is it right to go against your conscience?

5 Under what circumstances might it be morally permissible to break the laws of the state to follow your conscience?

6 What factors might make our conscience an unreliable guide?

7 Can you suggest some reasons for believing that conscience is a reliable **moral guide**?

8 In what ways do philosophers argue that conscience is linked to God?

9 What arguments might challenge a link between conscience and God or anything religious?

10 What are the strengths and weaknesses of the arguments that conscience is linked to right reason (Aquinas), intuition (Butler) or guilt (Freud)?

Task

1 In the 1990s, a group of Liverpool women broke into an British Aerospace factory and attacked a number of Hawk trainers that were to be delivered to Indonesia. They committed trespass and did criminal damage costing thousands of pounds. They maintained that the planes, which experts say can carry machine guns or light bombs for ground assault, had in the past been used in East Timor to attack civilians. The four women were cleared of damaging a jet fighter, despite admitting striking it with a hammer. They in turn accused British Aerospace of aiding and abetting the murder of civilians in East Timor. The jury found them not guilty.

   a Was the jury's decision correct?

   b Is it ever right to take the law into your own hands in a civilised society, or should the courts always be used to pursue grievances?

   c If an anti-abortionist was to destroy an abortion clinic, so preventing abortions – murder in his or her eyes – should he or she be prosecuted and, if so, on what basis?

2 Approximately 145 000 Jehovah's Witnesses live in the UK and the Republic of Ireland. They refuse to consent to blood transfusions, due to passages in the Bible that forbid the consumption of someone else's blood. In the event that a child of a Jehovah's Witness couple needs a blood transfusion, doctors may overrule the wishes of the parents and the child not to allow it. Should doctors or courts have the power to overrule parents and children who believe that the child's immortal soul would be in peril if such a procedure were to go ahead?

Religion and ethics

Extracts from key texts

Henry David Thoreau (1817–1862), *On the Duty of Civil Disobedience*, 1849

From paragraph 4

After all, the practical reason why, when the power is once in the hands of the people, a majority are permitted, and for a long period continue, to rule is not because they are most likely to be in the right, nor because this seems fairest to the minority, but because they are physically the strongest. But a government in which the majority rule in all cases can not be based on justice, even as far as men understand it. Can there not be a government in which the majorities do not virtually decide right and wrong, but conscience? – in which majorities decide only those questions to which the rule of expediency is applicable? Must the citizen ever for a moment, or in the least degree, resign his conscience to the legislator? Why has every man a conscience then? I think that we should be men first, and subjects afterward. It is not desirable to cultivate a respect for the law, so much as for the right. The only obligation which I have a right to assume is to do at any time what I think right.

Plato, *Crito*, 360 BCE

Scene: The Prison of Socrates

Socrates, the ancient Greek philosopher, was sentenced to death because his teaching was considered a corrupting influence on the young boy and a denial of the Gods. He could have easily escaped into exile and his friends encouraged him to do so. He refused to do so believing he had a duty to the laws of Athens which he had lived his life under.

Socrates: Then consider the matter in this way: Imagine that I am about to play truant (you may call the proceeding by any name which you like), and the laws and the government come and interrogate me:

'Tell us, Socrates,' they say; 'what are you about? are you going by an act of yours to overturn us – the laws and the whole State, as far as in you lies? Do you imagine that a State can subsist and not be overthrown, in which the decisions of law have no power, but are set aside and overthrown by individuals?' What will be our answer, Crito, to these and the like words? Anyone, and especially a clever rhetorician, will have a good deal to urge about the evil of setting aside the law which requires a sentence to be carried out; and we might reply, 'Yes; but the State has injured us and given an unjust sentence.' Suppose I say that?

Crito: Very good, Socrates.

Socrates: 'And was that our agreement with you?' the law would say, 'or were you to abide by the sentence of the State?' And if I were to express astonishment at their saying this, the law would probably add:

'Answer, Socrates, instead of opening your eyes: you are in the habit of asking and answering questions. Tell us what complaint you have to make against us which justifies you in attempting to destroy us and the State? In the first place did we not bring you into existence? Your father married your mother by our aid and begat you. Say whether you have any objection to urge against those of us who regulate marriage?' None, I should reply. 'Or against those of us who regulate the system of nurture and education of children in which you were trained? Were not the laws, who have the charge of this, right in commanding your father to train you in music and gymnastic?' Right, I should reply. 'Well, then, since you were brought into the world and nurtured and educated by us, can you deny in the first place that you are our child and slave, as your fathers were before you? And if this is true you are not on equal terms with us; nor can you think that you have a right to do to us what we are doing to you. Would you have any right to strike or revile or do any other evil to a father or to your master, if you had one, when you have been struck or reviled by him, or received some other evil at his hands? – you would not say this? And because we think right to destroy you, do you think that you have any right to destroy us in return, and your country as far as in you lies? And will you, O professor of true virtue, say that you are justified in this? Has a philosopher like you failed to discover that our country is more to be valued and higher and holier far than mother or father or any ancestor, and more to be regarded in the eyes of the gods and of men of understanding? also to be soothed, and gently and reverently entreated when angry, even more than a father, and if not persuaded, obeyed? And when we are punished by her, whether with imprisonment or stripes, the punishment is to be endured in silence; and if she leads us to wounds or death in battle, thither we follow as is right; neither may anyone yield or retreat or leave his rank, but whether in battle or in a court of law, or in any other place, he must do what his city and his country order him; or he must change their view of what is just: and if he may do no violence to his father or mother, much less may he do violence to his country.' What answer shall we make to this, Crito? Do the laws speak truly, or do they not?

Crito: I think that they do.

Socrates: Then the laws will say: 'Consider, Socrates, if this is true, that in your present attempt you are going to do us wrong. For, after having brought you into the world, and nurtured and educated you, and given you and every other citizen a share in every good that we had to give, we further proclaim and give the right to every Athenian, that if he does not like us when he has come of age and has seen the ways of the city, and made our acquaintance, he may go where he pleases and take his goods with him; and none of us laws will forbid him or interfere with him. Any of you who does not like us and the city, and who wants to go to a colony or to any other city, may go where he likes, and take his goods with him. But he who has experience of the manner in which we order justice and administer the State, and still remains, has entered into an implied contract that he will do as we command him. And he who disobeys us is, as we maintain, thrice wrong: first, because in disobeying us he is disobeying his parents; secondly, because we are the authors of his education; thirdly, because he has made an agreement with us that he will duly obey our commands; and he neither obeys them nor convinces us that our commands are wrong; and we do not rudely impose them, but give him the alternative of obeying or convincing us; that is what we offer and he does neither. These are the sort of accusations to which, as we were saying, you, Socrates, will be exposed if you accomplish your intentions; you, above all other Athenians.' Suppose I ask, why is this? they will justly retort upon me that I above all other men have acknowledged the agreement. 'There is clear proof,' they will say, 'Socrates, that we and the city were not displeasing to you. Of all Athenians you have been the most constant resident in the city, which, as you never leave, you may be supposed to love. For you never went out of the city either to see the games, except once when you went to the Isthmus, or to any other place unless when you were on military service; nor did you travel as other men do. Nor had you any curiosity to know other States or their laws: your affections did not go beyond us and our State;

we were your especial favorites, and you acquiesced in our government of you; and this is the State in which you begat your children, which is a proof of your satisfaction. Moreover, you might, if you had liked, have fixed the penalty at banishment in the course of the trial – the State which refuses to let you go now would have let you go then. But you pretended that you preferred death to exile, and that you were not grieved at death. And now you have forgotten these fine sentiments, and pay no respect to us, the laws, of whom you are the destroyer; and are doing what only a miserable slave would do, running away and turning your back upon the compacts and agreements which you made as a citizen. And first of all answer this very question: Are we right in saying that you agreed to be governed according to us in deed, and not in word only? Is that true or not?' How shall we answer that, Crito? Must we not agree?

Crito: There is no help, Socrates.

Socrates: Then will they not say: 'You, Socrates, are breaking the covenants and agreements which you made with us at your leisure, not in any haste or under any compulsion or deception, but having had seventy years to think of them, during which time you were at liberty to leave the city, if we were not to your mind, or if our covenants appeared to you to be unfair. You had your choice, and might have gone either to Lacedaemon or Crete, which you often praise for their good government, or to some other Hellenic or foreign State. Whereas you, above all other Athenians, seemed to be so fond of the State, or, in other words, of us her laws (for who would like a State that has no laws?), that you never stirred out of her: the halt [decrepit], the blind, the maimed, were not more stationary in her than you were. And now you run away and forsake your agreements. Not so, Socrates, if you will take our advice; do not make yourself ridiculous by escaping out of the city.'

'For just consider, if you transgress and err in this sort of way, what good will you do, either to yourself or to your friends? That your friends will be driven into exile and deprived of citizenship, or will lose their property, is tolerably certain; and you yourself, if you fly to one of the neighboring cities, as, for example, Thebes or Megara, both of which are well-governed cities, will come to them as an enemy, Socrates, and their government will be against you, and all patriotic citizens will cast an evil eye upon you as a subverter of the laws, and you will confirm in the minds of the judges the justice of their own condemnation of you. For he who is a corrupter of the laws is more than likely to be corrupter of the young and foolish portion of mankind. Will you then flee from well-ordered cities and virtuous men? and is existence worth having on these terms? Or will you go to them without shame, and talk to them, Socrates? And what will you say to them? What you say here about virtue and justice and institutions and laws being the best things among men? Would that be decent of you? Surely not. But if you go away from well-governed States to Crito's friends in Thessaly, where there is great disorder and license, they will be charmed to have the tale of your escape from prison, set off with ludicrous particulars of the manner in which you were wrapped in a goatskin or some other disguise, and metamorphosed as the fashion of runaways is – that is very likely; but will there be no one to remind you that in your old age you violated the most sacred laws from a miserable desire of a little more life? Perhaps not, if you keep them in a good temper; but if they are out of temper you will hear many degrading things; you will live, but how? – as the flatterer of all men, and the servant of all men; and doing what? – eating and drinking in Thessaly, having gone abroad in order that you may get a dinner. And where will be your fine sentiments about justice and virtue then? Say that you wish to live for the sake of your children, that you may bring them up and educate them – will you take them into Thessaly and deprive them of Athenian citizenship? Is that the benefit which you would confer upon them? Or are you under the impression that they will be better cared for and educated here if you are still alive, although absent from them; for that your friends will take care of them? Do you fancy that if you are an inhabitant of Thessaly they will take care of them, and if you are an inhabitant of the other world they will not take care of them? Nay; but if they who call themselves friends are truly friends, they surely will.'

'Listen, then, Socrates, to us who have brought you up. Think not of life and children first, and of justice afterwards, but of justice first, that you may be justified before the princes of the world below. For neither will you nor any that belong to you be happier or holier or juster in this life, or happier in another, if you do as Crito bids. Now you depart in innocence, a sufferer and not a doer of evil; a victim, not of the laws, but of men. But if you go forth, returning evil for evil, and injury for injury, breaking the covenants and agreements which you have made with us, and wronging those whom you ought least to wrong, that is to say, yourself, your friends, your country, and us, we shall be angry with you while you live, and our brethren, the laws in the world below, will receive you as an enemy; for they will know that you have done your best to destroy us. Listen, then, to us and not to Crito.'

This is the voice which I seem to hear murmuring in my ears, like the sound of the flute in the ears of the mystic; that voice, I say, is humming in my ears, and prevents me from hearing any other. And I know that anything more which you will say will be in vain. Yet speak, if you have anything to say.

Crito: I have nothing to say, Socrates.

Socrates: Then let me follow the intimations of the will of God.

Questions

1 What is Thoreau's problem with the rule of the majority?

2 Do you agree that unjust laws exist? Can you identify a law that could be said to be unjust, and then explain the moral argument against the law?

3 What are the respective benefits and difficulties with Thoreau's view that 'we should be men first, and subjects afterward' and that it's 'not desirable to cultivate a respect for the law, so much as for the right'?

4 What would Socrates' argument against Thoreau have been?

5 'Conscientious objection either to war, taxes or anything else is just a selfish refusal to accept the demands of living in society while living off its benefits.' Examine the arguments for and against this assertion.

6 How should courts respond to people who commit crimes on the grounds of conscience?

CHAPTER SUMMARY

Definitions and quotes:

■ Conscientious objectors refuse to fight wars that they disapprove of.

■ The synderesis rule, from the Greek word *synderessi*.

■ St Paul: an awareness of what is good and bad and observes it can be weak and mistaken (1 Corinthians 8:10–12).

- St Jerome: '... the spark of conscience ... with which we discern that we sin'.
- 'Conscience is thus ... the voice of our true selves which summons us ... to live productively, to develop fully and harmoniously. It is the guardian of our integrity.' (Erich Fromm)
- 'It is the reason making moral judgements or choice values.' (St Thomas Aquinas)

Conscience is the power of reason – St Thomas Aquinas (1224–1274):
- Conscience isn't an inner knowledge of right and wrong, but a device or faculty for distinguishing right from wrong actions.
- People basically tend to the good and away from evil (the 'synderesis rule').
- Conscience is 'reason making right decisions' (*Summa Theologica*, I–II, I).
- There are two parts to making moral decisions:
  - synderesis is right reason, an awareness of the moral principle to do good and avoid evil
  - conscientia distinguishes between right and wrong and makes moral decisions

Intuitive conscience – Joseph Butler (1692–1752):
- Conscience is the final moral decision-maker.
- Conscience distinguishes between approval and disapproval of human action.
- Humans are influenced by two basic principles, self-love and benevolence (love of others).
- Conscience directs us towards focusing on the happiness or interest of others and away from focusing on ourselves.
- Conscience determines and judges the rightness and wrongness of actions without introspection.
- 'Had it strength as it has right; had it power as it had manifest authority, it would absolutely govern the world.'
- Conscience is 'our natural guide, the guide assigned us by the Author of our nature'.

Conscience as guilt – Sigmund Freud (1856–1939):
- The human psyche is inspired by powerful instinctive desires which have to be satisfied.

- Children learn that the world restricts these desires.
- Humans create the ego, which takes account of the realities of the world and society.
- A 'super-ego' internalises and reflects anger and disapproval of others.
- A guilty conscience is created which grows into a life and power of its own, irrespective of the rational thought and reflection of the individual.
- The mature and healthy conscience is the ego's reflection about the best way of achieving integrity.
- The immature conscience (the super-ego) is a mass of feelings of guilt.
- The psychological account of conscience is modern, but can undermine both of the previous religious views.

Do we always obey our consciences?
- There's no objective way of measuring what some else's conscience is telling them, and why.
- We may be able to manipulate our consciences to justify our actions.
- It's possible to have a sense of knowing what one ought to do, but lack the strength or will to do it.

Is conscience a moral guide?
- Acting on your conscience is acting on your innermost convictions and involves an act of integrity.
- The Roman Catholic Church, following Aquinas, believes that conscience must first be informed.
- John Henry Newman (1801–1890) took a more intuitionist approach to conscience: 'I toast the Pope, but I toast conscience first.'

Difficulties with linking the conscience with God:
- Why do consciences sometimes conflict?
- Butler gives ultimate authority to conscience.
- Aquinas allows for a margin of error – consciences may be misled or misinformed.
- Atheists may claim that conscience is important to them.

Chapter 14

Secular ethics: egoism and humanism

Introduction

Key philosophers and works

Thomas Hobbes (1588–1679): *Leviathan*, 1651; *De Homine (On Human Nature)*, 1658

Adam Smith (1723–1790): *An Enquiry into the Nature and Causes of the Wealth of Nations*, 1776

David Hume (1711–1776): *Enquiry Concerning the Principles of Morals*, 1751 – Appendix II, 'Of Self Love'

Key terms

Altruistic, conditional egoism, ethical egoism, humanism, psychological egoism

What you will learn by the end of this chapter

- Secular arguments for morality.
- What is meant by psychological, ethical and conditional egoism.
- The strengths and weaknesses of egoism.
- What is meant by altruism and the arguments for and against it.
- What is meant by humanism.

Key questions

1 If God doesn't exist, is there any reason why we should be moral?
2 Is morality basically about putting others first?
3 Do humans invariably act out of selfish motives?
4 Is it moral to do what's in your own best interests?

Non-religious reasons for being moral

It is clear that religious believers have an obligation to uphold moral views in accordance with their religious traditions, but does the non-believer have any need for moral values? Jonathan Glover (1997, pp. 29–30) outlines the argument that general moral beliefs are needed for a number of reasons. First, he states that they are needed to avoid inconsistency. This inconsistency is illustrated by the view, held by many, that taxes should not go up but that hospitals should have more funding. To avoid this, we need to think about priorities and give each of them some value. The second reason is an argument about autonomy. It is important in our development into adulthood not simply to adopt the morals of our families or societies, but to come to our own opinion, which requires a degree of objectivity. Thirdly, we cannot always rely on intuitive responses when deciding what to do, as these may be clouded by self-interest or emotional disturbance.

In *Leviathan* (1651), Thomas Hobbes proposes a different view. Hobbes argues that humans are not naturally sociable. They construct civilised society for reasons of self-preservation. People are selfish, with a fundamental desire to take everything they can and, if possible, dominate the whole world.

Morality has come about to restrain us, so that – at night in our beds – we might not lie in fear of dying. Humankind's desire for domination is overcome by our reason, and by the realization that if we all act after our own desires, we are more likely to have a miserable time, ending with an untimely death. Given this fact, we reluctantly seek agreement with each other, making covenants to allow a mutual peace that is called the **social contract**. Humans must subject themselves in a governing contract to a supreme leader, the Leviathan, who enforces the natural law and protects everyone. This is done for entirely selfish reasons.

Alasdair MacIntyre (1966) argues that there is no anthropological or evolutionary evidence to back up Hobbes' theory that humans moved from a state of war to one of civilised society. Apes, our nearest ancestors, live in affectionate families and communities, and evidence suggests that humans have always done so (for his other arguments, see MacIntyre, 1966, pp. 135–139).

A prevailing ethical system based on self-centred thinking has developed and is called egoism, and to this we now turn.

Tasks

1 How convincing are Glover's non-religious reasons for being moral? Justify your answer.

2 Without restrictions on their freedom, are humans basically selfish and liable to violence?

What is egoism?

Morality is often viewed in terms of doing what is right irrespective of what the doer might want to do. To fail to consider the interests of others when deciding how to behave seems wrong. This altruistic view of morality is challenged by **egoism**. Reinhold Niebuhr has commented, 'The new life in Christ represents the perfection of complete and heedless self-giving which obscures the contrary impulse of self-regard. It is a moral ideal scarcely possible for the individual, and certainly not relevant to the morality of self-regarding nations.' (Niebuhr, 1965, p. 42) Egoism means putting my own interest above that of anyone else. In moral terms, such a view seems flawed. Kurt Baier (1997, p. 197) describes egoists as 'self centred, inconsiderate, unfeeling, unprincipled, ruthless self-aggrandizers, pursuers of the good things in life whatever the cost to others, people who think only about themselves or, if about others, then merely as means to their own ends'. There are three common forms of egoism: psychological egoism, conditional egoism for the common good and ethical egosim.

Psychological egoism

Psychological egoism is not a moral theory but a view of the way in which human beings work. Psychological egoists argue that all human actions are motivated by **self-interest**. We're programmed to act for ourselves. All our voluntary acts are things we want to do, which means that they are something we desire to do. If we act to satisfy our desire, our action is self-interested. Baier describes psychological egoism as a 'motivational pattern of people whose motivated behaviours is in accordance with a principle, namely, that of doing whatever and only what protects and promotes their own welfare, well being, best interest, happiness, flourishing, or greatest good, either because they are indifferent about that of others of because they always care more about their own than that of theirs when the two conflict'. (Baier, 1997, p. 198) Our actions express our dominant desires. This offers an explanation of human affairs – it is descriptive of human nature.

One argument against psychological egoism is that people act **charitably** for others. They give money to charity and do voluntary work. Members of the emergency services put their own lives in danger for the sake of others. Psychological egoism suggests that these actions are only superficially altruistic and have underlying egoistic motives. It's possible that some people give money to charity because they have a religious belief that their reward will be in heaven. Thomas Hobbes offered an egoistical explanation of charitable acts. We give to others out of a selfish desire to demonstrate our power to both look after ourselves and others (Hobbes, 1658). We may act out of pity for the situation that someone faces, but in pitying we are imagining that we may experience – in the future – the calamity that the other person is experiencing now. All apparent altruistic actions have egoistical undertones. People may think they are motivated by emotions such as anger, fear, love or compassion, but the underlying motive for human action is egoism.

Psychological egoists will admit that human beings don't always act in their own best interests as we can make mistakes. I may think that having an affair will give me great happiness, but this may prove false as my wife finds out and my family falls apart. I may be too weak willed to actually do what is needed. I know I should eat good and healthy food, but I'm tempted by those large chocolate bars that rot my teeth. Psychological egoists hold out that we do what we want to do. We fulfil our desires and those desires are selfish. They also maintain that actions which appear to be unselfish produce a sense of self-satisfaction in the person who does them. Giving to charity leaves my conscience clear when I walk past a homeless beggar on the street.

However, there are difficulties with psychological egoism. Joseph Butler noted that we may not want to do a certain thing, but that we choose to do it because the end is what we desire. Actions aren't born solely out of desire, but out of the ends that we seek. Even if all voluntary action is motivated by desire, that doesn't mean that it's self-interested. It is because someone is unselfish that he or she has the desire to give. The claim that charitable acts ease our guilty conscience is also flawed. Unselfish people derive satisfaction from acting for others. A selfish person wouldn't have a conscience in need of clearing. The conscience is evidence of selflessness. James Rachels observes that selfishness and self-interest aren't the same. It is in my interest to see a doctor when I feel sick, but this isn't being selfish. I'm being selfish when I refuse to allow my younger brother to have a go on my new computer game. A final critical difficulty lies with the fact that the essential claims of psychological egoism are no more than claims. While we may be able to suggest possible selfish motives for all altruistic acts, this doesn't provide proof, only potential explanations. Psychological egoism claims to know human motivation, but it can't provide factual evidence to back up such claims (see Baier, 1997, p. 199; Rachels, 1986, pp. 72–74).

Conditional egoism for the common good

Conditional egoism for the common good is an entrepreneurial form of the theory that maintains that entrepreneurs should be free to maximise their profit in business if the by-products of their success benefit the whole community.

This form of egoism is found in Adam Smith's *An Enquiry into the Nature and Causes of the Wealth of Nations* (1776). Smith, a great entrepreneur of the eighteenth century, argued for egoism as a practical ideal that benefits others. He believed that by granting entrepreneurs freedom to promote their own business interests and so maximise their profit, community benefits would be produced as by-products. He wrote: 'It is not from the benevolence of the butcher, the brewer, or the baker, that we expect our dinner, but from their regard to their own interest. We address ourselves, not to their humanity but to their self-love, and never talk to them of our own necessities but of their advantages.' (Smith, 1776, I.ii.2.) If I'm allowed the freedom to build up a strong business without being bound up by government red tape, the success of my business will lead to my employees having job security and guaranteed income which, in turn, will benefit the community, as their wages can support families and be spent in other businesses throughout the community. Allowing the entrepreneur to pursue his or own interests and succeed in business leads to a greater good for the community.

Conditional egoism is criticised because it offers no guarantee that trickle-down benefits would distribute themselves equally among the members of the community. My company may do well and some employees may benefit from my work, but this doesn't necessarily mean that all of them will – and it's far from clear whether their wage packets will ultimately help those not connected to my company. Baier (1997, p. 203) expresses doubts as to whether the common good would be reached by way of such an economic situation. It has not been demonstrated that unbridled capitalism leads to the improvement of the common good.

Ethical egoism

Ethical egoism is a theory, rather than a psychological pattern of behaviour. We tend to assume that morality requires us to act for the good of others. The boy scout sees an old man trying to cross the road and so helps the old man, because it's for the good of the old man to be helped in this way. Ethical egoism challenges this claim. Perhaps morality can be seen as doing things that are a means of our own self-fulfilment. For ethical egoists, moral actions are those that benefit the agent. In his work *Leviathan* (1651, Chapter 15), Thomas Hobbes argues that a moral principle is only acceptable if, by complying with it, the agent aims at his own greatest good. An action that doesn't lead me to my own greatest good is immoral. The only moral actions are those that suit my overall personal interests.

The writer William K. Frankena identifies two principles in ethical egoism. First, our basic and only obligation is to promote the greatest good over evil – which we can do. Secondly, when making judgements about others we should go by what is in our own best interest (Frankena, 1963, pp. 16–17). In his book *Ethics, Inventing Right and Wrong* (1977, p. 173), J. L. Mackie notes that egoism is a desirable moral principle. While this may seem to go against the grain of traditional morality, it seems reasonable to assume that it's right and proper for people to pursue what is in their own well-being.

Ultimately, however, Frankena doubts that ethical egoism is an acceptable form of morality. He gives an example of someone asking a friend for business advice. The principles of ethical egoism demand that the friend should advise what is in his own best interest, not what's best for the person asking for advice. Frankena believes this attitude is morally untenable (Frankena, 1963, p. 18).

In *Enquiry Concerning the Principles of Morals* (1751; Appendix II, 'Of Self Love'), David Hume argued that it is moral sentiment and feelings that engage us in concern and motivation for others. Love, friendship, compassion and gratitude play crucial roles in our behaviour. We're influenced by these feelings and we act on them. Psychological egoism fails to account for this fundamental element of human behaviour. Hume also criticises the attempts to reduce human motivation to a single cause – our own self-interest. This reduction is simplistic, as it doesn't consider the variety of complex motivations that affect human behaviour. If I help someone across the road, it may be because I have a sense of duty which I desire to be fulfilled. I may also have memories of my own grandparents, which stir feelings for the elderly in general. I may be thinking subconsciously about my own future old age, and be hopeful that I'll have such help from the young when I reach it. I may have heard about an accident on this road recently, which fuels concern for pedestrians on the crossing. A single cause belies that complexity, which involves fears, memories, experiences and beliefs.

Hume also points out that it's by no means clear that human desire is something that is in our interest to satisfy. My desire for food and water is in my own interest. My desire for large chocolate bars, cigarettes, alcohol and illegal substances may well be against my own best interests. I may have negative predispositions towards vanity, fame or vengeance that transcends any benefit they may bring. My desire to satisfy these predispositions might even be self-destructive (Hume, 1751).

Joseph Butler (*Fifteen Sermons*, 1726) argued that the motive of self-interest would have nothing to aim for unless the person had other motives to aim for. If you donate money to famine relief to alleviate starvation, your desire is that you don't want people to starve, not that you want to donate money. I have sympathetic concern for my friends' troubles for their interest, not mine. If we recognise that others are instrumental to our own satisfaction, and then we promote our own interests to an extent that doesn't diminish theirs, then we have made the first step to **altruism**. Altruism itself goes further, by saying that we should actively seek the advancement of the good of others.

Tasks

1 Suggest possible desires which, if pursued, wouldn't be in our self-interest.

2 Drinking water is in my self-interest. Bullying a younger pupil is selfish. Give other examples that demonstrate the difference between self interest and selfishness and try to explain what that difference is.

3 How could it be argued that it's in our own self-interest not to be selfish?

Christian altruism

Self-love has been seen by Judeo-Christian tradition as the basis for immorality. The Christian ethic stresses the claim of the other, and teaches that true selfhood can be gained only by a willingness to lose oneself. This is exemplified in Jesus' sacrifice for the good of humanity. The importance of the denial of self is also important to Buddhism, which maintains that enlightenment can't be attained without the denial of self. However, the commandment 'Love your neighbour as yourself' sheds light on a more complex Christian ethic present in the Scripture. This is related to the dignity of all human beings and maintains the paramount importance of the dignity of the human being (including the self), since to ignore it would be to the detriment of the human person and human life, the gift from God. Here, it's important to recognise that selfishness isn't the same as self-interest, and that the confusion of these two ideas causes many problems in the debates that surround egoism. If my actions don't take account of the detrimental effects that they have on others, then they are selfish. Self-interested actions might ensure that my personal integrity and dignity is affirmed, but this doesn't equate to selfishness. A Christian has a self-interest in this respect, but that doesn't prevent altruistic behaviour that maximises the good of others.

Humanism

While maintaining that morality exists, **humanists** reject both a divine basis for morality and Hobbes' idea that human beings are inherently wicked. They base their ethics on reason and common humanity (British Humanist Association, 2003a). Moral values are founded on human nature and experience alone, not a divine set of commands. Humanists believe that we should pursue happiness and the happiness of others: according to the nineteenth-century American humanist Robert G. Ingersoll, '... happiness is the only good; ... the time to be happy is now, and the way to be happy is to make others so' (Ingersoll, 1876). Humanists do not believe in a God who gives us moral codes; nor do they believe in an afterlife, in which the good will go to heaven and the bad to hell. Humanists believe that choice and freedom contribute to human happiness, so that human freedom is important, although they do believe in making responsible choices: 'They do not believe that basic moral principles are simply matters of personal preference or that they can vary much from place to place or time to time – humanists are not relativists' (British Humanist Association, 2003).

Humanists use a number of elements of theories to make moral decisions, looking at consequences, rights and wishes on the basis of reason, observation and respect for others. Humanists do not believe that moral values are dependent on religion but, instead, that they are found in human nature, experience and society. Communities develop shared values, as expressed in documents such as the Universal Declaration of Human Rights and, in making moral decisions, utilise principles such as 'Treat others as you would like to be treated'. Humanists do not all agree about different ethical issues, although they draw on a common corpus of secular, or secularised, principles and theories.

Questions

1 Outline a justified case to back up Hobbes' reasons for moral behaviour.

2 Identify possible sources of evidence to support the distinct forms of egoism.

3 Evaluate the arguments for and against the non-religious justifications for ethics.

4 Why is the concept of human rights important for humanism?

Non-religious reasons for morality:

- General moral beliefs are needed to avoid inconsistency, for our development into autonomous adults and to avoid inadvisable intuitive responses.
- In *Leviathan*, Thomas Hobbes argues that humans are not naturally sociable, but construct civilised society for reasons of self-preservation.
- Morality is needed to restrain us, so that – at night in our beds – we might not lie in fear of dying.
- Humans make a social contract that restricts their freedom, to allow a mutual peace.
- MacIntyre argues that there is no evidence to support Hobbes' theory that humans moved from a state of war to one of civilised society.

Egoism:

- Egoists are 'self centred, inconsiderate, unfeeling, unprincipled, ruthless self-aggrandizers, pursuers of the good things in life whatever the cost to others, people who think only about themselves or, if about others, then merely as means to their own ends.' (Kurt Baier)

Psychological egoism:

- It's a view of the way in which human beings work. The underlying motive for human action is egoism.
- Human actions, including ones that we think are altruistic, are motivated by self-interest.
- We may not want to do a certain thing, but we choose to do it because the end is what we desire.
- Actions are not born solely out of desire, but out of the ends that we seek.
- Even if all voluntary action is motivated by desire, that doesn't mean that it's self-interested. It's because someone is unselfish that he or she has the desire to give.
- Conscience is evidence of selflessness.
- Selfishness and self-interest aren't the same. It's in my interest to see a doctor when I feel sick, but this isn't being selfish. I'm being selfish when I refuse to allow my younger brother have a go on my new computer game.

Conditional egoism for the common good:

- It's an entrepreneurial form of the theory that maintains that entrepreneurs should be free to maximise profit in business if the by-products benefit the whole community (Adam Smith).
- Conditional egoism is criticised because it offers no guarantee that trickle-down benefits would distribute themselves equally among the members of the community.
- It's uncertain whether the common good would be reached in this way, and it hasn't been demonstrated economically.

Ethical egoism:

- Moral actions are those that benefit the agent (Thomas Hobbes).
- When making judgements about others, we should go by what is in our own best interest.
- It seems reasonable to assume that it's right and proper for people to pursue what's in their own well-being.

Criticisms:

- Moral sentiment and feelings engage us in concern and motivation for others (David Hume).
- Love, friendship, compassion and gratitude play crucial roles in our behavior.
- Human motivation can't be reduced to a single cause – our own self-interest. What about duty, upbringing, and so on?
- Desires can be self-destructive.

Christian altruism:

- Self-love is traditionally seen as immoral.
- Christianity promotes selflessness.
- Buddhism advocates the denial of self, for enlightenment.

Humanism:

- Humanists reject a divine basis for morality and base their ethics on reason and common humanity.
- Moral values are founded on human nature and experience.
- '… happiness is the only good; … the time to be happy is now, and the way to be happy is to make others so.' (Robert G. Ingersoll)

- Choice and freedom contribute to human happiness, so human freedom is important.
- 'They do not believe that basic moral principles are simply matters of personal preference or that they can vary much from place to place or time to time – humanists are not relativists.' (British Humanist Association)
- When making moral decisions, humanists consider consequences, rights and wishes, based on reason, observation and respect for others.
- Communities develop shared values, such as the Universal Declaration of Human Rights.

Part III

Ethical Issues

This final part considers a number of ethical issues of contemporary importance. Personal, medical, social and global issues related to ethics are considered. In many cases, discussions link back to ideas examined in Parts I and II.

Chapter 15

Sexual ethics and homosexuality

Introduction

Key terms

Affective and sexual complementarity, celibacy, contractarian, dualism, feminism, fidelity (*fides*), harm principle, homosexual inclination, libertarian, procreation (*proles*), sexual ethics, taboos, union (*sacramentum*)

What you will learn by the end of this chapter

- Ancient and modern views of sexual ethics.
- Natural law and biblical approaches to sexual ethics.
- Libertarian and feminist approaches to sexual ethics.
- Biblical, Catholic and liberal approaches to homosexuality.
- The strengths and weaknesses of these theories.

Key questions

1 What's the purpose of sex?
2 Is any sexual activity between adults acceptable if they consent?
3 On what basis might a sexual act be regarded as wrong?

What is sexual ethics?

Sexual ethics encompasses a wide variety of issues ranging from abortion and contraception to homosexuality, bisexuality and transexuality, marriage, cohabitation, masturbation, sexual acts, rape, prostitution, sex with animals, and pornography. Much of the debate about sexual ethics is related to and informed by religion, and this chapter considers religious views of sexuality in general and a study of homosexuality.

Three ancient views of sex

Pythagoreans and Stoics

The ancient Greek philosopher Pythagoras believed that humans should abstain from the physical, and live a quiet contemplative life. Pythagoreans believed that their souls were imprisoned in the body and that they had to free them to move to a new life form. The physical obstructs the soul's progress. Because sex inhibits this progress, it isn't holy. This division of the world between the physical and the spiritual is called **dualism**. The ancient Greek Stoics took a similar line and regarded with disapproval the sense of loss of control and animal instinct involved in sexual excitement and orgasm.

Cyrenaics

The Cyrenaics, established by Aristippus (fifth century BCE), were a group who celebrated physical pleasure and led a life of sensual enjoyment. They saw immediate physical pleasures as the supreme good and pursued them.

Ancient Hebrews

The ancient Israelites had a more positive attitude to sex and reproduction. This is seen in the Song of Songs, in which a couple express the sensual erotic beauty that they see in each other. There were also certain rules that recognised the importance of sex in marriage. Newly married men were excused from military service for one year to allow the couple to enjoy each other.

The context of sexual ethics

Today, sexual pleasure is often presented as a holy grail, pursued purely for its immediate physical satisfaction. This egoistical attitude observes that, with mutual consent, any form of sex is morally right. Monogamy and commitment beyond the moment are not required. Sex is an activity negotiated between the relevant parties and, as such, it falls outside religious teachings or absolute moral laws – beyond those described above – and marriage isn't a prerequisite. The freedom of the individual is paramount.

The paradox in contemporary Western culture is apparent in the rising concern over sexual crimes, rising teenage pregnancy rates and the proliferation of sexually transmitted diseases, most notably HIV and AIDS. People differ in their views over the nature of sex education in schools and when it should be taught, as well as the availability and nature of pornography. Some see the decay in Christian values as undermining the family and creating a social disaster, with more abortions than ever before and more children living in poverty as a result of marital breakdown. Others see those values as preventing the realisation of their true sexual identity. This chapter considers three approaches to sexual ethics: Christian, libertarian and feminist.

Christian approaches to sexuality

Christian attitudes to sex and marriage are influenced by the ancient cultures into and out of which the religion was born. Christian writers sometimes portrayed sex in a negative light – as with St Augustine who considered sex to be a sin, except for reproduction. Aquinas held a more positive view of the enjoyment of sex, although he still retained the link that sex had to be connected to reproduction.

Early Hebrew law regarded marriage as a purchase and assigned women the lowly status of the husband's property. The wife could not own or inherit property herself and divorce was a right that only men could exercise. This patriarchal approach has been rejected by a modern view of marriage, which sees men and women as equal in the relationship – although, in practice, this equality isn't evident in all marriages. Patriarchal views of the subservience of women and their role as principally for the raising of children are present in certain Christian communities, particularly fundamentalist evangelicals. The same is true of many other religious communities that are rooted in cultures that haven't experienced a process of the emancipation of women into society.

As with the Stoics and Pythagoreans, early Christians raised the status of celibacy as one that was more holy. Jesus didn't marry, although He did have a positive view of marriage. St Paul is notable for his negative view of sex, recommending celibacy in 1 Corinthians 7:25–40 in the light of the imminent end of the world. However, he acknowledges that celibacy is a special gift that is not for all, and he warns that it's better to be married than to commit sin and risk damnation. Almost all Christian monastic communities have been celibate and the Roman Catholic Church advocates celibacy for its priests, while Protestant denominations do not. Martin Luther left the monastery and married, while Erasmus praised marriage as the natural state and thought of celibacy as an unnatural state. He argued that marital sexuality was in part for the purpose of pleasure rather than reproduction alone.

Today, marriage is seen as the norm for lay people. Most Churches hold that sex outside marriage, adultery, masturbation and homosexual sex are all sinful. They come to those conclusions either from a scriptural standpoint – New Testament statements about marriage or sex forming the basis of moral judgements – or from a natural law standpoint, which uses Aquinas' theory to make judgements about the purpose of human beings, and from that to determine which sexual activities fit such a purpose and which don't.

Christianity saw the purpose of marriage as fidelity (*fides*) to one another, procreation (*proles*) and union of the parties (*sacramentum*). Christian ethics have focused on the purpose of sex as the key feature for making judgements on particular actions. There were two ways of establishing the purpose. One was to use sacred Scripture, and the other natural law. The Bible was interpreted as suggesting that sex was for having children – in Genesis, the Lord sent man forth to multiply, and that matched the view ascribed to by natural law. The proponents of natural law (most clearly expounded by Thomas Aquinas) believed that by identifying what the function of the human being was, he could see what should and should not be done. Sex led to reproduction, and so that was the purpose of the sexual organs. They should not be used for anything else other than reproduction, and contraception was forbidden as preventing God's purpose. Sexual activities that didn't lead to the birth of children, including masturbation, anal sex and oral sex, were also forbidden. Today, the use of artificial contraception is prohibited by the Roman Catholic Church, as it prevents God's purpose from taking place. As children require a stable environment, marriage is necessary. Extra-marital

Ethical issues

and pre-marital sex undermine the family, and risk bringing children into an insecure environment.

More recently, a greater emphasis has been given to the unitive element. Until the twentieth century, there was no link between sex and love in Christian theology. During the twentieth century, the Churches moved to develop an understanding of sex that is rooted in love. A number of documents illustrate the recognition of sex as a uniting, bonding, healing and affirming feature between a married couple. In its document *Marriage and the Church's Task* (1978), the Church of England notes that:

> ... The commitment is made in love for love.... It is a profound sharing of present experience. As such, it also anticipates the sharing of future experience. It is a commitment through time. It embraces the future as well as the present. It intends and promises permanence ... The polyphony of love finds expression in the lovers' bodily union. This is not to be comprehended simply in terms of the two individual's experiences of ecstatic pleasure. Such it certainly may be; but it is always more. It is an act of personal commitment which spans past, present and future. It is celebration, healing, renewal, pledge and future. Above all it communicates the affirmation of mutual belonging ... [Marriage] is a relational bond of personal love, a compound of commitment, experience and response, in which the commitment clothes itself in the flesh and blood of a living union.
>
> Church of England (1978), pp. 87, 88, 89 and 99

Similarly, the Roman Catholic Church has stated:

> This love is uniquely expressed and perfected through the marital act. The actions within marriage by which the couple are united ultimately and chastely are noble and worthy ones ... these actions signify and promote the mutual self-giving by which spouses enrich each other with a joyful and thankful will.
>
> *Pastoral Constitution*, Part 2, Chapter 1

Jack Dominion, the Catholic psychologist, has studied marriage and sexuality in detail and believes that a new definition or description of sex is needed. Taking these recent expressions from the Churches and developing them to take account of contemporary psychology, he writes in his book *Passionate and Compassionate Love* (1991, pp. 94–95) that sex is a personal expression. It communicates recognition and appreciation between the partners, it confirms the sexual identity of man and woman completely, it brings couples reconciliation and healing after dispute and hurt, it celebrates life and provides profound meaning, and it's a profound way of thanking each other for the loving partnership that they have. The sexual act is a model of total unity between the two people, which reflects the idea of sex in Genesis, restated by Jesus and St Paul. Jack Dominion separates children from this personal expression of love. The personal expression found in sex is present with or without the life-giving dimension.

Formally, Catholic Christianity maintains that the life-giving dimension of each act of sex is a primary function and, within the same documents as those quoted above, the Roman Catholic Church restates the traditional view: '... the true practice of conjugal love, and the whole meaning of family life which results from it, have this aim; that the couple be ready with stout hearts to cooperate with the love of the Creator and the Saviour, who through them will enlarge and enrich his own family day by day' (*Pastoral Constitution*, Part 2, Chapter 1).

Jack Dominion believes that Christianity has made a fundamental error by stressing the biological aspect of sex, and that this has had the effect of trivialising the act of sex. Until the twentieth century, there was no attempt to differentiate between sex as a biological act and making love as a personal expression.

The Catholic, Protestant and Orthodox Churches continue to maintain that sex is a practise exclusively for those who are committed to permanent loving relationships. However, among teenagers it is now far more common, in part due to the availability of more reliable contraception and more couples are living together before marrying. Such relationships have been traditionally referred to as 'living in sin'. Jack Dominion has observed that where the relationship is committed, loving and permanent, the criteria are met and, arguably, the lifestyle is morally acceptable by traditional Christian standards (Dominion, 1991, pp. 214–216) – although mainstream Churches reject this view.

The libertarian approach to sexuality

'Sex' is one of the most searched-for words on the Internet, and it finds itself on the cover of many magazines. It isn't unreasonable to say that the people of the twenty-first century are obsessed with sex. The ethic that underlies this presentation of sex is a libertarian one. This is the view that sex is morally permissible if there's mutual agreement or consent between the participating parties. This view is sometimes known as a **contractarian** view. There's no need to link sex either to marriage or, specifically, to reproduction, because there's no special traditional or religious view of the function of sex. Human freedom and autonomy are the most important principles or values.

Libertarianism does not allow for sexual crimes such as rape, as they go against the freedom principle – the rape victim is forced to have sex against his or her will. Libertarianism does not allow for sex with minors (children), as they can't be truly said to have free will – they don't have the ability to give informed consent. Sex involving any form of deception is also out of the question, as free choices can't be made if one party is kept in ignorance of issues that might be of importance.

Libertarians may also adopt the '**harm principle**' in their approach to sexuality. To observe the harm principle is to ensure that no harm is done to either party or to other third parties. This is an extension of the libertarian view of freedom. I'm allowed as much freedom as possible, without infringing other people's right to freedom, including freedom from harm. I may choose to do as I freely please, but if my actions impinge the freedom of another through the effects that they have on another, then my actions are called into question. If I like you and you like me, and we both want to have sex, then we can as long as we don't harm each other or anyone else. If the sex is adulterous and the betrayed spouse finds out and is harmed, then the act is called into question.

In the libertarian view, what is done in sex is again up to the individuals. There are no restrictions on the kind of sexual activity, no requirement to avoid sexual acts that don't lead to reproduction and so no prohibition of the use of contraception.

There are a number of advantages of the libertarian approach to sexuality. The view celebrates sexual liberation. It allows consenting adults to do as they please. Freedom is a basic principle that is highly regarded in today's society, particularly after centuries in which patriarchal traditions gave women subservient roles in marriage, and religion prescribed and enforced moral laws, such as the prohibition of homosexual sex. Libertarianism seems more tolerant and permissive of different sexual activities and lifestyles.

One weakness with libertarian approaches to sexuality regards free consent. It may be argued that adults can make free choices about sex, but what happens when there's an imbalance within the relationship? Consider the boss who makes unwanted advances to the secretary. Quitting the job may not help, as money is needed for dependents – and any reference written by the harasser may well be prejudiced. True freedom may not be present in relationships in which power isn't equally distributed between the parties. In his article 'Sex' (1991), Raymond Belliotti tells us about Rocco, a poor but honest barber's son who has a family in desperate need of money. His neighbour Vito has an unusual hobby of collecting peoples' middle fingers in exchange for $5000 and private medical care. Rocco agrees to have his middle finger chopped off and gets the money in return. Belliotti comments that Rocco's finger is treated as a commodity. He notes that although Rocco agreed to the procedure, there seems to be an important moral dimension that libertarianism can't account for (pp. 320–321).

Feminist approaches to sexuality

Feminists criticise both the traditional Christian approaches to sexuality and the liberal ones. Christian approaches rest on a defined cultural role for women, that of the child-bearer, wife and submissive companion. Implicit in the Christian approach is the Hebrew view of women as being created for the man, the property of the man, and in all senses secondary to the man. The defined socially constructed role of mother and wife effectively disempowers women by restricting their status in society and socialising them to meet the desires of men. Christianity relies on natural law – but this is the product of social conditioning, not nature. The result of this cultural background has been to give women a secondary role in society. The Hebrew and Greek view of women has meant that for hundreds of years they have had little access to politics or wealth, and very little free choice. This situation has affected sexual relationships. Sexual behaviour assumes male dominance and female submission. Most sexual crimes are committed against women. Marriage laws have only recently given equal status to women. Ultra Orthodox Jews today maintain that a divorce is only possible if the husband issues the 'Get' (the contract of divorce) and many women have found themselves locked into marriages, leaving them unable to remarry in the Faith. In some Protestant Christian Churches, the role of women is limited to that of home-maker and child-raiser.

Liberal approaches to sexuality are criticised by feminists because they assume a level playing field. They assume that men and women are in a position to enter freely into a sexual relationship. In a society that is patriarchal, that freedom is questionable. Just as there's an immorality in Rocco having to cut off his finger, so feminists argue that there's an immorality if a women has sex in the setting of an imbalanced social status or a culturally defined role. Women may be so conditioned that they are not even aware of their disempowered status.

Some feminists, such as Catharine Mackinnon (1987), argue that sexuality must be re-imagined and remade before moral sexual relationships become possible. Until this is done, sexual activity will be immoral. More extreme feminists, such as Jill Johnston (1974), argue for separation of men and women and for sex among women, as a political statement to undermine the domination and power of men.

Raymond Bellioti rejects the feminist idea that women are incapable of deciding for themselves. If women are indeed too socially conditioned to freely enter into relationships, then this is a justification for paternalism. Secondly, he doesn't see a problem with a women accepting a socially defined role if she chooses it. Thirdly, he challenges the assumption that sexuality is fundamental to the human person, and therefore as significant as feminists argue (Belliotti, 1991, pp. 324–325).

1 Consider how natural law, libertarianism and feminism might evaluate following sexual activities: masturbation, sex before marriage, adultery and contraception.

2 In your view, which provides the most convincing assessment, and why?

Christianity and homosexuality

In Western society – and in the UK in particular – there's a growing assumption that there's no moral issue about same-sex relationships beyond the issues that apply to heterosexual relationships. Nevertheless, there is still a stigma attached to homosexuality and there are strongly held views that it's immoral. The recent nail-bombing of a gay bar in London's Soho district illustrates the extent of the hostility felt by some towards the homosexual community. In the early part of the twentieth century, homosexual acts were crimes, and homosexuality was considered a mental illness for which appalling treatments were proposed. In medieval times, homosexuals were burnt at the stake.

Since the Wolfenden Report in 1957, and its recommendations for the Sexual Offences Act of 1957, there have been no criminal sanctions for consenting adults in private, who have reached the age of consent. Certain issues – such as adoption, sex education and the age of consent itself – still raise concern among the public, and discrimination in these areas is endorsed by the British government. For many gay men and women, the legal attitude and social stigma attached to homosexuality reflect the underlying cultural prejudice against homosexuality found in the Judeo-Christian tradition.

Christians have viewed homosexuality as wrong on many levels. There's no possibility of life arising from the sexual union, and so it's wrong on a natural law basis. Same-sex marriages haven't been permitted and so any kind of homosexual sex has taken place outside marriage which is sinful, along with all other forms of sex outside marriage. Finally, there are the specific scriptural sources that have implied a divine command against homosexuality. Church denominations differ somewhat in their views on homosexuality, and within Churches there are divisions.

The Bible and homosexuality

The Bible sees homosexual acts as freely chosen and is predominantly concerned with male behaviour only. In Leviticus we find 'You shall not lie with a man as with a women: that is an abomination' (Leviticus 18:22) and it's punishable by death (Leviticus 20:13). Deuteronomy 23:17–18 prohibits temple prostitution, and in Genesis 19:4–11, God destroys Sodom. This story is interpreted as showing God's displeasure with Sodom as resulting from His displeasure with homosexuality.

Many Christians look to Genesis 2:24, which says 'For this reason a man will leave his father and mother and be united to his wife, and they will become one flesh'. This is understood by many Christians as a definition of human relationships in heterosexual terms and is quoted by Jesus in the New Testament (Matthew 19:5 and Mark 10:7) and by St Paul (Ephesians 5:31).

In addition to these texts, St Paul's letters have influenced Christian teaching. In Romans 1:21–31, St Paul describes people engaging in same-sex sexual acts as 'dishonouring their bodies' and having 'unnatural relations' and he writes about 'men committing shameless acts with men'. In 1 Corinthians 6:9–11, a list of unrighteous kinds of people includes the words *malakoi* and *arsenokoitai*, which have been translated as 'male prostitute' and 'sodomite'.

These biblical texts have been used as a basis for the condemnation of homosexuality and homosexual acts in particular. God commands that it's wrong and so to behave in that way is sinful. There has also been a tendency to see homosexuality almost as a medical condition, to which sympathy should be given and for which a cure should possibly be found.

The Protestant Churches have a biblical basis for their teaching on homosexuality, which leads them to condemn the activity. The worldwide Anglican community has debated the issue of gay priests and gay marriage and commented that the ordinations of 'practicing homosexuals and the blessing of same sex unions call into question the authority of Holy Scripture'. In its *Book of Discipline* (1996), the United Methodist Church instructs that 'Homosexual persons are no less than heterosexual persons are individuals of sacred worth ... Although we do not condone the practice of homosexuality and consider this practice incompatible with Christian teaching ...'.

Critics of this approach don't accept that Scripture can be interpreted and applied in this way. John Boswell (1982) notes that other rules from similar texts are not so emphatically enforced. The Bible condemns hypocrisy and greed, but no one died at the stake in medieval times for these offences, while homosexuals perished. In *The Body in Context: Sex and Catholicism* (1992), Gareth Moore writes that while Christians are happy to follow the law set out in Leviticus, which says that it's immoral for a man to lie with a man, they reject the passage later on that advocates beheading as a punishment. Christians don't follow the requirement in Leviticus 19:19 that forbids the wearing of garments made of two kinds of material. Moore argues that we're ignoring the laws that we find inconvenient while pursuing those that attack minorities that we don't like (Moore, 1992, pp. 184–186). In other words, Scripture is being used inconsistently to reinforce prejudices. The story of Sodom and Gomorrah concerns a failure to meet the obligation of hospitality, rather than denouncing homosexuality (p. 191).

Gareth Moore also argues that St Paul's criticism of homosexual life comes from his assertion that the homosexual lifestyle is a product of a godless people. While that may have been St Paul's perception in the first century AD, the existence today of pious homosexual Christians doesn't fit his reason. Peter Vardy (1997, pp. 207–208) has noted that St Paul's notion that homosexual acts are against nature, as they are impure acts, seems to contradict the general rejection of the Jewish view of impurity found elsewhere in the New Testament. The text in 1 Corinthians 6:9–10 which purportedly describes homosexuals as unrighteous people is disputed by John Boswell. While later Christian writers translate these words as referring to homosexuals, Paul's meaning isn't clear, because the meanings of the words in first-century Greek are doubtful. The absence of specific teachings from the Gospels on the matter leave it open to interpretation.

The different approaches to Biblical interpretation have led to a fundamental divide in the Anglican Communion. In 2003, in the USA, the New Hampshire diocese chose as bishop an openly gay man, Gene Robinson, who lives with his partner. This act led to a crisis meeting of Anglican archbishops and many statements to the media that such a move could cause a split in the Communion.

The Roman Catholic Church and homosexuality

The Roman Catholic Church's teachings on homosexuality are summarised in the Catechism of the Catholic Church (paragraphs 2357–2359). The Church maintains that there's no sin involved in an **inclination** towards a member of the same sex, as such an inclination isn't freely chosen and is a trial for the person. The homosexual person should be treated with respect, compassion and sensitivity, and unjust discrimination should be avoided. The Church teaches that such people are called to chastity with the help of friendship, prayer and grace to achieve Christian perfection.

However, the Church maintains that homosexual acts don't proceed from a genuine affective and sexual **complementarity** (Catechism of the Catholic Church, paragraph 2357). The acts are sinful because of the biblical condemnation of homosexual acts as depraved and intrinsically disordered (Congregation for the Doctrine of the Faith, *Persona Humana*, 8) and the natural law ethic, which notes that no life can come from the acts. Thomas Aquinas' natural law theory advocates or prohibits actions depending on whether they advance or inhibit their purpose. Sex that doesn't allow for reproduction is unnatural and wrong, and so homosexual sex is wrong. The function of sex is either fully or partly to do with reproduction, and any sexual activity that doesn't allow for reproduction is immoral. Natural law passes no comment on homosexual inclinations, because they aren't freely chosen and are not actions. It's the actions themselves that are sinful.

There are difficulties with the natural law approach to homosexuality. It's arguable that the unitive act between a loving couple is a good enough purpose for sex, despite being non-reproductive. Many sexual acts – such as sex in the non-fertile part of the menstrual cycle, sex after the menopause, sex when one or both partners are infertile, and sex when the woman is pregnant – can't lead to reproduction. If we reject the reproductive imperative in sex, then natural law no longer opposes homosexual sex. In his article 'Homosexuality, morals, and the law of nature' (1997, pp. 250–251), Burton M. Leiser notes that a screwdriver can be used for a number of purposes, such as popping the cap of a bottle. Sexual organs are suited for reproduction and for the production of intense pleasure in oneself and others. Leiser argues that if the purpose of sexual organs is reproduction, then marriage between elderly couples who can't have children is unnatural. To condemn people for using their sexual organs for their own pleasure reveals the prejudices and irrational taboos of our society.

In their book *Catholics and Sex* (1992), Kate Saunders and Peter Stamford cite views of some Catholic cardinals about homosexuals which may fuel intolerance. In 1991, the Polish primate Cardinal Glemp referred to homosexuals as 'backyard mongrels', while Cardinal Razinger, of the Congregation of the Doctrine of the Faith, has written that 'the practice of homosexuality may seriously threaten the lives and well-being of a large number of people' (see Saunders and Stamford, 1992, p. 79). While the Church advocates tolerance and understanding, it approves discrimination against homosexuals in matters such as adoption and teaching. Arcigay, an Italian gay rights group, has linked the Church's teaching with violent expressions of intolerance. Arcigay estimates that, each year, between 150 and 200 gay men are murdered in Italy because of their sexual orientation (see http://www.religioustolerance.org).

Liberal Christian support for homosexuality

Liberal Christian writers challenge the traditional condemnation of homosexuality. They maintain that the quality of the relationship – be it heterosexual or homosexual – is what determines its moral value. The biblical basis for Christian opposition to homosexuality is disputable, and the natural law approach to Christian ethics is unsound. Liberal Christians draw on the teaching that all are made 'in the image and likeness of God'. If God creates men and women as homosexuals, then that nature and inclination must be good. Otherwise, it would suggest that God intentionally creates disordered human beings.

In his book *The Body in Context: Sex and Catholicism* (1992), Gareth Moore argues that there's a Christian basis for an inclusive attitude towards homosexuals, because Christianity is a religion that positively seeks to make room for the marginalised and outcasts in society (see 1 Corinthians 1:26–28).

On the website http://www.religioustolerance.org, B. A. Robinson notes that liberal Christians within the Methodist Church consider gay and lesbian ordination and same-sex marriage as **civil rights** issues. If human rights are for all, then ordination and marriage should be available to gay people as well as heterosexuals. They maintain that homosexuality is normal and natural, and isn't changeable or freely chosen. Recent debates within the Church of England have identified bishops who are, or have been, homosexual and there's a clear move by some to change the traditional teaching.

To produce a Christian ethic that regards homosexual lifestyles as positive and good requires a considerable re-evaluation of Scripture and a change in the assumptions about natural law. It's questionable whether a religion rooted in the heterosexual Hebrew culture, which saw man and woman as made for union with each other, can ever adequately incorporate homosexual marriage and lifestyle. However, Christianity has been able to reject its approval of slavery and its endorsement of female subservience – ideas that also have their roots in ancient Hebrew culture – so perhaps the view on homosexuality can change too.

Questions

1 What objections do some Christians have to homosexual sex?

2 What are the criticisms of the traditional Christian natural law and biblical approaches, and how convincing do you think they are?

3 Describe the ethical approaches to sexual ethics. What are their strengths and weaknesses?

CHAPTER SUMMARY

Ancient views of sex:

■ Pythagoreans and Stoics believed that humans should abstain from the physical, and live a quiet contemplative life to free them to move to a new life form.

- Cyrenaics celebrated physical pleasure as the supreme good and led a life of sensual enjoyment.
- Ancient Hebrews had a positive attitude to sex and reproduction.

Today:
- Sexual pleasure is often pursued in egoistical way – freedom of the individual is paramount.
- There are concerns over sexual crimes, rising teenage pregnancy rates and the proliferation of sexually transmitted diseases, most notably HIV and AIDS.

Christian approaches to sexuality:
- Christian writers sometimes portrayed sex in a negative light – as with St Augustine, who considered sex to be a sin except for reproduction.
- There was a patriarchal emphasis in early Hebrew law.
- Early Christians raised the status of celibacy as one that was more holy (monastic and priestly lifestyles).
- For lay people today, sex outside marriage, adultery, masturbation and homosexual sex are all sinful.
- The biblical and natural law purpose of marriage is fidelity, procreation and union – sexual acts are judged in terms of whether they meet this purpose.
- Recently, a greater emphasis has been given to the unitive love element over the reproductive emphasis.
- Christian Churches maintain that sex is exclusively for those committed to permanent loving relationships.

The libertarian approach to sexuality:
- Sex is morally permissible if there's mutual agreement or consent between the participating parties (contractarian).
- Human freedom and autonomy are the most important principles.
- Libertarianism does not allow for sexual crimes which go against freedom from harm.
- This view celebrates sexual liberation, is tolerant and permissive.
- Adults can make free choices about sex, but an imbalance within the relationship may threaten the freedom.

Feminist approaches to sexuality:

- Feminists criticise the traditional Christian approaches to sexuality, because there's a defined submissive cultural role for women, which disempowers them by restricting their status.

- Liberal approaches are criticised because they assume a level playing field, which doesn't exist – men and women aren't in a position to enter freely into a sexual relationship.

- Feminists argue that sexuality must be re-imagined before sexual activity can be moral.

- Extreme feminists have argued for separation of men and women.

- However, women may be able to make free choices. Despite their subservience a woman may freely choose a socially defined role and it's unclear whether sexuality is fundamental to the human person.

A summary of Christianity and homosexuality:

- There's a libertarian view that there's no moral issue about same-sex relationships, beyond the issues that apply to heterosexual relationships.

- Homosexual acts were crimes, homosexuality was considered to be a mental illness and homophobia exists too.

- Discrimination exists on issues such as adoption, sex education and the age of consent.

- Christians have seen homosexuality as wrong, because there's no possibility of life arising from the sexual union, same-sex marriages are not permitted, sex outside marriage is wrong, and scriptural sources imply a divine command against homosexuality.

The Bible and homosexuality:

- Bible extracts appear to prohibit homosexual acts.

- In Genesis, God destroys Sodom, perhaps because of his displeasure with homosexuality.

- St Paul describes people engaging in same-sex sexual acts as 'dishonouring their bodies' and having 'unnatural relations' and 'shameless acts'.

- Biblical texts have been used as a basis for the condemnation of homosexuality, and of homosexual acts in particular.

- Protestant Churches have a biblical basis for their teaching on homosexuality, which leads them to condemn the activity.

The Roman Catholic Church and homosexuality:

- The Roman Catholic Church believes that homosexual inclination isn't a sin, but that the acts are a sin.
- Homosexual acts don't proceed from a genuine affective and sexual complementarity, are depraved and intrinsically disordered, and no life can come from them.
- Critics of the natural law approach to homosexuality argues that the unitive act between a loving couple is a good enough purpose for sex, as many sexual acts can't lead to pregnancy.
- To condemn people for using their sexual organs for their own pleasure reveals the prejudices and irrational taboos of our society.
- Some argue that the Roman Catholic view of homosexuality fuels intolerance.

Liberal Christian support for homosexuality:

- Liberal Christians argue that the quality of the relationship, be it heterosexual or homosexual, is what determines its moral value.
- They challenge the biblical basis of opposition to homosexuality and the natural law approach to Christian ethics.
- Christians believe that all are made 'in the image and likeness of God'. If God creates men and women as homosexuals, then that nature and inclination must be good.
- There's a Christian basis for an inclusive attitude towards homosexuals, because Christianity is a religion that positively seeks to make room for the marginalised and outcasts in society.
- A positive Christian view of the homosexual lifestyle requires a re-evaluation of Scripture and a change in the assumptions about natural law.

Chapter 16

Life before birth: abortion

Introduction

Key terms

Abortion, consciousness, ectopic pregnancy, embryo, ensoulment, fertilised ovum, foetus, Hippocratic oath, liberty, life, personhood, sanctity of life, self-determination, women's rights

What you will learn by the end of this chapter

- The debates about the sanctity of life.
- The debates about personhood and the status of the foetus.
- The debates about the rights of women and the foetus.
- The strengths and weakness of these arguments.

Key questions

1 What does it mean to claim that life is sacred?

2 If a pregnant woman is killed, and her unborn child also, how many murders have there been, and why?

3 Is a foetus a person or a potential person, and how does your answer affect the rights it should have?

4 Should a foetus or embryo have the same rights as an adult human being?

5 Should abortion be available on demand, only in special circumstances, or under no circumstances?

Why is abortion so controversial?

Today, **abortion** is common for a number of reasons: sex is seen as being more for pleasure than procreation, women have a greater social and legal status, low child mortality has reduced the need for so many children, and foetal abnormalities can be detected. Abortion is commonplace in many countries, with tens of millions of abortions taking place each year. Although it's legal in many countries, its morality is disputed. Religious organisations such as the Roman Catholic Church campaign against the availability of abortion, while **women's rights** groups campaign for greater access.

The key ethical dimensions in the abortion debate include whether there should be an absolutist prohibition of abortion on the basis of divine law, natural law or human rights, or whether there are situations in which bad consequences would ensue as a result of going ahead with the pregnancy.

Christians and the sanctity of life

In ethics, abortion refers to the intentional destruction of a foetus in the womb. Ancient views of abortion differ, just as they do now. Aristotle favoured abortion to control the size of a family, but the Hippocratic oath prohibited it. No biblical text specifically prohibits abortion, although a number are cited as providing a framework for prohibiting abortion (see Genesis 4:1; Job 31:15; Isaiah 44:24, 48:1, 5; Jeremiah 1:5; Matthew 1:18; Luke 1:40, 42). It's prohibited in Christian writings such as the *Didache ton Apostolon* (a first-century AD Christian guide to living; see Staniforth, 1968) and those of Clement of Alexander and Tertullian. Christian writers disputed the point at which the soul infused with the body (ensoulment) and also whether early abortions were as morally grave as later ones, but essentially it was viewed as murder.

Christianity holds all human life to be sacred. To say that life is sacred implies reverence and respect. It's commonly assumed that killing is wrong, although there are justifications such as self-defence that allow it. The act of killing ends the life, the autonomy of the person and any possible future contributions that life could have made. It leaves friends and family bereaved, causing them the most acute emotional distress known to the human condition. However, none of these in themselves justifies a total prohibition of killing humans. There may be people who will make not positive contributions to life, such as compulsive serial killers, and there may be people who have no close friends or relatives who would mourn their passing. Capital punishment and killing in war have been justified to prevent undesirable consequences such as the deaths of innocents, and Christian acceptance of these is at odds with the attitude towards abortion.

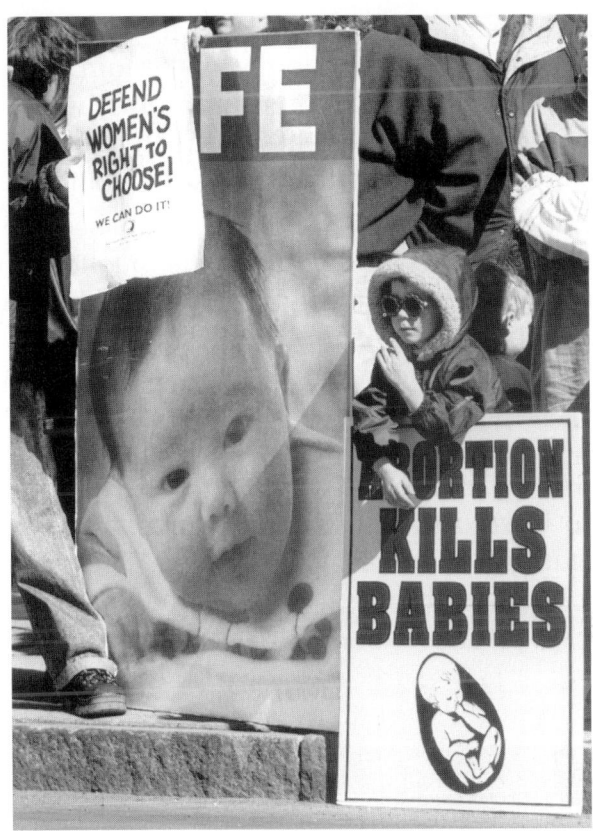

Religious arguments against abortion stress the limits of human authority over the taking of life. God is the life-creator and giver, and humans must not destroy what He has given. In the Judeo-Christian tradition, there's something inherently good about life, and about creating more life. Life is **sacred**, protected by divine authority.

Christianity rejects the taking of innocent life and so abortion is considered a grave sin. The Roman Catholic Church maintains that it is intrinsically evil and condemns it absolutely. Abortion goes against natural law and the Word of God, and there are no exceptions or scenarios that make it right. The foetus deserves the same status as a born human being. Those involved in procuring abortion leave themselves open to excommunication. Orthodox churches agree, as do fundamentalist evangelical churches, which oppose abortion on the basis that God alone is the author of life. David Smith (1997) identifies four principles that broadly summarise the Christian absolute rejection of abortion: God alone is Lord of life and death, humans do have no right to take life, human life begins at **conception** and so abortion at any stage is the murder of an innocent.

Liberal Protestant Christians oppose abortion in principle, and advocate the preservation of life, but allow for abortion in certain situations. These variously include abortion prior to the formation of the nervous system and brain, situations where the mother's life is threatened, in the case of rape or incest, and when the mother's mental or physical health is endangered.

An ectopic pregnancy is when the fertilised ovum becomes attached to the wall of the fallopian tube. To continue with the pregnancy would lead to the death of both the mother and the child. In these circumstances, the uterus is removed and the embryo dies. A Christian response to this makes use of the **'double effect'** rule. The doctors intend to save the mother, rather than killing the foetus, so the action is morally permissible. Peter Vardy and Paul Grosch (1994, p. 134) have identified a problem with the application of 'double effect' thinking in this particular example. New laser technology will enable women to have a safer operation which involves the foetus being 'lasered' rather than the fallopian tube removed. The result for the mother is much better, but it's difficult to suggest that the death of the foetus in this case is a secondary feature. All that is really different is the intention of the doctor.

Tasks

1 What moral principles imply that abortion is wrong in any situation?

2 Consider the scenarios in the list below, and suggest what ethical principles in each example challenge your answers to **1**:

a A woman aborts a child caused by rape.

b A woman aborts a child because the pregnancy is inconvenient for a film in which she's starring.

c A woman aborts her child because it's the product of incest.

d A woman aborts her child because she can't afford another child in her family.

e A woman aborts her child because it's so disabled that it will die at birth.

f A woman aborts a child because it's severely mentally handicapped, with no ability to communicate with or sense the world around it, or to think in a normal human way.

g A woman aborts a child because the pregnancy is ectopic and both will die unless abortion takes place.

h A woman aborts a child because she has a serious heart condition and may die in childbirth.

Personhood and the status of the foetus

The status of human life between conception and birth is central to the abortion debate. While some form of life is clearly present at conception, whether that form of life should get the full protection of the law is disputed. Not all human tissue is a person. Living cells such as human cancer cells are not persons. A baby born with no brain may be a human being, but it isn't a human person. A human being develops attributes throughout its life. When should full human rights status be conferred? Should status increase incrementally as the foetus becomes more like a born human being, or should it be bound to the point of conception or the point of birth?

Opponents of abortion argue that to kill a foetus is to murder a human person. In 1869, Pope Pius IX declared that a foetus is a human person from the moment of conception and so abortion is always murder. The claim that the foetus is a person is supported by the presence of all the necessary genetic material at conception, and the continuous development from conception to the born human being.

Critics of this position argue that the fertilised egg is too different from anything that we normally recognise as a person to be called the same thing. In 'A defence of abortion' (1971), Judith Jarvis Thompson accepts that there's continuous development in foetal growth, but suggests that there's a point at which it isn't a human being. There's a continuous growth from acorn to oak tree, but an acorn isn't an oak tree; just as a fertilised ovum – a newly implanted clump of cells – isn't a person. Jonathan Glover (1977, p. 123) writes that to call a foetus at the point of conception a person stretches the term beyond normal boundaries.

Perhaps personhood should be given when the foetus is viable, when it can survive a birth. There are two objections to this. First, the age which the foetus can survive outside the womb is reducing as medical technology progresses. Secondly, there are many people who are dependent on continual medical assistance, such as dialysis, in order to survive. We consider them to be persons despite their medical conditions.

Mary Anne Warren (1991, p. 313) argues that 'birth, rather than some earlier point, marks the beginning of true moral status'. She argues that if a foetus is a person, then sperm and ovum are persons. Birth provides a clear boundary, but Glover rejects this argument, because of the similarity between later foetuses and premature babies.

Consciousness may be suggested as a definition of personhood. Conciousness can't be applied to all living tissue, as it implies sensory experiences, the ability to feel pleasure and pain. However, consciousness would include many animals, and most would argue that animals are not persons in the same sense as humans are. The presence of rationality, and our ability to develop complex language and make complex tools, are distinctive features of personhood. However, studies of chimpanzees and dolphins show that many higher animals use complex communication and can make tools with which to manipulate their environments. Perhaps self-consciousness or self-awareness defines a human person. This includes a sense of our own past and future. However, very young babies are not self-aware in this sense, and most people would argue that killing babies is killing human persons. It could be argued that the foetus is a potential person, but this doesn't necessary imply that full legal status should be awarded on the basis of what it has the potential to be. A potential victory isn't the same as a victory. A potential person is not equal to a person.

The definition of personhood is unresolved, as is agreement over the point at which a potential human being becomes a full human being. Peter Vardy and Paul Grosch (1994, p. 155) note many attempts at drawing a dividing line at a particular point in the foetus' development, to indicate that before this point the foetus is tissue with potential and after this point a person, but there's no easy way of drawing the line with certainty. In 'Is the human embryo a person?' (1985), John Gallagher asks us to recognise that change is gradual. If an embryo is x at one time and James at another time, then there will be a time when it is part x and part James. While personhood doesn't provide a clear solution to the abortion debate, the moral status of the foetus is crucial. In 'The human person' (1998), Joseph Selling has argued that if a being qualifies as a person, then it has a direct moral standing, with rights and others have a duty towards it. Whether that duty extends to full human status remains in dispute.

Tasks

1 When is human life a person?
   a When the cells in the fertilised egg become differentiated?
   b When the heart starts to pump blood?
   c When the main organs are developed?
   d When there's movement?
   e When it feels pain?

2 A person is a being that deserves protection under the law equal to that of a born human. Examine this list and decide which should be given full status as human persons and which should not:
   a A baby boy.
   b A foetus.
   c A brain-dead woman.

d A baby born with no head.

e A chimpanzee or great ape.

f A dead person in a mortuary.

g A human skeleton.

h ET, the extra-terrestrial.

i A deranged psychopath who is unable to tell good from bad.

j Someone in a permanent vegetative state (PVS), kept alive by a life support machine.

k Someone with severe brain damage.

l A sufferer of severe Alzheimer's disease.

m Siamese twins, who share all major organs except the brain.

n Sperm.

o A 20-year-old woman.

p A dolphin.

3 Follow-up questions:

I Which caused the most disagreement, and why do you think this was?

II Does the ability to think make a difference?

III Does the ability to make moral decisions make a difference?

IV Which moral issues are affected by personhood?

V How might it be argued that some animals are moral persons?

Abortion and rights

The feminist position begins from the historical experience of female suppression and a patriarchal society, and the role of the Church in that history. Women were subordinated within the family and had their freedom limited by the constraints of motherhood and the unreliability of contraception. Women's roles have primarily been defined in terms of motherhood, and it was only towards the latter end of the twentieth century that women in large numbers began to have equal legal rights and equal opportunity of employment.

Mary Anne Warren (1991, 1997) puts forward a case for granting women the right to abort unwanted pregnancies, because if the state was to prohibit abortion undesirable consequences would follow. The absence in the past of safe legal access to abortion and contraception has meant that women in history have paid a terrible price. They have been forced to bear many children at short intervals, become debilitated and died young – a situation that aggravates poverty and places stress on families and whole societies. If the morality of an action is determined by its consequences, then women deserve access to abortion. Without it, they have a limited possibility of education and employment, and no reproductive autonomy. Abortion is essential for the health and well-being of individuals, families and society. Sex is an important, healthy part of life and so celibacy is not an option.

Warren maintains that abortion must be permissible to guarantee women's human rights of life, liberty and self-determination. The World Health Organisation (WHO) says that unsafe abortions kill 200 000 women every year. To be forced to bear a child is to be forced to undergo a risky process, that may lead to the possible giving up of work and education, and consequent hardship. Self-determination includes freedom from the infliction of bodily harm. Prohibition of abortion infringes on these rights. Warren argues that in most cases killing is wrong, but to prohibit abortion on demand would deny a woman's basic human rights. If the foetus is given equal rights then, in principle, a court could force a woman to go through with a dangerous birth rather than abort, because her life would be considered to be no more valuable than that of the foetus.

In 'A defence of abortion' (1971), Judith Jarvis Thompson sees abortion as an issue of self-defence. The foetus threatens the mother and so abortion is a defensive measure. However, while we have a right to kill in defence, it's unclear whether we have a right to kill an innocent in self-defence. Perhaps the foetus has the right of self-defence against the mother.

Task

You're on a sinking ship and there's one lifejacket left. You get the jacket and put it on, but another passenger arrives without one. If you keep it you will live, while the other passenger will die. Should you keep it or give it away, and why?

What are the ethical issues at stake in this situation, and how do they relate to abortion?

Extracts from key texts

Mrs Jill Knight, MP, 1966

House of Commons debate (in Glover, 1977, p. 120)

Babies are not like bad teeth to be jerked out just because they cause suffering. An unborn baby is a baby nevertheless. Would the sponsors of the Bill think it right to kill a baby they can see? Of course they would not. Why then do they think it right to kill one they cannot see? ... I have come to believe that those who support abortion on demand do so because in all sincerity they cannot accept that an unborn baby is a human being. Yet surely it is. Its heart beats, it moves, it sleeps, it eats. Uninterfered with, it has a potential life ahead of it of seventy years or more; it may be a happy one, or a sad life; it may be a genius, or it may be just plain average; but surely as a healthy, living baby it has a right not to be killed simply because it may be inconvenient for a year or so to its mother.

Judith Jarvis Thompson, The Violinist Example

In 'A defence of abortion' (quoted in Cahn and Markie, 1998, p. 738)

I propose, then, that we grant that the fetus is a person from the moment of conception. How does the argument go from here? Something like this, I take it. Every person has a right to life. So the fetus has a right to life. No doubt the mother has a right to decide what shall happen in and to her body; everyone would grant that. But surely a person's right to life is stronger and more stringent than the mother's right to decide what happens in and to her body, and so outweighs it. So the fetus may not be killed; an abortion may not be performed.

It sounds plausible. But now let me ask you to imagine this. You wake up in the morning and find yourself back to back in bed with an unconscious violinist. A famous unconscious violinist. He has been found to have a fatal kidney ailment, and the Society of Music Lovers has canvassed all the available medical records and found that you alone have the right blood type to help. They have therefore kidnapped you, and last night the violinist's circulatory system was plugged into yours, so that your kidneys can be used to extract poisons from his blood as well as your own. The director of the hospital now tells you, 'Look, we're sorry the Society of Music Lovers did this to you – we would never have permitted it if we had known. But still, they did it, and the violinist now is plugged into you. To unplug you would be to kill him. But never mind, it's only for nine months. By then he will have recovered from his ailment, and can safely be unplugged from you.' Is it morally incumbent on you to accede to this situation? No doubt it would be very nice of you if you did, a great kindness. But do you have to accede to it? What if it were not nine months, but nine years? Or longer still? What if the director of the hospital says, 'Tough luck, I agree, but you've now got to stay in bed, with the violinist plugged into you, for the rest of your life. Because remember this. All persons have a right to life, and violinists are persons. Granted you have a right to decide what happens in and to your body, but a person's right to life outweighs your right to decide what happens in and to your body. So you cannot ever be unplugged from him.' I imagine you would regard this as outrageous, which suggests that something really is wrong with that plausible sounding argument I mentioned a moment ago.

CHAPTER SUMMARY

- Today, abortion is common – it's legal in many countries, with tens of millions of abortions taking place each year.
- Religious organisations such as the Roman Catholic Church campaign against abortion, while women's rights groups campaign for greater access.

Christians and the sanctity of life:
- Abortion intentionally destroys a foetus in the womb, and biblical texts provide a framework for prohibiting abortion.
- Christianity holds all human life to be sacred – deserving of reverence and respect.
- The act of killing ends the life, the autonomy of the person and any possible future contributions that life could have made.
- Religious organisations argue that humans don't have authority over the taking of life as God is the life-creator and giver.
- Christianity rejects the taking of innocent life and so abortion is considered a grave sin – intrinsically evil, and condemned absolutely by the Roman Catholic Church, as it goes against natural law and the Word of God.
- God alone is Lord of life and death, and humans have no right to take life.
- Human life begins at conception and so abortion at any stage is the murder of an innocent.
- Liberal Protestant Christians oppose abortion in principle, and advocate the preservation of life, but allow for abortion in certain situations (where the mother's life is threatened, in the case of rape or incest, and

when the mother's mental or physical health is endangered).

■ The 'double effect' principle may be applied to allow for an abortion to save the life of a mother when otherwise neither the mother nor the foetus would live (for example, an ectopic pregnancy).

Personhood and the status of the foetus:

■ While some form of life is clearly present at conception, whether that form of life should get the full protection of the law is disputed.

■ Should status increase incrementally as the foetus becomes more like a born human being, or should it be bound to the point of conception or the point of birth?

■ Opponents of abortion argue that to kill a foetus is to murder a human person – the foetus contains the necessary genetic material.

■ Others argue that the fertilised egg is too different from anything that we normally recognise as a person to be called the same thing.

■ Personhood may be given when the foetus is viable, when it can survive a birth – although people who are dependent on continual medical assistance are considered to be persons despite their medical conditions.

■ The following are suggested as defining aspects of personhood: consciousness, rationality, self-awareness, and our ability to develop complex language and make complex tools.

■ Is a foetus a person or a potential person?

■ The definition of personhood is unresolved, as is agreement over the point at which a potential human being becomes a full human being.

Abortion and rights:

■ There's a historical experience of female suppression and a patriarchal society, defining women's roles in terms of motherhood.

■ Mary Anne Warren argues that women should have the right to abort unwanted pregnancies, because if the state was to prohibit abortion undesirable consequences would follow.

■ Illegal abortions would claim lives – and basic women's rights would be lost, as control over the reproductive system and process is essential if women are to experience basic rights to life, liberty and self-determination.

■ Judith Jarvis Thompson sees abortion as an issue of self-defence – although, arguably, the foetus has the right of self-defence against the mother.

Chapter 17

Life before birth: IVF and embryo research

Introduction

Key terms

Assisted reproductive technologies, *in vitro* fertilisation (IVF), artificial insemination (AI), embryo, personhood

What you will learn by the end of this chapter

- The nature of IVF and AI.
- Different religious and philosophical approaches to IVF.
- The legal context for embryo research in the UK.
- Religious and philosophical approaches to embryo research.

Key questions

1 Is the suffering caused by infertility more important than the loss of embryos involved in the IVF process?
2 Should reproduction be intrinsically linked to the act of lovemaking between committed couples?
3 Do I have a right to have a child?
4 Do I have a right to choose the 'sort' of child I want?
5 Can medical benefits that will save future lives justify the use of embryos under 14 days old for research?

Background

This chapter should be read in conjunction with Chapter 16 and 24, as both complement the discussion considered here.

Some couples are unable to have children naturally. For those who desire children, this can be painful and traumatic. Couples may feel that a major part of their life is impaired or limited by the lack of children, and women in particular can feel a sense of lacking or loss. For people in this position, medical advances in the area of Assisted Reproductive Technologies (ARTs) offer a chance to live life to the full as they see it, to fill a gap in their marriage and purpose. A whole chapter of their life may be opened up by the possibility of having their own children. It might be said that humans, like all living creatures, have a biological imperative to reproduce and that human life cannot be fully experienced if that option is beyond reach:

> I am an infertile man. I don't make babies ... My sperm, what there are of them, are immature, malformed, immotile ... I have known of my infertility for twenty years ... I vividly remember the indignity and pain of those appointments with the doctor ... If I cannot give my wife the baby she wants, I do not have anything worthy of giving to anyone I love ... My wife and I have come to a resolution of our infertility as a couple. We are the adoptive parents of a fine girl who thrives and finds our love ... I accept infertility, but I will never, fully, be reconciled to it.
>
> Glazer and Cooper (1988), pp. 38–42

AI and IVF

Artificial insemination (AI) involves injecting sperm through a catheter into the wife's reproductive tract. It is used to treat the husband's infertility due to physiological disorders. Usually, the husband's sperm are used, although donor sperm may also be provided.

In vitro fertilisation (IVF) refers to the procedure of retrieving eggs and sperm from the couple and placing them together in a laboratory dish to help fertilisation. Since 1978, there have been an estimated 30 000 so-called 'test tube babies'. Anthony Dyson describes the procedure:

> The female eggs (or ova) are placed in a culture medium in a glass or plastic flat shallow Petri dish or other appropriate laboratory container ... The male sperm is then introduced into the dish and the process of fertilisation takes place over the next twenty-four hours or so.

Second, following fertilization, some of the embryos are transferred to the woman's uterus (or womb), where it is hoped that implantation will take place, followed by a natural pregnancy.

Dyson (1995), pp. xi–xii

There are a number of factors that require consideration in evaluating the ethicality of IVF. The process involves the use of many embryos, which have to be stored. A recent survey found that there were 396 526 frozen human embryos in storage in the USA alone (Horsey, 2003). Many embryos not used for implantation are destroyed: for example, embryos may have been frozen for further attempts that, in the event, proved to be unnecessary. In addition, there is a high risk of failure causing distress to the couple involved. An extra factor is the use of donor eggs, sperm or indeed both, not to mention the involvement of surrogate mothers to provide wombs where a woman is unable to do this herself. IVF is also used to select healthy embryos in situations in which it is likely that the parents will produce embryos with a serious medical condition – or even where parents want a particular child with certain features to help another seriously ill child, although as yet it is not possible to choose features for non-medical purposes in the UK, such as selecting the gender of the child.

Tasks

The list below raises a number of important ethical questions. Consider the questions and in your answer explain how ethical and religious principles might affect peoples' views on them:

1 Should IVF be paid for by general taxation?
2 Is it right to involve the use of donors or surrogate mothers?
3 Does IVF infringe on marriage and fidelity?
4 Who should be allowed access to IVF?
5 Should homosexual couples be allowed to take advantage of IVF?
6 Should post-menopausal women be allowed to take advantage of IVF?
7 Is it right to harvest and store human embryos?

Approaches to IVF

Christian views

Different denominations have different perspectives on IVF depending, in part, on their attitude to the status of the foetus. The Catholic Church opposes IVF. In its document *The Gift of Life, Donum Vitae*, the Church restated the Vatican II teaching:

> Life, once conceived, must be protected with the utmost care; abortion and infanticide are abominable crimes.
>
> *The Gift of Life, Donum Vitae* (1987), para. 23

In the absence of any ability to detect a spiritual soul, this position – which informs the Church's view of abortion as well – makes any treatment involving the intended loss of a foetus unacceptable and immoral. The document goes on to state that:

> These [reproductive] procedures are contrary to the human dignity proper to the embryo, and at the same time they are contrary to the right of every person to be conceived and to be born within marriage and from marriage. Also, attempts or hypotheses for obtaining a human being without any connection with sexuality through 'twin fission', cloning or parthenogenesis are to be considered contrary to the moral law, since they are in opposition to the dignity both of human procreation and of the conjugal union. The freezing of embryos, even when carried out in order to preserve the life of an embryo – cryopreservation – constitutes an offence against the respect due to human beings by exposing them to grave risks of death or harm to their physical integrity, and depriving them, at least temporarily, of maternal shelter and gestation, thus placing them in a situation in which further offences and manipulation are possible from marriage.
>
> *Donum Vitae* (1987), para. 32

IVF and other reproductive technologies that take life creation outside the conjugal act are considered wrong because that process undermines sexual reproduction in marriage and in some way is disrespectful to the created embryo. The necessary storage of embryos is also considered disrespectful. The reasons for these principled views are theological. The Catholic Church maintains that life should be a sign of self-giving mutual love, and to preserve for the fidelity of the marriage no one else should be directly involved. The use of donor sperm or eggs infringes on the marital fidelity and infringes on the right that a child has of being born within and from marriage, as does the use of surrogate mothers. The Church also expresses its concern about the effects that the use of donor sperm or eggs might have on social unity. The children born may have concerns about their parentage, and where a spouse's biological traits are not involved in the child, this may cause family tensions and anxiety with regard to the child's identity.

The Church's philosophical acceptance of natural moral law underpins much of this thinking, as does the belief that sex within marriage is both unitive (mutual self-giving of love) and procreative. Reproductive technologies might aid and assist the requirement to reproduce found in Aquinas's primary precepts, but masturbation would be required, which is prohibited – and in any case that is not the only consideration, as marriage is considered by the Catholic Church to be a sacrament, and therefore has particular sanctity and holiness.

Protestant Christian churches have different ethical approaches to life before birth. While all consider human embryos as needing respect, some churches consider conception to be part of the process towards full human life, and do not afford the embryo the same status as a born human being. Indeed, those denominations that emphasise personal conscience in making moral decisions would not give direct guidance in the way the Catholic Church does. The Protestant writer Paul Ramsey (1974, p. 39), opposed artificial insemination by donor as it denies the unity of love between husband and wife, a love that should reflect the unity of love between Christ and his Church:

> [to] procreate beyond the sphere of love (AI, for example, or making human life in a test-tube) or to posit acts of sexual love beyond the sphere or responsible creation (by definition, marriage) – means a refusal of the image of God's creation.
>
> Ramsey (1974), p. 39

He was also concerned about the possibility of potential health risks of IVF to future babies, and on that basis rejected the procedure. On the other hand, Joseph Fletcher, champion of **situationism** and its person-centred ethics, challenged this view, arguing that the relationship was more important in the decision about the morality of AI, and that there is an exception in Deuteronomy 15:5–6 to the exclusive nature of husband–wife reproduction. He later described IVF in these terms:

> It seems to me that laboratory reproduction is radically human, compared to conception by ordinary heterosexual intercourse ...
>
> Fletcher (1976)

Fletcher does not see the involvement of medical science as detracting from the natural process, but as humanising it through the involvement of human creativity for compassionate reasons.

The diversity of approaches in Protestant ethics results from different approaches to using the Bible in ethical decision-making about issues in contemporary medical science.

Other ethical views

Philosophical approaches vary and produce differing conclusions. Kantian ethics might raise questions over the use of a number of embryos successfully to produce a single living child. The **categorical imperative** requires that people are treated as ends in themselves. Therefore, if an embryo is treated as a person, can the creation of many be justified for the sake of one born life? Does the fact that each embryo has the potential to be a born human circumnavigate the fact that most will not achieve that potential? Utilitarians have to consider whether to include the happiness of the individual embryos created, and have to measure that against the happiness of the couple and any child who comes of the treatment. A utilitarian might be concerned about the low success rate and might consider the chance of great disappointment caused by an unsuccessful attempt. Both approaches raise complex questions and each must clarify the status of the embryo.

Rights ethics might be applied in this context, but here too the differing rights of various interest groups, the couple, the embryos created, donors, the child created and society at large need to be taken into consideration. A couple might feel that they have a right to a child, and infertility could be seen as an illness that should be treated. The couple may feel that they have a right to access IVF technology, and beyond that to determine certain features of the child. In the event of donor sperm or eggs being used, there are also questions about the right to knowledge concerning the donor, to evaluate whether or not they want to use that particular donor. And if a donor is used, a child might also have a right to knowledge about the donor. The donor might have a right to anonymity, and a right to payment for the provision of his sperm or her eggs. Yet again there are questions about the rights of the unused embryos kept in storage, and about the rights of any embryos that are rejected because of mental or physical abnormalities, or because they are of the 'wrong' gender.

Decisions must be made about who should have rights, and about what claims they have over the rights of others. We cannot simply consider rights without also probing the motivation of the couple. In a consumer culture, there is a danger that children can be seen as simply another desired product, and this becomes more acute when particular features are requested. Children are not products and parents do not own them, so they cannot be treated as a commodity. Parents are custodians and this should bear on their motivation for wanting a child, and their desire for a particular child.

Read the following three passages and answer the questions below.

The 'sibling saviour'

Jamie Whitaker was brought into the world to save the life of his older brother Charlie, using IVF in the USA. Charlie, aged four, had Diamond Blackfan anaemia, a rare condition in which the bone marrow produces too few blood cells to take oxygen around the body, and he was undergoing regular painful treatments. The condition threatened to reduce the quality and length of his life, and the only hope for a cure was a bone marrow transplant from a child with perfect tissue match. Naturally, there is only a one in four chance of conceiving an exact match, but his parents wanted to improve the chance of success. The UK authority refused to give permission, so they went to the USA instead. In his article 'Down the slippery slope', Richard Nicholson (2003) says that we have no right to presume that the damage done to Jamie's self-worth will be countered by any sense of welcome he might feel for helping his brother. In an analogous case in 2003, the Court of Appeal overturned a similar judgment, so that a couple can now go ahead with a similar procedure. Is it right to create a child for the purpose of saving another child?

An IVF mix-up

In July 2002, black twins were born to two white parents because of an IVF mix-up, raising a number of ethical and legal questions: Who is the legitimate father? What rights do the biological and non-biological fathers have? What damage will be done to the family, children and adults involved for the sake of IVF?

The Diane Blood case

Stephen Blood contracted bacterial meningitis and fell into a coma in February 1995. Sperm samples were taken before he died. His wife Diane campaigned to be allowed to use the sperm to conceive a child, even though Stephen had not given consent. The Human Fertilisation and Embryology Authority refused permission as consent had not been given, but this decision was overturned by the Court of Appeal. Diane Blood has now had two children by her dead husband and has had him registered as the father.

1 For each of these situations, identify:

   a The ethical issues at stake.

   b Possible ethical approaches to successfully dealing with the dilemma.

2 Make a personal judgement for each case and justify your opinion.

Embryo research

Embryo experimentation has the potential to find cures for serious illnesses, using tissue or cells from embryos. It is possible that such work might help with the treatment of those suffering from Alzheimer's disease, Huntington's, chorea, diabetes and Parkinson's disease. This potential has led to increasing pressure to extend what is permissible in embryo research and experimentation. IVF itself is underpinned by such research and would not be possible without it. Recently, politicians in the UK voted to extend the research done on human embryos to allow stem cells to be taken from embryos at a very early stage of development, in the hope that this may lead to radical improvements in the treatment of a number of degenerative diseases.

Task

The Human Fertilisation and Embryology Authority (HFEA) grants licences for embryo research under the following conditions:

The HFEA cannot grant a licence unless it is satisfied the use of human embryos is necessary or desirable for the purposes of the research and may only be allowed for one of the following purposes

■ To promote advances in the treatment of infertility

■ To increase knowledge about the causes of congenital disease

■ To increase knowledge about the causes of miscarriages

■ To develop more effective techniques of contraception

■ To develop methods for detecting the presence of gene or chromosome abnormalities

HFEA (2003)

List the purposes given above in order of importance in your view, and decide which if any make a more convincing case for embryo research. Justify your conclusions.

Clearly, there are utilitarian arguments for embryo experimentation and research, but there are legal limits. A number of practices are prohibited in the UK including keeping an embryo past the appearance of the primitive streak of 14 days, placing a human embryo in an animal, replacing the nucleus of a cell of an embryo with the nucleus of another person (human cloning), and altering the genetic structure of any cell while it forms part of an embryo. Note that the primitive streak is a thickening in the surface of the embryo and that it results in the first stages of embryonic development (HFEA, 2003, p. 3).

Ethical debates about embryo experimentation start by considering the nature of the embryo; whether it is a person, a potential person or something else, and whether – and to what degree – rights are granted.

Peter Singer writes that it is possible to argue that up to 14 days after fertilisation an embryo (as opposed to a foetus) is not a human being, because at that time it can split into two or more genetically identical embryos (Singer, 1993, pp. 156–157). Before 14 days, we cannot be sure if we are looking at one or two individuals, and therefore there is no personal presence. For Singer, this justifies embryo experimentation.

The British Humanist Association agrees with this argument, noting that

> At the early stage where research is focused, an embryo has few of the characteristics we associate with a person. It is a fertilised human egg, with the capacity to develop into a person, but its cells have not yet begun to form into specialist cells that would form particular parts of the body (which is why they are potentially so useful). There is no brain, no self-awareness (or consciousness), no way of feeling pain or emotion, so an early stage embryo cannot suffer.
>
> British Humanist Association (2003b)

Others reject this, instead noting that even by day seven there are observable features of differentiation:

> The formation of the embryonic disk, and within that disk the epiblast, at about day seven, is a differentiation at least equally significant [as that occurring at about day 14]; in the epiblast are all or virtually all the 'embryo proper' cells. Indeed, the inner cell mass has differentiated from other parts of the embryo by about day five, and functional differentiation of the cells in the embryo begins even earlier ... The fact that some days elapse before one can identify which cells will become placenta and which 'embryo proper' in no way justifies any claim that during those days there is something other than an individual, self-developing human organism, fully continuous with – the very same individual being as – the adult human organism.
>
> Joint Committee on Bioethical Issues of the
> Catholic Bishops of Great Britain (1987)

Christian absolutists who argue for full rights from the point of conception do not believe that uncertainty about whether it is one or two beings is sufficient to merit the withdrawal of rights from the embryo. Biblical texts such as Jeremiah 1:3, Galatians 1:15, Ephesians 1:4 and Psalm 139 are often quoted to argue that our existence is ordained by God. Any interruption in the process of life interrupts God's plan for life and undermines the idea that God's image is reflected in each human being (Genesis 1:27).

The argument, held by some, that an embryo is a potential human being is rejected by Singer, who demonstrates its weakness by extending it to include sperm and eggs. They too could be seen as potential human beings, which simply require a human action for their potential to be realised. He notes that once an embryo is isolated in the laboratory, it too requires a human action for its potential to be realised, and so he does not see that an embryo is very different from sperm or eggs (Singer, 1993, pp.158–159). He gives an example of a laboratory assistant who tips some sperm and an egg down a sink and then notices later that the sink is blocked. According to those who argue from the position of potential, the two may well have formed an embryo and so it is wrong to clear the blockage.

Even if the embryo or foetus does not have full human rights, it may have some rights. If it feels pain, then it has an interest in not feeling pain (Singer, 1993, p. 164), but our knowledge of the activity of the brain in the early embryo and foetus is incomplete – which might, for some, be enough to apply a precautionary rule based on the chance that pain might be caused which we cannot detect.

However, Richard Doerflinger has argued that

> That way lies the moral approach of a totalitarian society, that thinks it can use and abuse individual human beings in accordance with some grand scheme promising 'the greatest good for the greatest number'. ... If, as modern embryology tells us, ... [genetically defective embryos] ... are indeed part of the continuum of human life, then the notion that genetic flaws enable us to destroy the 'imperfect' embryos has implications for the equal dignity of human beings after birth as well.
>
> Richard Doerflinger, quoted in Robinson (2001)

In recent times, the embryo research debate has been linked to stem cell research and human cloning. For further details on this dimension of the discussion, refer to Chapter 24.

Conclusions

There are a number of concerns over the use of embryos in research. Should they be used to help develop new treatments for degenerative diseases that harm many people? Does this turn human embryos into a commodity for the greater good of born humans? Should embryos have unique untouchable status irrespective of any benefit that they might give to others through experimentation? The debate over personhood is an important dimension in this discussion, as it is with abortion, and ultimately the view on when an embryo gains rights will heavily influence the ethical position that one takes on embryo research. Concerns about the use of one human being for another human being may come from the Kantian principle of treating all people as ends in themselves, a human rights ethic, or a **natural law** principle to preserve and protect innocent human life. It is conceivable to incorporate a utilitarian perspective into the natural law principle of life preservation, so that very many future lives are protected at the cost of a few lives now, although this would go against traditional formulations of natural law theory. Advocates of embryo research will justify their position on utilitarian grounds, claiming that the betterment of the quality and quantity of human life outweighs the cost of using embryos, which they are unlikely to consider as human beings.

Tasks

1 Why are there such contrasting views of IVF? Identify the principles that underpin those views and that lead to such disagreement.

2 Explore two differing philosophical approaches to embryo research and show why they reach their different conclusions.

CHAPTER SUMMARY

AI and IVF:

- Many couples suffer from infertility, and Assisted Reproductive Technologies (ARTs) offer a chance to live life to the full.

- Artificial insemination involves injecting sperm into the wife's reproductive tract, to treat the husband's infertile due to physiological disorders.

- *In vitro* fertilisation refers to the procedure of retrieving eggs and sperm from the couple and placing them together in a laboratory dish to help fertilisation.

- In the case of both AI and IVF, donors may be used.

- Issues of concern in IVF include storage, the destruction of unused embryos, the high failure rate, the use of donors, and the selection of healthy embryos or those with desired features.

The Roman Catholic Church:

- The Church opposes IVF, as many embryos are created and then destroyed in the process: the Church considers embryos to have a full human rights status from conception.
- The Church is also concerned that the involvement of donors and doctors impairs the conjugal act of lovemaking.
- Natural moral law underpins this belief in the protection of life, as does the belief that marriage is a sacrament and therefore has particular sanctity and holiness.

The different approaches of Protestant Christian churches:

- All consider human embryos as needing respect.
- Some churches do not afford the embryo the same status as a born human being.
- An emphasis on personal conscience leaves individual Christians to make their own moral decisions.
- Paul Ramsey opposed artificial insemination by donor, as it denies the unity of love between husband and wife.
- Joseph Fletcher argued that the relationship was more important in the decision about the morality of AI.
- The diversity of approaches in Protestant ethics results from the different approaches to using the Bible in ethical decision-making.

Other ethical views:

- In Kantian ethics, the categorical imperative requires that people are treated as ends in themselves, and perhaps embryos are persons.
- Utilitarians need to consider whether the happiness of the individual embryos created and not used is significant, and measure that against the happiness of the couple and the created child.
- A utilitarian might also be concerned about the low success rate, the cost of treatment set against other more reliable treatments, and the chance of disappointment caused by unsuccessful attempts.
- Rights theories must contend with the different groups claiming priority consideration, such as the couple, the embryos created, donors, the child created and society at large.
- In a consumer culture, there is a danger that children can be seen as simply another desired product, and this becomes more acute when particular features are requested.

Embryo research:

- Embryo experimentation has the potential to find cures for serious illnesses using tissue or cells from embryos.

- UK politicians have voted to extend the research done on human embryos to allow stem cells to be taken from embryos at a very early stage of development, in the hope that this may lead to radical improvements in the treatment of a number of degenerative diseases.

- There are utilitarian arguments for embryo experimentation and research for the greater good for the populace.

- Important in this discussion is the nature of the embryo and whether it is a person, a potential person or something else, and whether – and to what degree – rights are granted.

- Singer argues that up to 14 days after fertilisation, an embryo is not a human being.

- The British Humanist Association note that before 14 days an embryo has few of the characteristics that we associate with a person.

- Some argue that by day seven there are observable features of differentiation.

- Some Christian absolutists argue for full rights from the point of conception, because any interruption in the process of life interrupts God's plan for life and undermines the idea that God's image is reflected in each human being.

- Singer argues against potentiality as an argument, because sperm and eggs could be considered to be potentially human.

- Religious absolutists with strong pro-life beliefs see the use of embryos in this way as an indicator of a totalitarian society, one that thinks it can use and abuse individual humans for utilitarian reasons.

Conclusions:

- Some argue that embryo research helps to develop treatments for degenerative diseases.

- Should embryos be used to help develop new treatments for degenerative diseases that harm many people? Does this turn human embryos into a commodity for the greater good of born humans?

- The question of whether or not an embryo is a person fundamentally affects the view of IVF and embryo research.

Chapter 18

Voluntary euthanasia

Contents of Chapter 18

Introduction

Key terms

Assisted dying, autonomy, dignity, pro-euthanasia, sacred, self-determination, slippery slope, suffering, voluntary euthanasia

What you will learn by the end of this chapter

- What voluntary euthanasia is.
- The arguments in favour of voluntary euthanasia.
- The arguments against voluntary euthanasia.
- The strengths and weaknesses of the arguments for and against voluntary euthanasia.

Key questions

1 Should we have the right to take our own lives?
2 Is it wrong to kill humans who don't want to live?
3 Is there a difference between withdrawing life-sustaining treatment and delivering a lethal injection?

What is voluntary euthanasia?

Consider someone who has led a full and active life, but is now suffering from an incurable disease that slowly limits that person's ability to move, communicate with others and think as he or she used to do. While such a person still has some ability to control his or her own destiny, should that person be allowed to take his or her own life? Closely associated with this question is whether it's right for a doctor to assist with that process. Advocates of voluntary **euthanasia** point out that while they remain *able* to kill themselves, they have a quality of life that they do not want to end. What they want is for someone to help them to end their lives – or directly bring them to an end – once they have *lost* the ability to do so alone, and their quality of life is no longer desirable. Today, euthanasia is a criminal offence in virtually all countries, and it's strongly opposed by most governments and religious organisations. In Holland, about a thousand assisted deaths take place each year, and organisations such as the Voluntary Euthanasia Society (VES) campaign for a similar practice to be available in the UK. It's worth noting that the VES, along with most other pro-euthanasia groups, would never support ending someone's life against that person's will.

The Greek philosopher Hippocrates (460–370 BCE) wrote 'I will not prescribe a deadly drug to please someone, nor give advice that may cause his death'. Some doctors maintain this view, arguing that killing a patient doesn't fit with what a doctor should do. A doctor should heal, prevent diseases and assist people in living a healthy life. On the other hand, Francis Bacon (1561–1626) wrote that physicians are 'not only to restore the health, but to mitigate pain and dolours; and not only when such mitigation may conduce to recovery, but when it may serve to make a fair and easy passage' ('New Atlantis', 1627; in Vickers, 1996). Some doctors today feel that the need to preserve the patient's quality of life extends to a duty to help that patient to end his or her life in the way that he or she sees fit.

This chapter explores voluntary euthanasia and assisted dying. Should a person have the right to choose the manner and time of his or her own death, and should that person be given assistance in that process? The ethical arena of voluntary euthanasia is divided between those who tend to feel that it's right and merciful for us to have the freedom to decide the time and nature of our deaths, and those who claim that such autonomy would have harmful side-effects on society, or that it goes against religious beliefs.

Arguments for voluntary euthanasia

There are several arguments in favour of legal voluntary euthanasia.

Voluntary euthanasia is not murder

In his article 'Why physicians should aid the dying' (1977), Gregory E. Pence argues that killing humans who don't want to live is not wrong. It isn't wrong to help the dying to die, because they are actually dying.

Voluntary euthanasia is merciful

Voluntary euthanasia shows mercy for those suffering with intolerable pain from an incurable disease. The English humanist Thomas More (1478–1535) argued that when a patient suffers 'a torturing and lingering pain, so that there is no hope, either of recovery or ease, [they may] choose rather to die, since they cannot live but in much misery' (*Utopia*, 1516, Chapter 8). Voluntary euthanasia is a merciful opportunity to end needless suffering – one which we offer to animals and should offer to humans as well.

Voluntary euthanasia gives people autonomy

In his book *On Liberty* (1859), John Stuart Mill argued that in matters that do not concern others, individuals should have full autonomy: 'The only part of the conduct of any one, for which [a citizen] is amenable to society, is that which concerns others. In the part which merely concerns himself, his independence is, of right, absolute. Over himself, over his body and mind, the individual is sovereign.' We expect to have control over our bodies in matters of life, and it should be the same in matters of death. The VES (2001a) argues that every human being deserves respect and has the right to choose his or her own destiny, including how he or she lives and dies. Jack Kervorkian has said, 'In my view the highest principle in medical ethics – in any kind of ethics – is personal autonomy, self-determination. What counts is what the patient wants and judges to be a benefit or a value in his or her own life. That's primary.' (quoted in Richard M. Gula; in Hoose, 1998, p. 279) Advocates of voluntary euthanasia argue that it should be an option for a competent adult, who is able and willing to make such a decision. They argue that it should be on offer as one option among many, along with the kind of palliative care offered by hospitals and hospices.

Euthanasia goes on already

In 1994, the *British Medical Journal* published a survey that showed that some doctors already help patients to die. Doctors can legally give pain-relieving treatment in doses that will bring about people's deaths more quickly, and – in certain circumstances, such as in the case of the brain dead or comatose – they may also withdraw or withhold treatment even though a person will die. They can't directly help someone to die at that person's request. The VES hold that it would be more honest and much safer if voluntary euthanasia was legal and regulated. They argue that there's no ethical difference between withdrawing treatment and delivering a lethal injection.

Voluntary euthanasia maintains quality of life

Human beings should be able to maintain their dignity up until the ends of their lives. This isn't simply a matter of pain, but of self-respect. If my standard of living is such that I no longer want to live, then I should be able to end my life and, if necessary, be assisted in doing so. What's more, the quality of life worth living is one that only I can define. Having control over my life is a way of enhancing my human dignity.

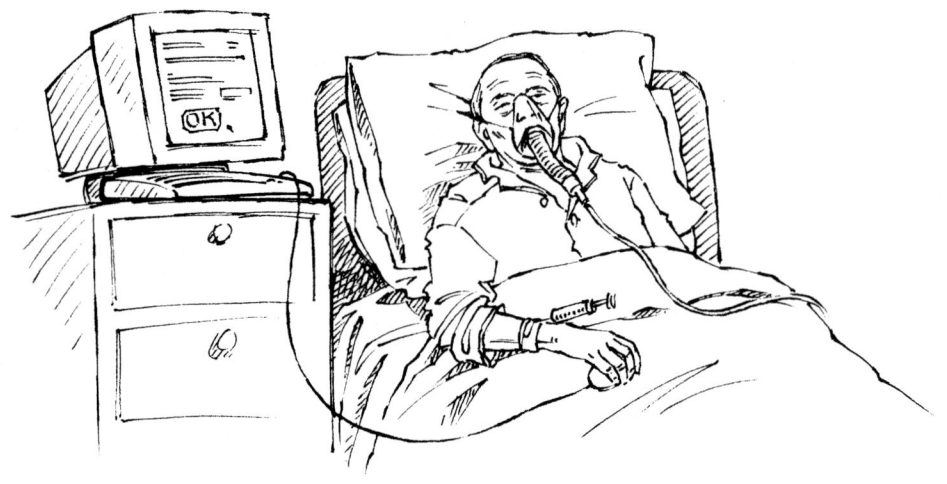

Religious arguments against voluntary euthanasia

Christianity, Islam, Judaism and Buddhism oppose euthanasia, including voluntary euthanasia, while Sikhism and Hinduism tend to leave it to the individual's conscience. Essentially, there are three arguments that come from a religious source.

Life is a sacred gift from God

At the Second Vatican Ecumenical Council, the Roman Catholic Church condemned crimes against life 'such as any type of murder, genocide, abortion, euthanasia, or willful suicide' (*Pastoral Constitution, Gaudium et Spes*, no. 27). Life is sacred and a gift from God, 'which they are called upon to preserve and make fruitful' (*Declaration on Euthanasia*, 1980). To take a life opposes God's love for that person, and rejects the duty of a person to live life according to God's plan. In the same declaration, the Roman Catholic Church made it clear that it was wrong to ask someone for an assisted death, and that an individual can't consent to such a death: 'For it is a question of the violation of the divine law, an offense against the dignity of the human person, a crime against life, and an attack on humanity.' The kind of autonomy that John Stuart Mill argues for is rejected by the Roman Catholic Church. We simply don't have that freedom, because we're made by God for the purpose of loving Him. He's created us for a purpose, and it's our duty to live and pursue that purpose.

Killing is forbidden

In the Hebrew Scriptures (the Christian Old Testament) the Sixth Commandment states 'Thou shalt not kill' (or murder) and traditionally, this has been interpreted by Christians and Jews to include euthanasia. The Quran says 'Take not life which Allah made sacred otherwise than in the course of justice' (Quran 6:151 and 17:33) and 'Do not kill (or destroy) yourselves, for verily Allah has been to you most Merciful' (Quran 4:29). In modern times, the First International Conference on Islamic Medicine endorsed the Islamic Code of Medical Ethics (Islamic Organization of Medical Sciences, Kuwait, 1981, p. 65), which states the following: 'Mercy killing, like suicide, finds no support except in the atheistic way of thinking that believes that our life on this earth is followed by void. The claim of killing for painful hopeless illness is also refuted, for there is no human pain that cannot be largely conquered by medication or by suitable neurosurgery ...'. The prohibition of killing is a moral absolute of Christianity, Judaism and Islam, and while exceptions have been made for warfare and self-defence, taking one's own life has traditionally been considered wrong.

Suffering has a special place in God's plan

Jesus died in pain on the Cross, and human suffering at the end of life connects us to the suffering that Jesus felt. This doesn't mean that Christians should refuse to take painkillers and should actively seek pain, but it does grant suffering the possibility of having a positive effect on the individual. It provides the chance that he or she may grow closer to God. (*Declaration on Euthanasia*, 1980). In an article on euthanasia (in Childress and Macquarrie, 1986), Thomas Wood writes that while suffering can seem meaningless, is terrible and is never sought, it isn't the worst evil – it can be an occasion for spiritual growth and it can have moral effects on those in attendance. It can have meaning in the context of a life lived in faith.

Tasks

1 How might it be argued that helping people to end their lives in the manner of their choosing supports human dignity?

2 Explain the religious principle that rejects the view that we should have control over the nature and timing of the ends of our lives.

3 Some assert that an argument about the quality of life could lead to dangerous assumptions about the disabled. Explain the possible danger here if voluntary euthanasia was to be legalised.

4 Some people argue that the religious view of suffering expressed by the Roman Catholic Church is outdated and insensitive. Why might they make this claim?

Other arguments against euthanasia

There are a number of other difficulties with legalised voluntary euthanasia.

Motives

When a person asks for death, can we be sure that the person isn't crying out in despair, rather than making a definitive decision? In desperate moments, I may feel that I want my life to end – that the pain is too great and life too agonising – but perhaps those moments will pass and I'll be glad that no one acted on my pleas. Can doctors be sure that I know and understand all the facts? Is it possible that I may have a fear of the future which will not be realised? Any euthanasia process would have to be able to establish, beyond any doubt, the true intentions of the patient who is requesting euthanasia and that the patient is fully aware of the situation. The risk of misinformation or a failure to comprehend the situation leaves the patient vulnerable to a decision that he or she might not truly want to make.

Mistakes

Can we be sure that mistakes will not occur? Suppose that someone chooses death because they have been diagnosed with a fatal incurable and painful illness. Then, after the person has died, it becomes apparent the diagnosis was incorrect (Hooker, 1997). There would have to be certainty about the diagnosis, but can there always be medical certainty about what the condition will entail and how long it will take to develop? There's an area of doubt here that could lead to terrible mistakes. Refusing to allow voluntary euthanasia safeguards us against this.

Abuse of the system

Would elderly relatives who think they are burdens to their families ask for voluntary euthanasia out of a sense of duty to the family? Jonathan Glover (1977) notes that people who feel they are burdens on their families sometimes commit suicide. On the other hand, could they be pressured into asking for assisted death by scheming relatives. The recent Shipman murders, where a general practitioner murdered dozens of elderly patients over a period of many years, highlights the power of doctors – especially over the elderly. A voluntary euthanasia system could allow such people even more scope for murder, by manipulating patients and documentation.

Impact on the community

What cultural effect might voluntary euthanasia have on society? Might it lead to other forms of euthanasia being supported – ultimately concluding with the kinds of involuntary euthanasia carried out by the Nazis on the sick, the elderly and the disabled? Glover rejects this argument as unconvincing, and Kusha has observed that this hasn't happened in Holland (Kusha, 1991, p.302). It's more likely that it might damage the care of patients who are dying. While opposing voluntary euthanasia, people have developed caring and sensitive provision for the terminally ill within the hospice movement, but legalisation would affect the culture in which that approach to care has been developed. If voluntary euthanasia was made legal, would people become concerned about visiting hospitals, fearful of what might happen? Perhaps they would be put off by a perceived risk of an unwanted assisted death. Ultimately, voluntary euthanasia, in its physician-assisted form, isn't simply a individual matter. It affects others and society as a whole – the doctor who assists, the nurses who are caring for the patient, the hospital in which it takes place and the wider community. The argument of an individual's right to die must be set against the community in which individuals exist. Acceptance of the practice of killing in hospitals could reduce the respect for life that civilizations uphold now more than ever in terms of human rights.

Tasks

1 Suggest procedures to ensure that a patient's request for euthanasia is truly meant and of his or her own accord (not manipulated by others).

2 In carrying out voluntary euthanasia, what dangers would you have to avoid?

3 Are your procedures reliable enough to permit voluntary euthanasia?

4 What impact do you think voluntary euthanasia would have on the community? Consider attitudes to the dying, hospitals and doctors.

Evaluating voluntary euthanasia

While euthanasia is prohibited in the UK, there are practices close to it that take place within the framework of the law. Some philosophers, such as Peter Singer, argue that there's no moral difference between the withdrawal of treatment (which is currently legal in the UK) and the active killing of a patient by a lethal injection. Consider someone standing by a canal, watching a boy drowning. The bystander fails to throw the ring to the boy and the boy drowns. This is morally reprehensible, but the bystander hasn't actually drowned the boy. In some countries, to pass a road accident where no one is attending the casualties is a criminal offence, but it's not the same as murder. This difference is acknowledged by the Roman Catholic Church, which approves the ending of treatment in situations in which death is inevitable and the treatment is precarious and burdensome (*Declaration on Euthanasia*, 1980).

The religious arguments against voluntary euthanasia carry the weight of theological and teaching traditions. Some have challenged those traditions. Catholic theologian Hans Kung has stated '... as a Christian and a theologian I am convinced that the all-merciful God, who has given men and women freedom and responsibility for their lives, has also left to dying people the responsibility for making a conscientious decision about the manner and time of their deaths' (VES, 2001b). This goes against the Judeo-Christian prohibition of killing. However, there have always been exceptions, such as killing in just wars and in self-defence. If a believer were to oppose all killing, taking a pacifist line with regard to personal and national moral behaviour, then euthanasia would be untenable. A Christian who endorses killing in war (see the section on 'Just war theory' in Chapter 17) or in self-defence might be able to find a starting-point for a theological case for euthanasia.

Many arguments in the euthanasia debate relate to consequences about which we can't be certain. It seems unlikely that a country following Holland's lead could ever slide into the kind of involuntary euthanasia that took place in Nazi Germany. There was an ideological system that underpinned that development. More likely dangers are to be found in the systems that might regulate the practice. Could they ever be foolproof? The protection of the system from error or deliberate misuse raises real concerns – and more so in the light of concerns already being raised about the power of doctors.

We can't predict the impact that voluntary euthanasia might have on peoples' perceptions of hospitals, or how it might affect an elderly person's perception of whether he or she is a burden. Holland can be used as a test case for detecting any **slippery slope** or negative impact that it may be having, but even within Europe cultures differ widely, and whether such a model could operate in a different society is open to question. Because of this, it isn't clear that a society that endorsed legalised voluntary euthanasia would ultimately be better than one where it existed only as an illegal practice.

These potential social dangers stand against the severe restrictions on individual autonomy that result from prohibiting voluntary euthanasia. If you decide that the risks to the community are too great, then you must reject the claims of those who want to avoid deaths that, in their eyes, are too painful and humiliating to accept. While the palliative care provided by organisations such as the hospice movement is undoubtedly a benefit to society, as it cultivates respect and sensitivity towards the terminally ill, and is a benefit to the individuals who receive the care, this will never satisfy those who claim that only the terminally ill can know that their lives are not worth living.

1 How might pre-existing religious teaching on the taking of life be used to support voluntary euthanasia?

2 Can you suggest reasons why people might say that voluntary euthanasia isn't just about the rights of the patient who wants to die?

3 A doctor withdraws treatment from a patient in a permanent vegetative state and then waits as the patient dies. Another doctor delivers a lethal injection to a patient in a identical state and the patient dies almost immediately. Are there any moral differences between what the two doctors have done? Which is better? Justify your view.

4 What are the religious and ethical arguments in favour of and against euthanasia?

CHAPTER SUMMARY

What is voluntary euthanasia?

- Should we have the ability to control our own destinies, by being offered assistance to take our own lives when we judge that the quality of our lives has deteriorated to the point at which they are no longer worth living?

- Euthanasia is a criminal offence in virtually all countries, and it's strongly opposed by most governments and religious organisations.

- In Holland, about a thousand assisted deaths take place each year.

- 'I will not prescribe a deadly drug to please someone, nor give advice that may cause his death.' (Hippocrates)

- Physicians are 'not only to restore the health, but to mitigate pain and dolours; and not only when such mitigation may conduce to recovery, but when it may serve to make a fair and easy passage'. (Francis Bacon)

Arguments for voluntary euthanasia:

- Voluntary euthanasia is not murder, as killing humans who don't want to live isn't wrong.

- It shows mercy to those suffering with intolerable pain from an incurable disease.

- It gives people autonomy – the right to choose their destiny, including how they live and die.

- Voluntary euthanasia should be an option for a competent adult who is able and willing to make such a decision.

- Euthanasia goes on already, in an uncontrolled and therefore unsafe way.
- It allows human beings to live dignified lives – the ends of their lives should be dignified.

Religious arguments against voluntary euthanasia:
- Life is a sacred gift from God, and humans are called upon to preserve it and make it fruitful.
- Killing is forbidden in the Hebrew Scriptures.
- For Christians, suffering has a special place in God's plan, because Jesus died in pain on the Cross, and human suffering can have meaning in the context of a life lived in faith.

Other arguments against euthanasia:
- Motives may be questionable – we may ask in moments of despair, or out of misplaced fears of the future.
- Mistakes could be made through faulty diagnosis.
- The system might be subject to abuse in the case of elderly relatives.
- Euthanasia might have a negative impact on the community by reducing the importance of care of patients who are dying, or by preventing people from going to hospital for fear of the possible consequences.
- Acceptance of the practice of killing in hospitals could reduce the respect for life that civilizations uphold.

Evaluating voluntary euthanasia:
- Some argue that there's no moral difference between the withdrawal of treatment and the active killing of a patient by lethal injection.
- The theological traditions that underpin the religious arguments have been challenged, as there are exceptions for the no-killing rule in the case of self-defence and war.
- The consequences of legalised euthanasia are uncertain.
- There would be flaws in the systems that might regulate the practice. Could they ever be foolproof?
- We can't predict the impact that voluntary euthanasia might have on peoples' perceptions of hospitals, or how it might affect an elderly person's perception of whether he or she is a burden.
- The potential social dangers stand against the restrictions of individual autonomy that result from prohibiting voluntary euthanasia.

Business ethics

Introduction

Key writers and works

Adam Smith (1723–1790): *An Enquiry into the Nature and Causes of the Wealth of Nations*, 1776

Karl Marx (1818–1883): *The Communist Manifesto*, 1848

Key terms

Business ethics, capitalism, corporate responsibility, ethical investment, profit motive, transnational corporation (TNC)

What you will learn by the end of this chapter

- The broad areas covered by business ethics.
- The perspectives of Adam Smith and Karl Marx on capitalism.
- Christian approaches to business ethics and the Catholic concept of the common good.
- Ethical issues raised by free global trade.
- What is meant by ethical investment and some of the issues that it raises.

Key questions

1 Is it wrong to steal a pencil from the company you work for? Why/why not?

2 Should a company stop producing arms if this means the loss of hundreds or thousands of jobs?

3 Should businesses be obliged to take into account anything other than profits, and if so what?

4 Is free trade in the interest of developing countries?

5 Are we responsible for the things done with our savings by banks?

Background

Business ethics covers the moral justification of economic systems and practices, the responsibilities of businesses and corporations, and the rights of workers. It is seen today in terms of ethical and unethical behaviour of corporations with regard to workers, consumers, the community and society at large and the environment, and is sometimes expressed as corporate responsibility.

Robert C. Solomon (1997, p. 254) observes that discussions about the rightness and wrongness of aspects of business life go back to the earliest writings. Aristotle approved of household trading (*oikonomikos*) as an essential part of society, but he considered trade for profit (*chrematisike*) as wholly devoid of virtue and he considered the people who did it to be parasites (Solomon, 1997, p. 355).

There are many examples of businesses acting unethically. Anthony Weston (2001, p. 304) notes that the A. H. Robins Corporation, maker of Chapstick and other household drugs, produced the Dalkon Shield, an intra-uterine device that caused infection, sterility and death in many of the 10 million women worldwide who used it. He also cites the example of a car fire hazard that the manufacturer could have easily corrected at a cost of $5–10 per car, but that they declined to put right, despite the knowledge that hundreds of people would be burnt as a result (Weston, 2001, p. 304).

Questions about the behaviour of companies are therefore an important feature of the discussion, but so are the principles behind the economic systems in which the companies operate, and debates about those principles must take account of Adam Smith and Karl Marx.

Adam Smith and Karl Marx

The moral philosopher Adam Smith is known for his works *The Theory of Moral Sentiments* (1759) and *An Enquiry into the Nature and Causes of the Wealth of Nations* (1776). In the first of these works, he argued that people were born with a moral sense, an innate conscience and a sense of natural fellow feeling, or sympathy, with others in our community. The second work proposes a system of political economy, and is not only an economic tract but also an assessment of social evolution.

Smith's account considered human evolution from hunters, through nomadic agriculture and feudal farming, until finally a stage was reached that he called perfect liberty, which meant that wages were determined by the market rather than by guilds, and trade and enterprise took place unconstrained by the government. This is known as *laissez-faire* capitalism and it reflects Smith's conviction that free market competition was the best way of encouraging entrepreneurs. He also thought that the benefits of those entrepreneurs would flow down throughout the community. A successful factory owner would employ more factory workers, who would gain from the stability of a good job. The community would gain from having higher employment. Government or guild controls would restrict the entrepreneur's ability to compete in the market and would reduce the success of the business. Smith believed that the free market system was counterbalanced by the natural fellow feeling or sympathy that individuals had for others in their community. This would mitigate against extreme individualism or selfishness. This point was subsequently forgotten by right-wing capitalists, who simply amplified the individualist doctrine of Smith's thought.

The term **capitalism** was brought to prominence by the work of Karl Marx, who used it pejoratively. He considered it

> ... the great feudal lords created an incomparably larger proletariat by the forcible driving of the peasantry from the land, to which the latter had the same feudal right as the lord himself, and by the usurpation of the common lands ... The old nobility had been devoured by the great feudal wars. The new nobility was the child of its time, for which money was the power of all powers.
>
> *Capital*, Karl Marx, Penguin Classics (1993)

Those who do not own the means of production (the proletariat or working class) must sell their labour, leaving the capitalist class (or bourgeoisie) with decisive bargaining powers.

Allen Wood summarises the Marxist criticism of capitalism as follows:

■ Capitalism has been responsible for colossal growth of human productive capacity.

■ Capitalism has a tendency to accumulate wealth in the hands of the means of production owners who bear few of the burdens the working class must bear, and the lot of the working class can only improve through their emancipation into means of production ownership.

Wood (1995), p. 120

The following extract from *The Communist Manifesto* outlines Marx's conviction that free trade capitalism leads to exploitation of the workers and creates more capital for those who own the means of production:

> It has resolved personal worth into exchange value. And in place of the numberless and feasible chartered freedoms, has set up that single, unconscionable freedom – Free Trade. In one word, for exploitation, veiled by religious and political illusions, naked, shameless, direct, brutal exploitation …

> … But does wage-labour create any property for the labourer? Not a bit. It creates capital, i.e., that kind of property which exploits wage-labour, and which cannot increase except upon condition of begetting a new supply of wage-labour for fresh exploitation.

> Marx (1888 edition), from Parts 1 and 2

Christianity and business

The Bible has no clear theory of economics, although it does discuss property. The commandment against stealing and the laws outlining the restoration of ill-gotten gains support the idea of the protection of privately owned property, although prophets denounced the rich for violating the rights and needs of others. Jesus was concerned about sharing wealth with the poor and meeting their needs: 'he has sent me to bring good news to the poor' (Jesus quoting Isaiah, in Luke 4:18).

After the Reformation, the virtues of thrift and enterprise were advocated by John Calvin and the English puritans. Max Weber wrote about the instrumental link between Protestant virtues and capitalism in *The Protestant Ethic and the Spirit of Capitalism* (1904–5), noting on p. 172 that:

> attainment of [wealth] as a fruit of labor in a calling was a sign of God's blessing, And even more important: the religious valuation of restlessness, continuous, systematic work in a worldly calling, as the highest means to asceticism, and at the same time the surest and most evident proof of rebirth and genuine faith, must have been the most powerful conceivable lever for … the spirit of capitalism. When the limitation of consumption is combined with the release of acquisitive activity, the inevitable practical result is obvious: accumulation of capital through ascetic compulsion to save.

> Weber (1904–5), p. 172

It has been suggested that Protestant theology is therefore too closely linked or individualistic to provide an effect criticism of industry (see Gunnemann, 1986, p. 68). An extreme extension of this is found among some Protestant churches that see business success as evidence of divine approval.

Roman Catholic thought has offered more critical teaching on industrial life. *Rerum Novarum* (1891), *Quadragesimo Anno* (1931), *Mater et Magistra* (1961) and *Populorum Progressio* (1967) took note of the exposed position of workers in the modern industrial age and argued for a right to work, for labour unions and for the obligation on the part of governments to protect the weak (see Gunnemann, 1986, p. 68):

> A tiny group of extravagantly rich men have been able to lay upon the great multitude of unpropertied workers a yoke little better than that of slavery itself.
>
> Pope Leo XIII, *Rerum Novarum* (1891), para. 2

and later

> Labour ... is not mere commodity. On the contrary, the worker's human dignity in it must be recognised. It therefore cannot be bought and sold like a commodity ... The right ordering of economic life cannot be left to a free competition of forces. From this source as from a poisoned spring have originated and spread all the errors of individualistic economic teaching ... An immense power and despotic economic dictatorship is consolidated in the hands of a few, who often are not owners but only the trustees and managing directors of invested funds which they administer according to their own arbitrary will and pleasure.
>
> Pope Pius XI, *Quadragesimo Anno* (1931), paras 83, 88 and 105

> The obligation to earn one's bread by the sweat of one's brow also presumes to right to do so. A society in which this right is systematically denied, in which economic policies do not allow workers to reach satisfactory levels of employment, cannot be justified from an ethical point of view, nor can that society attain social peace.
>
> Pope John Paul II, *Centisimus Annus* (1991), para. 43

Clifford Longley (1998) states that the idea of the common good is fundamental to Catholic social teaching. The concept has three main dimensions; that certain shared public values transcend the rights of individuals, that decisions should be taken at the lowest possible level of government ('subsidiarity') and that we are all responsible for one another ('solidarity') (p. 99). The Catholic Church criticises both communism and capitalism, and while it acknowledges that free market capitalism has shown itself superior in encouraging wealth creation and prosperity, it criticises the philosophical extension of the economic theory that the interests of the many are best served by individuals pursuing their own interests. This can lead to individual selfishness (p. 106). The Church argues that freedom in the economic sector should be circumscribed within a strong juridical framework that places it at the service of human freedom in its totality (Pope John Paul II,

Centisimus Annus, 1991, para. 42). In Longley's words, free markets can never be allowed to be sovereign, but must be watched, regulated and controlled in the name of the common good, because they are biased against the poor, tend to encourage selfishness among people and need a moral corrective (Longley, 1998, p. 111).

The profit motive and corporate responsibility

The maximisation of profit is sometimes identified as the driving force behind all business, and as the basic reason why business is unethical. This mentality sees making profit as the only purpose of business. Profit becomes the accumulation of wealth, and an extension of the vice of greed. To get a flavour of this outlook, here are two extracts from movies, one from the 1970s and the other from the 1980s:

> You have meddled with the primal forces of nature, Mr. Beale, and I won't have it, is that clear? You think you have merely stopped a business deal – that is not the case! The Arabs have taken billions of dollars out of this country, and now they must put it back. It is ebb and flow, tidal gravity, it is ecological balance! You are an old man who thinks in terms of nations and peoples. There are no nations. There are no peoples! There are no Russians. There are no Arabs! There are no third worlds! There is no West! There is only one holistic system of systems, one vast and immane ['immense' or 'brutal'], interwoven, interacting, multi-variate, multi-national dominion of dollars! Petro-dollars, electro-dollars, multi-dollars! Reichmarks, rubles, rin, pounds and shekels! It is the international system of currency that determines the totality of life on this planet!
>
> From *Network* (1976)

> The point is, ladies and gentlemen, greed is good. Greed works, greed is right. Greed clarifies, cuts through, and captures the essence of the evolutionary spirit. Greed in all its forms, greed for life, money, love, knowledge, has marked the upward surge of mankind and greed, mark my words, will save not only Teldar Paper but that other malfunctioning corporation called the USA ... Thank you.
>
> From *Wall Street* (1987)

One view of business ethics is that ultimately business is good at business, and that it should not get drawn into discussions about helping society or community projects. If it were to do that, the business activity might become less profitable – or even unprofitable – and risk failure, with all the harm to employees, investors and the wider community. Getting involved in charity or community projects is stealing from the shareholder. An extreme expression of this was aired by Milton Friedman in *The New York Times Magazine* on 13 September 1970, where he argued that the social responsibility of business was to increase its profits. To maximise profits is the only option, and corporations have no skills in the area of supporting charitable, health or education projects in the communities in which they are based.

Robert C. Solomon (1993) argues that this is an oversimplified view of what the profit motive is and why it is important. The pursuit of profit is one of many goals in business: 'we adopt a too narrow vision of what business is, e.g. the pursuit of profits, and then derive unethical or amoral conclusions'. Profits should be seen as 'a means of encouraging and rewarding hard work and investment, building a better business and serving society better' (p. 357). Profits get distributed and re-invested to ensure that the business grows and employees are rewarded.

Solomon sees a link between profit and social responsibility. Profit refers to productivity and social responsibility. A business aims to make a profit, but only by supplying quality goods and services, providing jobs and fitting into a community. Good businesses need to take the community into account, as a degree of social responsibility is necessary for business to be profitable and therefore productive. Businesses rest on shared interests and mutually agreed rules of conduct. Competition takes place in a community, which business serves and depends on: 'business almost always involves large co-operative and mutually trusting groups, not only corporations themselves but networks of suppliers, service people, customers and investors' (Solomon, 1993, p. 358).

Anthony Weston (2001, p. 305) illustrates this point. The pharmaceutical company Johnson & Johnson has a corporate credo, which lists its responsibilities. It first identifies doctors, nurses and patients, mothers, fathers and all others who use its products. It then lists its employees, the communities in which people live and work, and finally its stockholders. The stakeholders, the people who use the products and live and work in the locality, come above the stockholders, who invest in the company (the full credo is reproduced at the end of this chapter). When seven people were poisoned by cyanide-laced Tylenol capsules in Chicago in 1981, Johnson & Johnson pulled 22 million bottles off the shelf, offered to exchange any already purchased bottles, provided executives to talk to the media and took losses of $100 million. They re-introduced the drug in tamper-resistant packaging, which has become the industry standard, and quickly reclaimed their 80% market share, in Weston's words 'proving that doing the right thing by stakeholders also benefits stockholders too' (Weston, 2001, p. 305).

Transnational corporations and developing countries

Between 1958 and 1998, the value of global trade has increased by a factor of over 80. In 1998, the European Union produced 26% of the GDO wealth through exported goods and services (worth $2172 billion out of the total of $8346 billion) (De Schutter, 2001, p. 9). The foreign affiliates of trans-national corporations made $9.5 trillion in sales in 1997, a substantial increase on the previous year (UNDP, 1999, p. 31) and

> ... the gigantic corporations make or control between a half and two-thirds of the global production and of the international trade.
>
> Hugon (1999), p. 34

These statistics showing the global value of world trade and the importance of trans-national corporations in global production reflect a change in the production of goods, as noted by Lester Thurow, an American economist, writing in 'The fractures of capitalism':

> For the first time in the history of Mankind, any kind of product can be manufactured anywhere in the world, and sold anywhere in the world. A capitalist economy means manufacturing where costs are the lowest, and selling where prices and profits are the highest. Minimum costs and maximum profit, that's it; maximising profit lies at the core of capitalism. The sentimental affection for the country is not part of the system.
>
> Lester Thurow, quoted in EFTA (2001), p. 11

Capitalists argue that global free trade is the only way in which less developed countries (LDCs) can become prosperous. Transnational corporations (TNCs) enable capital and technology to be transferred to LDCs, attracted by low labour and other costs. This raises incomes, employment and trade even in developed countries, by exploiting comparative advantage.

However, others argue that unrestricted free trade can allow TNCs to restrict LDCs from exploiting their potential. There can be major losers in the free trade market. As Eduardo Galeano puts it:

> The division of labour among nations – resulting from the theory of comparative advantage – actually consists in the specialisation of countries: in 'victory' for some, in 'defeat' for others.
>
> Eduardo Galeano, quoted in EFTA (2001)

and, according to the sociologist and political expert Robert Fossaert,

> besides political dependence which is always conspicuous, there is also economic dependence, often masked by the apparent egalitarianism of trade, as if all the countries had equal currencies, equally powerful banks, and equally productive factories: the uneven development of economic structures is converted by the world market into captures of stocks, chronic debt burdens, unfair trade and other imperialistic effects that may be less conspicuous than those of colonialism, but of which the powerful driving force is accumulation at global level.
>
> Fossaert (1996), p. 144

There is also a question of the extent to which the profit benefits that TNCs gain from using the available comparative advantage of LDCs are shared with the LDCs themselves:

> The top fifth of the world's people in the richest countries enjoy 82% of the expanding export trade and 68% of foreign direct investment – the bottom fifth, barely more than 1%.
>
> UNDP (1999), p. 31

The global reach school of thought (named after the work of Richard J. Barnet – see Barnet and Müller, 1974; Barnet and Cavanagh, 1994) paints a picture of TNCs as global powers that are capable of reaching across boundaries, but that are obsessed with their own interests and that show a lack of concern for those who are affected. In *No Logo* (2001), Naomi Klein has chronicled many examples of cases of exploitation by TNCs of workers in LDCs: see the extract at the end of this chapter.

The global reach school argues that the disparity of benefits received in LDCs compared with the profits made by TNCs is a result of market imperfections that need corrective control. LDCs are not in an equal bargaining position with TNCs and are unable to protect their key national industries. Free trade between very powerful TNCs and powerless LDCs, with fragile economies and industries, is not free in the fullest of senses.

Unfortunately, as a result of the free trade capitalist mantra, aid and development packages have often been negotiated on condition of a lowering of trade barriers on the part of the LDC, sometimes with catastrophic affects when the global market has gone against the interests of the poorer country. Ironically, some of the richest countries, such as the USA, have very strong trade barriers to protect their national interests. Fair trade groups argue for a system of world trade as a source of well-being for all peoples – and for all the people of all peoples – and that the market must have controls to protect certain fundamentals, such as health and education projects, and the right to grow one's own food rather than just crops to be exported. The Trade Justice Movement campaigns for trade justice to benefit poor people, not free trade. They call on world leaders to:

- stop forcing poor countries to open their markets; and champion their right to manage their own economies
- regulate big business and their investments to ensure people and the environment come before profits
- stop rich countries promoting the interests of big business through trade interventions that harm the poor and the environment
- ensure trade policy is made in a fair, transparent and democratic way

Trade Justice Movement (n.d.)

Ultimately, the debate about global trade returns to the debate about capitalism and, as noted earlier, capitalism is the system that has shown itself to be the most effective form of wealth production. However, both religious and non-religious groups are concerned that free trade should be restricted to protect fundamental rights and uphold justice, but this appears to be much more difficult in the global community, where there is no strong independent judicial authority.

Tasks

1 What is meant by the phrases 'just trade' and 'free trade'?

2 If you were going to restrict the activities of companies, what limits would you place on the free market?

Ethical investment

1 Is it right to make money out of shares in tobacco companies?

2 Does it matter if your money, held in a bank account, is being used by that bank to invest in companies that are doing things that you consider to be morally wrong?

3 Should you borrow from banks that have holdings in arms manufacturers?

4 Are you responsible for the things that are done with your investments?

The profit motive versus corporate responsibility argument extends into investment. At one level, it could be argued that the most important thing that banks and other financial institutions can do with your money is to invest it in the companies that are most likely to make big profits, so that they can give you better rates of return on your investments. Supporters of the profit motive would maintain that this is what financial institutions are obliged to do. However, a case could be made for ethical investment, just as for corporate responsibility. The Ethical Investment Association argues that:

> socially responsible investment allows you to integrate your values and beliefs with your financial requirements. By investing in a socially and environmentally responsible manner, you are putting your money to work towards a better world and a more just society. You are voicing an opinion for positive social change, while helping to make it happen. You also know your money isn't going to finance businesses engaged in poor social and environmental practices. You are helping to create a sound and sustainable future.
>
> Ethical Investment Association (n.d.)

This may mean sacrificing the profit levels attained by 'unethical businesses', such as those connected to tobacco or arms manufacturing. A BBC news story from 2002 reported that the losses to investors in ethical portfolios have been greater than other losses (BBC News Online, 24 January 2002), although prior to that investments in ethical funds did slightly better than others (BBC News Online, 2000). One of the potential positive side effects of ethical investment is to encourage more companies to adopt socially and environmentally sustainable practices. The threat of litigation for poor practices, as well as bad publicity, may put pressure on business activities.

In the eighteenth century, the Quakers refused to invest in companies that were involved in the slave trade, and increasingly today people are less willing to invest in funds which in turn are invested in pornography or arms manufacturing, or which involve governments of doubtful ethical integrity. However, the question remains: Are the general public prepared to sacrifice personal profits for ethical reasons?

Extracts from key texts

Naomi Klein, *No Logo*

From pages 327–328

The Year of the Sweatshop

For a time that year, North Americans couldn't turn on their televisions without hearing shameful stories about the exploitative labor practices behind the most popular, mass-marketed labels on the landscape. In August 1995, the Gap's freshly scrubbed facade was further exfoliated to reveal a lawless factory in El Salvador where the manager responded to a union drive by firing 150 people and vowing that 'blood will flow' if organizing continued. In May 1996, U.S. labor activists discovered that chat-show host Kathie Lee Gifford's eponymous line of sportswear (sold exclusively at Wal-Mart) was being stitched by a ghastly combination of child laborers in Honduras and illegal sweatshop workers in New York. At about the same time, Guess jeans, which had built its image with sultry black-and-white photographs of supermodel Claudia Schiffer, was in open warfare with the U.S. Department of Labor over a failure on the part of its California-based contractors to pay the minimum wage. Even Mickey Mouse was letting his sweatshops show after a Disney contractor in Haiti was caught making Pocahontas pajamas under such impoverished conditions that workers had to nourish their babies with sugar water.

More outrage flowed after NBC aired an investigation of Mattel and Disney just days before Christmas 1996. With the help of hidden cameras, the reporter showed that children in Indonesia and China were working in virtual slavery 'so that children in America can put frilly dresses on America's favorite doll.' In June 1996, *Life* magazine created more waves with photographs of Pakistani kids – looking shockingly young and paid as little as six cents an hour – hunched over soccer balls that bore the unmistakable Nike swoosh. But it wasn't just Nike. Adidas, Reebok, Umbro, Mitre and Brine were all manufacturing balls in Pakistan where an estimated 10 000 children worked in the industry, many of them sold as indentured slave laborers to their employers and branded like livestock ... Scandal has dogged Nike, with new revelations about factory conditions trailing the company's own global flight patterns. First came the reports of union crackdowns in South Korea; when the contractors fled and set up shop in Indonesia, the watchdogs followed, filing stories on starvation wages and military intimidation of workers. In March 1996, *The New York Times* reported that after a wildcat strike at one Javanese factory, twenty-two workers were fired and one man who had been singled out as an organizer was locked in a room inside the factory and interrogated by soldiers for seven days.

From pages 338–339

Amnesty International, in a departure from its focus on prisoners persecuted for either their religious or political beliefs, is also beginning to treat multinational corporations as major players in the denial of human rights worldwide. More and more, recent Amnesty reports have found that people such as the late Ken Saro-Wiwa have been persecuted for what a government sees as a destabilizing anticorporate stance. In a 1997 report, the group documents the fact that Indian villagers and tribal peoples were violently arrested, and some killed, for peacefully resisting the development of private power plants and luxury hotels on their lands. A democratic country, in other words, was becoming less democratic as a result of corporate intervention. 'Development,' Amnesty warned, is 'being pursued at the expense of human rights ...'

The Johnson & Johnson credo

We believe our first responsibility is to the doctors, nurses and patients, to mothers and fathers and all others who use our products and services. In meeting their needs everything we do must be of high quality. We must constantly strive to reduce our costs in order to maintain reasonable prices. Customers' orders must be serviced promptly and accurately. Our suppliers and distributors must have an opportunity to make a fair profit.

We are responsible to our employees, the men and women who work with us throughout the world. Everyone must be considered as an individual. We must respect their dignity and recognize their merit. They must have a sense of security in their jobs. Compensation must be fair and adequate, and working conditions clean, orderly and safe. We must be mindful of ways to help our employees fulfill their family responsibilities. Employees must feel free to make suggestions and complaints. There must be equal opportunity for employment, development and advancement for those qualified. We must provide competent management, and their actions must be just and ethical.

We are responsible to the communities in which we live and work and to the world community as well. We must be good citizens – support good works and charities and bear our fair share of taxes. We must encourage civic improvements and better health and education. We must maintain in good order the property we are privileged to use, protecting the environment and natural resources.

Our final responsibility is to our stockholders. Business must make a sound profit. We must experiment with new ideas. Research must be carried on, innovative programs developed and mistakes paid for. New equipment must be purchased, new facilities provided and new products launched. Reserves must be created to provide for adverse times. When we operate according to these principles, the stockholders should realize a fair return.

CHAPTER SUMMARY

Introduction:

- Business ethics considers the moral justification of economic systems and practices, the responsibilities of businesses and corporations, and the rights of workers.

- Aristotle approved of household trading as an essential, but considered trade for profit as devoid of virtue.

Adam Smith and Karl Marx:

- Adam Smith proposed a system of political economy to reach 'perfect liberty', which meant wages determined by the market and enterprise free from government control (*laissez-faire* capitalism), in the context of moral sympathy towards others in the community.

- Smith believed that free market competition encouraged entrepreneurs and that the benefits would flow throughout the community.
- Karl Marx opposed capitalism as a system that concentrated wealth in the hands of those who owned the means of production by exploiting the workers.

Christianity and business:

- The Bible has no theory of economics, although it does discuss property.
- Jesus seemed concerned about sharing wealth with the poor and meeting their needs.
- Protestant reformers extolled virtues of thrift and enterprise, but this is too individualistic to provide an effective criticism of industry.
- Roman Catholic teaching took note of the exposed position of workers in the modern industrial age and argued for a right to work, for labour unions, and for the obligation on the part of governments to protect the weak.
- Clifford Longley notes that fundamental to Catholic social teaching is the idea of the common good, which means that certain shared public values transcend the rights of individuals, that decisions should be taken at the lowest possible level of government ('subsidiarity') and that we are all responsible for one another ('solidarity').
- The Catholic Church acknowledges the success of free market capitalism, but criticises the philosophical extension of the economic theory that the many are best served by individuals pursuing their own interests.
- Freedom in the economic sector should be permitted only within a strong juridical framework that places it at the service of human freedom in its totality.

The profit motive and corporate responsibility:

- The maximisation of profit is sometimes identified as the driving force behind all business, and as the basic reason why business is unethical.
- One view of business ethics is that ultimately business is good at business, and that it should not get drawn into discussions about helping society or community projects lest the business activity should become less profitable – or even unprofitable – and risk failure, with all the harm to employees, investors and the wider community.
- Profits should be seen as 'a means of encouraging and rewarding hard work and investment, building a better business and serving society better'. (Robert C. Solomon)

- A business aims to make a profit, but only by supplying quality goods and services, by providing jobs and by fitting into a community.
- A degree of social responsibility is necessary for a business to be profitable and therefore productive, as businesses rest on shared interests and mutually agreed upon rules of conduct.

Transnational corporations and developing countries:
- Global trade has increased enormously and is mostly under the control of gigantic corporations.
- 'Any kind of product can be manufactured anywhere in the world, and sold anywhere in the world.' (Lester Thurow)
- Capitalists argue that global free trade allows transnational corporations (TNCs) to enable capital and technology to be transferred to less developed countries (LDCs).
- Others argue that unrestricted free trade can allow TNCs to restrict LDCs from exploiting their potential.
- The rewards seem to be concentrated in the hands of the rich: 'The top fifth of the world's people in the richest countries enjoy 82% of the expanding export trade and 68% of foreign direct investment – the bottom fifth, barely more than 1%.' (UNDP)
- The global reach school of thought sees TNCs as global powers that are capable of reaching across boundaries, but that are obsessed with their own interests and show a lack of concern for those who are affected.
- Free trade between very powerful TNCs and powerless LDCs, with fragile economies and industries, is not free in the fullest of senses.
- Aid and development packages have often been negotiated on condition of a lowering of trade barriers on the part of the LDC, sometimes with catastrophic effects, while some of the richest countries, such as the USA, have very strong trade barriers to protect their national interests.
- Fair trade groups argue for just trade, rather than free trade, to protect the poorest countries and workers and their industries.
- Capitalism is the system that has shown itself to be the most effective form of wealth production, but free trade should be restricted to protect fundamental rights and justice.

Ethical investment:

It could be argued that the most important thing that banks and other financial institutions can do with your money is to invest it in the companies that are most likely to make big profits, so that they can give you better rates of return on your investments.

- Others argue for socially responsible investment that matches people's values and beliefs with their financial requirements. This may mean sacrificing the profit levels attained by 'unethical businesses' such as those connected to tobacco or arms manufacturing.

- One potential positive side effect of ethical investment is to encourage more companies to adopt socially and environmentally sustainable practices. The threat of litigation for poor practices, as well as bad publicity, may put pressure on business activities.

- In the eighteenth century, the Quakers refused to invest in companies that were involved in the slave trade.

Chapter 20

Environmental ethics

Contents of Chapter 20

Introduction

Key philosophers and works

Peter Singer (1943–): *Practical Ethics*, 1993

Terence R. Anderson: Environmental ethics (in Childress and Macquarrie, 1986)

Pope John Paul II: *Centesimus Annus*, 1991

Aldo Leopold (1887–1948): *A Sand County Almanac*, 1949; The land ethic (in LaFollette, 1997)

Scott I. Paradise: Rehabilitation for cosmic outlaws (in Stone, 1971)

Arne Naess (1912–) and George Sessions: Basic principles of deep ecology, *Ecophilosophy*, 1984

Key terms

Anthropocentric, biocentric, deep ecology, geocentric, holistic, theocentric

What you will learn by the end of this chapter

■ The main ethical areas of debate related to the environment.

■ Religious and non-religious approaches to problems within the environment.

■ The strengths and weaknesses of the different approaches.

Key questions

1 Does the environmental system have value in itself that must be respected?

2 Is it more convincing to argue that we should take care of the environment for its own sake or for our sake?

3 Do Christians have a moral obligation to look after the environment?

What is environmental ethics?

In his book *An Introduction to Christian Ethics* (2002), Roger H. Crook observes that technological advancement and scientific investigation had been seen as positive human activity, perhaps paving the way towards a better society, but that there is now a view that this activity is threatening humanity's long-term survival (Crook, 2002, p. 267). The term 'environmental ethics' covers a wide range of concerns, such as the preservation of endangered species, the conservation of natural habitats, the effects of over-fishing or deforestation, the depletion of the ozone layer, and the effects of pollution on human health and the natural world. Environmental ethics is concerned with our attitudes towards and impact on the biological and geological dimensions of the planet, in terms of how that impact affects humanity, whether it enhances or diminishes the well-being and diversity of other forms of life on Earth, and whether humanity maintains or disturbs the balance between the planet's different life forms and geological systems. In addition, Christians and other religious believers have a particular view of their duty and responsibility towards creation.

There are differences among scientists about both the exact nature of environmental problems and how to solve them. Exponents of environmental ethics, however, argue that the following is the case:

- The different delicate and interconnected systems that nurture and sustain life, providing clean air, water and soil, are breaking down through pollution and abuse. Deforestation and emissions of 'greenhouse gases' affect the atmosphere and threaten to disrupt or damage life on Earth.

- The world's finite natural resources are being depleted at an unsustainable rate because of our way of life and the increasing population. The reduction of non-renewable natural resources threatens international stability as well as the local inhabitants who depend on them.

- It is likely that environmental damage will disproportionately affect the poor, who tend to live in vulnerable areas. What is more, 80% of the world's resources are controlled by the richest 20% of the world's population, while 20% of humanity lacks clean water, adequate food, shelter and clothing. The rich take a greater proportion of what the environment has to offer than the poor.

- Industrialisation and technological and scientific development, often for commercial gain, has led to the destruction of grasslands and forests, the over-exploitation of oceans, and the extinction of species, reducing biodiversity.

A few people argue that this is a simplified distortion of a far more complex picture. In his work *The Skeptical Environmentalist: Measuring the Real State of the World* (2001), Björn Lomborg suggests that, for human beings, the situation in the world is getting better but is not yet good. He argues that we are not running out of energy resources, that fewer and fewer people are starving and that poverty has been reduced more in the past 50 years than in the preceding 500 years (p. 4). In other words, the picture of the planet's environmental state is far more complex and quite simply not as bad as many believe. His work is a survey of the research of others. His case is that development protects us from the environment, and enables us to counter the extremes of weather and failures of crops that, up until the last century, meant life or death for large numbers of humans. An environmental ethic that constrains development might actually make the situation for human beings worse. This does not mean that there is no place for environmental ethics, but that any such ethic should not be based on unproven assumptions.

Task

Consider the following extract and answer the questions.

KAKADU NATIONAL PARK in Australia's Northern Territory, contains rugged woodlands, swamps and waterways supporting a rich variety of life; it contains species found nowhere else, including some, such as the Hooded Parrot and the Pig-nosed Turtle, which are endangered. Kakadu affords aesthetic enjoyment and recreational and research opportunities. Many think it is a place of immense beauty and ecological significance. It is of spiritual significance to the Jawoyn aboriginals. Kakadu is also rich in gold, platinum, palladium and uranium, which some think should be mined. If this happens then, environmentalists claim, aesthetic, recreational and research opportunities will be reduced, the beauty of Kakadu will be lessened, species will disappear, ecological richness will decrease, the naturalness of the place will be compromised and the spiritual values of the Jawoyn discounted. Mining already goes on in the Kakadu area and there is pressure to allow more. Should more mining be allowed? Should any mining at all be allowed? How exactly might we reach answers to these ethical questions?

Elliott (1991), pp. 284–293

1 Should the mining in this example be allowed?

2 Should any mining at all be allowed?

3 How might we go about answering these ethical questions?

4 Do human beings have a greater claim to the planet's resources than any other life form?

5 Should humans be forced to accept a simpler lifestyle, to protect and preserve the environment?

Ethical issues

Christian approaches to environmental ethics

Christian views on the environment have been accused of placing an emphasis on human domination of the world. The account of creation in Genesis says 'let them [humans] have dominion over the fish of the sea, and over the fowl of the air, and over the cattle, and over all the earth, and over every creeping thing that creepeth upon the earth' (Genesis 1:26b), and this anthropocentric emphasis on the idea that the world is for human use is also seen in the writings of the ancient Greek philosopher Aristotle: 'Since nature makes nothing purposeless or in vain, it is undeniably true that she has made all animals for the sake of man' (*Politics* I, 3.1256b21). Similarly, Aquinas maintains that 'all animals are naturally subject to man'. Peter Singer is critical of this Christian tradition and argues that the Hebrew and Greek traditions place humans at the moral centre while the environment is regarded as morally insignificant. Genesis makes mankind dominant over the world and encourages him to multiply over it and subdue it. Singer notes that Aquinas did not recognise sin against the environment, and that the main Western view has been that the natural world exists for the benefit of humans: in this view, nature has no intrinsic value and its destruction cannot be sinful. Scott I. Paradise has suggested that certain common religious beliefs need to be revised, and below are his revisions:

1. 'Only man and the things he treasures have any value' must be replaced by 'All things have value.'

2. 'The universe exists for man's exclusive and unconditional use' must be replaced by 'Man has been given responsibility for the earth.'

3. 'In production and consumption, man finds his major fulfillment' must be replaced by 'In producing and consuming, man finds only a small part of his humanity.'

4. 'Production and consumption must increase endlessly' must be replaced by 'Improvement in the quality of life takes precedence over increasing the quantity of material production.'

5. 'The earth's resources are unlimited' must be replaced by 'Material resources are limited and are to be used carefully and cherished.'

6. 'A major purpose of government is to make it easy for individuals and corporations to exploit the environment for the amassing of wealth and power' must be replaced by 'A major purpose of government is to regulate the exercise or property rights and to supervise a planning process that will prevent the impairment of the quality of the environment.'

Paradise (1971)

It can be argued that the Christian tradition presents a more positive environmental ethics (see Anderson, 1986). Christian ethics is necessarily theocentric (God-centred) as God is the underlying reason for moral behaviour and this includes environmental ethics. It is also anthropocentric in that the Christian/agape love of neighbour is the fundamental principle for human relations, and as the condition of the environment can affect the quality and ease of human life. It is also arguably geo/biocentric, in that creation is God-made and good, and therefore must be preserved because it is a good in itself. Anderson notes that 'The recognition that nonhuman creatures have intrinsic value is present in the Christian tradition (Basil the Great, Chrysostom, Augustine, Francis)' (Anderson, 1986, p. 197). Crook argues that these latter obligations have authority because of God. Christians see their relationships with one another in terms of their relationship with God. The value that the environment has comes from its relationship with God – that which God created (Crook, 2002, p. 267).

The Christian view understands the environment in terms of God's sacred creation. The idea of stewardship is present in the Bible, which emphasises that humans are responsible to God for their use of *His* world. Humans are part of that creation: Roger Crook argues that human activity has worth as part of God's creative process, and so technology and science are not bad. God works in and through nature, and nature is important to God (see Psalm 19). He goes on to suggest that as human beings manipulate nature more than any other life form, they have a special responsibility to care for it. The irreparable damage being done to the planet and the natural order comes about because of human selfishness in taking a short-term view: 'Man is so intrinsically related to nature that when he sins against God, nature suffers; and when he obeys God, nature rejoices' (Barnette, 1972, p. 37). Pope John Paul II has written

> Man thinks that he can make arbitrary use of the earth, subjecting it without restraint to his will, as though the earth did not have its own requisites and a prior, God-given purpose, … Instead of carrying out his role as a co-operator with God in the work of creation, man sets himself up in place of God and thus ends up in provoking a rebellion on the part of nature, which is more tyrannised than governed by him.
>
> Pope John Paul II, *Centesimus Annus* (1991), Section 37

In a paper entitled 'The call of creation: God's invitation and the human response: the natural environment and Catholic social teaching', the Catholic Church argues that

> A way of life that disregards and damages God's creation, forces the poor into greater poverty, and threatens the right of future generations to a healthy environment and to their fair share of

the earth's wealth and resources, is contrary to the vision of the Gospel.

Catholic Bishops' Conference of England and Wales (July 2002)

Christians are duty bound to observe several principles, which imply a religious moral responsibility to care for the environment out of love for God, love for each other and love for God's creative work:

1 *Creation has value in itself and reveals God.* Genesis 1–2 records that God created everything and his creation is good and loved for its own sake. Creation has a distinct relationship with God – it glorifies and worships God (see Psalms 96:12; Isaiah 55:12). The environment is special not because humans need it but because it has value in itself as the work of God and to an extent reveals God. St Thomas Aquinas argued that the diversity of the life on earth reveals the richness of God's nature and therefore Christians are bound not to degrade or damage it.

2 *Human beings are dependent but responsible.* Human beings are co-creators with God as they use and transform the natural world. Human acts should reflect God's own love for creation and should show care for creation as human life depends on creation.

3 *Creation reveals human sin.* Sin has distorted the human relationship with the natural world damaging the balance of nature. This idea is in the Old Testament: 'The earth dries up and withers, the world languishes and withers; the heavens languish together with the earth. The earth lies polluted under its inhabitants; for they have transgressed laws, violated the statutes, broken the everlasting covenant' (Isaiah 24:4–5). 'Therefore the land mourns, and all who live in it languish; together with the wild animals and the birds of the air, even the fish of the sea are perishing' (Hosea 4:2–3). Our immoral treatment of the environment damages our relationships with God, with each another and between humanity and the earth.

4 *Creation participates in human redemption.* A Christian's relationship with God is affected by how he or she uses the gifts of creation. Loving God includes giving thanks and praise for these gifts, honouring and respecting them for their own sake and because they are destined by God to be fairly shared for all people. Care and respect must replace exploitative greed.

5 *Creation in the world to come.* Part of being a Christian is to work to bring about the Kingdom of God. Humans are called to renew the face of the earth until there is peace and harmony, life and health for all. In the words of Revelation, 'the curse of destruction will be abolished' (Revelation 22:1–3) and the bounty of the world shared among all peoples.

There must be a change of attitude towards material possessions:

> It is not wrong to want to live better. What is wrong is a style of life which is presumed to be better when it is directed towards

having rather than being and which wants to have more, not in order to be more but in order to spend life in enjoyment as an end in itself.

Pope John Paul II, Centesimus Annus (1991), Section 37

Humans must observe environmental justice, which means taking account of the impact of their lifestyles on others and the world. The desire for affluence and greater wealth can dominate. Advertising encourages the idea that we have a right to use the luxury goods of creation entirely as we wish. All people should remember the emphasis placed by the world religions on simplicity.

Tasks

1 Explain how a Christian environmental ethic could be anthropocentric, geo/biocentric and ultimately theocentric.

2 In your view, do the biblical sources support an environmental ethic?

3 Should a Christian's love of God necessarily extend to care for creation?

Deep ecology

Beyond religious attempts at an environmental ethic, there has been a great deal of work to produce a secular-based approach that recognizes value in all life forms, and perhaps even the geological and biological systems and diversity of planet earth, and rejects anthropocentric ethics. The term **deep ecology** refers to this project. Aldo Leopold led this attempt, calling in 1949 for a new ethic to deal with man's relationship to the land and to the animals and plants that thrive upon it. He sought to enlarge the boundaries of the moral community to include soils, waters, plants and animals, or collectively the land (Leopold, 1949). It is not enough to see the environment in terms of its contribution to human life. This tendency is illustrated well by the American poet William Cullen Bryant (1794–1878):

... The Hills
Rock-ribbed and ancient as the sun. – the vales
Stretching in pensive quietness between;
The venerable woods – rivers that move
In majesty, and the complaining brooks
That make the meadows green, and, poured round all
Old oceans grey and melancholy waste, –
Are but the solemn decorations all
Of the great tomb of man.

Bryant (1817)

Arne Naess argued that deep ecology sought to 'preserve the integrity of the biosphere for its own sake', not for any possible human benefits. Leopold says 'A thing is right when it tends to preserve the integrity, stability and beauty of the biotic community. It is wrong when it tends otherwise.' In a paper published in 1984, Arne Naess and George Sessions proposed that:

1. The well being of human and non-human life on Earth have value in themselves. These values are independent of the usefulness of the non-human world for human purposes.

2. Richness and diversity of life forms contribute to the realisation of these values and are also values in themselves.

3. Humans have no right to reduce this richness and diversity except to satisfy vital needs.

Naess and Sessions (1984)

Arguably, this ethic can be extended to include natural objects or systems and in *Deep Ecology* (1985), Bill Devall and George Sessions argue that 'all organisms and entities in the ecosphere, as parts of the interrelated whole, are equal in intrinsic worth'. Peter Vardy and Paul Grosch (1994) note that James Lovelock's Gaia hypothesis sees the ecosystem as a whole as an entity in its own right, which must be considered in any moral deliberation (Lovelock, 1979, p. 279); while Paul Taylor (quoted in Vardy and Grosch, 1994) argues that there should be respect for every life, as every living thing is 'pursuing its own good in its own unique way'.

However, the attempt to extend intrinsic value to all of the elements of the earth is problematic. Singer maintains that while all life forms can have value as part of the diverse interrelated 'geophysiological' structure of the planet, it is only justifiable to give intrinsic value to sentient life forms, as plants and other organisms cannot truly be said to desire to flourish or have experiences. Lovelock's use of the Greek goddess Gaia to describe the world may be appealing, but it seems to confer on the earth a consciousness that is not there (Singer, 1993, p. 282). There is a danger that by using metaphorical or romantic language we will confer sentiency on things that do not possess it.

1 Compare and contrast the contributions made by the Christian tradition and deep ecology to the environmental debate.

2 Are Singer's criticisms of Christian environmental ethics justified or not? Why/why not?

3 Apply environmental ethical theory to the issue of animal rights. Which approach is more effective: the Christian approach or deep ecology?

Extracts from key texts

Peter Singer, *Practical Ethics*, 1993

From page 266

And God said, Let us make man in our image, after our likeness: and let them have dominion over the fish of the sea, and over the fowl of the air, and over the Earth, and over every creeping thing that creepeth upon the Earth. So God created man in his own image, in the image of God created he him; male and female created he them. And God blessed them, and God said upon them, Be fruitful, and multiply, and replenish the Earth, and subdue it; and have dominion over the fish of the sea and over the fowl of the air, and over every living thing that moveth upon the Earth.

Today Christians debate the meaning of this grant of 'dominion'; and those concerned about the environment claim that it should be regarded not as a license to do as we will with other living things, but rather as a directive to look after them, on God's behalf, and be answerable to God for the way in which we treat them. There is, however, little justification in the text itself for such an interpretation; and given the example God set when he drowned almost every animal on Earth in order to punish human beings for their wickedness, it is no wonder that people should think the flooding of a single river valley is nothing worth worrying about. After the flood there is a repetition of the grant of dominion in more ominous language: 'And the fear of you and the dread of you shall be upon every beast of the Earth, and upon every fowl of the air, upon all that moveth upon the Earth, and upon all the fishes of the sea; into your hands are they delivered.' The implication is clear: to act in a way that causes fear and dread to everything that moves on the Earth is not improper; it is, in fact, in accordance with a God-given decree. The most influential early Christian thinkers had no doubts about how man's dominion was to be understood. 'Doth God care for oxen?' asked Paul, in the course of a discussion of an Old Testament command to rest one's ox on the Sabbath, but it was only a rhetorical question – he took it for granted that the answer must be negative, and the command was to be explained in terms of some benefit to humans.

Aldo Leopold, The land ethic (in LaFollette, 1997)

From pages 634–643

When god-like Odysseus returned from the wars in Troy, he hanged all on one rope a dozen slave girls of his household whom he suspected of misbehaviour during his absence. This hanging involved no question of propriety. The girls were property. The disposal of property was then, as now, a matter of expediency, not right and wrong.

Concepts of right and wrong were not lacking from Odysseus' Greece: witness the fidelity of his wife through the long years before at last his blackprowed galleys clove the wine darkseas from home. The ethical structure of that time covered wives, but had not yet extended to human chattels. During the three thousand years which have since elapsed, ethical criteria have been extended to many fields of conduct, with corresponding shrinkages in those judged by expediency only.

This extension of ethics, so far studied only by philosophers, is actually a process in ecological evolution. Its sequences may be described in ecological as well as in philosophical terms. An ethic, ecologically, is a limitation on freedom of action in the struggle for existence. An ethic, philosophically, is a differentiation of social from anti social conduct …

… The first ethic dealt with the relation between individuals; the Mosaic Decalogue is an example. Later accretions dealt with the relation between individual and society. The Golden Rule tries to integrate the individual into society; democracy to integrate social organisation to the individual.

There is as yet no ethic dealing with man's relation to land and to the animals and plants which grow upon it. Land, like Odysseus' slave girls, is still property. The land relation is still strictly economic, entailing privileges but not obligations.

The extension of ethics to this third element in human environment is, if I read the evidence correctly, an evolutionary possibility and an ecological necessity. It is the third step in a sequence. The first two have already been taken. Individual thinkers since the days of Ezekiel and Isaiah have asserted that the despoilation of land is not only inexpedient but wrong. Society, however, has not yet affirmed their belief. I regard the present conservation movement as the embryo of such an affirmation ...

All ethics so far rest upon a simple premise: that the individual is a member of a community of interdependent parts. His instincts prompt him to compete for his place in the community, but his ethics prompt him also to cooperate. The land ethic simply enlarges the boundaries of the community to include soils, waters, plants, and animals, or collectively: the land.

This sounds simple: do we not already sing our love for and obligation to the land of the free and the home of the brave? Yes, but just what and whom do we love? Certainly not the soil, which we are sending helter-skelter downriver. Certainly not the waters, which we assume have no function except to turn turbines, float barges, and carry off sewage. Certainly not the plants, of which we exterminate whole communities without batting an eye. Certainly not the animals, of which we have already extirpated many of the largest and most beautiful species. A land ethic of course cannot prevent the alteration, management, and use of these 'resources,' but it does affirm their right to continued existence, and, at least in spots, their continued existence in a natural state.

CHAPTER SUMMARY

What is environmental ethics?

- Environmental ethics is concerned with our attitudes towards and impact on the biological and geological dimensions of the planet and humanity.

Some argue that –

- Earth's systems, which nurture and sustain life, are breaking down.
- Finite natural resources are being depleted unsustainably.
- Environmental damage disproportionately affects the poor.

- Industrialisation and technological and scientific development have reduced biodiversity.

Others argue that –

- This is a simplified distortion of a far more complex picture.
- The situation is improving.
- We are not running out of energy resources.
- Fewer and fewer people are starving.
- Development protects us from the environment.
- An environmental ethic that constrains development might actually make the situation worse for human beings.

Christian approaches to environmental ethics:

- Singer argues that the Hebrew and Greek traditions leave the environment as morally insignificant.
- Singer points to a Judeo-Christian emphasis on human domination of the world.
- 'All animals are naturally subject to man.' (St Thomas Aqunias)
- A positive view is that Christian environmental ethics is theocentric, anthropocentric (love of neighbour) and geo/biocentric, as creation is God-made and so is good in itself.
- 'The recognition that nonhuman creatures have intrinsic value is present in the Christian tradition.' (Terence R. Anderson)
- The concept of stewardship in the Bible means that humans are responsible to God for their use of *His* world.
- As human beings manipulate nature more than any other life form, they have a special responsibility to care for it.
- 'Man is so intrinsically related to nature that when he sins against God, nature suffers; and when he obeys God, nature rejoices.' (Henlee H. Barnette)
- 'A way of life that disregards and damages God's creation, forces the poor into greater poverty, and threatens the right of future generations to a healthy environment and to their fair share of the earth's wealth and resources, is contrary to the vision of the Gospel.' (The Roman Catholic Church)
- God's creation is good and is loved for its own sake. Humans are co-creators with God, but sin distorts the human relationship with the natural world.

- A Christian's relationship with God is affected by how he or she uses creation. Humans are called upon to bring peace and harmony, life and health for all.

Deep ecology:
- Deep ecology is an attempt to provide a secular environmental ethic.
- Aldo Leopold enlarges the moral community to include soils, waters, plants and animals, or collectively the land.
- Arne Naess argued that deep ecology sought to 'preserve the integrity of the biosphere for its own sake', not for human benefits.
- The well-being of both human and non-human life on Earth is of value.
- Humans can only reduce the earth's richness and diversity to satisfy vital needs.
- Richard Sylvan and Val Plumwood say that humans must not 'jeopardise the well being of natural objects or systems without good reason'.
- Bill Devall and George Sessions argue that 'all organisms and entities in the ecosphere, as parts of the interrelated whole, are equal in intrinsic worth'.
- Naess and Sessions propose the principles that the flourishing of human and non-human life is intrinsically valuable and that the richness and diversity of life forms also has value.
- James Lovelock sees the ecosystem as a whole as an entity in its own right (Gaia), which must be considered in any moral deliberation.
- Paul Taylor argues that there should be respect for every life, as every living thing is 'pursuing its own good in its own unique way'.
- Singer argues that it is only justifiable to give intrinsic value to sentient life forms, as plants and other organisms cannot truly be said to desire to flourish or have experiences.

Chapter 21

Justice and punishment

Introduction

Key philosophers and works

Plato (428–347 BCE): *The Republic*

Thomas Hobbes (1588–1679): *Leviathan*, 1651

John Stuart Mill (1806–1873): *On Liberty*, 1859

Jean-Jacques Rousseau (1712–1778): *The Social Contract*, 1762

John Rawls (1921–2002): *A Theory of Justice*, 1971 and 1999

Robert Nozick (1938–2002): *Anarchy, State and Utopia*, 1974

James Rachels (1941–): Punishment and desert (in LaFollette, 1997)

Bertrand Russell (1872–1970): *Why I Am Not a Christian*, 1927

Key terms

Justice, social contract, social justice, distributive justice, original position, veil of ignorance, maximin rule of game theory, entitlement, deterrence, retribution, reformation

What you will learn by the end of this chapter

- Pre-20th-century philosophical theories of justice.
- A Christian approach to justice.
- Rawls' and Nozick's contrasting theories of justice, and their weaknesses and strengths.
- The deterrence, retribution and reformation theories of punishment, and their weaknesses and strengths.

Key questions

1 What is meant by the word 'justice'?
2 Are the rich morally obliged to help the poor?
3 Should the rich be taxed more heavily to pay to help the poor?
4 Is it right that some are born into rich inheritances while others are born into debt?
5 Why do we punish?
6 Do criminals deserve to be punished?
7 Is it more important to let the victims feel vindicated than change the behaviour of the criminals?

Justice

The word **justice** comes from the Latin meaning 'right' or 'law', but an understanding of justice requires a look at the ancient Greek philosopher, Plato.

Plato: the just city

In his work *The Republic*, Plato said that the perfect state will 'obviously have the qualities of wisdom, courage, self-discipline and justice' (427e, p. 197). A person who keeps the first three of these in balance acts justly and, likewise, a state that keeps all three in balance is a just state. Justice in the state mirrors justice in an individual.

In his book *Understanding Plato* (1987, pp. 75ff), David Melling notes that Plato believed that individual human beings are not self-sufficient, but that they gather in communities so that they can meet each other's needs and provide mutual support, and also provide welfare to those in need. This was called the '*polis*' (city–state). A community in which individuals all tried to complete all of the tasks of life – farming, carpentry, medicine and politics – would not be as effective as one in which people specialised in the areas in which they were most skilled. A *polis* is a social unit in which economic functions are differentiated and specialised, so that all of the community's needs are fulfilled.

In a just state, the various parts work harmoniously together and while individuals must rule themselves, the state must be ruled by philosopher guardians who have the wisdom to ensure that the proper balance is retained and that justice remains:

> The society we have described can never grow into a reality or see the light of day, or there will be no end to the troubles of state, or indeed, my dear Glaucon, of humanity itself, till philosophers become kings in this world.
>
> Plato, *The Republic*, 473d, p. 263

Plato was suspicious of democracy, as it could represent the views of the ignorant. He believed that a structured order organised by a philosopher king would be a more reliable way of establishing a just city–state.

Christianity and justice

There are many biblical sources for **justice**. God both loves justice and does justice: 'I the Lord, love justice' (Isaiah 61:8, cf. Psalms 37:28), 'The Lord works righteousness and justice for all the oppressed' (Psalms 103:6) and 'I know that the Lord secures justice for the poor and upholds the cause of the needy' (Psalms 140:12). N. P. Harvey (1995) writes that God's justice is seen in His anger with those who disobey His commands. It is a practice of retributive justice (p. 17) and we are encouraged to do justice too: 'Follow justice and justice alone' (Deuteronomy 16:20) and 'Let justice roll on like a river, righteousness like a never-failing stream' (Amos 5:24).

In *Christian Ethics, An Introduction* , Bernard Hoose describes the different dimensions to the Christian view of justice. The Hebrew Scriptures refer to *Mishpat*, which concerns duties and responsibilities that embody life in the covenant with God and each other, and *Sedakah*, which means God's righteousness and bringer of judgement.

Christians are created to work for God's kingdom of justice and peace, and injustice is a manifestation of sin (Hoose, 1998, pp.167–168). **Social justice** has been a central component of the Christian view of justice. Amos denounced those who trample the poor into the ground (Amos 5:24) and Church fathers saw the rich as robbers who kept bread belonging to the hungry. The plight of the poor and oppressed forms a litmus test to measure the justice and injustice in the world (Hoose, 1998, p. 168).

Liberation theologians have argued for the epistemological privilege of the oppressed, so justice is not just about distribution but also who has the power to distribute. In his book *A Theology of Liberation* (1994), the liberation theologian Gustavo Gutierrez writes:

> The struggle for a just world in which there is no oppression, servitude, or alienated work will signify the coming of the Kingdom. The Kingdom and social injustice are incompatible ... salvation embraces all men and the whole man; the liberating action of Christ ... is at the heart of the historical current of humanity; the struggle for a just society is in its own right very much a part of salvation history.
>
> Gutierrez (1994), p. 168

The Roman Catholic idea of **social justice** refers to the duty that an individual has to the community, and society should be structured in a way that allows all people to meet their duties. At the Second Vatican Council, the Church declared its *Pastoral Constitution, Gaudium et Spes*, in which it says:

Furthermore, while there are just differences between peoples, their equal dignity as persons demands that we strive for fairer and more human conditions. Excessive economic and social disparity between individuals and peoples of the one human race is a source of scandal and militates against social justice, equity, human dignity, as well as social and international peace.

Roman Catholic Church, Gaudium et Spes, para 29

Christians are enjoined to pursue the common good. There can be no marginalisation or powerlessness in a Christian just world.

Hobbes, Mill, Rousseau and the social contract

Thomas Hobbes dealt with the topic of establishing a just society in his book *Leviathan* (1651). He presented an individualistic account of human society. Hobbes argued that all humans had the same needs for food, shelter and so on, but that there was a limited supply of those things. Humans had an essential equality of power and were basically focused on looking after their own self-interests. As a result of these factors, humans lived in continual fear that someone else was going to deprive them of their possessions or their lives, and they lived in a state of competitive warfare against each other. This was the basic state of nature, and the only way out of it was through agreement to a 'social contract', under which people agreed not to deny the freedoms of others. Hobbes wrote, 'The passions that incline men to peace are: fear of death; desire of such things as are necessary to commodious living; and a hope by their industry to obtain them' (Hobbes, 1651, Ch. 13). An external authority enforced the social contract.

Will Kymlicka sees Hobbes' approach in terms of morality as mutual advantage. There is nothing wrong in harming another person, but people are better off if they do not. It is mutually advantageous not to harm others, as there is then no need to waste resources on the defence of property and life. To injure others is not inherently wrong, but we gain by not doing it .

For John Stuart Mill, the principle whereby the authority would act was based on harm. In his essay *On Liberty* (1859), he stated that acts that cause harm should be suppressed:

> The only purpose for which power can be rightly be exercised over any member of a civilised community against his will is to prevent harm to others

Mill (1859), p. 56

and

> The liberty of the individual must be thus far limited; he must not make himself a nuisance to other people.

Mill (1859), p. 56

This ensures an individual 'rights-based interests' approach. People are left free to develop, but not if they cause harm to others. In his work *The Social Contract* (1762), the French philosopher Jean-Jacques Rousseau stated his belief that this process would enable humans to move from a self-focused lifestyle to one that took account of others, and therefore a transition would be made from a state of nature to a civilised society.

For the most part, theories of justice are identified as either individualistic or communitarian. Plato's approach was **communitarian**, as was Rousseau's, while Hobbes' is individualistic. Two recent thinkers have made important contributions to each of these approaches, and special attention will be given to each below.

Questions

1 Should the poor get preferential treatment in the distribution of wealth and the power to distribute wealth?

2 Is a wise dictator preferable to an ignorant democracy?

John Rawls: *A Theory of Justice*

In his book *A Theory of Justice* (1971, revised edn 1999), Rawls responds against the utilitarian ethic applied to society. He notes that at first glance it might be natural to transpose a utilitarian approach of individuals to the community at large. An individual would seek out the greatest good even at the expense of other more immediate goods, so that the greatest good would be achieved. However, there would be no guarantee that wealth would be distributed in a fair way:

> The striking feature of the utilitarian view of justice is that it does not matter, except indirectly, how this sum of satisfactions is distributed among individuals any more than it matters, except indirectly, how one man distributes his satisfactions over time ... Thus there is no reason in principle why the greater gains of some should not compensate for the lesser losses of others; or more importantly, why the violation of the liberty of a few might not be made right by the greater good shared by many.
>
> Rawls (1999), p. 23

The rights of an individual can be violated if that in turn benefits the majority. A few slaves with no rights might live in profound unhappiness, but this is justified by the happiness of the majority, who benefit from slave labour.

Rawls proposes an approach to justice that embraces the idea that the dispossessed should be protected. In his first chapter, 'Justice as fairness', Rawls argues that

> justice denies that the loss of freedom for some is made right by a greater good shared by others. It does not allow that the sacrifices imposed on a few are outweighed by the larger sum of advantages enjoyed by many.
>
> Rawls (1999), p. 3

In other words, liberties of equal citizenship are taken as a given in a just society. Rawls' idea of justice as fairness means that there can be no arbitrary advantage of power, wealth or position in society. Free and rational people would agree on a basic structure of society, underpinned by common principles of justice, and they would accept an initial position of equality as defining the fundamental terms of their association. Rawls proposes an **original position** corresponding to a state of nature. In this hypothetical state or community of rational equal and self-interested individuals, people are to establish guidelines for living, to cover all rights and duties. In this state of nature, there is an essential feature that

> no one knows his place in society, his class position or social status, nor does anyone know his fortune in the distribution of natural assets and abilities, his intelligence, strength, and the like ...
>
> Rawls (1999), p. 11

With people unsure what position they are going to hold in their future lives, existing behind what Rawls calls a 'veil of ignorance', they would ensure that if they should have the misfortune to be the most dispossessed, the system would protect them. With this in mind, they would propose principles of justice that would preserve and protect the least fortunate. People would ensure that no one was either advantaged or disadvantaged by the system adopted.

Rawls goes further, to propose two principles of justice that, from this position, rational people would go on to choose:

> First: each person is to have an equal right to the most extensive scheme of equal basic liberties compatible with a similar scheme of liberties for others.
>
> Second: social and economic inequalities are to be arranged so that they are both (a) reasonably expected to be open to everyone's advantage, and (b) attached to positions and offices open to all.
>
> Rawls (1999), p. 53

In other words, Rawls advances the assumption of distribution of equal rights, duties, wealth and power. Inequalities will emerge once people live out their lives and make their own judgements and choices. If everyone was given the same money to start off with, sooner or later some would make more money and would have more than others. To ensure that the most dispossessed are protected, Rawls requires that any advancement of wealth and power must be accompanied by an increase in responsibilities for the least well off in society (Rawls, 1999, p. 13). Inequalities are only permissible if the second rule is applied. Any hardships that people may encounter cannot be to the benefit or greater good of many others. The rich must sacrifice some of their wealth for the benefit of the poor. Greater goods can only be earned while the lot of the least well off is improved, and each individual has a duty to look out for the most dispossessed. It is only justifiable that some are elected to govern, as having a government allows people to get on with life. It would be impractical for all people to be involved in government.

For Rawls, these two principles apply to the basic structure of society and government, the assignments of rights and duties, the regulation and distribution of social and economic advantages, basic liberties including political liberty (voting and holding office), freedom of speech and assembly, liberty of conscience and freedom of thought, the freedom of the person, the right to hold property and freedom from arbitrary arrest and seizure as defined by the concept of the rule of law.

Rawls applies the **maximin rule** of game theory. He argues that the best outcome is the one where the least well off person has the least bad result. Vardy and Grosch (1994) illustrate this using the game of snakes and ladders. If you need to throw a six to get into the game, some players will never even start, because they will never throw a six. Instead, you should simply allow all players to start with their first throw. A six will still be better than any other throw, but even a one will allow a person to enter the game. Rawls believes that there is a greater set of possible outcomes if everyone remains in the game.

Fundamentally, Rawls' approach puts justice, the law, the courts and the judges as the protectors of the weak, and this can be seen not just in terms of protection from other individuals but protection from the state or government as well. It is rather ironic that young people often see law enforcement and the workings of justice as the tool of government against the freedom of individuals; yet, critically, it is the only bastion or guardian of those rights and freedoms against the imposition of government.

Tasks

1 Which of the following represents the fairest allocation of a school's resources, and why?

   a The same resources to each person.

   b Resources divided according to students' ability to use them.

   c Resources divided according to students' productive success in using them.

   d Resources divided according to students' needs.

   e A higher percentage of resources allocated to those students who are most in need.

2 Which of the following do you find most convincing, and why?

   a The state should share what the wealthy do not need with those who need it in order to survive, whether or not the wealthy agree.

   b It is wrong for the government to take from me forcibly what I have earned justly.

3 Is it fair:

   a To allow the rich to pass on their wealth to their children?

   b For governments to claim death duty taxes to redistribute a portion of that wealth?

4 Isn't it unfair to say that the rich have a greater duty to the poor than the poor have to the rich? Why/why not?

Robert Nozick: justice as entitlement

In his book, *Anarchy, State and Utopia* (1974), Robert Nozick criticises Rawls' view that such a complex and universal model of justice can be imposed on society. He argues that Rawls unfairly benefits the poor at the expense of the rich, and fails to consider that people are entitled to legitimately acquired natural assets: 'Rawls' construction is incapable of yielding an entitlement or historical conception of distributive justice' (p. 202). Nozick thinks it is unreasonable to discard the possibility that people in the original position might approve just or historical acquisition as a principle to govern distribution.

Nozick proposes a more individualistic approach to justice. He sees justice as **entitlement**. I am entitled to my possessions, my earnings and my acquisitions as long as I remain within the law. The same is true for you as well. Nozick's account has three main principles:

Ethical issues

1. A person who acquires a holding in accordance with the principle of justice in acquisition is entitled to that holding.

2. A person who acquires a holding in accordance with the principle of justice in transfer, from someone else entitled to the holding, is entitled to the holding.

3. No one is entitled to a holding except by (repeated applications of 1 and 2

... a distribution is just if everyone is entitled to the holdings they possess under the distribution.

Nozick (1974), p. 151

In contrast to Rawls, Nozick argues that we have no moral obligation to anyone except ourselves. He takes an individualist and minimalist position, and disputes that there is a just basis for Rawls' suggestion that those who have power and wealth have a duty to share their earnings with the least wealthy and powerful. Nozick's approach is libertarian: people own themselves, while the world and everything in it is originally unowned, although an individual can acquire rights over a disproportionate share of the world as long as in doing so they do not worsen the lot of others.

Considering Rawls and Nozick

Utilitarians object to Rawls because due to his adoption of the maximin approach, his theory doesn't maximise utility. Libertarian's object to Rawls because his theory infringes on liberty through taxation of the rich for the benefit of the poor, and it can be argued that people should be made to suffer the consequences of their actions. Nozick's view is that ideal distribution can only be achieved if we don't interfere with individual liberty. In providing a safety net, the incentive to achieve is diminished. People who choose to work hard to earn more income should not be required to subsidise those who have chosen a more leisurely poorer route. In effect, Nozick's case is that it is not the job of justice to determine economic distribution, but merely the rules governing the acquisition and transfer of goods.

However, it could be argued that people should not suffer consequences of circumstances over which they have no control – and in terms of family wealth, physical and emotional ability, status or class, an unjust world gives some people great advantages from birth, which are denied to others. One unpalatable consequence of Nozick is the conclusion that we have no obligation to help the poor, in the context of a world in which the distribution of wealth benefits a tiny proportion of the planet's population, while a large proportion live in poverty. Nozick's approach might be seen as akin to the person who walks past someone drowning in a canal and chooses not to throw that person a lifebelt. According to Hugh LaFollette, this means giving luck a disproportionate influence on our life experiences:

Children in developed countries have better life prospects than children in the third reason for one reason alone: luck. I did not deserve to be born to parents who could provide for me, in a country with an education system like the US; certainly I did not deserve it more than a poor child in Addis Ababa, Baghdad or Jakarta. So why should I have a relatively cushy life, while they fight to stay alive, simply because of luck? Should luck play such a large role in determining our fates? Or should morality seek to limit luck's influence?

LaFollette (1997), p. 517

Nevertheless, there is a degree of common sense behind the idea that people are rewarded for their effort and contribution, and that a system that seeks to raise the overall standard of living by rewarding effort and achievement is plausible, and certainly commonplace in British schools. To be fair to Nozick, he argues that the acquisition of wealth for some should not disadvantage others, and so he wouldn't necessarily accept all aspects of the global market.

Iris Marion Young (1997a) is concerned that both Rawls and Nozick focus far too much on distributive approaches to justice. She writes that it leads to a view that justice is simply about things such as 'resources, income and wealth or on the distribution of social positions, especially jobs'. This ignores the 'social structure or institutional context that often help determine distributive patterns'. Issues of decision-making power and procedures, division of labour and culture are left out. Justice must have a broader scope, including politics and the extent to which social institutions inhibit or liberate people. Justice must ensure that individuals are free to learn, and to control both their actions and the conditions of their actions, and are not naive about property and trade.

Interestingly, Nozick's approach strongly supports the principle that justice should protect the individual from the state, as does Rawls account, and it is important to acknowledge that the approaches have some common ground.

Tasks

1 What criticism does Rawls make of a utilitarian form of justice?
2 Explain what is meant by the original position and suggest a criticism of it.
3 Apply Rawls' two principles of justice to a situation.
4 Explain what Nozick means by the phrase 'justice as entitlement', and state and evaluate arguments for and against the theory.
5 Outline the case that Rawls and Nozick focus far too much on distributive approaches to justice.

Punishment

LaFollette (1997, p. 467) observes that any system of justice must be morally justified: 'we must determine the circumstances under which the state can justifiably deprive someone of her life or liberty, and we must decide what the morally appropriate punishment would be'. Traditionally, there have been three theories of punishment: deterrence, retribution and reformation (or rehabilitation).

Deterrence theory

A utilitarian approach sees punishment as a deterrent. Punishment discourages others from doing the same, by focusing minds on the consequences that will befall them should they choose to follow the same course of action. The suffering inflicted on the criminal creates an example for others. Deterrence theory assumes that most criminal acts are rational behaviour, and that possible future criminals will be dissuaded from criminal activity because of the risk and threat of the same punishment. To put this another way, people will engage in criminal and deviant activities if they do not fear apprehension and punishment. If a stretch of road has a speed camera in operation, drivers will slow down to avoid a fine – they are deterred from committing a speeding offence. Deterrence is sometimes referred to as rational choice theory, because of the importance of the idea of a human rational decision not to commit a crime because of fear of what might happen.

Bernard Hoose (1998, p. 199) notes that a utilitarian would justify the harm done to the criminal on the basis of an overall greater good caused by discouraging more criminal acts, although he calls into question whether or not this sort of deterrence actually works. Prisons have been described as colleges of crime: if a relatively small-time criminal is imprisoned in a place in which he or she mixes with more hardened criminals, and if he or she has a sense of injustice about the imprisonment, then the feelings that the criminal might harbour may make him or her more of a liability upon release. Hoose notes examples of evidence from countries that have abandoned the death penalty and have seen a reduction in the rate of murder. Ruth Morris (1989, p. 110) argues that when the state resorts to brutal acts, it brutalises its people into doing more harm. Punishment can have a corrupting influence rather than a deterrent influence. Roger Crook notes that

> Psychiatric and sociological studies, however, show that this kind of threat does not prevent such serious crimes as murder, rape or trafficking in drugs.
>
> Crook (2002), p. 224

C. L. Ten argues that punishment may embitter and alienate a person from society, so that the person may be more likely to commit crime again, and so punishment could cause crime to increase (Ten, 1997, p. 369). In the USA, a number of states have adopted a '3 Strikes' policy, whereby if a third offence is committed the criminal will end up serving from 25 years to life. At the time, this policy was hailed as leading to a reduction of crime in New York, but there is also criticism that it simply clogs up prisons with petty criminals and does not reduce crime.

Retribution theory

The theory of **retribution** sees punishment as something that is owed to the criminal as payment for the crime committed:

> When someone who delights in annoying and vexing peace loving folk receives at last a right good beating, it is certainly an ill, but everyone approves of it and considers it as good in itself, even if nothing further results from it.
>
> Kant (1788), p. 170

James Rachels writes that the idea that 'wrongdoers should be "paid back" for their wicked deeds – fits naturally with many people's feelings', and that people are satisfied when murderers and rapists 'get what they have coming' and they are infuriated when villains 'get away with it' (Rachels, 1997, p. 470). While this may seem primitive or unenlightened, Rachels argues that treating people as they deserve on the basis of past actions is an appropriate response. He gives an example of whether a job should be given to an applicant who does the bare minimum or to one who has gone far beyond expectations and saved a company by his actions. It is clear that the job should be given to the hard-working applicant, on the basis of his past actions. Rachels outlines the principle of just deserts:

> People deserve to be treated in the same way that they have (voluntarily) treated others. Those who have treated others well deserve to be treated well in return, while those who have treated others badly deserve to be treated badly in return.
>
> Rachels (1997), p. 473

Rachels argues that this approach is good because it encourages the realisation that the only way in which we can succeed as individuals is through our good treatment of others. This gives people control over how others will treat them, because they are in control of their free actions (Rachels, 1997, pp. 473–474). Secondly, he suggests an egalitarian principle concerning equal distribution of social benefits for adopting retributionism. The hard worker gave up leisure time that was available to the slacker, and so the hard worker must be recompensed. Thirdly, he suggests that reciprocity is an integral part of morality. People are moral in part because they hope to be treated in a moral way in return. If morality had no good return and immorality no bad consequences, people would be less inclined to be moral. It would be a viola-

Ethical issues

tion of justice if murders and rapists had no deserts for their actions, and it is a matter of justice that they do receive their just deserts. A criminal can be said to have brought the punishment upon him- or herself. Being law-abiding incurs some discomfort and restrictions on what can be done.

D. W. Van Ness (1995) notes that retributionist punishment is said to accomplish a number of things:

> 1. it helps define and reinforce community values; 2. it affirms individual responsibility; and 3. it satisfies the desire for redress which results when law-abiding members of the community observe a law-breaker. Fairness requires that those who have forgone ill-gotten gains by obeying the law should be vindicated when others reap the benefits of crime.
>
> Van Ness (1995), p. 711

Retributionist punishment raises questions of the nature of the punishment and its extent: Should the punishment be a prison term or fine, and if so, how many years and how much money? (Hoose, 1998, pp. 202–204.) There is also the question of the circumstances. How is a contract killer punished in comparison with either a drunk driver who killed a child or a brutalised wife who murdered her husband after years of abuse? Is punishment always necessary, and is it right to think of punishment in terms of satisfaction and revenge? Ten (1997, p. 367) notes that retribution theory restricts punishment to those who have broken the law knowingly. Those who did it accidentally cannot be blamed, even though they broke the law. Arguably, this is questionable, as there is a case that the law must be upheld even if the crime was unwitting.

One contemporary extension of this approach is found in the idea of restorative justice, whereby criminals and victims are given the opportunity to meet, so that the criminal can experience or be presented with the suffering that he or she has caused to the victim. This presents the possibility of satisfying the victim's personal desire to see that the wrongdoer realises the harm done and it may in fact lead on to the next main theory of punishment, reformation. Clearly, this approach can only be beneficial with common consent by both the criminal and the victim, and it is not appropriate in certain situations.

Reformation (or rehabilitation) theory

The theory of **reformation** seeks to convert the criminal through correction and **rehabilitation**. Jeremy Bentham (1789, p. 170) wrote: 'All punishment is mischief: all punishment in itself is evil.' This rejection of the idea of retribution is often coupled with the idea that crime is caused in part by problems of social care, education, mental or physical health or poverty, and that the solution is to correct the problems rather than simply criticising and harming the wrongdoer in some way. Reformation is far more interested in punishment that removes causes of crime. Bertrand Russell put it in these terms:

> No man treats a motorcar as foolishly as he treats another human being. When the car will not go, he does not attribute its annoying behaviour to sin; he does not say, 'You are a wicked motorcar, and I shall not give you any more petrol until you go.' He attempts to find out what is wrong and to set it right.
>
> Russell (1927), p. 40

Reformative punishment may be a far more humane and effective approach than the other models. The Prison Reform Trust (n.d.) notes that the UK imprisons more of its people than almost any other European country, and argues it does not reform or deter – half of all prisoners re-offend within two years. Some credence is given to Bertrand Russell's view through the fact that up to a third of prisoners have some identifiable psychiatric disorder, and this may be linked to their criminal behaviour.

> We assume that being behind bars with nothing to do but build up resentments or go mad will make him emerge from prison a better man, renewed and chastised. Imprisonment is certainly no guarantee of success.
>
> Hospers (1972), p. 390

Nevertheless, personal reformation only happens when the individual freely embraces the means, and there is no proof that punishment is reformatory. It is the educational and psychiatric facilities that help with the reformation, rather than the actual taking away of liberty (Hoose, 1998, pp. 204–205). It is questionable whether there is a clear reliable method of actually reforming a criminal.

It is also questionable whether the criminal behaviour is a result of some failure in upbringing or a particular mental state, rather than simply a free decision to commit a crime. It could also be argued that people have a right to be different, and that the state does not have the right to try to change the beliefs and ideas of individuals who choose activities that come into conflict with the law (Encyclopædia Britannica, 1999). This is brutally illustrated in Stanley Kubrick's film *A Clockwork Orange*, where electric shock treatment is used to try to create feelings of aversion towards immoral criminal behaviour. In the film, the brutality of the treatment is comparable with the brutality of the original criminal acts. There is a political dimension to the reformation approach, which is equally disturbing. This could be illustrated by looking at countries in which certain political opinions or religious beliefs have been outlawed, and where the state has sought to change those views by employing physical and psychological torture.

Ethical issues

Crook comments on Hospers' compromise view that punishment should meet two conditions:

> it should be deserved, and it should do some good to someone: the offender, the victim, society, or all three ... the penal system should not focus on punishment but on treatment.
>
> Crook (2002), p. 224

Crook (2002, pp. 224–225) notes the similarity between Hospers' suggestion and the traditional Christian concept of reconciliation. In *The Divine Imperative* (1942), Emil Brunner draws a similarity between the punishment of the criminal and the Christian idea of atonement for our sins. Christ expiates our sins and reconciles us to God. In terms of crime, something must be done to provide satisfaction (Catholics use the word 'penance' for this) and this satisfaction should be between the criminal and society. Reconciliation requires a change of heart in the criminal, akin to reformation, which includes a realisation that wrong was done and that people suffered as a result, and a desire not to offend again. It also includes satisfaction being made to the individuals affected, to society and to God, which might in part meet the desire for retribution, but there must also be acceptance and recognition of change by society and the victims.

Questions

1 Is it possible to defend the argument that punishment acts as a deterrent, and can you justify your answer?

2 How might Rachels' argument of retributionist punishment be justified?

3 Consider the arguments for and against reformative punishment. Which are more convincing, and why?

Extracts from key texts

John Rawls, *A Theory of Justice*, 1971

From pages 3 and 53

> In justice as fairness the original position of equality corresponds to the state of nature in the traditional theory of the social contract. This original position is not, of course, thought of as an actual historical state of affairs, much less as a primitive condition of culture. It is understood as a purely hypothetical situation characterized so as to lead to a certain conception of justice! Among the essential features of this situation is that no one

knows his place in society, his class position or social status, nor does any one know his fortune in the distribution of natural assets and abilities, his intelligence, strength, and the like. I shall even assume that the parties do not know their conceptions of the good or their special psychological propensities. The principles of justice are chosen behind a veil of ignorance. This ensures that no one is advantaged or disadvantaged in the choice of principles by the outcome of natural chance or the contingency of social circumstances. Since all are similarly situated and no one is able to design principles to favor his particular condition, the principles of justice are the result of a fair agreement or bargain. For given the circumstances of the original position, the symmetry of everyone's relations to each other, this initial situation is fair between individuals as moral persons, that is, as rational beings with their own ends and capable, I shall assume, of a sense of justice. The original position is, one might say, the appropriate initial status quo, and thus the fundamental agreements reached in it are fair. This explains the propriety of the name 'justice as fairness': it conveys the idea that the principles of justice are agreed to in an initial situation that is fair. The name does not mean that the concepts of justice and fairness are the same, any more than the phrase 'poetry as metaphor' means that the concepts of poetry and metaphor are the same.

...

The first statement of the two principles reads as follows.

> First: each person is to have an equal right to the most extensive scheme of equal basic liberties compatible with a similar scheme of liberties for others.

> Second: social and economic inequalities are to be arranged so that they are both (a) reasonably expected to be to everyone's advantage, and (b) attached to positions and offices open to all ...

... These principles primarily apply, as I have said, to the basic structure of society and govern the assignment of rights and duties and regulate the distribution of social and economic advantages. Their formulation presupposes that, for the purposes of a theory of justice, the social structure may be viewed as having two more or less distinct parts, the first principle applying to the one, the second principle to the other. Thus we distinguish between the aspects of the social system that define and secure the equal basic liberties and the aspects that specify and establish social and economic inequalities. Now it is essential to observe that the basic liberties are given by a list of such liberties. Important among these are political liberty (the right to vote and to hold public office) and freedom of speech and assembly; liberty of conscience and freedom of thought; freedom of the person, which includes freedom from psychological oppression and physical assault and dismemberment (integrity of the person); the right to hold personal property and freedom from arbitrary arrest and seizure as defined by the concept of the rule of law. These liberties are to be equal by the first principle.

The second principle applies, in the first approximation, to the distribution of income and wealth and to the design of organizations that make use of differences in authority and responsibility. While the distribution of wealth and income need not be equal, it must be to everyone's advantage, and at the same time, positions of authority and responsibility must be accessible to all. One applies the second principle by holding positions open, and then, subject to this constraint, arranges social and economic inequalities so that everyone benefits.

Robert Nozick, *Anarchy, State and Utopia*, 1974

From pages 151–153

If the world were wholly just, the following inductive definition would exhaustively cover the subject of justice in holdings.

1. A person who acquires a holding in accordance with the principle of justice in acquisition is entitled to that holding.

2. A person who acquires a holding in accordance with the principle of justice in transfer, from someone else entitled to the holding, is entitled to the holding.

3. No one is entitled to a holding except by (repeated) applications of 1 and 2.

The complete principle of distributive justice would say simply that a distribution is just if everyone is entitled to the holdings they possess under the distribution.

A distribution is just if it arises from another just distribution legitimate means. The legitimate means of moving from one distribution to another are specified by the principle of justice in transfer. The legitimate first 'moves' are specified by the principle justice in acquisition. Whatever arises from a just situation by just steps is itself just. The means of change specified by the principle of justice in transfer preserve justice. As correct rules of interference are truth-preserving, and any conclusion deduced via repeated application of such rules from only true premisses is itself true, so means of transition from one situation to another specified by the rinciple of justice in transfer are justice-preserving, and any situation actually arising from repeated transitions in accordance with the principle from a just situation is itself just. The parallel between justice-preserving transformations and truth-preserving transformations illuminates where it fails as well as where it holds. That it a conclusion could have been deduced by truth-preserving means from premisses that are true suffices to show its truth. That from a just situation a situation *could* have arisen via justice-preserving means does *not* suffice to show its justice. The fact that a thief's victims voluntarily *could* have presented him with gifts does not entitle the thief to his ill gotten gains. Justice in holdings is historical; it depends upon what actually has happened ...

... The general outlines of the theory of justice in holdings are that the holdings of a person are just if he is entitled to them by the principles of justice in acquisition and transfer, or by the principle rectification of injustice (as specified by the first two principles). If each person's holdings are just, then the total set (distribution) of holdings is just. To turn these general outlines into a specific theory we would have to specify the details of each of the three principles of justice in holdings: the principle of acquisition of holdings, the principle of transfer of holdings, and the principle of rectification of violations of the first two principles.

CHAPTER SUMMARY

Justice:

Plato –

- Plato said that the perfect state will 'obviously have the qualities of wisdom, courage, self discipline and justice'.
- Plato believed that individual human beings are not self-sufficient, but that they gather in communities to provide mutual support and welfare to those in need.
- In a just state, the various parts work harmoniously together.

Christianity and justice –

- God loves justice and does justice, and Christians are encouraged to do justice and work for God's Kingdom of justice and peace.

- There can be no marginalisation or powerlessness in a Christian just world.

Hobbes, Mill, Rousseau and the social contract –

- Thomas Hobbes argued that all humans have the same needs, the same power and are focused on looking after their own self-interests, but as a result live in continual fear of murder or theft.
- According to Hobbes, the only way out is through agreement to a 'social contract': people agree not to impeach the freedoms of others, this being enforced by an external authority.
- Also according to Hobbes, it is mutually advantageous not to harm others, as there is then no need to waste resources on the defence of property and life.
- John Stuart Mill argued that the state should only prevent acts that cause harm to others.
- Jean-Jacques Rousseau believed that humans would change from being self-focused to being other-focused, from the state of nature to a civilised society.

John Rawls: *A Theory of Justice* –

- Rawls rejects the application of the utilitarian ethic to society, as there would be no guarantee that wealth would be distributed in a fair way.
- A few slaves with no rights might live in profound unhappiness, but this is justified by the happiness of the majority, who benefit from slave labour.
- Rawls' theory ensures that the dispossessed are protected.
- Liberties of equal citizenship are taken as given in a just society.
- Justice as fairness means that there can be no arbitrary advantage of power, wealth or position in society.
- Rawls proposes an original position or a community of rational equal and self-interested individuals, in which people decide their principles from behind a veil of ignorance, and so propose principles of justice that preserve and protect the most dispossessed.
- Rawls goes further, to propose two principles of justice: everyone has an equal right to the most extensive scheme of equal basic liberties compatible with a similar scheme of liberties for others; and social and economic inequalities must be open to everyone's advantage, and attached to positions and offices open to all.
- For Rawls, these principles apply to the structure of society and government, the assignments of rights and duties, the regulation and distribution of social and economic advantages, and basic liberties.

- Rawls applies the maximin rule of game theory. He argues that the best outcome is the outcome where the least well off has the least bad result.

Robert Nozick: justice as entitlement –

- Nozick criticises Rawls' idea that a complex model of justice should be imposed universally on society.
- Rawls' theory unfairly benefits the poor at the expense of the rich.
- It is unreasonable to discard the possibility that people in the original position might approve other principles of justice.
- Nozick proposes an individualistic approach to justice as entitlement. We are entitled to that which we justly acquire, transfer and distribute.
- We have no moral obligation to anyone except ourselves.

Considering Rawls and Nozick –

- Utilitarians object to Rawls for not maximising utility.
- Libertarians object to Rawls because his theory infringes on liberty through taxation of the rich for the benefit of the poor.
- Nozick argues that ideal distribution can only be achieved if we don't interfere with individual liberty.
- Nozick believes that it is not the job of justice to determine economic distribution, but merely the rules governing the acquisition and transfer of goods.
- However, people should not to suffer consequences of circumstances over which they have no control.
- One unpalatable consequence of Nozick is the conclusion that we have no obligation to help the poor.
- Hugh LaFollette argues that Nozick gives luck a disproportionate influence on our life experiences.
- Nevertheless, common sense says that people should be rewarded for their effort.
- Iris Marion Young argues that both Rawls and Nozick focus far too much on distributive approaches to justice, ignoring the 'social structure or institutional context that often help determine distributive patterns'.

Punishment:

- There are three traditional theories of punishment: deterrence, retribution and reformation (or rehabilitation).

Deterrence theory –

- A utilitarian approach sees punishment as a deterrent by focusing on the consequences that will befall those who commit crimes.
- The theory assumes that most criminal acts are rational behaviour, and that possible future criminals will be dissuaded from criminal activity because of the risk and threat of the same punishment.
- Bernard Hoose notes that a utilitarian would justify the harm done to the criminal on the basis of an overall greater good caused by discouraging more criminal acts.
- Hoose disputes that punishment deters – some call prisons colleges of crime, and some countries that have abandoned the death penalty have seen a reduction in the rate of murder.
- If the state resorts to brutal acts, it brutalises its people, and so punishment can have a corrupting influence.

Retribution theory –

- The theory of retribution sees punishment as paying back wrongdoers their just deserts.
- This approach encourages the realisation that the way to succeed as individuals is through our good treatment of others.
- This gives people control over how others will treat them, because they are in control of their free actions.
- The theory suggests an egalitarian principle concerning equal distribution of social benefits for adopting retributionism.
- Reciprocity is an integral part of morality, and people are moral in part because they hope to be treated in a moral way in return:
  - Bernard Hoose raises questions about deciding the precise nature and extent of punishment.
  - Ten notes that the retribution theory restricts punishment to those who have broken the law knowingly.

Reformation (or rehabilitation) theory –

- Reformative punishment seeks to convert the criminal through correction and rehabilitation.
- Crime is caused in part by problems of social care, education, mental or physical health, or poverty.
- Arguably, reformative punishment is more humane than earlier more brutal modes.
- The UK imprisons more of its people than many countries, but half of all prisoners re-offend within two years.

- However, Hoose notes that personal reformation only happens when the individual freely embraces the means, and there is no proof that punishment is reformatory.
- Educational and psychiatric facilities help with rehabilitation without any loss of individual liberty.
- Is there a reliable method of reforming a criminal?
- Is criminal behaviour a free decision to commit a crime, rather than the result of some early influence?
- Perhaps people have a right to be different.

Chapter 22

War and peace

Introduction

Key philosophers and works

St Augustine of Hippo (AD 334–430): *De Civitate Dei* (*The City of God*)
St Thomas Aquinas (1224–1274): *Summa Theologica*, 1273
Reinhold Niebuhr (1892–1971): *Moral Man and Immoral Society*, 1932

Key terms

Authority, cause, Christian realism, intention, *jus ad bellum*, *jus in bello*, just war theory, justice, last resort, pacifism, proportionality, realism, success

What you will learn by the end of this chapter

- The key thinkers behind, and principles of, just war theory – and how to apply it.
- The theories of ethical and religious pacifism.
- The theory of realism.
- The relative strengths and weaknesses of these theories.

Key questions

1 Does a country have a right to defend itself from attack?
2 Suggest some limits to what a country can do in defence of itself against an unprovoked attack.
3 Can civilians ever be a just target in war?
4 Should a Christian defend a weaker neighbour from attack?

War and religion

Wars in the West against the Muslim control of Jerusalem in the eleventh, twelfth and thirteenth centuries were sometimes seen as **holy wars** or crusades. At the beginning of the twentieth century, many churchmen saw the First World War as a war in the cause of the Kingdom of God (Jones, 1998). A holy war is a good war, guided by God. Today, mainstream Christian Churches have rejected the holy war concept, that war can be good. Islam also has a concept of a holy war called a 'jihad' (the Arabic for 'fight', or 'battle'), which is a religious duty to spread or defend Islam by waging war. In the modern world, the Muslim emphasis is on waging war with one's inner self. Modern theologians reject holy war, which seems to take a simplistic view of God that supports one particular national interest and rejects mercy for the enemy.

This chapter will consider three other approaches to war:

- **Just war theory**, which maintains that war may be justified if fought only in certain circumstances, and only if certain restrictions are applied to the way in which war is fought.
- **Pacifism**, which rejects the use of violence and the taking of human lives.
- **Realism**, which maintains that normal moral rules can't be applied to how states conduct themselves in war.

Just war theory

Many Christians have taken the view that war may be justified under certain circumstances, and only if fought observing certain rules of conduct. Just war theory attempts to clarify two questions: 'When is it right to fight?' and 'How should war be fought?' Today, just war theory is the standard method of assessing the morality of war. It's a basic moral guide for Christians today.

Ancient philosophers such as Aristotle and Cicero wrote that a war of self-defence was just (Aristotle in *Politics* I, 3.1256b23–27, fourth century BCE, and Cicero in *De officiis* I, II). In the fourth and fifth centuries AD, the Christian thinkers St Ambrose of Milan and St Augustine of Hippo, the latter in *De Civitate Dei* (*The City of God*), justified the use of war to defend the Church against those who threatened the Faith. They based their justification on stories in the Old Testament that portray God as leading the Hebrews to victory in battle (see, for example, Deuteronomy 1:30; 20:4; Joshua 2:24; Judges 3:28) and the writings of St Paul in Romans 13:4, where he says that rulers are servants of God when they execute God's wrath on domestic wrongdoers (see also Regan, 1996 p. 7).

In the thirteenth century, St Thomas Aquinas drew together the strands of Christian thinking on just war, and listed right authority, just cause and just intention as the key moral dimensions. In the sixteenth and seventeenth centuries, Francisco Suarez and Franciso de Vitoria added three additional conditions: **proportionality** in the conduct of war, only entering into war as a last resort, and only fighting if there is reasonable chance of success (in *Reflectiones: De Indis et de jure belli* and *De triplici virtute theological: de caritate, disputatio 13 [de bello]*; taken from Regan, 1996). This set of principles became the established criteria for just war theory, which was accepted formally by the Roman Catholic Church and expounded fully in the Catholic Bishops of America's Pastoral Letter *The Promise of Peace: God's Promise and Our Response* (1983). We shall consider each condition. The quotes from Aquinas are from the *Summa Theologica* (Part II, Question 40, answers to the first four questions).

When it's right to fight: conditions for *jus ad bellum*

Just authority

Aquinas wrote that just authority meant that war could only be started by legitimate authority: 'the authority of the sovereign by whose command the war is to be waged'. The phrase 'competent authority' is used by the Catholic Bishops: 'In the Catholic tradition the right to use force has always been joined to the common good; war must be declared by those with responsibility for public order, not by private groups or individuals.' (*The Promise of Peace*, 1983, para 87) There can be no private armies of individuals who can start a war and, equally, an incompetent government or sovereign doesn't have the authority to initiate war.

Just cause

Just cause was described by Aquinas in the following terms: '... those who are attacked, should be attacked because they deserve it on account of some fault ...'. The Catholic Bishops elaborate the condition further, saying 'War is permissible only to confront "a real and certain danger," ...' which includes protecting innocent life, preserving a decent human existence and guaranteeing basic human rights. The state can't fight a war of **retribution** (*The Promise of Peace*, 1983, para 86). This leaves open the possibility of war on behalf of a third party, a neighbouring state that's under attack, and even military action against a state that's persecuting a group of its own people.

Just intention

Aquinas wrote that the war had to be fought with just intention, for 'the advancement of good, or the avoidance of evil'. Sovereigns could not fight wars for immoral intentions. They had to have good motives. The Bishops elaborated in their letter, stating that 'war can be legitimately intended only for the reasons set forth above as a just cause. During the conflict, right intention means pursuit of peace and reconciliation, including avoiding unnecessarily destructive acts or imposing unreasonable conditions (e.g., unconditional surrender).' (*The Promise of Peace*, 1983, para. 95) Soldiers can't use or encourage a hatred of a minority in war. Their intentions must be virtuous.

Proportionality

There had to be proportionality between the injustice that led to the war and the damage done by war, in terms of suffering and loss of human life. In other words, a state should not wage a war that causes substantially more suffering and destruction than the actual wrong done by the enemy. According to the Catholic Bishops, '... proportionality means that the damage to be inflicted and the costs incurred by war must be proportionate to the good expected by taking up arms'. Excessive violence, death and damage should be avoided (*The Promise of Peace*, 1983, para. 99). For example, it would have been disproportionate for the UK to have launched a nuclear strike on Argentina in response to their invasion of the Falkland Islands.

Last resort

War must be the last resort. All peaceful attempts at resolution must have been exhausted before violence is used. War can't be chosen as a first response – or, indeed, before attempts have been made to establish peace via normal political routes.

Reasonable chance of success

There should a fair chance that the war will be won. It's immoral to enter into a hopeless war, thus magnifying the suffering and loss of life for no constructive purpose. This is 'to prevent irrational resort to force or hopeless resistance when the outcome of either will clearly be disproportionate or futile' (*The Promise of Peace*, 1983, para. 98).

Comparative justice

Lastly, the American Bishops add a requirement for comparative justice. In other words, both sides to the conflict must be fairly considered.

How war should be fought: conditions for *jus in bello*

There have always been rules of conduct in war, although such rules have often been ignored. Since the twentieth century, international agreements such as the Geneva and Hague conventions have attempted to limit certain kinds of warfare. With the increasing numbers of civilians affected in war, these agreements are both timely and yet seemingly ineffective. However, at the end of the Second World War, Nazi officers were tried for crimes against humanity and, more recently, senior Serb commanders have been successfully tried for war crimes. Recently, a Serb commander was tried for running a rape centre prison camp, where women and girls as young as 12 were repeatedly raped by the Serb soldiers. In the Christian tradition, there are conditions of conduct that limit the degree of destruction and who may be killed. The principles are proportionality – which essentially means that only the minimal force necessary should be used – and discrimination between combatants and non-combatants.

Proportionality demands that only necessary destructive force and weapons are used to achieve the peace desired. In particular, the Bishops reject the use of nuclear weapons, which could lead to wholesale and long-lasting effects. An act of war aimed indiscriminately at the destruction of entire cities, or of extensive areas along with their populations, is a crime against God and humanity, and should be condemned.

The Bishops also insist on a degree of discrimination over targets. The text specifically mentions the carpet incendiary bombing in the Second World War, which destroyed large civilian populations rather than selective military targets. A warring Christian country should not use nuclear, biological or chemical weapons in this way, should not target crops or homes, and should not harness any other new technology that affects whole civilian populations. Such 'total war' is rejected and the deliberate taking of innocent lives is prohibited. Innocent lives are defined as 'non-combatant' and 'non-military' – although the Bishops recognise that these groups can provide political, social and economic support for a fighting nation and acknowledge that there is ambiguity here. However, the Bishops identify the following who could never be classed as combatants: schoolchildren, hospital patients, the elderly, the ill, the average industrial worker producing goods not directly related to military purposes, and farmers.

Evaluating just war theory

Just war theory attempts to maintain core moral principles in a framework to permit the use of violence in controlled circumstances and against certain targets. It recognises the need the act against a tyrannical aggressor, that is intent on aggression against civilians and minority groups within its boundaries and in other countries. The framework doesn't allow for wanton acts of violence in the national interest, but only for the use of minimal force. It's not a green light for states to ignore basic human rights and it takes account of the importance that Christians accord to justice.

Realists argue that the just war conditions are ambiguous, open to question or too simplistic and impractical. Jeff McMahan (1991) writes that wars are caused by complex reasons, and that it's unrealistic to try to see the act of waging war in terms of a single 'just' cause. He also notes that the outcomes of war are difficult to calculate. It isn't always clear that peace will be the result of a military action, or that success is likely. America lost the war in Vietnam despite its overwhelming military superiority. Finally, he notes that the conduct of armies and individual soldiers is difficult to control: to expect fighting soldiers who have to kill their opponents to keep their thoughts free from from malice or prejudice towards those opponents is unrealistic.

In addition to the problems with the criteria for deciding if it's just to go to war, there are problems deciding who might be a just target in war. The 1983 pastoral letter states 'the lives of innocent persons may never be taken directly, regardless of the purpose alleged for doing so'. (*The Promise of Peace*, 1983, para. 104) A soldier is a combatant, but in the Second World War, when munitions workers went to fight on the front line, women replaced them and were arguably fair targets. If a civilian population supports the actions of its army and government in launching an unprovoked war, that population is less innocent than the army of the country that's being attacked.

Those who provide the economic power to the war machine are an essential part of the war effort. The RAF bombed Germany's industrial centres because they powered the armies, even though they were not directly military in nature. If civilians are part of the cause of the war machine, then they, like combatants, may be targeted. Just war theory doesn't endorse bombing industrial targets populated by civilians. However, if military targets are in residential areas, civilians will invariably be affected by the bombing, even with today's high-technology laser-guided bombs. Perhaps a soldier fighting for a just cause should have scope for using violence against a wider range of people.

Tasks

1 Consider which of the following are innocent and should not be attacked, under the just war theory, and then in your own opinion:

   a Politicians and generals who launch and direct wars.

   b Soldiers, pilots and seamen, and women who fight.

   c Medics who heal the soldiers.

   d Munitions workers who approve of the war.

   e Non-military factory workers who support the war.

   f Civilians who approve of the war.

   g Children who approve of the war.

   h The elderly who approve of the war.

   i The infirm who approve of the war.

   j Civilians who oppose the war and do nothing to contribute to it.

2 Make an argument that the following actions are just, and then consider how convincing your argument is:

a To launch a preventive strike against an enemy that's about to launch an attack against you.

b To use violence in the rescue of nationals of your country, who are held prisoner in a foreign country.

c To sponsor terrorism against a government that's causing the suffering and death of many of its own people.

d To use military force against a country that's posing an economic threat that is crippling your economy.

e To use military force to settle territorial claims – in other words, to take back territory that was once yours.

Pacifism

Just war theory comes under criticism from those who advocate **pacifism**. Pacifists argue that just war theory ignores the essential pacifist stance taken by Jesus. He rejected the option to use physical force even in defence of himself against unjust aggressors. They maintain that war is always wrong. Richard Norman notes that an analogy is often made between the right to self-defence and fighting against an aggressor state. We consider it just to use force in our personal self-defence and draw an analogy with fighting against an invading force. In his article 'Moral restraints in warfare' (Norman, 1998, p. 13), he questions whether our right to defend ourselves with force necessarily transfers to our right to defend our sovereignty. After all, it may not be a matter of life and death. Is the defence of a culture or way of life sufficient to justify the use of violence?

In its most extreme form, pacifism is the opposition to all forms of violence as a means of settling disputes, either between individuals or between countries. A form of pacifism is found in the ancient history of Buddhism and Christianity. Siddharta Gautama, the founder of Buddhism, required that his followers renounce violence. Early Christians refused to fight in the Roman Imperial army, perceiving pacifism in Jesus' teachings about loving our neighbours as ourselves and turning the other cheek, and from His order to Peter to drop his sword (Matthew 22:39, 5:38–39, 26:52). Christians modelled themselves on Jesus, who didn't resist capture, and who suffered torture and death, forgiving those who executed Him.

This early form of pacifism changed when Christianity became the official religion of the Roman Empire, although several Reformation Churches in the sixteenth and seventeenth centuries were and still are pacifist, including the Mennonites, the Moravians, the Society of Friends and the Church of the Brethren. Members of these groups refuse to bear arms and fight. They conscientiously object to violence and have often been persecuted as a result. More recently, in the early twentieth century, the International Fellowship of Reconciliation link movement was formed, advocating the principle Christian duty of seeking reconciliation and rejecting the taking of life.

While several religious denominations have upheld pacifist principles, Richard Regan (1996, p. 5) notes that many pacifists today are pacifist for philosophical reasons. They maintain that killing or physically attacking another human is intrinsically wrong. Life has an absolute value. Pacifists argue that the loss of life, human suffering and tremendous economic, social and moral damage caused by war is too great, and that it should be abandoned as a tool of national governments. They maintain that non-violence and non-resistance will change the minds of, or disarm, those who use violence. They encourage non-violent resistance, essentially a refusal of the public to co-operate with a conqueror so causing considerable inconvenience.

There are a number of difficulties with Pacifism. Jeff McMahan (1991) insists that pacifism is difficult to maintain, especially as it takes away from the victim the right to judge whether a violent response is just. The widespread use of mass deportations, and even mass exterminations, shows the weakness of pacifist principles. The persecutions of Christian pacifists and Jews in the Middle Ages and under the Nazi regime has led to foreign domination of invaded countries, sometimes by the most fanatical and ruthless powers (see Moseley, 1998).

Tasks

1 Make a case for the claim that the teachings of Jesus are pacifist.

2 Suggest Gospel incidents or stories that could be used to challenge the case you have made in **1**.

3 Give examples of what could be meant by passive resistance.

4 Make a philosophical argument against the use of violence in self-defence.

5 Make a historical argument against the effectiveness of pacifism.

Realism

Some Christians have rejected pacifism, choosing instead a position known as 'Christian realism'. In his book *Moral Man and Immoral Society* (1932), Reinhold Niebuhr argued that because human nature was evil, human communities have to use force to maintain a just and ordered society. The usual moral rules that restrict individual actions, such as those that stop us harming or killing each other, don't apply to communities or states, which have special rights necessitated by their status. Realism argues that special moral rules apply once you have a human community with special political responsibility, which goes beyond the individual responsibility that human beings have. This means that war that serves the national interest is morally acceptable. Niebuhr rejected pacifism as a heresy that assumed that love is guaranteed victory over the world. Pacifists expect God's will to prevail without realising that they have a duty to be proactive in the world. They don't recognise that God rules through human institutions such as governments and the courts. Jeff McMahan (1991, pp. 384–385) questions the special rights that national governments are granted by realism. He argues that there's no moral difference just because a number of human 'actors' are gathered together.

Pacifism seems to place extraordinary limitations on individual rights of self-defence which, in an era of weapons of mass destruction and the practice of genocide, may ultimately appear unacceptable for a state. Realism seems to provide virtually no limitations to a government's actions in war and, in an era of war crimes against large civilian populations, there's a case that there should be some limitations on governments in war.

Tasks

1 What are the philosophical principles in realism?
2 On what theological grounds did Niebuhr challenge pacifism?
3 Explain what's meant by just war theory.
4 Consider two or more criticisms of just war theory.
5 Compare and contrast just war theory and realism.
6 Consider the strengths and weaknesses of pacifism.

Extracts from key texts

St Thomas Aquinas, *Summa Theologica*, 1273

Part II, Question 40: part of the answers to the first four questions

In order for a war to be just, three things are necessary. First, the authority of the sovereign by whose command the war is to be waged. For it is not the business of a private individual to declare war, because he can seek for redress of his rights from the tribunal of his superior. Moreover it is not the business of a private individual to summon together the people ... And just as it is lawful for them to have recourse to the sword in defending that common weal against internal disturbances, when they punish evil-doers, according to the words of the Apostle (Rm. 13:4): 'He beareth not the sword in vain: for he is God's minister, an avenger to execute wrath upon him that doth evil'; so too, it is their business to have recourse to the sword of war in defending the common weal against external enemies. Hence it is said to those who are in authority (Ps. 81:4): 'Rescue the poor: and deliver the needy out of the hand of the sinner'; and for this reason Augustine says (Contra Faust. xxii, 75): 'The natural order conducive to peace among mortals demands that the power to declare and counsel war should be in the hands of those who hold the supreme authority.'

Secondly, a just cause is required, namely that those who are attacked, should be attacked because they deserve it on account of some fault. Wherefore Augustine says (Questions. in Hept., qu. x, super Jos.): 'A just war is wont to be described as one that avenges wrongs, when a nation or state has to be punished, for refusing to make amends for the wrongs inflicted by its subjects, or to restore what it has seized unjustly.'

Thirdly, it is necessary that the belligerents should have a rightful intention, so that they intend the advancement of good, or the avoidance of evil. Hence Augustine says (De Verb. Dom. [*The words quoted are to be found not in St Augustine's works, but Can. Apud. Caus. xxiii, qu. 1]): 'True religion looks upon as peaceful those wars that are waged not for motives of aggrandizement, or cruelty, but with the object of securing peace, of punishing evil-doers, and of uplifting the good.' For it may happen that the war is declared by the legitimate authority, and for a just cause, and yet be rendered unlawful through a wicked intention. Hence Augustine says (Contra Faust. xxii, 74): 'The passion for inflicting harm, the cruel thirst for vengeance, an unpacific and relentless spirit, the fever of revolt, the lust of power, and such like things, all these are rightly condemned in war.'

CHAPTER SUMMARY

Just war theory:

- Just war theory asks 'When is it right to fight?' and 'How should war be fought?'
- Ancient philosophers such as Aristotle and Cicero wrote that a war of self-defence was just.
- The Christian thinkers St Ambrose of Milan and St Augustine of Hippo in the fourth and fifth centuries AD justified the use of war to defend the Church against those who threatened the Faith.
- St Paul, in Romans 13:4, says that rulers are servants of God when they execute God's wrath on domestic wrongdoers.
- St Thomas Aquinas in the thirteenth century, Francisco Suarez and Franciso de Vitoria in the sixteenth and seventeenth centuries and the Catholic Bishops of America's Pastoral Letter formulated the theory.

When it's right to fight – conditions for *jus ad bellum*:

- Just authority – a head of state, not a private army or an individual, may start a war.
- Just cause – not a war of retribution.
- Just intention – war for the advancement of good, or the avoidance of evil.
- Proportionality – reasonable use of force only.
- Last resort – all other means tried first.
- A reasonable chance of success – don't fight hopeless wars, thus magnifying the suffering and loss of life for no constructive purpose.
- Comparative justice – both sides to the conflict must be fairly considered.

How war should be fought – conditions for *jus in bello*:

- Certain acts in war are always wrong.
- Proportionality demands that only necessary destructive force and

weapons are used to achieve the peace desired – the indiscriminate destruction of entire cities is a crime against humanity.

- No indiscriminate targeting – civilians should not be targeted.

Evaluating just war theory:

- It maintains core moral principles in a framework permitting violence in controlled circumstances and against certain targets.
- It recognises the need the act against a tyrannical aggressor that is intent on aggression.
- It prohibits wanton acts of violence in the national interest.
- Realists argue that the just war conditions are ambiguous, open to question or too simplistic and impractical.
- Outcomes of war are difficult to calculate.
- There is uncertainty about which people are just targets.

Pacifism:

- Pacifists argue that just war theory ignores the essential pacifist stance taken by Jesus.
- A right to self-defence doesn't correspond to a right to defend sovereignty.
- Pacifism opposes all forms of violence.
- Siddharta Gautama, the founder of Buddhism, required that his followers renounce violence and early Christians refused to fight.
- In the early twentieth century, the International Fellowship of Reconciliation link movement was formed, advocating the principle of the Christian duty of seeking reconciliation and rejecting the taking of life.
- Many pacifists today are pacifist for philosophical reasons, maintaining that killing or physically attacking another human is intrinsically wrong, as life has an absolute value.
- Jeff McMahan insists that pacifism removes the victim's right to judge whether a violent response is just.
- The widespread use of mass deportations, and even mass exterminations, shows the weakness of pacifist principles.

Realism:

- Christian realism argues that human communities have to use force to maintain a just and ordered society.

Ethical issues

- The moral rules that restrict individual actions don't apply to communities.
- A war that serves the national interest is morally acceptable.
- Niebuhr rejected pacifism as a heresy that assumed that love is guaranteed victory over the world.
- God rules through human institutions such as governments and the courts.
- Jeff McMahan questions the special rights that national governments are granted by realism.
- Pacifism seems to place extraordinary limitations on individual rights of self-defence.
- Realism provides few if any limitations to a government's actions in war.

Chapter 23

Rights: human and animal

Introduction

Key terms

Animal experimentation, animal liberation, animal rights, duties, entitlement, equality, human rights, immunities, protections, liberty/freedoms, life, moral community, non-moral beings, powers, preference utilitarianism, speciesism, Universal Declaration of Human Rights, virtue

What you will learn by the end of this chapter

- The historical background to human rights.
- The different kinds of rights and different theories of rights.
- The strengths and weaknesses of human rights ethics.
- Three different approaches to animal rights.
- The relative strengths and weaknesses of these animal rights theories.

Key questions

1 What or who can be the subject of a right?
2 What kind of things can there be a right to?
3 Are rights ever absolute, or are there always circumstances when rights can be overruled for the benefit of the majority, the common good?

Human rights

Background

Human rights have a history that dates back to the Stoics' belief in a universal moral law that human conduct can be judged against and brought into harmony with. Later, the Magna Carta (1215) put in place the idea that 'right' was not just what the king did. In England, the Petition of Right (1628) and the Bill of Rights (1689) suggest the view that human beings are endowed with eternal and inalienable rights. In the seventeenth century, the English philosopher John Locke argued that human individuals have certain rights including the rights to life, liberty and property. In the eighteenth century, Thomas Jefferson described his countrymen as 'free people claiming their rights as derived from the laws of nature and not as the gift of their Chief Magistrate'. The Declaration of Independence, proclaimed by the 13 American Colonies on 4 July 1776, states that 'We hold these truths to be self-evident, that all men are created equal, that they are endowed by their Creator with certain unalienable Rights, that among these are Life, Liberty and the Pursuit of Happiness.' This was followed by the Declaration of the Rights of Man (26 August 1789), which defines 'liberty' as including the right to free speech, freedom of association, religious freedom, and freedom from arbitrary arrest and confinement.

With the creation of the Universal Declaration of Human Rights in 1948, a set of principles was established to guarantee equality before the law; protection against arbitrary arrest; the right to a fair trial; freedom from *ex post facto* criminal laws; the right to own property; freedom of thought, conscience and religion; freedom of opinion and expression; and freedom of peaceful assembly and association. The following rights are all included: to work and freely choose one's work, to receive equal pay for equal work, to form and join trades unions, to rest and leisure, to an adequate standard of living, and to education.

The rights expressed in the Universal Declaration take different forms. Some are claims which generate duties that others have. For example, the right to have a loan repaid is a claim that generates a duty to repay the loan. Other rights are powers that we might have in law, such as the right to choose who will inherit your wealth after your death and who cannot. Rights may also be liberties, or freedoms, such as not having to give evidence against your own spouse, or evidence that might prejudice your case in court. Lastly, rights can be immunities, or protections from certain actions, such as violence from another individual, slavery or discrimination due to your political or religious views.

What are rights?

The case for human rights is set against a backdrop of political leaders failing to respect freedom and equality in their treatment of people. For hundreds of years, class structures ensured that the rich and powerful dominated and enslaved the poor and weak. Even in democratic Athens, only certain men were full citizens. Women, foreigners, traders and slaves didn't have the same status under the law, despite making up the majority of the population. The widespread practice of slavery in the ancient and medieval worlds, coupled with numerous acts of tyranny against civilian populations up to the present age, have built a case for human rights to be enshrined in law. They have become a political mainstay of democracies. But what of the ethical basis of rights? What are rights anyway?

There's a link between the idea of rights and the idea of a **divine law** that's above and beyond human law, as expressed by St Thomas Aquinas in his natural moral law theory. Human rights aren't validated by law: they seem to exist in themselves. The law can be morally wrong while human rights are not. The Kantian idea of humans being ends in themselves, who can't be used for any other purpose, supports rights ethics. There is something special about human beings, which means that these rights apply in dealing with humans.

Rights tend to express a deontological or absolute ethical point of view. More right-wing expressions of rights ethics are found in Robert Nozick's book *Anarchy, State and Utopia* (1974). Nozick is a deontologist who maintains that we have rights – to life, liberty, and legitimately acquired property – that are absolute. It isn't just for the state to decide what we can earn or keep, or what we must do with our earnings or property. Similarly, Ronald M. Dworkin, in *Taking Rights Seriously* (1977), argues that rights are like moral trump cards. Just because I have wealth and you don't, it doesn't follow that you can have a share of my money, even if you're in dire need of it.

Where do rights come from?

Originally, rights were seen to come from God. Because we're made by God, we have a special **sacred** status that gives us rights. This religious view remains popular today and emerges clearly in the abortion debate, although many atheists would reject such a link. Another traditional origin of rights is nature. Secular documents expressing rights have linked them to a quasi-spiritual status that human beings have by virtue of their being human. Some argue that rights come from the duties or responsibilities that we have towards others. The Late Chief Rabbi Lord Jakobovits said, '... could it be that the greatest moral failure of our time is the stress on our rights, on what we claim from others – human rights, women's rights, worker's rights, gay rights and so on – and not on our duties, on what we owe to others?' and the Labour politician Jack Straw has warned '... the ethics and politics of dutiless right, demand-satisfaction and self-realization through unimpeded freedom of action have been a costly moral failure in the corrupted liberal orders'.

The danger of a rights-based ethic seems to be that it may become an individualistically based ethic – one that rejects the interests of the common community of humanity. My enjoyment of my rights depends upon the respect of others and, in turn, they depend upon me respecting their rights. In her book

Values for a Godless Age (2000), Francesca Klug maintains that this approach never explains who or what authority decides this flow of duties and rights (p. 214). We don't always expect duties from 'rights holders'. We wouldn't expect a baby human being to have any responsibilities to anyone, and yet we would give it rights.

In Chapter 3 of her book *An Intelligent Person's Guide to Ethics* (1999), Mary Warnock acknowledges that ethics can be discussed in terms of rights to life, but doubts that there can be an ethical system based on rights (p. 54). She argues that rights may be conferred by a person's absolute need – a satisfaction of something that he or she is entitled to. The abolition of slavery recognised pre-existing rights – entitlements that humans had on the basis that not to have such an entitlement was wrong absolutely. Discussions about rights return us to the debate about how we decide what's right and wrong in a given situation (p. 59).

While the advent of a focus on human rights is of great importance, especially as a tool for identifying immoral behaviour on the part of individuals and governments, ultimately it seems that rights ethics must be linked either to the law or to God, or to some other ethical system of actually determining and justifying those rights.

Tasks

1 Decide which of the following would you give full rights (FR) to, which you would give limited rights (LR) to and which you would give no rights to (NR), and explain your reasoning:

   a A day-old pre-embryo.

   b A 24-week-old foetus.

   c A whale.

   d An old age pensioner in a persistent vegetative state, with no hope of recovery.

   e The Moors murderer Myra Hindley.

   f A chimpanzee.

   g A two-year-old toddler.

   h A 400-year-old oak tree.

   i A serial killer.

   j An incurable paedophile.

   k A human corpse.

   l Adolf Hitler (if he were alive).

2 Identify three historical documents in the development of human rights and state what they contribute to the rights debate.

3 Explain the link that people have made between rights and the law and God.

4 Explain the dangers of observing rights alone in moral debates.

5 Consider the basis on which human rights can be taken away. Think about crime, national and majority interests.

Racism, discrimination and preference

The rise of the notion of human rights is closely related to the civil rights movement. Longstanding discriminatory practices involving the treatment of minority groups, such as slavery and segregation, have been challenged periodically over the past two centuries, although the extent to which equality exists in practice varies within nations and across nations.

Ethical discussions have arisen over the appropriateness of positive discrimination – in effect, preferential treatment for minority groups, to counter years of discrimination. Bernard R. Boxhill (1997, p. 333), notes two arguments for preferential treatment. The first is a teleological case that the future consequence of treating minority groups preferentially is a more harmonious society in which the damage done by racism has finally been addressed. This consequence justifies the immediate apparent injustice of preferring certain traditionally disadvantaged groups over others, an action that creates a more egalitarian society in which racism diminishes.

The second argument sees this preferential treatment as compensation for the past wrongs done to members of those groups. An equal opportunity approach must address the unequal starting points that people have in life, according to their racial or ethnic backgrounds. This practice has been criticised as causing resentment towards the minority groups through the imposition of an apparently unfair system, and stigmatising the individuals who – under preferential treatment over more qualified majority candidates – benefit from their preference.

Others note that members of minority groups who have suffered past injustices did so to different degrees, and that a simple preference on account of race or ethnicity benefits those who need no additional help at the expense of others who might. Nevertheless, the reality that most societies experience considerable degrees of discrimination towards race in particular suggests that human rights have yet to be fully realised in many contexts.

Ethical issues

Animal rights

At one time, animals were considered to be a resource for us to use and enjoy as we pleased. There's now growing concern about the suffering that we cause to animals. We use animals to carry burdens and we use them in sporting events. We keep them in zoos and rear them for their products. We also experiment on them for research. Around the world, billons of animals die every year because of these activities.

Some – such as Michael A. Fox and Carl Cohan – argue that humans have no moral obligation to animals at all, while others – such as Tom Regan and Peter Singer – argue that animals should not be eaten, should not be used in sports or for hunting, and should not be experimented upon, either for cosmetic and or medical purposes. Another view, expressed by Roger Scruton, argues that there are important moral considerations about animals, such as sustaining a balance in the natural world and preventing moral decay by allowing cruel or vicious treatment.

We have no moral obligation to animals

In his book *The Case for Animal Experimentation* (1986), Michael A. Fox argued that animals are not members of the moral community and that we have no moral obligation towards them. He defined a moral community as 'a social group composed of interacting autonomous beings where moral concepts and precepts can evolve and be understood. It's also a social group in which the mutual recognition of autonomy and personhood exist.' (p. 50) These can't exist where animals are concerned and so they are not morally significant creatures. Fox eventually changed his mind completely – rejecting his earlier belief – but others, such as Carl Cohan, have not. In his article 'The case for the use of animals in biomedical research' (1998), Cohan argues that animals have no rights. Rights can only exist between people, who can make moral claims on each other (p. 830). This moral capability arises from a number of faculties that animals don't have. These include an inner consciousness of free will, the grasp by reason of moral law, and human membership in a moral community. Humans confront choices that are moral and lay down moral laws: animals don't. They lack free moral judgements and so don't have rights.

The difficulty with attempts at defining the characteristics that make humans morally significant is the fact than human beings sometimes don't display these characteristics. Human babies and toddlers don't display the moral capability that Cohan requires of animals. Nevertheless, we give them moral status and regard them as deserving of special protection. Crimes against young children are considered particularly abhorrent, precisely because they are more vulnerable due in part to their lack of sophistication.

This attitude that animals are simply not worth considering in the moral picture was illustrated in December 1974, when an American public television network brought together Robert Nozick and three scientists whose work involves animals. Nozick asked 'whether the fact that an experiment will kill hundreds of animals is ever regarded, by scientists, as a reason for not performing it'. One of the scientists answered, 'Not that I know of.' Nozick pressed his question: 'Don't the animals count at all?' Dr A. Perachio, of the Yerkes Center, replied 'Why should they?', while Dr D. Baltimore, of the Massachusetts Institute of Technology, added that he didn't think that experimenting on animals raised a moral issue at all ('The price of knowledge', broadcast in New York on 12 December 1974; quoted from Singer, 1995). At the very least, these scientists displayed a lack of sensitivity. Arguably, they were exhibiting a degree of callous disregard for the animals involved in experimentation, and few scientists would be prepared to make such comments openly today.

Animals deserve the same respect as humans

In his article 'The case for animal rights' (1985), Tom Regan argues for the total abolition of the use of animals in science, the total dissolution of commercial animal agriculture and the total elimination of commercial and sport hunting and trapping. He argues that it isn't simply the pain that we put animals through but the whole system that's wrong. It's wrong to view animals as our resource, here for us – to be eaten, surgically manipulated, or exploited for sport or money. A mentally normal mammal is subject of a life, and this life has inherent value and requires treatment as an individual. All beings who have inherent value have it equally. A difficulty with Regan's position is that it gives us no guidelines for action where values conflict (Gruen, 1991, p. 343). Consider the following situation.

> [I]magine five survivors are on a lifeboat. Because of limits of size, the boat can only support four. All weigh approximately the same and would take approximately the same amount of space. Four of the five are normal adult human beings. The fifth is a dog. One must be thrown overboard or else all will perish. Whom should it be?
>
> Regan (1983), p. 285

In the end, Regan argues that we should kill the dog, as the death of a human is a greater loss than the death of the dog, but this seems inconsistent with his general view.

Peter Singer's book *Animal Liberation* (1995), offered a new system of ethics for our treatment of animals. He argued that by treating animals differently we're guilty of being speciesist: 'If a being suffers, there can be no moral justification for refusing to take the suffering into consideration. No matter what the nature of the being, the principle of equality requires that suffering be counted equally with the like suffering – in so far as rough comparisons can be made – of any other being.' (Singer, 1995)

The point that animals are different from humans should not mean that we treat them differently. Not all humans are of equal worth to society or are equal in what they can do, but they receive equal treatment. If we're prepared to carry out experimentation on a chimpanzee, then it must be for a purpose so grave that we would be prepared to use a retarded human being (Singer, 1995, pp. 75, 77–78). If we're unwilling in principle ever to use a retarded human being in such experimentation, then we should not carry out experimentation on animals with a similar mental capability. To discriminate against animals in this way is speciesist.

We allow procedures on animals which give them pain. Animals feel pain and they respond to painful experiences just as we respond, by screaming or withdrawing from the source of the pain, in the same way as humans do. We kill animals for food, in sport or in experimentation, and yet we would never do so to humans. The 'sanctity of life' argument is arbitrarily reserved for humans alone.

> Why is it that we lock up chimpanzees in appalling primate research centres, and use them in experiments that range from the uncomfortable to the agonising and lethal, and yet we would never think of doing the same to a retarded human being at a much lower mental level? The only possible answer is that the chimpanzee, no matter how bright, is not human, while the retarded human, no matter how dull, is … This is speciesism, pure and simple, and it is just as indefensible as the most blatant racism. There is no ethical basis for elevating membership of one particular species into a morally crucial characteristic. From an ethical point of view, we all stand on an equal footing – whether we stand on two feet, or four, or none at all.
>
> Singer (1985)

Singer argues that the principle of equality that we apply for men and women and people of different races should also operate with animals. This doesn't mean that we think that animals are equal to humans, but that our treatment of all humans and animals should be equal. Singer is a modern utilitarian in many respects and he builds his case on Bentham's 'each to count for one and none for more than one'. He doesn't think that animals should necessarily be treated in the same way as humans, but that they should receive equal preference. Singer is a preference utilitarian.

Singer's approach is a mainstay of the animal liberation movement, but it is radical. It would require a commitment to vegetarianism, and would place considerable limitations on science. Inevitably human experimentation would become more prevalent, as only humans can give informed consent. For many, the extreme conclusions of preference utilitarianism are unpalatable.

Animals should not be treated in a way that depraves humanity

In his book *Animal Rights and Wrongs* (2000), Roger Scruton rejects Singer's thinking. He maintains that animals don't have the same moral status and therefore should not receive equal preference. Animals are non-moral beings, because they don't have rationality, self-consciousness, personality and so on. Full members of the moral community have rights and duties, as we do, and such rights and duties could never be given to animals. You could never gain their consent before taking them into captivity, training them, domesticating them or using them in any other way. Animals can't fulfil the obligations and duties that membership of the moral community requires (pp. 79–81). If dogs were to commit crimes, then they would be punished. If they killed rabbits, they would be considered as murderers. Scruton maintains that to grant equal status to animals is impractical and immoral, as it places an unreasonable burden of duty and responsibility on animals.

Scruton does, however, argue that our treatment of animals may be deemed immoral if it makes us less virtuous and encourages vice. Inflicting pain on animals for its own sake, or for the enjoyment of the spectacle, is morally wrong because it encourages a vicious character – it contributes to moral corruption. Activities such as dog-fighting and bear-baiting are morally

Ethical issues

depraved, because of the impact that they have on the viewers. Many people take offence to bull-fighting because of the goading and the pain inflicted on the bull. If the spectator's interest were cruel or sadistic, bull-fighting would be immoral. Advocates of bull-fighting maintain that the interest is in the skill and bravery of the matador, but Scruton questions a practice where the courage of the matador counts for everything and the sufferings of his victim count for nothing. Arguably, this shows a lack of sympathy on the part of the crowds (pp. 97–98). If anglers take pleasure in torturing live fish with hooks, we could consider fishing to be immoral. But if they take pleasure in the angling rather than the torture, then the activity is moral.

This view is echoed by the Labour politician Roy Hattersley, who wrote in *The Guardian* (21 April 1990): 'I have long supported whoever it was who said that the real objection to fox-hunting is the pleasure that the hunters get out of it … If killing foxes is necessary for safety and survival of other species, I – and several million others – will vote for it to continue. But the slaughter ought not be fun.'

This concern about our relationship with animals extends to our attitude to wildlife, zoos, livestock and experimentation. The demands of sympathy, piety and human virtue mean that it's wrong to take pleasure in the suffering of a wild animal. Zoos are of questionable morality, because they take wild animals out of their habitats, preventing them from enjoying the benefits of the wild (p. 99). We have a duty to 'protect their habitats, to secure, as best we can, the balance of nature, and to inflict no pain or fear that is not a necessary part of our legitimate dealings with them'. Animals should not be kept in conditions where they can't appreciate the joys of nature simply in order to reduce costs. This displays a failure to show sympathy or pity towards them. Scruton doesn't think that these things are wrong in themselves, or that animals have rights as such, but he's concerned that our attitude towards animals does have moral significance. Many argue that experiments on animals are necessary for the advancement of science, and are permissible when suitably controlled. Scruton maintains that experimentation may become immoral if it encourages a degree of callousness. To experiment on a higher mammal such as a chimpanzee, in a way that destroys their higher abilities, suggests a failing of sympathy towards the animal (pp. 106–107). We become better people if we're sympathetic towards animals and worse people if we treat them in a cruel or callous way.

One consequence of this virtue approach is that, while animals have no rights, we have duties towards them depending on our relationship with them. We have a special duty to pets that are dependent on us or, in the case of farmers, to livestock. That relationship has moral significance and we have a particular duty to look after such animals: 'we have a duty to provide a fulfilled life, an easy death and the training required by their participation in the human world'. To ignore such duties wouldn't make us more virtuous people. It would be cruel to torture a pet that was dependent on us.

Scruton is critical of our sentimental approach to wild animals: we're far more concerned about the tiger and the elephant than the difficulties of the toad and the stick insect. He also argues that we should maintain the balance of nature. Fishing using massive suction devices which draw in all fish of all ages, young and mature, distorts the balance of nature and now threatens the fish stocks. This disregard for animal species does not enhance us as human beings, although the hunting and shooting of wild animals may, in the right circumstances, be permissible and even be a positive good.

This approach draws on the idea of **virtue ethics**, which is interested in how we become better people. While some who reject animal rights see the treatment of animals as having no moral relevance, the virtue approach is concerned not just with what is done to animals but also the attitudes that underpin those actions. Equally, Scruton's approach avoids the difficulty of choosing between an animal and a human, because it doesn't argue for equal status between animals and humans, or equal treatment.

Tasks

1 In your own words, summarise the three basic views on animal rights.
2 What are the moral differences between killing animals for food, pleasure and scientific purposes?
3 Which animals are potential candidates for being given rights, and why?
4 Give an example of a situation that highlights the problem of giving animals rights equal to those of humans.

Extracts from key texts

Jeremy Bentham, *Principles of Morals and Legislation*, 1789

Chapter 1, Introduction, page 7, footnote

The day may come when the rest of the animal creation may acquire those rights which never could have been withholden from them but by the hand of tyranny. The French have already discovered that the blackness of the skin is no reason why a human being should be abandoned without redress to the caprice of a tormentor. It may one day come to be recognized that the number of the legs, the villosity of the skin, or the termination of the os sacrum are reasons equally insufficient for abandoning a sensitive being to the same fate. What else is it that should trace the insuperable line? Is it the faculty of reason, or perhaps the faculty of discourse? But a full-grown horse or dog is beyond comparison a more rational, as well as a more conversable animal, than an infant of a day or a week, or even a month, old. But suppose they were otherwise, what would it avail? The question is not, Can they reason? nor Can they talk? but Can they suffer?

Peter Singer, *In Defence of Animals*, 1985/*Animal Liberation*, 1975

If a being suffers there can be no moral justification for refusing to take that suffering into consideration. No matter what the nature of the being, the principle of equality requires that its suffering be counted equally with the like suffering – in so far as rough comparisons can be made – of any other being. If a being is not capable of suffering, or of experiencing enjoyment or happiness, there is nothing to be taken into account. So the limit of sentience (using the term as a convenient if not strictly accurate shorthand for the capacity to suffer and/or experience enjoyment) is the only defensible boundary of concern for the interests of others. To mark this boundary by some other characteristic like intelligence or rationality would be to mark it in an arbitrary manner. Why not choose some other characteristic, like skin color?

The racist violates the principle of equality by giving greater weight to the interests of members of his own race when there is a clash between their interests and the interests of those of another race The sexist violates the principle of equality by favoring the interests of his own sex. Similarly the speciesist allows the interests of his own species to over ride the greater interests of members of other species. The pattern is identical in each case.

How can a man who is not a sadist spend his working day heating an unanesthetized dog to death, or driving a monkey into a lifelong depression, and then remove his white coat, wash his hands, and go home to dinner with his wife and children? How can taxpayers allow their money to be used to support experiments of this kind? And how can students go through a turbulent era of protest against injustice, discrimination, and oppression of all kinds, no matter how far from home, while ignoring the cruelties that are being carried out on their own campuses?

The animal liberation movement ... is not saying that all lives are of equal worth or that all interests of humans and other animals are to be given equal weight, no matter what those interests may be. It is saying that where animals and humans have similar interests – we might take the interest in avoiding physical pain as an example, for it is an interest that humans clearly share with other animals – those interests are to be counted equally, with no automatic discount just because one of the beings is not human. A simple point, no doubt, but nevertheless part of a far-reaching ethical revolution. (*In Defence of Animals*)

Douglas Adams *The Restaurant at the End of the Universe* (1980)

From pages 91–92

A large dairy animal approached Zaphod Beeblebrox's table, a large fat meaty quadruped of the bovine type with large watery eyes, small horns and what might almost have been an ingratiating smile on its lips.

"Good evening," it lowed and sat back heavily on its haunches, "I am the main Dish of the Day. May I interest you in parts of my body?" It harrumphed and gurgled a bit, wriggled its hind quarters into a more comfortable position and gazed peacefully at them.

Its gaze was met by looks of startled bewilderment from Arthur and Trillian, a resigned shrug from Ford Prefect and naked hunger from Zaphod Beeblebrox.

"Something off the shoulder perhaps?" suggested the animal, "Braised in a white wine sauce?"

"Er, your shoulder?" said Arthur in a horrified whisper.

"But naturally my shoulder, sir," mooed the animal contentedly, "nobody else's is mine to offer."

Zaphod leapt to his feet and started prodding and feeling the animal's shoulder appreciatively.

"Or the rump is very good," murmured the animal. "I've been exercising it and eating plenty of grain, so there's a lot of good meat there." It gave a mellow grunt, gurgled again and started to chew the cud. It swallowed the cud again.

"Or a casserole of me perhaps?" it added.

"You mean this animal actually wants us to eat it?" whispered Trillian to Ford.

"Me?" said Ford, with a glazed look in his eyes, "I don't mean anything."

"That's absolutely horrible," exclaimed Arthur, "the most revolting thing I've ever heard."

"What's the problem Earthman?" said Zaphod, now transferring his attention to the animal's enormous rump.

"I just don't want to eat an animal that's standing here inviting me to," said Arthur, "it's heartless."

"Better than eating an animal that doesn't want to be eaten," said Zaphod.

"That's not the point," Arthur protested. Then he thought about it for a moment. "Alright," he said, "maybe it is the point. I don't care, I'm not going to think about it now. I'll just ... er ..."

The Universe raged about him in its death throes.

"I think I'll just have a green salad," he muttered.

"May I urge you to consider my liver?" asked the animal, "it must be very rich and tender by now, I've been force-feeding myself for months."

"A green salad," said Arthur emphatically. "A green salad?" said the animal, rolling his eyes disapprovingly at Arthur.

"Are you going to tell me," said Arthur, "that I shouldn't have green salad?"

"Well," said the animal, "I know many vegetables that are very clear on that point. Which is why it was eventually decided to cut through the whole tangled problem and breed an animal that actually wanted to be eaten and was capable of saying so clearly and distinctly. And here I am."

It managed a very slight bow.

"Glass of water please," said Arthur.

"Look," said Zaphod, "we want to eat, we don't want to make a meal of the issues. Four rare steaks please, and hurry. We haven't eaten in five hundred and seventy-six thousand million years."

The animal staggered to its feet. It gave a mellow gurgle.

"A very wise choice, sir, if I may say so. Very good," it said, "I'll just nip off and shoot myself."

He turned and gave a friendly wink to Arthur.

"Don't worry, sir," he said, "I'll be very humane."

Rights: human and animal

1 Summarise the views of Arthur and Zaphod regarding eating the animal.

2 What aspects of this fictitious story reflect some attitudes to animals today?

3 From a position in support of animal rights, use this extract to argue against current practices in agriculture and the food manufacturing process.

CHAPTER SUMMARY

Human rights:

- The Magna Carta (1215), The Petition of Right (1628) and the English Bill of Rights (1689).

- In the seventeenth century, the English philosopher John Locke argued for human rights.

- 'We hold these truths to be self-evident, that all men are created equal, that they are endowed by their Creator with certain unalienable Rights, that among these are Life, Liberty and the Pursuit of Happiness.' (Declaration of Independence)

- The Universal Declaration of Human Rights instituted a set of principles to uphold certain rights for all human beings.

- Rights may be claims that generate duties, powers, liberties or freedoms, and provide immunities or protections from certain actions.

What is the ethical basis of rights?

- Divine laws have expressed beliefs about the treatment of human beings.

- Kant saw human beings as ends in themselves – they can't be used for any other purpose.

- Rights express a deontological or absolute ethical point of view.

Where do rights come from?

- Rights are seen as coming from God, nature or from duties or responsibilities that we have towards others.

- To see rights as individualistic doesn't explain where they come from or who confers them – they are community-based.

- Mary Warnock doubts that there can be an ethical system based on rights, because you need an ethical system to establish the rights.
- Rights ethics are linked either to the law or to God, or to some other ethical system of actually determining and justifying those rights.

Racism, discrimination and preference:
- Human rights are closely related to the civil rights movement.
- The extent to which equality exists varies in practice.
- Ethical discussions have arisen over the appropriateness of positive discrimination.
- Arguably, the future consequence of treating minority groups preferentially is a more harmonious society in which the damage done by racism and other forms of discrimination has finally been addressed.
- Another argument sees this preferential treatment as compensation for the past wrongs done to members of those groups.
- Preferential treatment may in practice cause resentment towards minorities from the majority population groups.
- Members of minority groups who have suffered past injustices have done so to different degrees.

Animal rights:
- Animals were considered to be a resource for us to use and enjoy as we pleased.
- Concerns exist regarding how we use them for work, sport, as food and in experimentation.

We have no moral obligation to animals:
- Some argue that animals are not members of the moral community, because they can't conceive of morality, and so we have no moral obligation towards them.
- Rights can only exist between people who can make moral claims on each other, which requires an inner consciousness of free will, the grasp by reason of moral law, and membership of a moral community.
- Human babies and toddlers don't display moral capability yet we give them moral status and special protection.

Animals deserve the same respect as humans:
- Tom Regan argues for the total abolition of the use of animals in

science, the total dissolution of commercial animal agriculture and the total elimination of commercial and sport hunting and trapping.

- The systematic use of animals is wrong – living beings who have inherent value have it equally.
- A difficulty with Regan's position is that it gives us no guidelines for action where values conflict between animals and humans.
- Peter Singer argues that by treating animals differently, we're guilty of being speciesist.
- Singer's approach is a mainstay of the animal liberation movement, but has radical implications for how humans live.

Roger Scruton:

- Scruton rejects Singer's emphasis on animal suffering, arguing that animals don't have the same moral status because they can't be expected to have the moral obligations and duties that humans have.
- To grant equal status to animals is impractical and immoral, as it places an unreasonable burden of duty and responsibility on animals.
- Scruton argues that our treatment of animals is immoral if it makes us less virtuous.
- 'I have long supported whoever it was who said that the real objection to fox-hunting is the pleasure that the hunters get out of it … If killing foxes is necessary for safety and survival of other species, I – and several million others – will vote for it to continue. But the slaughter ought not be fun.' (Roy Hattersley)
- Although animals have no rights we have duties towards them depending on our relationship with them (pets and livestock).
- 'We have a duty to provide a fulfilled life, an easy death and the training required by their participation in the human world.' (Scruton)
- We have a moral obligation to maintain the balance of nature.

Chapter 24

Human cloning

Introduction

Key terms

Cloning, embryo, ethical gradualism, genetic engineering, genetics, infertile, stem cell, therapeutic cloning

What you will learn by the end of this chapter

- Why human cloning is an ethical issue.
- The main religious and ethical debates related to human cloning.
- The strengths and weaknesses of those debates.

Key questions

1. Is genetic engineering 'playing at God' or is it an exercise in morally valid scientific freedom?
2. Should cloning technology be used to determine features of our children?
3. Should the technology be used to help infertile couples to reproduce?
4. Would you be happy to have a clone made using your genes?
5. Would you be happy knowing that you were the clone of your parent?

Genetics in ethical debates

There are a number of ethical debates concerning the use of genetic engineering today. The following extract from *The Economist* highlights many of these debates.

Read the following extract:

> Step forward to a dinner party in 2025. Your hostess warns you that the tomatoes are the new cholesterol reducing ones. Your host grumbles as he eats only organic food. Your gay neighbour tells you how his clone (should you think of it as his son or brother?) is doing at school. Somebody mentions the amount the Smiths have paid to make sure their next daughter has blue eyes. Wouldn't it have been better spent on making her musical? Somebody jokes about the couple who could have had a Margaret Thatcher clone but instead chose a Bill Clinton. On the drive back, the headlines are about attempts to raise the retirement age to 95.
>
> 'Perfect?', *The Economist*, 14 April 2000, page 15

Identify the different moral issues raised by this extract:

1 Is genetic engineering 'playing at God' or is it exercising morally valid scientific freedom?

2 Should cloning technology be used to determine features of our children?

3 Should the technology be used to help infertile couples reproduce?

4 Would you be happy to have a clone made using your genes?

5 Would you be happy knowing that you were the clone of a parent?

The above task touches on some of the possible applications of the developing techniques in genetic engineering. This chapter is exclusively concerned only with one of these new applications – human cloning.

What is cloning and why is cloning technology useful?

On 24 February 1997, Ian Wilmot and his fellow scientists at the Roslin Institute near Edinburgh announced to the world that they had cloned a lamb named Dolly. Pictures of Dolly were on the front page of every newspaper in the world. At the time, there was a media frenzy, which quickly turned into a panic. Governments took action to prevent the technology being used to clone human beings, but in March 2001 an Italian doctor claimed that he was only months away from starting to clone babies for infertile couples. There are a number of strong medical arguments in favour of the use of cloning technologies, as well as ethical and religious arguments against.

Understanding these arguments requires a basic knowledge of the scientific processes involved in cloning.

Cloning is the creation of an embryo using the genetic material from another being. Cloning technology uses embryos because embryos are a rich source of a special type of cell called a stem cell. Stem cells can replicate themselves and generate more specialised cell types as they multiply. Stem cells from an embryo are much more versatile than those from an adult. The procedure works by taking a fertilised ovum (an embryo) with its stem cells, removing the genetic contents of that ovum and replacing them with the genes from another animal. You could take an ovum that has been fertilised by male A and female B. You would then replace the newly created genetic material (combining elements from male A and female B) in that ovum with genetic material from male C. The resulting life would be a genetic copy of male C.

One possible use of this technology would be for infertile couples who could not conceive. They could use donor eggs and sperm in order to obtain the necessary embryonic stem cells and then replace the genetic material with (for example) the woman's genetic imprint. The resulting child would be a genetic copy of the mother. Note that, normally, new life has a unique genetic imprint and is made up of elements from both parents. This isn't the case in this example. Currently such a practice is prohibited in the UK and some other countries, although if the demand is strong enough it seems likely that it will happen somewhere in the world.

There are a number of other possible medical applications using therapeutic cloning. At a recent conference (see BBC News Online, 2001), Professor Wilmot argued that 'There are tens of thousands of people with different degenerative diseases and it would be a great shame it we failed to develop treatments for them because of irresponsible people somewhere else.'

The human body's specialised cells can't be replaced by natural processes. Medical conditions that seriously damage them, or leave them diseased – such as Alzheimer's disease and Parkinson's disease – are particularly difficult to treat. There's an acute shortage of donated healthy organs, and cloning technology could be used to grow the required cell tissue using embryonic stem cells. Once the cells had been grown, they could be injected back into the patient:

> In the long term there could be considerable potential for the use of tissues derived from stem cells in the treatment of a wide range of disorders by replacing cells that have become damaged or diseased. Examples might include the use of insulin-secreting cells for diabetes; nerve cells in stroke or Parkinson's disease; or liver cells to repair a damaged organ ... In addition to this potential to develop tissue for use in the repair of failing organs, or for the replacement of diseased or damaged tissues, the technique of cell nuclear replacement might be applied to treat some rare but serious inherited disorders. Repairing a woman's eggs (oocytes) by this technique gives rise to the possibility of helping a woman with mitochondrial damage to give birth to a healthy child which inherits her genes together with those of her partner.
>
> Department of Health (2000a), pages 6–7

These possible benefits have been used by scientists to encourage the British government to permit research using embryo stem cells. The go-ahead has been given for research using human embryos under the control of the Human Fertilisation and Embryology Authority, with a particular focus on increasing understanding and developing treatments for mitochondrial diseases involving stem cells derived from embryonic sources. However, the government will prohibit the mixing of human adult (somatic) cells with the live eggs of any animal species, and the transfer of an embryo created by cell nuclear replacement into the uterus of a woman (so-called 'reproductive cloning') should remain a criminal offence (Department of Health, 2000b). Since these conclusions were drawn, Westminster MPs have voted to the relax existing rules so that stem cells can be taken from embryos at a very early stage of development and used for therapeutic cloning.

Tasks

1 Why do embryos have to be used for this research?
2 Summarise the possible benefits of cloning technology.

The ethical debate

There are a number of moral dimensions concerning the act of originating a child through cloning. Cloning is opposed on the basis that the act of cloning is intrinsically wrong, a deontological approach, and also because the consequences are harmful. These arguments appeal to God's will or to the unnaturalness of the act. They maintain that from conception onwards the embryo has full human status, thus allowing no research or use that isn't to the benefit of the embryo. Any technology that involves the creation of dispensable embryos is rejected. This represents the traditional Christian view, which leads Christians to reject abortion, *in vitro* fertilisation and embryo research and experimentation. God creates life, and it isn't for humans to destroy even its embryonic form. The former Roman Catholic leader of Scotland, Cardinal Winning, recently said that even though the 'end is good', the 'means are immoral', as they result in the death of 'tiny cloned human beings' (BBC News Online, 2000a). Dr Michael Jarmulowicz, Honorary Secretary of the Guild of Catholic Doctors, notes that it has always been accepted in British law that the earliest human embryo should be treated with respect and accorded a special status (see Guild of Catholic Doctors, 1999). He argues that to use the human embryo for basic science research that hasn't yet been undertaken in animals would end the special status that embryos deserve. He also maintains that therapeutic cloning could become possible from adult cells in the future, which would save the lives of the embryos used in the research and, finally, that to allow therapeutic cloning would invariably lead on to human cloning.

Cloning is also rejected because of the harmful impact that it might have on human society, the family or the child. These consequentialist objections identify harm that might be done to the individual being cloned and to society as a whole. Leon Kass opposes cloning in his article 'The wisdom of repugnance' (1998). He sees the common repugnance that people express towards cloning as a revolt against the excess of human wilfulness and a warning not to do something that is profoundly unspeakable. It's a sign that human nature no longer commands respect. In his article, Kass goes on to make three points.

Human cloning will harm the created child by threatening a confusion of identity and individuality, because 'She is the work not of nature or nature's God but of man, an Englishman' (pp. 13–14). Because the cloned person will be in genotype and appearance identical to another human being, possibly a parent, the child will have a crisis of identity (p. 27).

Human cloning represents a step towards turning reproduction into manufacturing: '… if sex has no intrinsic connection to generating babies, babies need have no necessary connection to sex …' (p. 16). In natural sexual reproduction, each child has two complementary biological progenitors. Cloning turns begetting into making. Procreation becomes manufacture, which makes man another part of man-made things. In natural procreation, human beings come together, complementarily male and female, to give existence to another being who is formed. A cloned human being is a product of intention and design (pp. 29–30).

Finally, Kass argues that cloning represents a form of despotism of the cloners over the cloned, and represents a blatant violation of the inner meaning of parent–child relationships. A child stems from and unites two lineages. The exact genetic constitution is decided by nature and chance, not human design. He believes that these biological truths express truths about our identity and our human condition. Reproduction that doesn't involve sex isn't natural and rejects common family relations (pp. 30–31).

Donald Bruce (2000), director of the Church of Scotland's Society, Religion and Technology project, rejects not only human cloning but also the use of cloned embryos for therapeutic cloning: 'It is my view the creation and use of cloned embryos for procedures such as these should not be allowed … I believe we should stop in our tracks, and not continue to use embryos routinely for cell therapy.' He argues that it isn't consistent to allow for an embryo to be created but then prevent it from coming to full term. It's wrong to create an embryo as a resource for others. It should be afforded dignity in itself. Bruce also voices concern about 'ethical gradualism' – allowing far reaching ethical processes by a series of small steps, the first of which is therapeutic cloning.

Some supporters of cloning argue principally for the use of embryos for medical research, on the basis that the results will bring such benefit as to merit the medical process that the embryos have to go through. They maintain that the early embryo is no more than a ball of cells. As it is undeveloped and wouldn't survive outside the womb, research is permissible. The beneficial consequences wholly justify the action. At a recent conference (see BBC News Online, 2001), Professor Wilmot made clear his view supporting therapeutic cloning but opposing reproductive cloning: 'Although I'm a very strong advocate of cloning as a possible means of therapy, I am still a strong critic of people who say they want to clone humans … It would be a great shame if irresponsible attempts to produce people would provoke a backlash against research with human embryos …'. He believes that the overall benefits of cloning, the possible treatments that could be made available to suffers of conditions such as Alzheimer's disease and Parkinson's disease, far outweigh any objections to the use of embryos in experimentation and research. Some Christians have adopted this middle view, which rejects human cloning but allows therapeutic cloning on the basis of the good consequences that it produces. In 1996, the Church of Scotland affirmed the special status of the embryo as created by God, but also recognised the potential benefits of embryo research under limited circumstances.

Ethical issues

There are also those who argue that full reproductive human cloning is morally acceptable. In 'Will cloning harm people?' (1998, pp. 115–128), Gregory E. Pence argues human cloning wouldn't be harmful as embryos can't be harmed. While human embryos are lost in the cloning process, this doesn't harm any person. Pence points out that 40% of human embryos fail to implant in normal sexual reproduction. Thousands of embryos can be stored and many couples decline to pay fees for preserving embryos. He's implying that we're using double standards if we allow one but prevent the other. In his view, embryos are not sentient and can't experience pain. They are not persons and so there's no objection to their use in cloning. Pence believes that the objection to human cloning is an irrational fear.

In 'Dolly's fashion and Lois's passion' (1998), Stephen Jay Gould, the Harvard palaeontologist, argues that there are no new ethical questions raised by human cloning. He suggests that identical twins share more properties than Dolly did with her mother. Conjoined twins differ in personalities and achievements, and so human cloning raises no new ethical questions: 'We know that identical twins are distinct individuals, albeit with peculiar and extensive similarities. We give them different names. They encounter divergent experiences and fates. Their lives wander along disparate paths of the world's complex vagaries. They grow up as distinctive and undoubted individuals, yet they stand forth as far better clones than Dolly and her mother.' (pp. 106–107) A cloned human being would live in a different time and culture from the source of the gene code. Identical twins are more alike than Dolly and her mother.

In 'Wrongful life, federalism, and procreative liberty' (1998), the law professor John Robertson argues that the use of cloning for reproduction is entirely acceptable: 'If a couple is willing to take the risk that embryos won't form or cleave, that they won't implant, that there will be a high rate of miscarriage, that the child will be born with some defect, and that they will then rear the child, it is hard to see why this is any worse than the other practices that could lead to physically-damaged offspring.' (p. 8) He sees reproductive cloning as another reproductive technology alongside IVF. For some people, it is their only opportunity to have children.

If the cloning debate is addressed in terms of its consequences, one must balance the resulting good against the resulting bad. Childless couples seeking children would have the potential to have children. Those suffering from a number of terrible degenerative diseases might have the chance of a cure. But these goods must be weighed against the potential bad. The cloned individual might be psychologically or emotionally damaged. There may be erosion in society's attitude to life and reproduction. The technology could be used by those with dubious motives.

A deontological approach looks to the rightness or wrongness of the action in itself. If the embryo has full human status from conception, then embryo research and human cloning is immoral, because a number of embryos would die. To create life in an asexual way is unnatural: it attacks the dignity of sexuality and therefore human dignity. The nature of the ethical debate will depend upon whether the proponents take deontological or teleological approaches. It will be subject to the proponents' fears about what will happen if either therapeutic or reproductive cloning comes about. It would appear that we're soon going to find out what the consequences are. Therapeutic cloning is already taking place in the USA, and it may only be a short time before reproductive human cloning is a reality.

Tasks

1 What links the Roman Catholic Church's criticism of human cloning with that of IVF, abortion and embryo research?

2 What other specifically religious reasons are there opposing human cloning?

3 How might human cloning change our understanding of sex and, in your view, would this be a positive or negative development?

4 What possible harms might human cloning cause to the individual?

5 What possible harms might human cloning cause to society?

6 How might it be argued that a clone raises no more ethical questions than an identical twin?

7 Outline the argument for a person's right to clone.

Extracts from key texts

Leon Kass, 'The wisdom of repugnance', 1998

From page 20

> People are repelled by many aspects of human cloning. They recoil from the prospect of mass production of human beings, with large clones of look-alikes, compromised in their individuality; the idea of father–son or mother–daughter twins; the bizarre prospects of a women giving birth to and rearing a genetic copy of herself, her spouse or even her deceased father or mother, the grotesqueness of conceiving a child as an exact replacement for

another who has died; the utilitarian creation of embryonic genetic duplicates of oneself, to be frozen away or created when necessary, in case of need of homologous tissues or organs for transplantation; the narcissism of those who would clone themselves and the arrogance of others who think they know who deserves to be cloned or which genotype any child-to-be should be thrilled to receive; the Frankensteinian hubris to create human life and increasingly to control its destiny; man playing God. Almost no one finds any of the suggested reasons for human cloning compelling: almost everyone anticipates its possible misuses and abuses. Moreover, many people feel oppressed by the sense that there is probably nothing we can do to prevent it from happening. This makes the prospect all the more revolting.

CHAPTER SUMMARY

- On 24 February 1997, Ian Wilmot and his fellow scientists at the Roslin Institute near Edinburgh announced to the world that they had cloned a lamb named Dolly.
- Cloning is the creation of an embryo using the genetic material from another being.

Uses:

- One possible use of this technology would be for infertile couples who could not conceive.
- There are a number of other possible medical applications using therapeutic cloning.
- New treatments could be developed for medical conditions that seriously damage or leave the human body's specialised cells parts diseased – such as Alzheimer's disease and Parkinson's disease.
- There's an acute shortage of donated healthy organs, and cloning technology could be used to grow the required cell tissue using embryonic stem cells.
- The British government supports extending embryo research activity to develop treatments.

The ethical debate:

- Those who argue that from conception the embryo has full human status reject cloning as an embryo is destroyed in the process.

- Leon Kass argues that human cloning will harm the created child by threatening a confusion of identity and individuality, because it represents a step towards turning reproduction into manufacturing, and also a form of despotism of the cloners over the cloned, and a blatant violation of the inner meaning of parent–child relationships.

- Donald Bruce rejects not only human cloning but also the use of cloned embryos for therapeutic cloning.

- Some supporters of cloning argue principally for the use of embryos for medical research, on the basis that the end justifies the means.

- Gregory E. Pence argues that human cloning wouldn't be harmful because embryos can't be harmed.

- Stephen Jay Gould argues that there are no new ethical questions raised by human cloning, as identical twins share more properties than Dolly did with her mother.

- Amongst the consequential factors, childless couples seeking children would have the potential to have children, and those suffering from a number of terrible degenerative diseases might have a chance of a cure. Weighing against this is the chance of a psychologically or emotionally damaged cloned individual, or the erosion of society's attitude to life and reproduction.

- Therapeutic cloning is already taking place in the USA and an Italian doctor has claimed that he will be able to offer reproductive cloning to childless couples soon.

Glossary

a posteriori A statement is *a posteriori* if it's knowable after experience. See **Kantian ethics** and **emotivism**.

a priori A statement is *a priori* if it's knowable without any reference to any experience we may have had. The statement 'all bachelors are men', is *a priori* because we don't need to establish that they are all men by proving it because of the nature of the word 'bachelor'. See **Kantian ethics** and **emotivism**.

abortion In ethics, the term is usually used to mean the termination of a pregnancy by artificially induced means. Ethical debates in abortion centre on whether an unborn human is a full or potential person and therefore receives full or partial **rights**, the extent of the mother's rights, the father's rights, whether women depend on access to abortion for full fertility control and therefore full emancipation into human society, and the extent of autonomy in this area. Religious beliefs about life and the human being play a major part in the debate, as do scientific factors such as the levels of pain felt by a **foetus** being aborted.

absolutism/ethical absolutism An objective moral rule or value that is always true in all situations and for all people – expressed by the ancient Stoics as 'Let justice be done though the heavens fall.'

act utilitarianism A teleological or consequentialist theory that uses the outcome of the particular action to determining its rightness or goodness. General rules can never force us to act if in a given situation better ends can be reached by doing something different. Jeremy Bentham was an act utilitarian. It contrasts with **rule utilitarianism**. See also **utilitarianism**.

action guiding The idea that ethical principles prescribe behaviour and guide actions, rather than simply describing beliefs; found in **prescriptivism**.

agape love From a Greek word meaning 'love'. Agape love is distinct from erotic love or familial love. In Christian terms, it refers to the unconditional love that they must show their neighbours. For Joseph Fletcher's **situation ethics**, moral decision-making must centre around determining the most agape-loving thing to do in a situation.

agnosticism The belief that nothing is known or can ever be known about the existence or nature of God or anything beyond the material world.

altruism 'Other-centeredness' – acting out of selfless concern for others. Christians are commanded to love their neighbours as themselves. Altruism can be contrasted with selfishness or egoism. See also **ethical egoism**.

amoral To have no moral rules or principles at all.

analytic statement A classic term used by Kant, meaning a statement that is true by definition. A statement is analytically true if the clauses or predicates within the statement say something that is necessarily true of all instances of the subject. For example, all spinsters are women. It isn't possible to be a spinster if one is not a woman. See **Kantian ethics** and **emotivism**.

animal experimentation   A term referring to the experimentation on animals for medical, scientific, cosmetic or nutritional purposes. See also **animal liberation**.

animal liberation   A term describing a state of freedom for animals from human experimentation and use for sport and food. See also **animal experimentation**.

anthropocentric environmental theory   An environmental theory that prioritises human interests over and above any other interests of living things in discussions about the environment.

antinomian ethics   The view that there are no moral principles or rules at all.

arête   The Greek word for 'excellence' or 'virtue'. The virtue of an Olympic swimmer is in swimming well, and the virtue of a national leader lies in motivating people to work for the common good.

argument   A set of statements consisting of premises and a conclusion.

artificial insemination (AI)   The injection of sperm through a catheter into the wife's reproductive tract. It is used to treat the husband's infertility due to physiological disorders.

assisted dying   Where an individual takes his or her own life with the help of another person, such as in the provision of drugs. 'Physician-assisted suicide' infers that this person is a doctor. See also **euthanasia**.

Assisted Reproductive Technologies (ARTs)   Technologies such as artificial insemination and *in vitro* fertilisation that give infertile couples a better chance of having children.

atheism/atheist   The belief that God does not exist/adherents to that belief. Philosophers who were atheists include Karl Marx, Friedrich Nietzsche, Bertrand Russell and Jean-Paul Sartre.

autonomous moral agent   Someone who makes moral decisions freely. Many philosophers, such as Kant, hold that you can only be responsible for actions which you undertake of your own will. Libertarians believe that we have this freedom. It's usually contrasted with 'heteronomy', meaning rule by others. To believe that people are autonomous is to adopt a position opposed to **determinism**. See also **autonomy, libertarianism**.

autonomy   Self rule or government. Etymologically, the term is made up of *autos* meaning 'self' and *nomos* meaning 'rule'. It is generally used with reference to countries that rule themselves, but in ethics refers it to the individual. See **autonomous moral agent**.

belief   A belief is an opinion or supposition. It can mean 'know' (I believe 2 + 2 = 4), or 'think' (I believe you're telling the truth), but is more usually associated with religious doctrines or dogmas and sometimes philosophical and ethical positions.

benevolent   To be helpful, friendly.

bigamy   Marriage to a second wife while a previous marriage is in force. This is a crime in Western countries, but is more common in Middle Eastern cultures.

biocentric environmental theory   An environmental theory that considers the biological nature and diversity of the planet to be of prime importance in ethical discussions about the use of the environment.

bioethics/biomedical ethics   The application of ethics to the biological sciences, medicine, genetics, health care and public policy with regard to these areas. Judaism and Roman Catholicism have strong traditions regarding bioethics, and issues such as **abortion**, **euthanasia**, reproductive technologies, organ transplantation and human **cloning** are all included in this topic. See also **sexual ethics**.

blameworthy   To be morally responsible for a wrong or bad act or outcome.

business ethics   The moral justification of economic systems and practices, the responsibilities of businesses and corporations, and the rights of workers.

capital punishment   The use of the death penalty as a punishment determined by a legally empowered court. Traditionally there was some debate within the Christian tradition as to whether or not capital punishment was justifiable. Debates range from whether the commandment 'Thou shall not kill' in fact only refers to murder to how it can be held alongside the Christian centrality of love and the preservation of life. It's held as an effective deterrent and ultimate retribution where it's practised, but those who oppose the death penalty cite the dangers of potential miscarriages of justice and the importance of reform. See also **just war theory** and **punishment**.

capitalism   The system of the free market economy, in which the means of production is privately owned and market forces guide production and distribute income.

categorical imperative   An unconditional command which, for Kant, told us our duty by pointing to actions which were good in themselves, and in the pursuit of the *summum bonum* (the supreme good). For Kant, this included his **universalisability** maxim, 'Always act in such a way that the maxim of your action can be willed as a universal law.' See also **Kantian ethics**.

celibacy   A state of not entering into sexual relations with another person, usually found among religious ministers, such as Catholic or Orthodox priests.

Christian realism   The belief that Christians may use violent means to bring about the kingdom of God and to secure peace on Earth.

civil disobedience   To disobey or resist the state because of a point of ethical principle. Mahatma Gandhi and Martin Luther King stand out as examples of leaders who practised civil disobedience against the British in India and campaigned for **civil rights** for black people in the USA, respectively. Henry David Thoreau is associated with this term, as is his influential essay 'Civil resistance': 'Must the citizen ever for a moment, or in the least degree, resign his conscience to the legislator? Why has every man a conscience then? I think that we should be men first, and subjects afterward ... The only obligation which I have a right to assume is to do at any time what I think right.' See also **conscience**.

civil rights   Legally enforced and protected **rights** belonging to people by virtue of their citizenship of a state. Examples of civil rights are freedom of expression and of religious belief. Ethical debates have included whether these rights proceed from **human rights** or natural rights. Great civil rights activists include Mahatma Ghandi and Martin Luther King.

cloning A form of **genetic engineering** whereby a human or animal is created with the same genetic identify as another. The technique is currently used in breeding animals and crops. Human cloning is banned in many countries and has not taken place at the time of publication – although it is possible.

communitarianism A collectivist philosophy that considers group rights to be primary over individual rights and explicitly rejects individualism.

compatibilism The belief that it's possible to maintain both **determinism** and **free will**, because while some aspects of our nature are determined, our ability to make moral decisions is not. See also **libertarianism, soft determinism**.

conditional egoism A form of egoism proposed by Adam Smith, which believes that free commercial activity should be allowed if it has a trickle-down beneficial impact on the wider community.

conscience Aquinas called it 'the mind of man making moral judgements'. It's variously understood as meaning the voice of God within us (Butler), our sense of moral right and wrong, or our super-ego enforcing the rules of behaviour implanted within us when we were young (Freud). Ethical issues surrounding conscience include the conflict between state law or religious belief and individual conscience (**civil disobedience**), the justification of conscience as a reason for moral behaviour, and the difficulties in defining and relying on conscience as a guide for moral behaviour. Cardinal Newman said 'I toast the Pope but I toast conscience first.'

conscientious objector Someone who refuses to fight for a state because he or she disapproves of the conflict for religious, political or ethical reasons.

consequentialism Any ethical view that establishes the rightness or wrongness of actions by the good or bad produced by its consequences. See also **situation ethics, teleological, utilitarianism**.

contractarian The view that an activity is morally permissible if there's mutual agreement or consent between the participating parties. The term emphasises freedom and so is libertarian. It is found in **sexual ethics**. See also **libertarianism**.

corporate responsibility The idea that businesses have a responsibility to consider the interests of their customers, their workers and the community in which they exist, as well as investors' or owners' interests.

cultural relativism The form of relativism which maintains that what is good or bad, right or wrong, for a person varies in relation to the culture in which the person lives. These different values are equally valid because there are no moral absolutes (nor discernible moral absolutes). For example, polygamy is permitted in some Islamic societies but is a crime in most Western societies. Neither position is more valid than the other. See also **relativism** and **subjectism**, and their opposites **absolutism** and **objectivism**.

deep ecology A secular-based approach to environmental ethics, which recognises value in all life forms and perhaps even the geological and biological systems and diversity of planet earth, and rejects anthropocentric ethics.

definism See **ethical naturalism/ethical cognitivism**.

democracy Rule by the people either directly (where each citizen votes on policy, and so sovereignty rests with them) or through representation (where citizens elect politicians and give them authority to make policy decisions, thereby giving sovereignty to the elected group).

deontological ethics Actions are intrinsically right or wrong. They are right or wrong in themselves, irrespective of their consequences. The term is traditionally associated with Kantian **duty**, but can also be linked to ethical systems that uphold absolute moral norms and human **rights**. Deontologists hold that one can't undertake immoral acts, such as torture of spies, even if the outcome is morally preferable, such as the early ending of a war. It's contrasted with **teleological/consequentialist** ethical theories. See also **absolutism, Kantian ethics, natural moral law, objectivism**.

descriptive ethics A term for an ethics that doesn't advocate a particular moral outlook (as **prescriptivism** does) and doesn't seek to determine the rightness or wrongness of moral actions (as **normative ethics** do). Descriptive ethics simply identifies and compares different ethical systems that exist in different cultures. In this sense, it's anthropological.

determinism The view that choices are influenced by factors other than the will of the individual. See also **compatabilism, free will, hard determinism, libertarianism, soft determinism**.

deterrence The theory that punishment discourages others from doing the same, by focusing minds on the consequences that will befall them should they choose to follow the same course of action.

distributive justice Theories of justice that focus on resources, income and wealth, or on the distribution of social positions.

divine command theory The ethical theory that maintains that actions are right or wrong depending on whether or not they correspond to God's commands. It is part of the **Euthyphro dilemma**.

double effect A theory used to justify the termination of a **foetus** if the intention is to save the life of the mother and the action has the secondary effect of killing the foetus. An ectopic pregnancy, where the fertilised ovum lodges itself in the fallopian tube, is an example of this. If the pregnancy continues the mother and foetus will die. The double effect theory morally justifies the removal of the fallopian tube, because the intention is to save the mother's life even though the effect of doing so leads to the death of the foetus.

dualism The belief that a human is comprised of a material or physical element (the body) and a spiritual element (the soul).

duty A motive for acting in a certain way which indicates moral quality. It's important in **Kantian ethics**, where doing good means rationally determining and then following duty. For W. D. Ross, the *prima facie* duties are a set of ultimate moral obligations which, if followed, will ensure that we're acting morally. Duty was also important for the **naturalist** F. H. Bradley, who also felt that being good meant doing one's duty.

effacement The radical removal of detrimental qualities of mind necessary for moral behaviour. An idea in Buddhism.

ego The psychological term for the self. It is important for egoism and for the Freudian view of **conscience**.

embryo A term for a human being in the first eight weeks from conception. After eight weeks, the term **foetus** is used.

emotivism A theory in **descriptive ethics** that holds that all moral judgements are simply expressions of positive or negative feelings and that, as such, all moral statements are meaningless as they can't be verified. It was made prominent by **logical positivists** and the **Vienna Circle**; in particular, by A. J. Ayer and C. L. Stevenson.

empiricism Concerning facts that are verifiable by testable sense experience. In ethics, **naturalism** maintains that moral truths can be scientifically proven, while **intuitionism** and **emotivism** reject the principle.

Enlightenment, the The intellectual movement in modern Europe from the sixteenth until the eighteenth centuries, that maintained that human reason could understand the world and guide all human conduct.

entitlement, justice as Nozick's theory: I am entitled to my possessions, my earnings and my acquisitions as long as I remain within the law. The same is true for you as well.

Epicureanism The ancient Greek movement that held that the good life is gained by the sensible and moderate pursuit of pleasure.

ethical absolutes See **absolutism**.

ethical egoism 'Self-centeredness' – a moral theory that commonly states that each person ought to act in his or her own self-interest.

ethical gradualism Also known as the **slippery slope** theory, this refers to the view that an ethical wrong is achieved by permitting lesser wrongs in succession.

ethical investment The idea that investment should be made only in businesses that behave in an ethical manner, and that investors have a responsibility to ensure that they do not invest in organisations that are unethical.

ethical naturalism/ethical cognitivism (definism) The ethical theory that moral values can be derived from empirical sense experience. **Naturalists** believe that statements of fact ('is') can imply statements of moral obligation ('ought'). The contrary ethical position is **ethical non-naturalism/ethical non-cognitivism**. See also **empiricism, naturalistic fallacy**.

ethical non-naturalism/ethical non-cognitivism The ethical view that ethical statements cannot be derived from empirical sense experience. **Intuitionism** and **emotivism** are examples of this view. See also **empiricism, ethical naturalism/ethical cognitivism, naturalistic fallacy**.

ethics Ethics (sometimes known as **moral philosophy**) includes the following sorts of questions: How should we live? What's right and what's wrong? What do we mean by the word 'right' and the word 'good'? How can we measure goodness and badness? Are some things always wrong or does it depend on the point of view or situation? Ethical theory examines the different philosophies or systems used to explain and make judgements about 'right', 'wrong', 'good' and 'bad'. **Practical, or applied, ethics** is more focused on subjects that invite ethical questioning, such as **abortion** and **euthanasia**. The term 'ethics'comes from the Greek word *ethikos*, from the root *ethos*, meaning 'character'. Ethical theory is subdivided into three: **normative ethics**, which asks whether actions are right or wrong; comparaitve or **descriptive ethics**, which simply describes and compares differing ethical practices; and **meta-ethics**, the study of the meaning of ethical language, the definitions of words such as 'good', 'right', and so on.

euthanasia   Literally meaning 'a good death', the term is used to descibe the doctor-assisted death for a patient with a painful terminal condition, the switching off of life support machines for those in comas, and the killing of the elderly or disabled. Ethical debates range over the right ever to take life, the right to choose the manner and time of death with dignity, and the safe application of legalised euthanasia.

Euthyphro dilemma   Does God command moral behaviour because it's good, or are the morals good because God commands them? The dilemma was first identified by Plato in *Euthyphro*.

extrinsically good action/extrinsic good   Something that is good not within itself but because of the goodness of the effects or consequences that it has; the opposite of **intrinsically good**.

feminism   The theory that advances the emancipation of women in society, advocates equal preference and opportunities for women, and in some forms positive discrimination to redress the historical preference towards men. Feminist theories hold strong views on women's access to **abortion** and equality in **sexual ethics**.

freedom/free will   See **autonomy**.

foetus   A term for a human being after eight weeks have passed since conception. For the first eights weeks the term **embryo** is used.

genetic engineering   A term that describes the technology and practice of **cloning**, gene therapy and genetic manipulation

geocentric environmental theory   An environmental theory that considers the geological nature and diversity of the planet to be of prime importance in ethical discussions about the use of the environment.

Golden rule theory   The maxim that we should act morally as we would expect to be treated. It's found in various ancient and modern sources, most notably the Christian 'Do unto others as you would have them do unto you.' Thomas Hobbes held that we only act morally because we don't want to be acted against in a immoral way. Moral behaviour has selfish roots.

good and bad   Ethics that question definitions of the 'good' are known as **meta-ethics**. Plato held that the good was an **absolute** that existed in a truer form than the things we perceive around us. **Relativists** hold that goodness is determined by the traditional value system of a given culture. Trying to define and determine what the good is the preoccupation of the student of ethics. 'Bad' is the opposite of 'good', meaning a thing that is immoral, and is used by theories within **normative ethics** to refer to an action or outcome that should not be sought.

gradualism   Also known as the **slippery slope argument**, in ethics this is used to describe the dangers of theories that allow for moral laws to be broken in certain circumstances. The dangers are stated as being that once lesser moral laws are broken, greater ones are then broken, and ultimately all moral **absolutes** are abandoned. **Situation ethics** is identified as a theory that could over-step certain ethical boundaries. In applied ethics, some argue that to legalise **euthanasia** would eventually lead to the justification of all sorts of of dubious moral practices, including infanticide.

hard determinism   The belief that people don't have free will to act in moral situations, that all moral actions have uncontrollable prior causes. Determinism has the difficulty that if people aren't free to act morally then it seems unreasonable to hold them responsible for their actions.

harm principle   The belief that an act or consequence is morally permissible if no harm is done.

hedonic calculus   Bentham's utilitarian computation by which the good and bad effects of an action can be measured.

hedonism   The belief that pleasure is the chief 'good'.

heroic society   A time reflected by ancient Greek literature which emphasises the importance of virtues such as courage, honour and strength.

Hippocratic oath   The oath taken by physicians.

holistic environmental theory   An environmental theory that considers the interests of a broad range of factors, including balance within the ecosystem.

holy war   A war fought out the belief that it's approved of or commanded by God, such as the crusades.

human rights   See **rights**.

humanism   An attitude of mind that gives central importance to human beings and human values, rather than to any religious ideas.

'hurrah/boo' theory   Another term for **emotivism**.

hypothetical imperative   A conditional, 'if', command, such as 'If you want to lose weight, go on a diet.' Some philosophers have claimed that morality is only a system of hypothetical imperatives, while others, such as Kant, maintained that morality is a matter of **categorical imperatives**.

immoral   An immoral act is one that is considered bad or wrong.

intention   In ethics, questions can be asked about whether intentions make a difference to the moral value of the action. If they do, then it could be argued that to give to charity to show off in order to gain praise is a right but bad action. For **consequentialist** theories of ethics, intention is important, as intention is what you hope to achieve by the action – arguably, all moral actions have an element of this. For Kant, intention can make all the difference, as acting out of feelings is wrong, while acting using reason to perceive **duty** is right.

intrinsically good   Good in itself, without reference to consequences; the opposite of **extrinsically good**.

intuitionism/ethical non-naturalism   A meta-ethical theory that states that moral truths are known by intuition, a special kind of perception.

***in vitro* fertilisation (IVF)** The procedure of retrieving eggs and sperm from a couple and placing them together in a laboratory dish to help fertilisation.

jus ad bellum Justice in the decision to wage war.

jus in bello Justice in the conduct of war.

just war theory The belief, expounded by the Roman Catholic Church and some Protestant Churches, that a war is justified and morally acceptable if it meets certain criteria.

justice, theory of The principles underpinning law and their relationship to those laws. Ethical debates in this area surround the definition of justice and how to make justice operate effectively in the community. There are two main theories. Individualistic theories maintain that communities are made up of individuals and therefore justice should preserve the **rights** of individuals. Individualism is characterised by Margaret Thatcher's claim that 'There is no such thing as society' and Thomas Hobbes' theory that individuals make rules to live by for selfish reasons – that it's in their best interests. Communitarian theories hold that society is more than the sum of its parts and has some organic dimension. Plato recognised the importance of community in his city–state. Karl Marx, Alasdair MacIntyre and John Rawls developed communitarian theories of justice.

Kantian ethics The ethical theory defined by Kant, consisting of the primacy of **duty**, good will and the **categorical imperative**.

kingdom of ends This term was used by Kant to describe a world in which people acted not in a way that treated others as means but, rather, only as ends. he argued that we ought to act as if all people did this in our dealings.

law A moral or legal code of conduct. It can be used to refer to legislation of the state (in the UK, Acts of Parliament), Church rules (Canon Law in the Roman Catholic Church), moral guidelines either written in nature or in the hearts of all people (Aquinas) or simply developed individually as part of a personal value system. Ethical debates that mention law may be in discussions of whether natural or absolute laws exist outside human-created ideas, whether they should be applied universally or according to legal custom, and the reconciliation between laws of the state and moral laws. See also **absolutism, conscience, natural moral law, relativism**.

legalistic ethics An ethical system that contains rules for every situation and/or the association of doing good with simply following those rules.

libertarianism The view that humans are free to make moral choices and are therefore responsible for their actions; an opposite stance to **determinism**.

logic The study of argument and reasoning – of whether certain conclusions follow from their premises and, if so, why.

logical positivism The view that the only real things are those that are either empirically provable (we can test them) or logically necessary ($1 + 1 = 2$). All religious, superstitious and supernatural statements are meaningless. This philosophy was propagated by a group called the **Vienna Circle** and later came to be associated with A. J. Ayer and **emotivism**.

love A key concept in Christian ethics, where people must love their neighbours as they do themselves. It's also important for **situation ethics**, wherein it forms the central rule by which the value of moral behaviour is assessed – what is the most loving thing to do. The kind of love here is **agape love**, meaning unconditional love, which is not dependent on any return and is very different from the love of family and erotic love.

maximin rule of game theory Rawls' view that the best outcome is the outcome where the least well off person has the least bad result. An aspect of his theory of **justice**.

means Another term for actions. In ethics, 'means' are often contrasted with 'ends', so that some ethical theories focus on the intrinsic goodness of an action while others look at the consequences of actions.

meta-ethics The study of the meaning of ethical statements and terms such as 'good', 'bad', 'right' and 'wrong'.

moral agent A phrase used to describe a being who can make moral decisions or judgements, or who can be judged on moral grounds.

moral autonomy See **autonomy**.

moral philosophy See **ethics**.

moral responsibility See **blameworthy**.

morality Morality comes from the Latin word *moralis* – concerned with which actions are right and which are wrong, rather than the character of the person. Today, morality and **ethics** are often used interchangeably.

motive See **intention**.

natural law/natural moral law Ethical theories that hold that there's a good natural order to the human world which ought to be adhered to. The natural order is determined either by a deity or some other supernatural power. The origins of natural law in the West go back as far as the ancient Greeks (Sophocles, Antigone) but were famously developed by St Thomas Aquinas, who deduced that the fundamental natural law was to protect oneself and protect the innocent, and that from these can be derived the rules, to live, to procreate, to create a civil society and to worship God. The Roman Catholic Church is a prominent exponent of natural moral law today and this is manifested in its teaching against the use of artificial contraception.

naturalism See **ethical naturalism**.

naturalistic fallacy G. E. Moore's claim that good can't be defined as it's simple and indefinable. Moore famously compared it to yellow which, if defined was no longer yellow.

nihilism The belief that there's no value or truth – a belief in nothing (*nihil*).

non-cognitivism The belief that moral judgements or exclamations don't have truth value and therefore can't be known. An example of this is **emotivism**.

normative ethics   See **ethics**.

objective moral norm   A phrase meaning the same as 'ethical absolute'. See **absolutism**.

objectivism   Truth is objectively real irrespective of one's individual or cultural viewpoint or value system. Things that are right and wrong are absolutely right and wrong.

original position   A hypothetical state or community of rational, equal and self-interested individuals who are to establish guidelines for living to cover all rights and duties. In this state, people exist under a veil of ignorance whereby they do not know what position they are going to hold in their future lives, and so will be inclined to construct a system that protects the most dispossessed.

'ought' implies 'can'   The argument that an act must be possible before it can be required.

pacifism   The belief that acts of violence are wrong. Some forms allow self-defence, but the stronger varieties don't believe that any violent action is morally acceptable.

personhood   A term used in debates about the extent to which embryos are considered to be human beings with rights, such as abortion, embryo research and IVF. Views on what defines a human being as a person vary from consciousness, to sentiency, to self-awareness to self-sufficiency.

personalism   The ethic that demands that human beings are not treated as 'means' (Kant) but are subjects. Personalism argues that human are interrelational social beings, part of the physical and spiritual world. Personalism affirms self-conscious experience. Ultimately, it puts the person in the centre of any moral or ethical dilemma.

positivism   The situational principle that Christians freely choose faith that God is love, so giving first place to Christian love.

practical, or applied, ethics   The study of ethical issues such as **abortion** or **justice**, as opposed to purely ethical theories such as **natural moral law** and **utilitarianism**.

pragmatism   The principle that moral commands must have a chance of a successful end.

predestination   The belief that God has decided who will enter heaven and who will not.

prescriptivism   An ethical theory that contends that moral statements are not simply describing an opinion but have an intrinsic sense such that others ought to agree and follow that moral view. This contrasts with **descriptive ethics** and to some extent **emotivism**.

prima facie   In Latin, 'at first glance'. In ethics, the term is associated with W. D. Ross and his *'prima facie* duties' – a duty that must be followed unless a stronger duty exists, which may override it.

principle of utility   The utilitarian maxim that seeks the greatest good for the greatest number.

profit motive The idea that the principal motivation behind business is to make profits, on the basis that only in that way is the business viable, and that only through such profits will the customers, workers, owners and investors gain any produce.

proportionality/proportionalism The concept of proportionality is found in St Thomas Aquinas' consideration of **just war theory**. He argued that warring activity should be proportionate to the aggression made and not excessive to that aggression. It's present in modern formulations of just war theory, and questions actions such as the atomic bombing of Hiroshima and Nagasaki during the Second World War. It's also found in the Roman Catholic teaching on **euthanasia**, which holds that while euthanasia is wrong, the excessive or overburdensome treatment of terminally ill patients may also be wrong, especially if the pain caused is disproportionate to the result of the procedure. Proportionalism is a relatively new ethical theory that tries to bridge the gap between the traditional Christian **natural moral law** ethic and the modern relativist Christian ethic, **situationism**. It maintains that there there are basic moral laws which are only broken in extreme circumstances.

psychological egoism The doctrine that all human motivation is ultimately selfish or egoistic.

purpose This is important in **natural moral law**, which maintains that moral goodness or badness can be deduced from whether or not an action accords with human purpose.

punishment Loss or suffering inflicted as a result of an offence.

Qur'an The holy book of Islam, believed by Muslims to be the spoken words of Allah, recorded verbatim by Muhammad (PBUH), and of central authoritative importance to their faith and life.

realism Traditionally, ethical realism holds that moral facts exist. The term also describes the theory that, in fact, it's never possible to make good choices, as sin is present in all people, and therefore we ultimately have to choose between the lesser of two evils.

realism and war The belief that personal moral codes of conduct do not apply to international politics. The defence of the community allows for individual moral principles, such as 'do not kill', to be ignored.

reason This plays a central role in some ethical theories. Kant and Aquinas believed that moral behaviour means acting in accordance to reason as opposed to emotion. Aquinas believed that conscience is reason making moral decisions.

reformation (or rehabilitation) A theory that seeks to convert the criminal through correction and rehabilitation.

relativism Relativism takes several forms. **Descriptive** ethical relativism maintains that different cultures and societies have differing ethical systems. **Normative** ethical relativism claims that each culture's beliefs or value system are right within that culture, and that it's impossible validly to judge another culture's values externally or objectively. As such, there are no absolute moral norms. Some relativists hold that moral absolutes may exist, but that they are unknowable. J. L. Mackie is a famous contemporary relativist philosopher.

retribution   A theory that sees punishment as something that is owed to the criminal as payment for the crime committed.

rights   Entitlements to do something without interference from other people, granted by divine, natural or secular authority by virtue of being human or being the citizen of a state.

rule utilitarianism   Instead of looking at the consequences of a particular act, rule utilitarians first establish the best general course of action to follow in these circumstances and then always follows that course. So, the general rule of driving on the left-hand side of the road is established as the best rule to follow in the UK, even though in a particular instance the left lane is slow-moving while the other lane is empty. John Stuart Mill is an example of a rule utilitarian. See also **act utilitarianism**, **utilitarianism**.

sentiment   A word used by Hume to describe the source of moral opinions, separate from factual knowledge or information.

sexual ethics   Ethical issues related to sex, including pre-marital sex, extra- marital sex, homosexuality, contraception, masturbation, contraception, and so on.

Shari'a   The systemised law based on the Qur'an and Hadith; the agreement of their meaning and interpretation, grounded in divine wisdom.

situation ethics/situationism   An alternative Christian ethical theory promulgated by Joseph Fletcher in the 1960s, that rejected legalistic codes of ethics in favour of a more relativist model. Fletcher argued that the morally right thing to do was that which was most loving in that particular situation. The love that Fletcher meant was **agape love** or unconditional love. The theory has been rejected by some Christian Churches, most notably the Roman Catholic Church. **Proportionalism** is a more moderate form of situation ethics .

slippery slope argument   See **gradualism**.

social contract   An agreement between the ruled and the rulers identifying the rights and duties that each has. This is important in the work of Thomas Hobbes, John Locke and Jean-Jacques Rousseau.

social justice   An ideal state and approach to justice that Christians are created to work for, seen as an indicator of the presence of God's kingdom of justice and peace.

soft determinism   See **determinism**.

state of nature   The original state that human beings live in. It was identified by Thomas Hobbes as being a state of aggressive war that must be overcome by a social contract and, conversely, argued by Jean-Jacques Rousseau to be a state of pre-civilised paradise.

subjective/subjectivism   An extreme version of **relativism**, which argues that each person's values and beliefs are relative to that person alone and can't be judged externally or objectively.

summum bonum   The supreme good that Kant argues we pursue through moral behaviour.

Sunnah (or Sunna)   The body of social and legal traditions, customs and practices of the Prophet, and essential to the Muslim community as recorded in the Hadith.

synthetic   Synthetic statements are statements which may be true or false but can be demonstrated using experience or sense perceptions. 'The squirrel is behind the tree' is synthetic – you can look and it's either there or not there.

teleological/teleological ethics   Ethical theories that establish the rightness or wrongness of a given act by consideration of the consequences. See also **consequentialism, utilitarianism.**

theocentric environmental theory   An environmental theory that prioritises the interests of God, His will and His creation over and above any other interests.

transnational corporation   A business that is registered and that operates in more than one country.

Ummah   The community is the instrument through which the ideals and commands of the Qur'an are applied at the social level, so that Muslims are accountable to both God and the community.

universalisability   A moral law that is obeyed every time everywhere. Kant maintained that the only maxims which are morally good are those which can be universalised.

utilis   A Latin word meaning 'useful'.

utilitarianism/utility theory/utility principle   A teleological theory that maintains that an action is right if it produces the greatest good for the greatest number. It was formulated by Jeremy Bentham and developed by John Stuart Mill. Utilitarianism measures the potential goodness produced using the **hedonic calculus** and thereby draws conclusions about which action is the best. **Deontological** theories are contrary to this theory. Critics point out that utilitarianism provides no justice for minorities and ignores the possibility of intrinsically bad acts, such as torturing babies. See also **act utilitarianism, consequentialism, rule utilitarianism.**

verification   The process of checking – using logic or sensory evidence – the validity of statements.

vice   A wrong that is habitually done.

Vienna Circle   A group of philosophers who held that moral statements were meaningless because they could not be verified.

virtue/virtue ethics   To habitually do what is right. Virtue ethics is a theory that claims that being good requires the practice of a certain kind of behaviour. Aristotle advanced virtue ethics and it has been recently redefined by Alasdair MacIntyre. Debates range on how we determine what these ethical virtues are and whether being good is something that we can practice at at all.

Bibliography

General reference works

Cahn, S. M. and Markie, P. (1998) *Ethics, History, Theory, and Contemporary Issues*, Oxford University Press, Oxford.

Childress, James F. and Macquarrie, J., eds (1986) *A New Dictionary of Christian Ethics*, SCM, London.

Encyclopædia Britannica (1994–1999); http://www.britannica.com/and DVD edition.

LaFollette, Hugh, ed. (1997) *Ethics in Practice. An Anthology*, Blackwell, Oxford.

McGrath, Alister E. (1994) *Christian Theology, an Introduction*, Blackwell, Oxford.

Singer, P., ed. (1991 hardback, 1993 paperback, 1997 paperback reprint) *A Companion to Ethics*, Blackwell, Oxford.

Specific texts

Anderson, Terence R. (1986) Environmental ethics. In: *A New Dictionary of Christian Ethics* (ed. Childress, James F. and Macquarrie, J.), SCM, London.

Annas, Julia (1992) Ancient ethics and modern morality. In: *Philosophical Perspectives, 6: Ethics* (ed. Tomberlin, J. E.), Ridgeview, Atascadero, California, pp. 119–136.

Aquinas, St Thomas (1273) *Summa Theologica*, transl. by the Fathers of the English Dominican Province, Benziger Bros, USA, 1947.

Anscombe, G. E. M. (1958) Modern moral philosophy. *Philosophy*.

Aristotle (fourth century BCE) *The Nicomachean Ethics*, translated with an introduction by W. D. Ross, Oxford University Press, Oxford, 1980.

Augustine, St, Bishop of Hippo (392) *Acta seu Disputatio Contra Fortunatum Manichaeum* (*Acts or Disputation Against Fortunatus, the Manichaean*); http://www.newadvent.org/fathers/1404.htm

Augustine, St, Bishop of Hippo (n.d.) De Trinitate. In: William of Auvergne, *The Trinity, or the First Principle (De Trinitate, Seu De Primo Principio)*, Medieval Philosophical Texts in Translation, No. 28, Marquette University Press, USA, 1989.

Augustine, St, Bishop of Hippo (n.d.) De Civitate Dei (The City of God). In: *Concerning the City of God Against the Pagans*, Penguin, Harmondsworth, 1984.

Austin, John (1832) *The Province of Jurisprudence Determined*, John Murray, London.

Ayer, A. J. (1936) *Language, Truth and Logic*, Victor Gollancz, London.

Ayer, A. J. (1959) *Philosophical Essays*, Macmillan, London.

Barnet, Richard J. and Cavanagh, John (1994) *Global Dreams, Imperial Corporations and The New World Order*, Simon & Schuster, New York.

Barnet, Richard J. and Müller, Ronald E. (1974) *Global Reach: the Power of the Multinational Corporations*, Touchstone, Simon & Schuster, New York.

Barnette, Henlee H. (1972) *The Church and the Ecological Crisis*, Eerdmans, Grand Rapids.

Baier, Kurt (1991) Egoism. In: *A Companion to Ethics* (ed. Singer, P.), Blackwell, Oxford, pp. 197–204.

BBC News Online (2000a) Churchman attacks cloning as 'immoral'. 27 November; http://news.bbc.co.uk/hi/english/uk/scotland/newsid_1042000/1042869.stm

BBC News Online (2000b) How to be an ethical investor. 24 January; http://news.bbc.co.uk/1/hi/uk/616511.stm

BBC News Online (2001) Cloning ethics in the spotlight. 7 April; http://news.bbc.co.uk/hi/english/uk/scotland/newsid_1042000/1042869.stm

BBC News Online (2002) Losing money with a conscience. 31 July; http://news.bbc.co.uk/1/hi/business/2161135.stm

Belliotti, Raymond (1991) Sex. In: *A Companion to Ethics* (ed. Singer, P.), Blackwell, Oxford, pp. 315–326.

Bentham, Jeremy (1776) *A Fragment on Government* (ed. Montague, F. C.), Greenwood Press, London, 1980.

Bentham, Jeremy (1789) *Principles of Morals and Legislation*, Prometheus, London, 1988.

Boswell, John (1982) *Rediscovering Gay History: Archetypes of Gay Love in Christian History*, Gay Christian Movement, London.

Boxhill, Bernard R. (1997) Equality, discrimination and preferential treatment. In: *A Companion to Ethics* (ed. Singer, P.), Blackwell, Oxford.

Bradley, F. H. (1927) *Ethical Studies*, 2nd edn, Oxford University Press, Glasgow (first published 1876).

British Humanist Association (2003a) A humanist way of ... thinking about ethics; http://www.humanism.org.uk/site/cms/contentViewArticle.asp?article=1209

British Humanist Association (2003b) A non-religious perspective on ... embryo research; http://www.humanism.org.uk/site/cms/contentViewArticle.asp?article=1230

Bruce, Donald (2000) *The Tablet*, 26 August, p. 1127.

Brunner, Emil (1942) *The Divine Imperative*, trans. Olive Wyon, Lutterworth Press, London.

Bryant, William Cullen (1817) Thanatopsis. *North American Review*, September.

Butler, J. (1726) *Fifteen Sermons*, Bell, London, 1964.

Campbell, C. A. (1976) On selfhood and Godhead. In: *Philosophy: Paradox and Discovery* (ed. Minton, A.), McGraw-Hill, New York.

Cohan, Carl (1998) The case for the use of animals in biomedical research. In: *Ethics, History, Theory and Contemporary Writings* (ed. Cahn, S. M. and Markie, P.), Oxford University Press, Oxford, pp. 829–837.

Crook, Roger H. (2002) *An Introduction to Christian Ethics*, Prentice Hall, New Jersey.

Dancy, Jonathan (1991) Intuitionism. In: *A Companion to Ethics* (ed. Singer, P.), Blackwell, Oxford, pp. 411–420.

Denny, Frederick M. (1985) Ethics and the Qur'an: community and world view. In: *Ethics in Islam* (ed. Hovannisian, R. G.), Undena 1985, Malibu, California.

Department of Health (2000a) Stem Cell Research: Medical Progress with Responsibility, June 2000, pages 6–7.

Department of Health (2000b) Government response to the report 'Stem Cell Research: Medical Progress with Responsibility', August.

De Schutter, René (2001) What is at stake in world trade. In: *Fair Trade Yearbook*; http://www.eftafairtrade.org/pdf/YRB2001Ch01_EN.pdf, p. 9.

de Silva, P. (1997) Buddhist ethics. In: *A Companion to Ethics* (ed. Singer, P.), Blackwell, Oxford, pp. 58–68.

Devall, Bill and Sessions, George (1985) *Deep Ecology: Living as if Nature Mattered*, Gibbs Smith, Layton, Utah.

Dominion, Jack (1991) *Passionate and Compassionate Love, a Vision for Christian Marriage*, DLT, London.

Dostoyevsky, Fyodor Mikhailovic (1879–1880) *The Brothers Karamazov*, transl. by David McDuff, Penguin, Harmondsworth, 1993.

Dworkin, Ronald M. (1977) *Taking Rights Seriously*, Harvard University Press, Cambridge, Massachusetts.

EFTA (European Free Trade Association) (2001) *EFTA Yearbook: Challenges of Fair Trade 2001–2003*; http://www.eftafairtrade.org/yearbook.asp

Elliott, Robert (1991) Environmental ethics. In: *A Companion to Ethics* (ed. Singer, P.), Blackwell, Oxford, pp. 284–293.

Encyclopædia Britannica (1999) Theories and objectives of punishment – rehabilitation. DVD edition.

Ethical Investment Association (n.d.) http://www.ethicalinvestment.org.uk/

Fletcher, Joseph (1963) *Situation Ethics, the New Morality*, Westminster Press, Philadelphia.

Fletcher, Joseph (1971) *Ethical Aspects for Genetic Controls*, New England Journal of Medicine, pp. 776–783.

Fossaert, Robert (1996) *L'avenir du socialisme*, Editions Stock, Paris.

Fox, Michael A. (1986) *The Case for Animal Experimentation*, University of California Press, Berkeley.

Frankena, William K. (1963) *Ethics*, Prentice-Hall, Englewood Cliffs, New Jersey.

Freud, Sigmund (1938) *The Outline of Psychoanalysis*, trans. by James Strachey.

Friedman, Milton (1970) The social responsibility of business is to increase its profits. *New York Times Magazine*, 13 September.

Gallagher, John (1985) Is the human embryo a person? *Human Life Research Institute Report*, number 4.

Glazer, S. and Cooper, S. L. (1988) *Without Child: Experiencing and Resolving Infertility*. Lexington Books, Lexington, Massachusetts.

Glover, Jonathan (1977) *Causing Death and Saving Lives*, Penguin, Harmondsworth.

Gould, Stephen Jay (1998) Dolly's fashion and Lois's passion. In: *Flesh of my Flesh, the Ethics of Human Cloning* (ed. Pence, G.), Rowman & Littlefield, Oxford, pp. 101–110.

Gruen, Lori (1991) Animals. In: *A Companion to Ethics* (ed. Singer, P.), Blackwell, Oxford, pp. 343–353.

Guild of Catholic Doctors (1999) Comments to the Chief Medical Officer's Expert Group on Cloning, 29 October.

Gunnemann, Jon P. (1986) Business ethics. In: *A New Dictionary of Christian Ethics* (ed. Childress, James F. and Macquarrie, J.), SCM, London, pp. 68–71.

Gutierrez, Gustavo (1994) *A Theology of Liberation*, SCM, London.

Hare, R. M. (1952) *The Language of Morals*, Oxford University Press, Oxford.

Hare, R. M. (1963) *Freedom and Reason*, Clarendon Press, Oxford.

Haring, Bernard (1954) *The Law of Christ*, tr E. G. Kaiser, Westminster, Newman Press.

Harvey, N. P. (1995) Justice and peace. In: *New Dictionary of Christian Ethics and Pastoral Theology* (ed. Atkinson, D. *et al.*), IVP, Leicester, pp. 15–21.

Herodotus (fifth century BCE) *Histories*, transl. by George Rawlinson, Wordsworth Classics, Ware, 1996.

HFEA (Human Fertilisation and Embryology Authority) (2003) Human embryo research; http://www.hfea.gov.uk/PressOffice/Backgroundpapers/Humanembryo research

Hobbes, Thomas (1651) *Leviathan*, Oxford University Press, Oxford, 1998.

Hobbes, Thomas (1658) *De Homine (On Human Nature)* See *Man and Citizen: Thomas Hobbes's De Homine*, trans. by Charles T. Wood, T. S. K. Scott-Craig and Bernard Gert, Harvester Press, Brighton, 1978.

Honderich, Ted, ed. (1995) *The Oxford Companion to Philosophy*, Oxford University Press, Oxford.

Hooker, Brad (1997) Rule utilitarianism and euthanasia. In: *Ethics in Practice. An Anthology* (ed. LaFollette, H.), Blackwell, Oxford, pp. 42–52.

Hoose, Bernard (1987) *Proportionalism: the American debate and its European roots*, Georgetown University Press, Washington.

Hoose, Bernard, ed. (1998) *Christian Ethics, an Introduction*, Cassell, London.

Horsey, Kirsty (2003) Results of US embryo storage survey published. 18 May; http://www.ivf.net/artman/publish/article_322.shtml

Hospers, John (1972) *Human Conduct*, Harcourt Brace Jovanovich, New York.

Hugon, Philippe (1999). In: *Collectif Gemdev: Mondialisation. Les mots et les choses*, Editions Karthala, Paris.

Hume, David (1748) *An Enquiry Concerning Human Understanding*. In: *Enquiries Concerning Human Understanding and Concerning the Principles of Morals*, Clarendon Press, Oxford, 1975.

Hume, David (1751) *Enquiry Concerning the Principle of Morals*. In: *Enquiries Concerning Human Understanding and Concerning the Principles of Morals*, Clarendon Press, Oxford, 1975.

Hume, David (1739–1740) *A Treatise of Human Nature* (three volumes), Fontana, Glasgow, 1962.

Ingersoll, Robert G. (1876) *On the Gods and Others Essays*, Prometheus Books; (September 1990).

Islamic Organization of Medical Sciences, Kuwait (1981); http://islam.org/ Science/euthanas.htm, at http://islamicity.com/default.shtml

Johnston, Jill (1974) *Lesbian Nation: the Feminist Solution*, Simon and Schuster, New York.

Johnson & Johnson, Credo, http://www.jnj.com/our_company/our_credo/index.htm

Jones, Richard G. (1998) Peace, violence and war. In: *Christian Ethics, an Introduction* (ed. Hoose, B.), Cassell, London, p. 212.

Kant, Immanuel (1781) *Critique of Pure Reason*, transl. by Norman Kemp Smith, Macmillan, London, 1933.

Kant, Immanuel (1785) *Groundwork for the Metaphysics of Morals*, trans. by H. J. Paton, Routledge, London, 1948.

Kant, Immanuel (1788) *Critique of Practical Reason*, trans. by L. W. Beck, Bobbs-Merrill, Indianapolis, 1977.

Kant, Immanuel (1797) *The Metaphysics of Morals*, Cambridge University Press, Cambridge, 1996.

Kass, Leon (1998) The wisdom of repugnance. In: *Flesh of my Flesh, the Ethics of Human Cloning* (ed. Pence, G.), Rowman & Littlefield, Oxford, pp. 13–38.

Keenan, James F. (1998) Virtue ethics. In: *Christian Ethics, an Introduction* (ed. Hoose, B.), Cassell, London, pp. 84–94; see also *Dialogue, a Journal for Religious Studies and Philosophy* 15, November 2000.

Kelly, Kevin T. (1992) *New Directions in Moral Theology*, Chapman, London.

Kierkegaard, Søren (1843) *Fear and Trembling*, Penguin, Harmondsworth, 1985.

Klein, Naomi (2001) *No Logo*, Flamingo, London.

Klug, Francesca (2000) *Values for a Godless Age: the Story of the UK's New Bill of Rights* , Penguin, Harmondsworth.

Kusha, Helga (1991) Euthanasia. In: *A Companion to Ethics* (ed. Singer, P.), Blackwell, Oxford, pp. 294–302.

Kymlicka, W. (1997) The social contract tradition. In: *A Companion to Ethics* (ed. Singer, P.), Blackwell, Oxford, pp. 186–196.

Leibniz, Gottfried Wilhelm (1686) *Discourse on Metaphysics*, ed. and trans. by Daniel Garber and Roger Ariew, Hackett, Indianapolis, 1991.

Leiser, Burton M. (1997) Homosexuality, morals, and the law of nature. In: *Ethics in Practice. An Anthology* (ed. LaFollette, H.), Blackwell, Oxford, pp. 242–253.

Leopold, Aldo (1949) *A Sand County Almanac*, OUP, Oxford 1949.

Leopold, Aldo (1997) The land ethic. In: *Ethics in Practice. An Anthology* (ed. LaFollette,

H.), Blackwell, Oxford, pp. 634–643.

Lomborg, Bjorn (2001) *The Skeptical Environmentalist: Measuring the Real State of the World*, Cambridge University Press, Cambridge.

Longley, Clifford (1998) Structures of Sin and the Free Market, The New Politics, Catholic Social Teaching for the twenty-first century, SCM, London.

Louden, Robert (1997) On some vices of virtue ethics. In: *Virtue Ethics* (ed. Crisp, R. and Slote, M.), Oxford University Press, Oxford, Chapter 10.

Lovelock, James (1979) *Gaia: a New Look at Life on Earth*, Oxford University Press, Oxford.

Lucretius (first century BCE) *De Rerum Natura* (ed. Kenney, E. J.), Cambridge University Press, Cambridge, 1977.

MacIntyre, Alasdair (1966) *A Short History of Ethics*, Routledge, London.

MacIntyre, Alasdair (1985) *After Virtue, a Study in Moral Theory*, 2nd edn, Duckworth, London.

Mackie, J. L. (1977) *Ethics, Inventing Right and Wrong*, Penguin, London.

MacKinnon, Catharine A. (1987) *Feminism Unmodified: Discourses on Life and Law*, Harvard University Press, Cambridge, Massachusetts.

Marx, Karl (1848) *The Communist Manifesto*.

McMahan, Jeff (1991) War and peace. In: *A Companion to Ethics* (ed. Singer, P.), Blackwell, Oxford, pp. 385–386.

McQuilkin, Robertson (1995) *An Introduction to Biblical Ethics*, Tyndale House, Carol Stream, Illinois.

Melling, David (1987) *Understanding Plato*, Oxford University Press, Oxford.

Mill, John Stuart (1859) *On Liberty*, Harmondsworth, Penguin, 1982.

Mill, John Stuart (1861) *Utilitarianism*, Hackett, Indianapolis, 1979.

Mill, John Stuart (1869) *On the Subjugation of Women*, Wordsworth Classics, Ware, 1996.

Moore, G. E. (1903) *Principia Ethica*, Cambridge University Press, Cambridge, 1993.

Moore, Gareth (1992) *The Body in Context: Sex and Catholicism*, SCM, London.

More, Thomas (1516) Of their slaves, and of their marriages. Chapter 8 of *Utopia*; http://csf.colorado.edu/mirrors/marxists.org/reference/archive/more/works/utopia/ch8.html

Morris, Ruth (1989) *Crumbling Walls ... Why Prisons Fail*, Mosaic Press, London.

Morton, Adam (1996) *Philosophy in Practice*, Blackwell, Oxford.

Moseley, Alexander (1998) *Internet Encyclopedia of Philosophy*; http://www.utm.edu/research/iep/j/justwar.htm

Naess, Arne and Sessions, George (1984) Basic principles of deep ecology. *Ecophilosophy*, 6.

Nanji, Azim (1997) Islamic ethics. In: *A Companion to Ethics* (ed. Singer, P.), Blackwell, Oxford.

Neilson, Kai (1959) An examination of the Thomistic theory of natural moral law.

Natural Law Forum, IV; reprinted in Paul E. Sigmund, ed. (1988) *St Thomas Aquinas on Politics and Ethics*, Norton, New York.

Newman, John Henry (1947) *A Grammar of Assent* (ed. Harold, C. F.), David McKay and Co., London.

Nicholson, Richard (2003) Down the slippery slope. *The Tablet*, 28 June; http://www.thetablet.co.uk/cgi-bin/archive_db.cgi?tablet-00758

Niebuhr, Reinhold (1932) *Moral Man and Immoral Society*, Scribner, New York.

Niebuhr, Reinhold (1935) *An Interpretation of Christian Ethics*, Meridian, New York, 1956.

Niebuhr, Reinhold (1965) *Man's Nature and his Communities: Essays on the Dynamics and enigmas of Man's Personal and Social Existence*, Scribner, New York.

Norman, Richard (1998) Moral restraints in warfare. *Dialogue, a Journal for Religious Studies and Philosophy*, issue 11, November, pp. 12–17.

Nozick, Robert (1974) *Anarchy, State and Utopia*, Basic Books, New York.

O'Connell, Timothy E. (1990) *Principles of Catholic Morality Revised Edition*, HarperCollins 1990, New York.

Owen, H. P. (1965) *The Moral Argument for Christian Theism*, George Allen & Unwin, London.

Palmer, Michael (1991) *Moral Problems: a Coursebook for Schools and Colleges*, The Lutterworth Press, Cambridge.

Paradise, Scott I. (1971) Rehabilitation for cosmic outlaws. In: *A New Ethic for a New Earth* (ed. Stone, Glenn C.), Connecticut, Friendship Press, pp. 133–142.

Pence, Gregory E. (1997) Why physicians should aid the dying. In: *Ethics in Practice. An Anthology* (ed. LaFollette, H.), Blackwell, Oxford, p. 254, pp. 21–32.

Pence, Gregory E., ed. (1998) *Flesh of my Flesh, the Ethics of Human Cloning*, Rowman & Littlefield, Oxford.

Perry, R. B. (1954) *Realms of Value*, Harvard University Press, Cambridge, Massachusetts.

Peters, Ted (1997) *Playing God?: Genetic Determinism and Human Freedom*, Routledge, London.

Phillips, D. Z. (1966) God and ought. In: *Christian Ethics and Contemporary Philosophy* (ed. Ramsey, I.), SCM, London, p. 137.

Pigden, Charles R. (1991) Naturalism. In: *A Companion to Ethics* (ed. Singer, P.), Blackwell, Oxford, pp. 421–430.

Plato (fifth–fourth century BCE), Crito and Euthyphro. In: *The Last Days of Socrates*, transl. by Hugh Tredennik, Penguin Classics, London, 1969.

Plato (fifth–fourth century BCE) *The Republic*, trans. by Desmond Lee, 2nd edn, Penguin, Harmondsworth, 1979.

Prichard, H. A. (1912) Does moral philosophy rest on mistake? *Mind*; reprinted in *Moral Obligation: Essays and Lectures*, Clarendon Press, Oxford, 1949.

Prison Reform Trust (n.d.) Why Prisons Reform?; http://www.prisonreformtrust.org.uk/aboutus1.html

Rachels, James (1971) God and human attitudes. *Religious Studies*, 7, 334.

Rachels, James (1986) *Elements of Moral Philosophy*, McGraw-Hill, New York.

Rachels, James (1991) Subjectivism. In: *Companion to Ethics* (ed. Singer, P.), Blackwell, Oxford, pp. 438–439.

Rachels, James (1997) Punishment and desert. In: *Ethics in Practice. An Anthology* (ed. LaFollette, H.), Blackwell, Oxford, pp. 470–479.

Ramsey, Paul (1950) *Basic Christian Ethics*, Westminster/John Knox, Louisville, Kentucky.

Ramsey, Paul (1974) *Fabricated Man, the Ethics of Genetic Control*, Yale University Press, New Haven, Connecticut.

Rawls, John (1971) *A Theory of Justice*, The Belknap Press of Harvard University Press, USA (revised edn 1999).

Regan, Richard R. (1996) *Just War, Principles and Causes*, CUA Press, Washington, DC.

Regan, Tom (1985) The case for animal rights. In: *In Defence of Animals* (ed. Singer, P.), Blackwell, Oxford.

Robertson, John (1998) Wrongful life, federalism, and procreative liberty. In: *Flesh of my Flesh, the Ethics of Human Cloning* (ed. Pence, G.), Rowman & Littlefield, Oxford, pp. 85–100.

Robinson, B. A. (2001) Human embryo research: all sides to the disputes. Ontario Consultants on Religious Tolerance, 1 May; http://www.religioustolerance.org/res_emb.htm

Robinson, John A. T. (1963) *Honest to God*, SCM, London.

Ross, W. D. (1930) *The Right and the Good*, Clarendon Press, Oxford.

Ross, W. D. (1939) *The Foundations of Ethics*, Oxford University Press, Oxford.

Rousseau, Jean-Jacques (1762) *The Social Contract*, Wordsworth Classics, Chatham, 1998.

Russell, Bertrand (1927) *Why I Am Not a Christian*, Watts, London.

Saunders, Kate and Stamford, Peter (1992) *Catholics and Sex*, Heinemann, London.

Schaller, Walter (1990) Are virtues no more than dispositions to obey moral rules? *Philosophy*, 20 (July), 1–2.

Scruton, Roger (2000) *Animal Rights and Wrongs*, 3rd edn, Metro, in association with Demos, London.

Selling, Joseph (1998) The human person. In: *Christian Ethics, an Introduction* (ed. Hoose, B.), Cassell, London, pp. 95–109.

Sidgwick, H. (1874) *The Methods of Ethics*, Macmillan, London, 1962.

Singer, P., ed. (1985) *In Defence of Animals*, Blackwell, Oxford.

Singer, P. (1993) *Practical Ethics*, Cambridge University Press, Cambridge.

Singer, P. (1995) *Animal Liberation*, Pimlico, London.

Smedes, Lewis B. (1983) *Mere Morality*, Lion Paperbacks, Tring.

Smith, Adam (1776) *An Enquiry into the Nature and Causes of the Wealth of Nations*.

Smith, David (1997) Abortion: a moral controversy. *Dialogue, a Journal for Religious Studies and Philosophy*, Issue 8 (April), 9–14.

Solomon, Robert C. (1993) Business ethics. In: *A Companion to Ethics* (ed. Singer, P.), Blackwell, Oxford, pp. 354–365.

Spinoza, Benedict (1674) *Ethics (Ethica Ordine Geometrico Demonstrata [Ethics Demonstrated with Geometrical Order])*, Everyman's Library no. 481, Letchworth, 1950.

Staniforth, Maxwell, transl. (1968) Didache ton Apostolon. In: *Early Christian Writings*, Penguin, Harmondsworth.

Stevenson, C. L. (1937) The emotive meaning of ethical terms. *Mind*, **XLVI**.

Stevenson, C. L. (1938) Persuasive definitions. *Mind*, **XLVI**.

Stevenson, C. L. (1945) *Ethics and Language*, Yale University Press, New Haven, Connecticut/Oxford University Press, London.

Stone, Glenn C., ed. (1971) *A New Ethic for a New Earth*, Connecticut, Friendship Press.

Sumner, William Graham (1906) *Folkways*, Ginn, Boston.

Temple, William (1923) *Mens creatrix: an Essay*, Macmillan, London (reissue of 1917 edition).

Ten, C. L. (1997) Crime and punishment. In: *A Companion to Ethics* (ed. Singer, P.), Blackwell, Oxford, pp. 366–372.

Thera, Ñanamoli, ed. (1987) *The Practice of Loving-Kindness (Metta), as taught by the Buddha in the Pali Canon*, The Wheel Publication No. 7, Buddhist Publication Society, Kandy.

Thera, Nyanaponika, ed. (1988) *The Simile of the Cloth and The Discourse on Effacement, Two Discourses of the Buddha from the Majjhima Nikaya*, The Wheel Publication No. 61/62, Buddhist Publication Society, Kandy.

Thompson, Judith Jarvis (1971) A defence of abortion. *Philosophy and Public Affairs*, 1(1).

Thoreau, Henry David (1849) *On the Duty of Civil Disobedience* (original title: *Resistance to Civil Government*); ftp://uiarchive.cso.uiuc.edu/pub/etext/gutenberg/etext93/civil10.txt

Tillich, Paul (1951, 1957 and 1963) *Systematic Theology*, three vols, The University of Chicago Press, Chicago.

Trade Justice Movement (n.d.), *About the Trade Justice Movement*; http://www.tradejusticemovement.org/about.shtml

Trethowan, D. I. (1970) *Absolute Value: a Study in Christian Theism*, George Allen & Unwin, London.

UNDP (1999) *Human Development Report*, New York, 1999.

Van Ness, D. W. (1995) Punishment. In: *A New Dictionary of Christian Ethics and Pastoral Theology* (ed. Atkinson, D. et al.), IVP, Leicester, pp. 710–712.

Vardy, Peter (1997) *The Puzzle of Sex*, Fount, Glasgow.

Vardy, Peter and Grosch, Paul (1994) *The Puzzle of Ethics*, Fount, Glasgow.

Vickers, Brian, ed. (1996) *Francis Bacon*, Oxford University Press, Oxford.

Voluntary Euthanasia Society (VES) (2001a) Factsheet: the case for; http://www.ves.org.uk/DpFS_For.html

Voluntary Euthanasia Society (VES) (2001b) Factsheet: religion; http://www.ves.org.uk/DpFS_Rel.html

Warnock, Mary (1999) *An Intelligent Person's Guide to Ethics*, Duckworth, London.

Warren, Mary Anne (1991) Abortion. In: *A Companion to Ethics* (ed. Singer, P.), Blackwell, Oxford, pp. 303–314.

Warren, Mary Anne (1997) On the legal and moral status of abortion. In: *Ethics in Practice, An Anthology* (ed. LaFollette, H.), Blackwell, Oxford, pp. 79–90.

Weber, Max (1904–5) *The Protestant Ethic and the Spirit of Capitalism*, new introduction and translation by Stephen Kalberg, Fitzroy Dearborn, Chicago/London, 2001.

Weston, Anthony (2001) *A 21st Century Ethical Toolbox*, Oxford University Press, Oxford.

Williams, Bernard (1973) *Utilitarianism: For and Against,* Cambridge University Press, Cambridge.

Wood, Allen (1995) *Capitalism* In: *The Oxford Companion of Philosophy* (ed. Honderich, Ted), Oxford University Press, Oxford, pp. 119–120.

Young, Iris Marion (1997a) Displacing the distributive paradigm. In: *Ethics in Practice. An Anthology* (ed. LaFollette, H.), Blackwell, Oxford, pp. 541–558.

Young, Robert (1997b) *The implications of determinism.* In: *A Companion to Ethics* (ed. Singer, P.), Blackwell, Oxford, p. 535 .

Church teaching documents

Roman Catholic Church

Acta Synodalia Concilii Vaticani II, vol. IV, part 7, p. 502, n.37.

Centisimus Annus, Encyclical Letter, Pope John Paul II, 1991. In: *The Common Good and the Catholic Church's Social Teaching*, a statement by the Catholic Bishops' Conference of England and Wales, Gabriel Communications, Manchester, 1996.

Charter of the Rights of the Family, published by the Holy See, (24).

Humanae Vitae, Encyclical Letter, Pope Paul VI, 1968, 14.

Joint Committee on Bioethical Issues of the Catholic Bishops of Great Britain, Statement responding to recommendations of the British government's Warnock Committee, July 9, 1987. See 17 *Origins* 144-7 (July 30, 1987) at 145. Quoted from http://www.usccb.org/prolife/issues/bioethic/embryo/embryapp.htm, Secretariat for Pro-Life Activities, 2003, United States Conference of Catholic Bishops website.

Mater et Magistra, Encyclical Letter, Pope John XXIII, 1961; http://www.vatican.va/holy_father/john_xxiii/encyclicals/documents/hf_j-xxiii_enc_15051961_mater_en.html

On the Dignity of Procreation – Respect for Human Life Congregation for the Doctrine of the Faith – *Donum Vitae* 1987.

Pastoral Constitution, Gaudium et Spes. From Vatican Council II (1996) *Constitutions, Decrees, Declarations* (ed. Flannery, A.), Dominican Publications, USA.

Persona Humana: Declaration on Certain Questions Concerning Sexual Ethics, Sacred Congregation for the Doctrine of the Faith, CTS, London, 1975.

Pope John Paul II (1994) *Catechism of the Catholic Church*, Geoffrey Chapman, London.

Populorum Progressio, Encyclical Letter, Pope Paul VI, 1967; http://www.vatican.va/holy_father/paul_vi/encyclicals/documents/hf_p-vi_enc_26031967_populorum_en.html

Quadragesimo Anno, Encyclical Letter, Pope Pius XI, 1931. In: *The Common Good and the Catholic Church's Social Teaching*, a statement by the Catholic Bishops' Conference of England and Wales, Gabriel Communications, Manchester, 1996.

Rerum Novarum, Encyclical Letter, Pope Leo XIII, 1891. In: *The Common Good and the Catholic Church's Social Teaching*, a statement by the Catholic Bishops' Conference of England and Wales, Gabriel Communications, Manchester, 1996.

Roman Catholic Church (n.d.) The call of creation: God's invitation and the human response: the natural environment and Catholic social teaching; http://217.19.224.165/resource/GreenText/index.htm

Sacred Congregation for the Doctrine of the Faith *Declaration on Euthanasia*, 5 May 1980.

The Promise of Peace: God's Promise and Our Response, Catholic Bishops of America Pastoral Letter, CTS, USA, 1983.

Veriatatis Splendor, Encyclical Letter, Pope John Paul II, CTS, London, 1993.

United Methodist Church

United Methodist Church (1996) The nurturing community, section on social principles. In: *Book of Discipline*, Abingdon Press, para. 66.

The Anglican Communion

Church of England, Marriage Commission (1978) *Marriage and the Church's Task: the Report of the General Synod Marriage Commission*, CIO Publishing, London.

Index

Page references in italics indicate tables or illustrations

Temple, William 102
Ten, C.L. 265–6, 267
Theocentrism 246
Thera, Nyanaponika 135–6
Therapeutic cloning 309–10, 311, 312, 314
Thompson, Judith J. 195, 198, 199–200
Thoreau, Henry D. 153
Thurow, Lester 232
TNCs (Transnational corporations) 232–4
Trethowan, D.I. 126
Truth 13, 14–15, 151; moral truths 17, 65–6, 128

Ummah 140
Universal Declaration of Human Rights 291
Universalisability 58, 61–2, 83, 84

Utilitarianism 7, 18; act and rule 43–4; and ARTs 207; Bentham and 38–40, 47–8; evaluating 45–7; and justice 259; Mill and 42, 49–50; and punishment 265
Utility principle 39, 42, 43, 47–8

Values 16, 17, 103, 162; ancient 116; humanism and 168
Van Ness, D.W. 267
Vardy, Peter 185; & Grosch, Paul 30, 31, 81, 194, 196, 261
Verification (of knowledge) 77
Vices 113, *114*; Buddhist 135–6
Vienna Circle 77
Virtue theory 15, 112, 114–15; and animal rights 299–300;

Aristotle and 113–14, *114*, 117–18; evaluating 115–16; MacIntyre and 112–13, 115, 118–19; Roman Catholicism and 137
Virtues 27, 113, *114*; Buddhist 135–6
Voluntary euthanasia *see* Euthanasia, voluntary

War; Christian realism and 285; just war theory 106–7, 278–82, 286–7; pacifism 283–4; and religion 278
Warnock, Mary 293
Warren, Mary A. 195, 197
Weber, Max 228
Wilmot, Ian 308, 309, 312
Women; and abortion 192, 197–8; social role 182, 197
Wrong *see* Right and wrong